CW01209171

UNDER THE RAINBOW

UNDER THE RAINBOW

INSIDE JOHN BRUTON'S COALITION GOVERNMENT

SHANE KENNY

GILL BOOKS

Gill Books
Hume Avenue
Park West
Dublin 12
www.gillbooks.ie

Gill Books is an imprint of M.H. Gill and Co.

© Shane Kenny 2024

9781804581865

Designed by Bartek Janczak
Typeset by Jen Patton, Liz White Designs
Edited by Jane Rogers
Proofread by Sally Vince
Indexed by Fergus Mulligan
Printed and bound in the UK using 100% renewable electricity at CPI Group (UK) Ltd
This book is typeset in Minion Pro.

The paper used in this book comes from the wood pulp of sustainably managed forests.

For permission to reproduce material, the author and publisher gratefully acknowledge Geraldine Kennedy/*Irish Times*.
For permission to reproduce the back cover image, the author and publisher gratefully acknowledge John Donohoe/*Meath Chronicle*.

All rights reserved.
No part of this publication may be copied, reproduced or transmitted in any form or by any means, without written permission of the publishers.

A CIP catalogue record for this book is available from the British Library.

5 4 3 2 1

*For my beloved wife, Victoria Martos, and Simon, Ann and Toby.
I also dedicate this book to the memory of former
Taoiseach John Bruton, a great Irish democrat
and an honourable man, who died on 6 February 2024.*

CONTENTS

Introduction 1
1 Learning the game 3
2 A budget springing leaks 14
3 A plot to wreck a peace plan 21
4 Joint Framework Documents launched 36
5 Bruton meets Clinton in the US 54
6 Hugh Coveney's phone call 80
7 Moscow, Paris and Cannes 95
8 Arms disposal crisis 116
9 Victory in the divorce referendum 133
10 Peace deal as Clinton arrives 137
11 London Docklands IRA bomb 172
12 Summit sets talks date 197
13 Clinton's Middle East peace summit 210
14 'Gateway' election and all-party talks 222
15 Veronica Guerin's murder 259
16 British debacle at Drumcree 268
17 Bruton addresses the US Congress 286
18 EU presidency seals euro deal 298
19 The hepatitis C disaster 312
20 Lowry's fall and Haughey's money 318
21 A peace deal with Tony Blair 339
   Afterword 371
   Acknowledgements 374
   Select bibliography 375
   Index 378

INTRODUCTION

THE RAINBOW COALITION: THAT WAS how the media described the Fine Gael, Labour and Democratic Left coalition government that was in power from late 1994 to June 1997. It was the first three-party Irish government, and arguably the most left-wing government in the history of the state; and the name became indelibly fixed in the popular imagination.

Despite a generally held view that Bertie Ahern and Tony Blair, with a nod in the direction of John Hume and Albert Reynolds, solved the Northern problem with the Belfast Good Friday Agreement in 1998, the historical facts are very different. The Belfast Agreement depended heavily on foundations put in place by Taoiseach John Bruton and Tánaiste Dick Spring of the Rainbow government, and by British Prime Ministers John Major and Tony Blair.

There were six critical pillars of the peace process. Three were created before the Rainbow government took power. I have adopted this pillars approach to illustrate the key actions and developments that paved the way to peace in Ireland. The first pillar was a dialogue between John Hume, leader of the Social Democratic and Labour Party (SDLP) in Northern Ireland and Gerry Adams, leader of Sinn Féin, seen as the political arm of the IRA, leading to an agreed joint document. Into this context, a forward-looking UK Northern Ireland secretary, Peter Brooke, made a historically important speech in 1990 declaring that Britain had 'no selfish strategic or economic interest' in Northern Ireland and would accept unification, if the people wanted it. This was the basis for the second pillar, the Downing Street Declaration made by the British Prime

Minister John Major and Taoiseach Albert Reynolds. This was followed by the third pillar, an IRA ceasefire in August 1994.

Three more vital pillars of the peace process were put in place by Bruton and Spring with Major, despite the effective loss of his majority in parliament and a powerful Tory right wing opposing him. Bruton and Major agreed the Joint Framework Documents in late February 1995. This was the blueprint of the Belfast Agreement and the fourth pillar. Then, against the backdrop of the extraordinarily joyful historic visit of President Bill Clinton to Ireland in December 1995, Bruton and Major agreed the fifth pillar, an International Body on the disposal of paramilitary weapons, bringing the former US Senate leader George Mitchell and the Clinton administration into the heart of the Irish peace process. The sixth pillar – all-party talks chaired by Mitchell – were launched in June 1996. These talks later negotiated the Belfast Agreement.

Without these crucial pillars already in place, there would have been no agreement on Good Friday 1998; it would have taken much longer. After Major's election defeat in May 1997, John Bruton and Tony Blair, in the space of two months, were able to agree on all measures required to restore the ceasefire (which had been broken by the IRA in 1996) to bring Sinn Féin into the already existing sixth pillar of the peace process, before the Ahern government took power. The full story is told here.

I'm writing about the Rainbow government from my own perspective and direct involvement as government press secretary, providing readers with the atmosphere, as well as the facts, together with anecdotes and quotations from notes I took on events, tapes that I made of all interviews and media 'doorsteps' with Bruton, together with the assistance of government papers in both Britain and Ireland. This work is also informed by wide reading on this crucial period of Irish history. I wrote a substantial part of this work when the Rainbow government lost office after a seriously mistaken decision to hold an early general election in June 1997, which I opposed for economic and political reasons as well as for the unfinished business of the government. This is a story of political and economic achievement, and of tragedy, both political and human.

1
LEARNING THE GAME

THE NEGOTIATIONS BETWEEN FINE GAEL, Labour and Democratic Left to form the Rainbow government in December 1994 were interrupted by tragedy. Peter Wilson, the son of Senator Gordon Wilson, died after a motor accident. The senator had become a nationally respected figure because of the dignity and grace he showed after the death of his beloved daughter Marie in the IRA Enniskillen Remembrance Day bombing on 8 November 1987. That bombing killed 11 people and injured 63, including 13 children, with a further fatality much later, a man who had been in a coma for 13 years. Gordon Wilson, who was injured in the bombing, had gone with Marie to see the annual parade commemorating British military war dead, and both were buried in rubble by the explosion. Unable to move, he held his badly injured daughter's hand under the rubble, repeatedly asking her if she was alright and trying to comfort her. Rescuers pulled them out of the collapsed building, but Marie died in hospital shortly afterwards. Her heartbroken father gave an extraordinary interview to the BBC. Under the rubble, as they lay hand in hand, Marie's last words to him, minutes before they were freed, were 'Daddy, I love you very much.' The interview was notable both for the intensely moving description of his last moments with Marie and also for his quietly spoken words, 'I bear no ill will. I bear no grudge.' He was revered and admired for his attempts to promote reconciliation and an end to Northern violence after the bombing. He forgave the bombers and said he would pray for them, while he asked loyalists not to take revenge for Marie's death. In consequence, Gordon Wilson was nominated to Seanad Éireann.

There would be a substantial attendance of politicians from the Republic at Peter Wilson's funeral. The leaders of Fine Gael and Labour, John Bruton and Dick Spring, headed north to attend. They knew that the eyes of the media would be focused on them; they were the key players in an unfolding political drama. Albert Reynolds' government of 'historic compromise' between Fianna Fáil and Labour had finally collapsed some weeks before, after months of internal tension, disagreement over tax concessions for expatriates, and the publication of the Beef Tribunal report. That tribunal had investigated government export guarantees given by Reynolds, and he issued a press release in advance of the report's publication asserting that he had been cleared of any wrongdoing claimed by his critics, principally Desmond O'Malley, leader of the Progressive Democrats. As taoiseach, he had had sight of the report and he got his retaliation in first. Then there was the appointment of Attorney General Harry Whelehan as president of the High Court, without the full consent of Tánaiste Dick Spring. It had been discovered that a Northern Ireland extradition warrant for a convicted paedophile priest, Father Brendan Smyth, had lain unattended for seven months in the attorney general's office. Albert Reynolds claimed that a deal had been done with Spring on the Whelehan appointment some weeks previously.

An attempt to stitch the Fianna Fáil coalition together again, replacing Reynolds with Bertie Ahern, had failed, so Labour had to turn to the opposition to find new government partners. Not that *they* were reluctant. John Bruton was very anxious to do a deal; his continued leadership of Fine Gael almost certainly depended on it. I was the presenter of RTÉ radio's *News at One* at the time and one of Bruton's able young lieutenants, Ivan Yates, joined me for an interview in which he warned publicly that if Fine Gael were not in government after the political debacle, John would be given 'time and space' to assess his future. In other words, time to go gracefully. Bruton had already faced down a challenge to his leadership just nine months previously. He survived, but the party was deeply divided, with consequences that would sorely affect the future government. But all that dissolved into the shadows cast by the political spotlight of the moment. Fine Gael grandee Jim Mitchell believed that Bruton would never become taoiseach because of his 'charisma deficit', but now he was the man of the hour. It was either John Bruton for taoiseach – or a general election.

Dick Spring's Labour Party had thrown away a golden chance to negotiate for their objective of rotating taoisigh, which would have been a first since the foundation of the state. They had rebuffed Fine Gael after the Reynolds resignation, and had then attempted to reconstruct the Fianna Fáil arrangement. When further public revelations erupted in the Father Brendan Smyth affair – a report in the *Irish Times* revealed that other members of Reynolds' cabinet had also had vital information about the delayed extradition warrant – Labour abandoned Fianna Fáil. Spring told Fergus Finlay, his close adviser, that he could not trust them in government. In Finlay's memoir he quotes Spring saying, 'We're never going to be out of trouble with these guys, are we?' So Labour had a reduced hand of cards, but they were playing them as hard as they could.

When Fine Gael's general secretary, Ivan Doherty, drove to John Bruton's country home at Dunboyne, County Meath, to accompany him to Peter Wilson's funeral in Enniskillen on 10 December 1994, the vital share-out of cabinet places was an issue that Doherty raised with Bruton. Labour wanted the Department of Finance as part of the deal. In coalition with Fianna Fáil, Labour had succeeded in winning foreign affairs and the new giant Department of Enterprise and Employment, but swapping the latter for control of Ireland's purse strings would be unprecedented for a left-wing party; and in a Fine Gael-led coalition, it would smack distinctly of weakness. John Bruton was keenly aware of this. His immediate reaction had been to reject the demand outright, muttering, 'If they want an election – let's give it to them.' But then he agonised about it. It was just before Christmas. The polls had clearly indicated that the public did not want an election. Doherty said to Bruton: 'Do you want to be taoiseach? That's the question. You're going to be taoiseach, so it doesn't matter who has finance.' John Bruton's instinct was the same. A government formed out of these negotiations would be historic – the first in the history of the state formed without an election. Bruton was so preoccupied with the negotiations that he forgot to bring a suitable overcoat to the funeral on that bitterly cold December day. When they reached Enniskillen, he borrowed his general secretary's fine Crombie, leaving Ivan with a casual anorak from the car, while Bruton rang his negotiators to let them know he had arrived, and then they went into the church.

John Bruton and Dick Spring saw each other at the service but there was no contact. They left by different doors, with separate photos captured by the press. Bruton phoned his negotiators in Dublin again for a longer session on the agreed policy programme which he noted on one of the school copybooks he used for notes. Afterwards they got into Bruton's car and headed for home. Bruton read out the details from his copybook and as they neared the border, he was relaxed, comfortable that he was going to be taoiseach of the new government: 'Let's have a drink on it,' he said as they drove into Derrylin. They found an open pub and, to the bemusement of early drinkers in the sleepy Northern border town who were used to having the pub to themselves, toasted the formation of the Rainbow government – a unique experiment in Ireland's history. When the new administration was established, Ivan Doherty became programme manager for Enda Kenny, Minister for Tourism and Trade in the Rainbow coalition.

There were other hurdles to be jumped, including last-minute negotiations over Democratic Left's representation at the cabinet table. It was agreed to include Democratic Left's Pat Rabbitte as a super junior minister who could attend cabinet but would not have voting rights; and the party's leader, Proinsias De Rossa, became Minister for Social Welfare. A new junior ministry was later created for Fine Gael's Donal Carey. Two years earlier, during the coalition negotiations between all parties after the November 1992 election, Bruton had made the mistake of ruling out including Democratic Left in a coalition. When Spring rang him to check before he finally did the deal with Fianna Fáil, Bruton had said the party was still a 'red line'; it would be unacceptable to Fine Gael as a government partner. Now, Democratic Left *was* acceptable, despite its position further left than Labour, and concerns over reports that it had received money from the Soviet Union. Anchoring the RTÉ radio *Election '92* programme, I had trouble reaching Proinsias at his constituency count, and joked that he 'must be in the Kremlin basement looking for the money documents', to gales of laughter from the panel (astonishingly reported in the *Irish Times* the next day), but this was no longer a red-hot issue. Bruton actually developed friendly relations with the senior members of the party in opposition, and even more so in government; they shared his approach to Northern Ireland.

A fundamental psychological barrier had been crossed. A Fine Gael leader could live with a Labour finance minister and with the more radical Democratic Left. For Labour, having finance as well as foreign affairs would help them to forget about the taoiseach's office – at least during this administration. It would also mean that, at a time of growing prosperity, Labour could put its stamp on taxation and general economic policy while at the same time demonstrating that the party could act responsibly with the country's finances. The hope was that it would contribute to the stability of the enterprise. There were plenty of doom-mongers, though. Vincent Browne mused in his *Irish Times* column that the government might not survive its first budget, which was just six weeks away. In fact, the budget was to initiate the government's first crisis, but not over the financial differences that Vincent foresaw. As for the rotating taoiseach idea, it would eventually fall to the *second* three-party government – Fianna Fáil, Fine Gael and the Greens – of 2020 to finally have a rotating taoiseach, the position being shared between Micheál Martin, leader of Fianna Fáil, and Leo Varadkar, the Fine Gael leader, later replaced by Simon Harris.

I never had any direct connection with Fine Gael before I began working for the taoiseach. My father was a Fianna Fáil cumann chairman for a short period in later life. He resigned because he became disillusioned with the party he had supported for most of his life. An uncle, Hugh O'Gorman, who had been in the anti-Treaty IRA, was interned in Finner camp between Bundoran and Ballyshannon during the bitter winter of 1922–3. He died young and my mother blamed the imprisonment for breaking his health. My parents became floating voters, at a time when that was rare. John Bruton had approached me in January 1994 to become communications director of Fine Gael, and I turned down the offer. So when he was on the way to becoming taoiseach, I first thought wryly of what might have been. I was truly surprised when the offer of the press secretary's job came. We had always had a good journalist–politician relationship, and after the defeat of the second Fine Gael–Labour coalition of 1982–7, Bruton was very helpful, doing a substantial background interview for my first book, *Irish Politics Now*, co-written with Fergal Keane, with inputs from RTÉ staff involved in the 1987 election.

Unlike many of my colleagues, I did not write Bruton off as a serious player in politics. I considered him thoughtful, intelligent and, as an interviewee, a man who could roll with the punches. He never resented a tough encounter, as long as it was fair, and he had been through many rugged interviews during his sometimes embattled career, from the collapse of Garret FitzGerald's first coalition with Labour in 1981–2 because of Bruton's planned imposition of VAT on children's shoes, to the challenge to his own leadership of Fine Gael in early 1994. The tax on children's shoes, which was hung around Bruton's neck in the media for years, was not in fact his doing, though he never shirked his ministerial responsibility or tried to share the blame. He had rejected it when it was put forward by senior finance officials – on the strange grounds that women with small feet could avoid the tax – but Bruton was overruled by the taoiseach, who took the officials' side. FitzGerald admitted as much in a late-night news conference after the government fell. The foundation of Irish prosperity was in fact laid down by Bruton in his 1987 budget, which could not be put before the Dáil because Labour had left the government. But his budget was implemented by Haughey's Fianna Fáil government, formed after the 1987 general election. Media and historians have given all the credit for this budget to Minister for Finance Ray MacSharry and to Charles Haughey, an issue that needs to be reviewed.

There was no honeymoon for the Rainbow government when it took power mid-term. One piece of scripted hyperbole for Bruton was to become an albatross around me and my colleagues' necks. After his election as taoiseach, John Bruton told the Dáil that he would conduct his government 'as if behind a pane of glass'. During the political turmoil of the previous months, much had been made of the need for openness, transparency and accountability. Dick Spring in particular had stressed the need for these qualities in a speech after leaving Reynolds' government. So the new administration had set the bar very high. Too high, was the response of my predecessor as press secretary, Seán Duignan, when he heard Bruton's 'pane of glass' speech. 'That'll be the day,' was his verdict.

The Dáil committee established to investigate the overhanging issues from the previous administration continued its hearings. It took statements from all the key players, but little new information emerged from the evidence. I became convinced that events which had happened, and facts revealed, were often exaggerated and even given sinister meaning because of the failure of trust between Dick Spring and Albert Reynolds. That breakdown poisoned relations between the two coalition partners and divided key figures in Labour. For example, I was stunned when Pat Magner, a key Labour figure, responded to a casual question with a sharp denunciation of some senior Labour figures' attempts during the crisis to get Spring back into government with Fianna Fáil. I asked how relations were now, and he said, 'Better, but you don't get over that lightly.'

The whirlwind of media attention that the peace process could generate after the IRA announced a 'complete cessation' of military action more than three months before was brought home to me on my first day in the Office of the Press Secretary in Government Buildings, 19 December 1994. Before I had any time to settle in, I faced a deluge of phone inquiries from the home media, as well as from British, Northern Irish and other journalists, about Bruton's first meeting as taoiseach with John Major, due to take place in London the following day. It was a baptism of fire. I was simultaneously trying to absorb the brief for the visit and making the logistical arrangements for the traditional doorstep interviews at 10 Downing Street, as well as further interviews to be conducted later with RTÉ, BBC, ITN, *Channel 4 News* and a host of others. There was huge interest in the meeting because of the new man on the pitch. In terms of content, however, it could only be a getting-to-know-you session. We flew to RAF Northolt on the government jet, my first flight on the magnificent Gulfstream IV, a twin-jet US business plane. From Northolt we were taken by limousine, fronted by police outriders, to the prime minister's office, where John Major personally greeted us with a handshake at the door. I felt that I was walking into another world, and that was the reality. Diplomatic relations between states operate on another plane – and those between Britain and Ireland exist on a special dimension because of the troubled past and now the peace process that was history in the making.

I was accompanied by John Foley, who had been nominated deputy government press secretary by Dick Spring during the Fianna Fáil–Labour government. He had remained at his post when the Labour ministers had left the government because the appointment was to the Department of the Taoiseach, and he now continued in that role under the new administration. His role, I found out much later in Fergus Finlay's book *Snakes and Ladders*, was to 'mark' me. We took the opportunity of the leaders' meeting to get to know my opposite number, the Downing Street press secretary, Christopher Meyer. He took us to his tiny office where we had a drink in front of a comforting coal fire on a cold winter's night. When the meeting between the two leaders was ending, Chris and I were called into the cabinet room to hear the wrap-up and to assist if needed with the formula of presentation to the media outside. This was our first Rainbow encounter at government-to-government level with the issue of the decommissioning of arms. Decommissioning IRA weapons and explosives in the context of a ceasefire was the British government's objective, as well as decommissioning the arms of Protestant loyalist paramilitaries. It was also a concern for democratic parties in the Republic, Northern Ireland and the UK generally. The argument was that this was no longer necessary if the IRA's 'cessation' was really complete. The British were unhappy and distrustful because the word 'permanent' was not used, and that word was prescribed in the Downing Street Declaration. The main objective was to get John Major to agree that it was 'not a single-item agenda' and, while decommissioning was important, it was not the only issue that had to be dealt with. The first meeting between Major and Bruton went well. Both men trotted out this line to the assembled journalists from the doorstep of Number 10, and then John Bruton repeated the mantra to BBC *Newsnight*, *Channel 4 News* and other interviewers later that evening.

I shared an official car with Fergus Finlay on the way back to the Irish embassy. Fergus remarked to me that in accepting our 'not a single-item agenda' line on decommissioning, the British had softened a bit. This phrase was to be repeated by Bruton a number of times in the new year, including saying it should not be used as a 'blocking' item on the agenda for dealing with other important matters about how to achieve a Northern Ireland settlement. The issue was to become a symbolic power struggle between Sinn Féin/IRA and the British government that was almost impossible to resolve. The following day, before our return to Dublin, Bruton had his first meeting as taoiseach with Labour leader Tony Blair and Shadow Northern Ireland Secretary Mo Mowlam over coffee and biscuits in the elegant drawing room of the embassy. After an hour, they and Bruton gave short interviews to British and Irish correspondents in the foyer of the embassy. After they left, we retreated upstairs, and John remarked to me with satisfaction: 'They're in our column too.'

The taoiseach had a brief meeting with Gerry Adams at Dublin Airport on the way back; Adams was flying out somewhere. Bruton had already had a very brief encounter with Adams at an event after he became taoiseach, where he had told Adams jokingly, 'not to worry'; he was 'a teddy bear'. There wasn't much time again at this meeting, but enough to make the exchange useful and straightforward, though non-committal. Bruton reassured Adams that he and the new government had a strong commitment to the peace process; he raised the arms issue on the basis of his talk with Major, and the question of continuing punishment beatings. Adams told him then that arms decommissioning would not take place until there was a final settlement. They talked briefly about the issue of Republican prisoners in Ireland, with releases held up after the killing of a Northern postman that autumn; and Bruton also told him that he'd brought up with Major the issue of support for the Belfast-based Irish-language school Meánscoil Feirste, and it had been promised attention.

Later in January a group of Irish prisoners was released, but not without a tussle with the Department of Justice. Negotiations had begun in December with the IRA men insisting that, under the terms of the 1939 Offences Against the State Act, they did not have to sign forms pledging good behaviour to get an early release. Sinn Féin got legal advice on this. Justice officials were concerned that the releases would be seen as an amnesty. The three government party leaders met to discuss this issue. The Department of Justice accepted that the forms were not legally necessary – but they were still demanding signatures. The Provos would give only oral statements, which could be written down. Democratic Left leader and Minister for Social Welfare, Proinsias De Rossa, who had been an active republican, told his colleagues: 'The same thing happened to me when I was locked up – and I wouldn't sign!' The matter was resolved shortly afterwards without signed forms. An important first hurdle had been crossed. The week ended with the Christmas break – and all seemed well.

The problem with the 'pane of glass' concept is that the nature of government is to try to control events, not let them spin out of control. Exercising that control means that openness and transparency are also effectively controlled, but not necessarily abandoned. Add to that the complications of the peace process, which was the biggest story around, and there was an immediate recipe for apparent conflict between words and reality. I raised this matter with the taoiseach, who told me that by 'behind a pane of glass' he meant that all decisions would be made public after they were taken. He said the media was interested in conflict. While differences of opinion in a coalition, or even a single-party cabinet, were normal before issues were thrashed out and agreement reached, these differences could be presented in the media as splits and divisions in the government. He had also intended his words as a warning to ministers that they should behave with discretion, and not tell journalists about all the internal workings of the government. I pointed out to him that papers come out every day, and radio and TV are hungry for news all the time, so we had to take that into account and manage it as best we could with a flow of accurate information. But nothing really changed.

Bruton admired the way Liam Cosgrave, taoiseach in the 1970s, largely ignored the media, and spent his time getting on with the job. But that had been twenty years earlier.

I knew the story of the peace process from a journalist's perspective, and I was familiar with all the main personalities. But assistant press secretary Tony Heffernan and I, in particular, had to learn a new, and sometimes byzantine, diplomatic language to ensure that in our briefings we did not cause an unnecessary rift on any of the sensitive fronts – with London, the SDLP, Sinn Féin, the Unionist and loyalist parties or the bipartisan approach in the Dáil, which did not last long. Sinn Féin were in many ways the masters of peace process language and were rigorous in ensuring that different party interviewees in the media used the same language. They drove a coach and four through their interlocutors in this way. It was a tough discipline for the spokespersons of a new administration who were determined not to drop the ball. In fact, though the media gave the Rainbow government the reputation of being a very closed administration, it proved to be one of the leakiest ever. The first major crisis, which was already coming down the tracks, was caused by a leak. We had a minor skirmish over the appointment of two extra ministers of state – bringing the total to 17 – but when I met Des O'Malley, former Progressive Democrat leader, in Leinster House in mid-January, he cheerfully warned me, 'It hasn't even started yet – just wait till the Dáil gets back!' He was right.

2

A BUDGET SPRINGING LEAKS

A WEEK OR SO BEFORE the budget was announced, the papers carried copious stories with highly accurate information. It didn't come through the press secretary's office. There was nothing new in this, however. In recent years, extensive budget leaks before the day had become almost normal. Pretty well all the main changes were public knowledge 24 hours before the presentation of the budget statement by Ruairí Quinn, Minister for Finance. John Bruton was anxious. He called me from his car phone on the morning of the last cabinet meeting before the budget: 'The government could be destabilised by all these leaks. What's your assessment?' I was deeply concerned. I had no idea where the stream of newspaper stories was coming from, and I told him so. But I was also able to tell him that I saw no sign of concern from Labour, and their man was in charge at finance. When I had spoken to John Foley about it the previous evening, he had said that everybody seemed to be comfortable with it. If Labour hadn't had something to do with the leaks, all hell would be breaking loose. My predecessor, Seán Duignan, had warned me that Labour were 'masterful' at the art of leaking.

When I thought more deeply about this, there was a case to be made for ensuring that different measures in the budget got a good showing in the media, and that has become the norm, up to the present day. Otherwise, many items frequently get lost on budget day because the main news story from the speech dominates. It's one thing to make a decision to reveal financial measures, obviously the case now, but we weren't at that stage in 1995; the leaks were of information supposed to be budget secrets. Despite the opposition clamouring that the level of budget leaks was unprecedented, I expected that after the minister's speech, analysis of the content would begin to dominate media coverage. However, on budget day the leaks story was to take an unexpected and explosive turn.

I was sitting in my office at about 12.15 p.m. on budget day, looking forward to handling a good news story for a change, when a devastating phone call arrived from Joe Lennon, then press officer in the Department of Finance: 'I've just got a call from the *Evening Press* demanding a comment on a press statement they've just received from the minister of state at Finance, Phil Hogan, containing the key elements of the budget.' Joe Lennon was clearly annoyed. I was deeply shocked. It didn't matter that most of the information in Phil Hogan's statement was already in the public domain – this was a very public breach of the principle of budget confidentiality by a Fine Gael junior minister, hours before the senior minister was due to make his budget speech to the Dáil. If it was a press release the *Evening Herald* would have it as well. This was serious.

Clearly the *Evening Press* would splash the story on its front page, and the opposition now had an advantage: they could rekindle the leaks story, which was a major issue in itself; and they had a big wedge they could drive between the government parties. It was one thing for Ruairí Quinn to be sanguine about anonymous budget leaks – but how would he react if a Fine Gael junior minister in his Department stole his thunder with a statement to the press? I rushed to the taoiseach's office to tell John Bruton what had happened. He was dismayed. Neither of us could believe that a minister or a ministerial adviser could be unaware of the protocols dealing with the formal release of budget information. Phil Hogan's statement had been issued three hours before Quinn was due to get to his feet in the Dáil.

A worried man, I made my way past the neo-classical columns of the hallway from the taoiseach's office back to my own room wondering if this was already the beginning of the end. John Bruton was trying to get Dick Spring on the phone as I left. The situation looked ominous. Ahead of me I saw an equally worried Phil Hogan trudging up the hallway towards the taoiseach's office. 'This is disastrous,' he said as we met. 'Yes,' I said simply. He began to explain that he'd prepared a statement for the evening papers on the budget so they could catch it in their later editions. But issuing it before the minister gave his speech? How could a minister not know that would be disastrous? John Bruton was waiting for him, I told him, and he wearily continued on his way. I was very sad for Phil, whom I liked personally. He was a bundle of energy and respected in the Dáil for his affable nature. No one wanted to see him fall – but damage had been done.

(Many years later Phil became the biggest victim of what became known as 'Golfgate', a media 'scandal' about the Oireachtas Golf Society holding a political insiders' golf outing and dinner at a County Galway hotel during the Covid-19 pandemic. It became a giant story, built up by the media, and caused public outrage. This led to the resignation of both the Minister for Agriculture, Dara Calleary, and Phil, who was by then the EU Commissioner for Trade, a heavyweight brief held by an influential senior member of the European Commission. It was little comfort that years later the charges brought against the organisers of the event based on government pandemic regulations were dismissed by a court.)

My meeting with Phil a few steps from the taoiseach's office was the beginning of a long day's journey into night. The gloom had lifted a little after lunch when I went to see Bruton again. My cryptic note made at the time reads 'Problems about release. Taoiseach talked to tánaiste. Hogan personal statement? Dick Spring not going to look for heads.' The phone conversation had gone relatively well in the circumstances, but what was to be done? Could Phil Hogan explain it in a statement, or would he have to go? Fianna Fáil and the PDs hammered away at the issue in the Dáil and on TV and radio during the afternoon and evening. Then, when asked about the affair during an RTÉ *Prime Time* budget special, Ruairí Quinn appeared to leave the door open to some sort of action against Phil Hogan, saying that what happened to him was now 'a matter for the taoiseach'. This sounded ominous. Quinn was reported to have been the Labour minister who had gone, with others, to Albert Reynolds' office before the fall of his government just two months before, saying 'We've come to get a head.'

The taoiseach called an evening crisis meeting in the conference room adjoining his office. It was already dark on this cold January day. Among those who attended were Seán Barrett, then a minister of state and chief whip; Michael Lowry, Minister for Transport, Energy and Communications; the taoiseach's programme manager, Seán Donlon; his political adviser, Roy Dooney; and myself. Phil Hogan spent some considerable time alone with the taoiseach and then began drafting a statement of the facts in a private office that also adjoins the taoiseach's own room. What emerged indicated a breakdown in communications between Hogan and his political adviser, who had sent the statement to the evening papers. The adviser was clear in his mind that the minister knew what he was doing with the statement when he sent it out. The minister, on the other hand, could not recall any exchange which could be interpreted as an endorsement of the early release of his budget statement.

After several hours trying to talk our way around this, there was a distinct atmosphere of crisis. The taoiseach did not want to leave the office that night until he knew what he was going to say in the Dáil about the affair the next day. He wanted to know the facts, but there was a clear conflict of evidence. By 4 a.m. everyone was bleary-eyed, nerves were frayed, and the atmosphere was very tense. Phil Hogan's adviser had joined the meeting and described in detail his recollection of his contacts with the minister, and his understanding of his tasks. After several hours, he departed. Then Phil wrestled with his story. I had an eerie sense of déjà vu, combined with early hours surrealism. It was in this room that, ten weeks before, Albert Reynolds and his ministers had struggled to write the botched Dáil statement on the Father Brendan Smyth affair, attempting to save his government during the November crisis. The majority consensus was that unless Phil could say clearly that he knew nothing about the leak of the budget statement, he would have to resign. If he did make such a statement, it would place the blame on his adviser, which would be seen as wrong since, as minister, he should bear responsibility; and it could potentially expose a conflict of evidence which, if unresolved, would throw petrol on the flames. Phil was understandably reluctant to accept that he could lose his job at the Department of Finance because of this fiasco. There were some who felt the approach was too purist, but John Bruton was determined to apply rigorous standards – as he had promised on taking office – and we were all aware of this.

I was acutely aware of the danger we now faced – making decisions or drafting half-baked statements in the small hours with no one in a fit state to think clearly would be a mistake. I pleaded with the taoiseach to adjourn the meeting and go home for a few hours' sleep. Thankfully, there was general agreement. At that stage – though no one was saying it outright – there was an acceptance among those present that Phil would have to go, and with a few hours to contemplate everything he would see this himself. When I got to the office the next morning, the situation had resolved itself. Phil had had further discussions with John Bruton and decided to resign to protect the government's integrity. Later that day he made a personal statement to the Dáil setting out his reasons. Mayo TD Jim Higgins took over his job at finance, breaking the ice caused by the anti-Bruton heave – he had been among those opposed to Bruton.

In retrospect, it does appear that Hogan had to fall on his sword for what in practical terms seemed a relatively small transgression. Given that information in his statement was already in the public domain, his offence could be seen as a technical breach. But at the time the principle of the thing loomed very large. A junior minister in the Department of Finance had publicly upstaged the Department chief before his budget speech, and the affair has to be seen in the context of the collapse of the previous government. Some opposition speakers protested that they had not called for his resignation – Phil had been made to walk the plank to save the government's skin. But his departure ended the crisis for a young and mainly inexperienced administration. For some months afterwards, Phil Hogan's principled departure from the government became the centrepiece of John Bruton's stump speech at gatherings around the country. Hogan was portrayed as a hero and used as a model of correct behaviour, taking the rap when something had gone wrong. That, and constant praise for Albert Reynolds for his part in the peace process, eventually got to people. As the summer of 1995 approached, several ministers asked me to tell Bruton to drop the two subjects and move on. I was reluctant to do so – but I discovered later that the message had been passed to Bruton by other means.

No sooner was the budget affair out of the way than the government hit its first major controversy over Northern Ireland.

John Bruton, Dick Spring and Proinsias De Rossa had their first formal meeting with Gerry Adams and a Sinn Féin delegation early in the new year of 1995. The government had made assurances, both public and private, that it would continue to fully support the peace process. Sinn Féin was also aware that the taoiseach had tried to get Martin Mansergh, Fianna Fáil's Northern Ireland adviser, to stay on with the Rainbow to work on the process; and that also contributed to confidence-building. This move was suggested to him by the former taoiseach, Fine Gael's Garret FitzGerald, and was supported by Tánaiste Dick Spring. In his biography of Mansergh, Kevin Rafter says his 'declining the opportunity to remain with the new coalition administration', and thus no longer playing a key role in the peace process, made the Sinn Féin president very angry. A close contact of Adams is quoted, in Martin Mansergh's biography, as saying: 'Gerry Adams was very upset with Martin's decision. He was furious with him.' If Mansergh had accepted the offer, it is possible that an unnecessary and bloody breakdown in the ceasefire could have been avoided. No one in the Department of the Taoiseach had Mansergh's long-standing relationship with Adams or his long years of experience on Northern policy. There was no one who might have been trusted by and able to explain to Adams and Sinn Féin the increasingly constrained political context in which John Major found himself. Mansergh would have known and understood the House of Commons scene. From this point on, Major might need the nine Ulster Unionist Party (UUP) MPs to keep his government in office. The unionists had already supported him in 1993 on a key vote in the Commons about the EU Maastricht Treaty; Major had survived, first of all, because of Speaker Betty Boothroyd's casting vote, then on a recount by a miscounted one vote. The IRA decommissioning issue, which Major made a precondition of all-party talks, was central to Major's relationship with the unionists. It certainly suited his political needs in the House of Commons to have the UUP MPs by his side, but it was probably a deeply felt trust issue for Major as well.

However, the overture to Mansergh was declined; he later became a Fianna Fáil TD and a junior minister in government. Rafter says in his biography that Mansergh, in briefing Bruton on the peace process, advised 'that there was a serious lack of personnel in the Department of the Taoiseach to deal with policy on the North. He made suggestions on personnel from the Department of Foreign Affairs whose transfer would address the issue.' I believe the person he had in mind was the head of the Anglo-Irish Division of the Department of Foreign Affairs, Seán Ó hUiginn, a gifted and highly respected second secretary of the Department, who had been deeply involved in drafting the Downing Street Declaration and the Joint Framework Documents. Seán would have been an excellent choice, but I doubt that the tánaiste, Dick Spring, would have wanted to lose his services. No move was made.

3

A PLOT TO WRECK A PEACE PLAN

THE RAINBOW'S NEXT SHOCK WAS to come from London and the unionists. On 1 February *The Times* led with the dramatic headline 'Anglo-Irish Plan for Joint Body: Document reveals proposals that will alarm Ulster Unionists'. The first paragraph of the story would have alarmed those unionists even more. It read: 'The British and Irish Governments have drawn up a document that brings the prospect of a united Ireland closer than it has been at any time since partition in 1920. The constitutional deal, to be discussed at a summit between John Major and John Bruton, the Irish taoiseach, is certain to be seen as a sell-out by the Unionist community.' The paper went on to quote from what it described as a draft text of the main Joint Framework Document which outlined the creation of a joint North–South body with 'radical executive powers, including the right to deal with Brussels', and a 'declaration of the birthright of everyone born in either jurisdiction to be part, as of right, of the Irish nation'.

The quid pro quo was an Irish promise to change Articles 2 and 3 of the Constitution, which laid out the Republic's territorial claim to Northern Ireland, though the paper said the language was not precise, suggesting that the exact terms were yet to be agreed. According to *The Times*, the proposals for the new body went 'further even than the 1973

Sunningdale Agreement that led to the Ulster Workers' Council strike the following year'. That strike had brought about the collapse of the first power-sharing government in Northern Ireland and an embryonic North–South Council of Ireland. The newspaper also said that relations between Ulster Unionists and the Northern Ireland Office were at their lowest since the Downing Street Declaration, which had been agreed by Taoiseach Albert Reynolds and John Major, and the unionists considered themselves effectively excluded from the consultative process.

Significantly, it said that several members of the British cabinet, led by Viscount Cranbourne, were warning in private that the proposed deal would never be accepted by the Protestant community in the North. Cranbourne was seen as a bulwark against progress in the peace process as John Major's Commons majority disappeared and his grip on power was markedly weakened by his opponents within the Conservative Party. *The Times* went further in an editorial attacking the document for proposing the 'harmonisation' of policy on health, education, social services, agriculture and economic affairs. 'Nationalists – then [at the Sunningdale conference in 1973] and now – regarded harmonisation of policy across the border as the logical prelude to unification,' the editorial said. It saw even worse to come. 'The document makes clear that the new institution will extend its powers as the years pass.' The remit of the body, the editorial quotes from the leaked material, 'should be dynamic, enabling progressive extension of its functions to new areas'.

The Times went on to give a simplistic view of the destruction of Sunningdale with its Council of Ireland two decades before, failing to mention that it collapsed because Harold Wilson's new Labour government had allowed the lawless Ulster Workers' Council to take power in Northern Ireland without lifting a finger to stop it. The newspaper said that that 'should act as a warning to those who believe that cross-border institutions can be established without provoking Unionist outrage'. In an ominous tone, 'The Thunderer' of Fleet Street concluded: 'A road has been marked out which leads – if it leads anywhere – to joint authority and eventual unification. It is for the British and Irish governments to prove that it also leads to peace.'

The Framework Documents set out the thinking of the two governments on an agreed resolution of the Northern problem. These documents were so important that they were subjected to intense examination by the new Irish government over two days in early January, with critical probing by Bruton and De Rossa. The text negotiation was carried out by a group of Irish and British officials called the Liaison Group. The taoiseach wanted his own input and scrutiny, so the secretary general of his Department, Paddy Teahon, and the secretary general of the Department of Justice, Tim Dalton, joined the team. It was important that the taoiseach had ownership of drafting an outline settlement of the Northern Ireland question. There was much time-consuming and torturous wrangling over language, because of the groundbreaking and historic nature of the material, and the leak to *The Times* was clearly designed to blow it off track. It caused consternation in both Dublin and London. I got my first call about it at home at 2 a.m. from John Armstrong on the night desk of the *Irish Times*, who had got hold of a first edition of the London newspaper. It was the first of many calls – but it didn't come as a total surprise because we had been alerted that a story was on the way.

The British side used early morning radio and television to respond. The Northern Ireland secretary, Sir Patrick Mayhew, was everywhere on nearly every television and radio station dismissing as 'absolute rubbish' and 'untrue' the suggestion that the main document brought the prospect of a united Ireland closer than at any time since 1920. If agreed, he said, it would not bring a united Ireland 'closer by one minute'. The British strategy was clear – blast the story for its 'false' conclusions and the leak for its destructive political agenda, while journalists sought to establish the status of the text. Sir Patrick agreed that he recognised 'some language, some phrases', but he largely succeeded in damning the motivation of the leakers – who wanted to 'destabilise the process' – and insisting that nothing would be imposed. In his BBC Radio Ulster interview, Mayhew spoke about not knowing if the document 'ever will be agreed with the Irish government', so the taoiseach's office wanted to nail this down immediately.

Before the Dáil met that morning at 10.30, the taoiseach tried to speak to Major on the phone. That wasn't possible, so at 10.35 Seán Donlon agreed a joint response with Rod Lyne, one of Major's key officials in Downing Street, that neither government would be thrown off course in the peace process, and the next key step would be to complete the Framework Documents as soon as possible. The message was passed to the taoiseach in the Dáil and he was able to put it on the record. That was an important first response through official channels. The British had been frustrating progress on the documents, even rowing back on previously agreed text precisely because they feared a unionist backlash, and we wanted to limit as much as possible the potential for backsliding.

A meeting between Dick Spring and Patrick Mayhew in the third week of January had not, as expected, wrapped up the negotiations. We were assured that Mayhew would be making a statement to the House of Commons to follow up on his broadcasting broadside. And, as contacts continued between Government Buildings and Downing Street, it was clear the British were deeply angered by the leak. Our hope was that John Major would be so angry at this blatant attempt to force his hand in public that it would stiffen his resolve. The UUP had been warning about the Liaison Group officials' talks for some time in advance of a meeting between their leader, Jim Molyneaux, and John Major the previous week. We now heard that the meeting had not gone well. Molyneaux had been very negative and did not think his party would accept the Framework Documents. Major's reassurances to him were to no avail.

It was obvious that the British were nervous and the difficulties in the Liaison Group were caused by British ministers changing texts their officials had presented to them. In the afternoon, we were briefed by Downing Street that John Major would make a special statement to the nation on BBC television that night. These events are as rare in the British system as they are in our own. It was Major's third such broadcast – the others were during the Gulf War and after the Downing Street Declaration in 1993, which laid out the agreed principles of the two states, Ireland and the UK, for a peaceful resolution of the Northern problem. This underlined his concern. During the broadcast, which took over the prime nine o'clock slot before the BBC news, Major stressed that the Joint Framework would be a 'consultation paper' for the parties to discuss; any North–South bodies must be accountable to people in the North; and the outcome would be subject to a referendum. But the peace process, and the document negotiations, would continue. I spoke on the phone to John Bruton and Dick Spring immediately after Major's broadcast because I felt we should sign off the day with a statement in accord with the prime minister's remarks. Some journalists had already been seeking a response. So I ended a trying day ringing around the political correspondents, stressing our agreement with Major that the proposals should be judged 'as a whole' when the documents were published. The Framework Documents were an important part of the strategy for dealing with the conflict in Northern Ireland and laid the foundations for the Belfast Good Friday Agreement.

The peace process grew out of the failure of successive Irish and British government attempts to marginalise and defeat those on the political extremes and those using violence, particularly the Provisional IRA. I believed too that some republican activists realised that the 'war' with the British had reached a stalemate, and that violence was a cul-de-sac. The policy of 'an Armalite in one hand and a ballot box in the other' was leaving the ballot boxes very light. Sinn Féin, led by Adams, wanted to co-operate with and join the constitutional political process while still pursuing its goals, so the Hume–Adams dialogue remained a powerful propelling political force, the first pillar of the peace process; this, together with the efforts of the ambitious new taoiseach, Albert Reynolds, had paved the way to the Major–Reynolds Downing Street Declaration on 15 December 1993. This was the second pillar of the peace process. Despite the fact that Sinn Féin and the IRA never formally accepted or endorsed the Declaration, it was followed in late August 1994 by the IRA declaring a 'complete cessation' of military activities, followed by the loyalists' end to their campaigns, the third pillar of the process. There were rocky moments, however, on the path to the joint declaration, including leaks, well documented in Rafter's biography of Martin Mansergh.

I was presenting RTÉ radio's *News at One* in 1993 during the sometimes heated discussions between John Major and the new Fianna Fáil taoiseach, Albert Reynolds, about a significant deal on a joint declaration. I covered their testy summit meeting at Dublin Castle in early December that year and stayed close to my contacts after the meeting. I got the final tip-off just before the next summit, so we were able, overnight on 15 December, to relocate the *News at One* to be broadcast from the Irish embassy in London, and Taoiseach Reynolds joined me live in our makeshift studio straight from Downing Street after the Declaration was agreed, leaving the officials celebrating with Major's champagne. Reynolds told me, and the Irish people on the air, that he was confident that the Declaration would pave the way to peace. Despite the Declaration never being endorsed by Sinn Féin, the IRA declared its 'compete cessation' eight months later.

In the Declaration the British government reiterated the important statement made by a previous Northern Ireland secretary, Peter Brooke, in November 1990, that the British government had 'no selfish strategic or economic interest' in Northern Ireland. There was no statement from the British that they would act as 'persuaders' for the united Ireland that Sinn Féin wanted. Rather, the Declaration statement said the governments' aim was to 'foster agreement and reconciliation leading to a new political framework founded on consent and encompassing arrangements within Northern Ireland, for the whole island, and between these islands'. These were the three dimensions or strands of the overall British–Irish proposals to come in the Framework Documents then being considered by senior Irish and British officials. But, crucially, the Declaration statement said:

> The British government agree that it is for the people of the island of Ireland alone, by agreement between the two parts respectively, to exercise their right of self-determination on the basis of consent, freely and concurrently given, North and South, to bring about a united Ireland, if that is their wish.

This built on the terms of the 1985 Anglo-Irish Agreement, signed by Taoiseach Dr Garret FitzGerald and British Prime Minister Margaret

Thatcher, which embedded the principle of consent for any constitutional changes to take place on the island of Ireland. Reynolds formally conceded on behalf of the Irish government that 'the democratic right of self-determination by the people of Ireland as a whole must be achieved and exercised with and subject to the agreement and consent of a majority of the people of Northern Ireland.' Britain would not stand in the way of unity, if a majority in Northern Ireland expressed that desire.

Republicans were not overly pleased. Their view of the self-determination of the Irish people was that it must be exercised on an all-Ireland basis. This of course exposes the fact that unionists are a minority in this context (graphically illustrated in the Sinn Féin landslide in the all-Ireland election in 1918) and the Sinn Féin view was that this minority should not be able to exercise a veto over the wishes of the majority community in Ireland as a whole. On a strictly logical level, this in fact is true; Ireland was a geopolitical entity for many centuries. However, constitutional nationalist politicians, North and South, had long accepted as far back as the Sunningdale Agreement in 1973 that unionists and loyalists could not be coerced into a united Ireland, and consent would be a necessity for a peaceful settlement. However, despite Sinn Féin's non-endorsement of the Downing Street Declaration, and repeated calls for clarification by Gerry Adams, Reynolds insisted that it was a considerable breakthrough and continued to press the party and the IRA for a significant response.

It was the first time that the British government had spoken of the 'self-determination' of the Irish people, albeit in a heavily qualified context, and they were now to be promoters of 'agreement' in Ireland. Their role would be 'to encourage, facilitate and enable the achievement of such an agreement', echoing John Hume's 'agreed Ireland' formula. The British even accepted that such an agreement may 'as of right, take the form of agreed structures for the island as a whole, including a united Ireland achieved by peaceful means'. For the unionists, Reynolds pledged in the context of a settlement to 'put forward and support proposals for change in the Irish Constitution which would fully reflect the principle of consent in Northern Ireland'. In other words, by dropping the claim to Northern Ireland in Articles 2 and 3 of the Constitution and providing a guarantee of consent. The Declaration also directly addressed Sinn Féin and the IRA:

> Democratically mandated parties which establish a commitment to exclusively peaceful methods, and which have shown that they abide by the democratic process, are free to participate fully in democratic politics and to join in dialogue in due course between the governments and the political parties on the way ahead.

In media interviews Mayhew and Major said that three months after a ceasefire, Sinn Féin/IRA would be invited to exploratory talks, but Mayhew made clear in his interviews that these talks would, *inter alia*, be about decommissioning weapons to demonstrate that violence was ended. In an interview referenced by Paul Bew and Gordon Gillespie in their 1996 book, Mayhew said: 'If they hold on to arms, if you know they have got them, then quite patently they are not giving them up for good.' In the Dáil, Dick Spring, tánaiste of the Reynolds administration, had spoken of the question of proving that a cessation of violence was permanent. 'We are talking about the handing up of arms and are insisting that it would not be simply a temporary cessation of violence to see what the political process offers. There can be no equivocation in relation to the determination of both governments in that regard.'

It was a view that he changed later when the British government stubbornly used decommissioning as a barrier to talks, until they got what they demanded – evidence of putting arms beyond use to establish trust. After the IRA finally announced 'a complete cessation of military operations' as of midnight, Wednesday 31 August 1994, almost at once the debate began over what 'a complete cessation' meant. Major questioned it because the word 'permanent' was not used. John Bruton, leader of Fine Gael (before he became taoiseach), took it 'on good faith' that it was permanent. Albert Reynolds viewed it as permanent and said 'the long nightmare is over'.

Martin McGuinness eased some scepticism by declaring that he took the IRA statement at face value, and it meant a complete cessation of military operations 'under all circumstances'. There was general media and public celebration of a historic moment. The cessation was not time-limited, and it was to transform people's lives in Northern Ireland over the next 17 months, while it lasted, and beyond. The ceasefire was eventually broken, but because of the duration of the ceasefire, a Rubicon had been crossed by republicans and the political landscape was changed in ways that could not be reversed. Sinn Féin seriously gained political ground, ironically in a Northern election they strongly opposed. They could interact with the British and Irish administrations, meeting ministers and having talks with Reynolds, Bruton, Spring, Mayhew and senior officials of both governments. This in turn was expected to lead to all-party negotiations where the parties would negotiate to achieve their aims through exclusively peaceful and democratic means. Underpinning that was a need for the two governments to set out the parameters of what they felt could be achieved.

The key Framework paper, 'A New Framework for Agreement', on which Dick Spring and Anglo-Irish Liaison Group officials had worked hard for more than a year was effectively a first draft of a settlement, a blueprint for a deal that could be supported by nationalists and unionists. It was to initiate the negotiating process by providing the parties with an agenda – and it was clearly understood that 'nothing is agreed until everything is agreed'. However, it did elucidate the two governments' thinking about what was attainable. The emphasis on North–South collaboration, with the establishment of North–South bodies made up of ministers from both sides of the border, that had the potential to grow across all areas – economic, social and cultural – and interact with the EU, was an undeniably powerful feature. Also undeniably powerful was the emphasis on consent for any constitutional change, which was threaded through the main Framework Document, along with guarantees that the proposed new bodies would be accountable to the people of Northern Ireland through their elected representatives. It was hoped that this would be a new beginning for Northern Ireland – but an attempt was made to undermine it by the intentionally damaging leak to *The Times*.

John Bruton had a good reputation with unionists for being fair-minded towards them, so he immediately put out feelers to see if there could be a meeting. Against the background of what had been disclosed, there was some surprise when a top-secret meeting between Jim Molyneaux and the taoiseach was agreed, and arrangements were made for it to take place at the home of Unionist MP Ken Maginnis, north of the border, on 5 February 1995. When Dick Spring heard about the meeting, he demanded that he accompany the taoiseach. The Unionist leaders were particularly distrustful of Spring, so there were fears that Molyneaux would pull out, but that didn't happen. The meeting was cordial and lasted for a couple of hours. Molyneaux was upset at his treatment by the British over the Framework Documents. He had been given sight of the Downing Street Declaration so that it could be explained to his constituents. He was offered similar access for the Framework Documents, but when he went to see Mayhew in December 1994, he was told there was as yet no document because so much remained to be agreed. He was offered a sight of it shortly before the leak, but he declined because it was too late.

Both Molyneaux and Maginnis thought *The Times* leak very damaging. Attitudes were struck over the language in the report, and they wanted to see it watered down. Bruton and Spring spelt out the advantages: language on changing Articles 2 and 3, to which Fianna Fáil was also committed; and a copper-fastening of Northern Ireland's position within the UK, based on the principle of consent. Molyneaux struck an odd note for the taoiseach and tánaiste by declaring little concern for Articles 2 and 3 (claiming the Republic's territorial rights to Northern Ireland), which he saw as historical curiosities with little real effect. Northern Ireland's position in the UK, he said, was already guaranteed by previous Irish government agreements. His real aim was to focus on diluting the cross-border bodies envisaged in the document.

The main document foresaw a far-reaching 'default mechanism' that proposed that North–South bodies would be automatically put in place by the sovereign governments if the unionists tried to renege on a deal. Molyneaux wanted that proposal dropped. Molyneaux and Maginnis wanted any cross-border bodies to be agreed by the new Northern Assembly before being put into effect by the two sovereign governments. Molyneaux's view was that the Northern Ireland Assembly would be duty-bound to set up such bodies if they had been agreed by all-party talks. They felt the Assembly would be neutered in an undemocratic way by any pre-agreement. It was, as usual, down to matters of trust. Nationalists and republicans would be wary of dropping the 'default mechanism', given that unionists would have a majority in any Assembly. Bruton and Spring made it clear that 'understandings' would not be enough. Any referendum on Articles 2 and 3 was unlikely to be successful without cross-border institutions that met the needs of the Northern minority.

Little enough comfort was taken from the meeting at the time, despite the friendly atmosphere. The default mechanism, which was modified to mollify the unionists, was a tactical device with a dual purpose. It aimed to put pressure on the unionists to agree some cross-border institutions they could stomach, lest the two governments go ahead and set up cross-border arrangements that would deepen the very limited 'joint authority' over the affairs of Northern Ireland established by the Anglo-Irish Agreement of 1985. It was a constant source of unionist irritation that Maryfield, an office of Irish officials on the outskirts of Belfast set up under this agreement, could hear evidence of discrimination, heavy-handed treatment of nationalists by the British Army, the Royal Ulster Constabulary (RUC) or the Ulster Defence Regiment (UDR), and a host of other nationalist complaints about the internal affairs of Northern Ireland. The Irish government was empowered by the agreement to make representations to the British about these matters on behalf of the minority community.

About a week or so after this sub rosa meeting across the border, I got a call from a political journalist claiming possession of information that Bruton had a secret meeting in the North with Molyneaux, now wanting confirmation and further information from the taoiseach. I said I would call Bruton and get back. Bruton was furious that there had been a leak. At first, he angrily said, 'This is so dangerous for Molyneaux; you'll have to deny it.' I said that was not going to happen. In fairness,

Bruton dropped his request immediately; he had just overreacted. We believed the leak had come from Labour sources.

The taoiseach and I discussed how to handle this sensitive leak. His fear was that dramatic publicity about the secret meeting across the border could endanger Molyneaux, who might be branded a kind of 'Lundy' (the man who urged opening the gates of besieged Derry to the army of James II in 1689) by the Democratic Unionist Party (DUP) and loyalists; he might even be physically attacked and harmed. The breach of confidence would damage relations with the Ulster Unionist leader at a time when the Framework Documents were imminent and would need some unionist acceptance. Bruton and I mulled over the possibility of throwing ourselves at the mercy of the journalist by admitting the meeting had been held, but pleading for the story not to be used on the grounds of national interests and security, and the danger of serious, even fatal, harm to Molyneaux. Bruton asked me to contact Peter Prendergast, a former government press secretary in Garret FitzGerald's administration, then in Brussels and working for the European Commission. Prendergast and I had a useful conversation, Peter agreeing with the 'plea for non-use approach' and adding that the journalist should be promised that it would be made up for with other stories.

After consulting with Bruton, who agreed with this approach, I added that he should ensure that a minister or another person should be the source of any 'exclusives'. I needed to be able to honestly deny that they came from me. He agreed. Then, taking a deep breath, I rang the journalist. I confirmed the meeting, but immediately asked that it not be published, in the national interest, and I spelt out graphically the potential personal harm to Molyneaux from this poisonous leak. I also assured the journalist that if the story was not published, it would be made up for by the taoiseach through another channel. There was silence on the line for a minute or more after I'd finished talking. Then the journalist took a big breath and finally said, 'I'll think about that.' I just said 'Thank you' and we rang off. Bruton and I waited anxiously for the newspaper the next day. I didn't sleep until I'd seen the first edition, and with great relief I saw that it was not covered. It never did appear.

The fact of the meeting was eventually published years later, deep into Eamonn Mallie and David McKittrick's book about the peace process, *The Fight for Peace*. It could have been a front-page exclusive for the journalist at the time, coming as it did just a few weeks before the Framework Documents. I was very grateful. The journalist and I never spoke of it again and I know nothing about the 'compensation' stories, and frankly I saw nothing that stood out. I often wondered if I could have resisted the temptation of such a hot story at the time, had I been in the journalist's place.

The Irish and British governments shared a fundamental objective in the peace process: that all-party talks between the Northern Ireland political parties, not further bilateral government agreements, were to be the source of agreement on the immediate future. The Anglo-Irish Agreement in 1985 had changed unionist thinking in a way that was not fully appreciated in the Republic a decade later. James Molyneaux described it as 'the beginning of the end of the Union as we have known it'. It had shown unionists that they could not trust a British prime minister – even one as right-wing and as well-disposed to their views as Margaret Thatcher – not to do another deal with the Republic, despite unionist objections, if it suited the interests of the rest of the UK. The unionists could be persuaded, it was hoped, to do a deal with the other parties in the North about sharing power so they could have real influence over how Northern Ireland was to engage with the Republic. At the time Bruton was concerned about getting unionists into the peace process with Sinn Féin, but it was clear that unionist parties' outright opposition to the Framework Documents would simply have to be ignored. 'No surrender, not an inch' had been the unionist default position for more than a century, though the wiser among them knew an accommodation would have to be reached.

Much later, in 2016, Brexit breathed new life into the old unionist dogma, explaining why unionist parties continuously defied the popular vote in the North, where 57 per cent voted in favour of staying in the EU. It gave the diehard unionists another unexpected barricade to man with 'no surrender, not an inch'. To illustrate the historical significance of the phrase, this is what Captain E.L. MacNaughton said in a letter to Hugh Kennedy, attorney general of the fledgling Irish Free State, in 1922 about the power of the Protestant Orange Order:

> It practically amounts to this, that the Protestant mob, noisy, ignorant, bigoted almost beyond belief, rule and hold sway in the 'Northern' area. They are the real masters. There is no genuine leadership. The leaders do not lead; they merely follow. They fear the machine; they cannot control it; they give utterance to those sentiments which will please this gang; to breathe a word about rapprochement would be for them political suicide.

This was quoted in UCD Professor Tom Garvin's seminal work *1922: The Birth of Irish Democracy*, which should have been obligatory reading during the years of centenary commemorations.

These words, which I call the MacNaughton rule, predicted the fate of unionist leaders who agreed, or just seemed willing to agree, to some rapprochement. Brian Faulkner (Sunningdale Agreement) lost the leadership of the UUP. David Trimble (Belfast Good Friday Agreement) lost the leadership of the UUP. Arlene Foster (Northern Ireland Protocol) lost the leadership of the DUP for suggesting that Northern Ireland would seek to make the best of the British protocol with the EU that established a commercial border with Britain in the Irish Sea, essentially keeping the North within the EU single market to avoid a hard border with the Republic. Unionist William Craig became a victim for simply suggesting a voluntary coalition with nationalists; he lost the leadership of his hardline Vanguard movement. There are others, as we shall see. On a visit to the European Parliament in Strasbourg in the late 1970s, I joined a prominent senior unionist leader for some late-night drinks in a bar in that beautiful city. I was surprised when he confessed that: 'I would not have a problem with much closer relations between North and South, or some form of shared cross-border structure, *if*, and it is a big if, I could bring my people with me.'

So after a couple of weeks of final negotiations in the shadow of this potentially destabilising leak, the Framework Documents were finally agreed, but not without some drama at Iveagh House, the seat of the Department of Foreign Affairs on Stephen's Green. Sir Patrick Mayhew forced the adjournment of a crucial day-long meeting demanding 'softer' language around the North–South bodies, until a text was produced that satisfied him, and the content still met Dick Spring's wishes.

A summit meeting between John Bruton and John Major was secretly arranged for 22 February. It was to take place at Hillsborough in County Down, the official residence of the Secretary of State for Northern Ireland. I spent some time on the phone with my opposite number in Downing Street, Chris Meyer, making arrangements for the media handling of what was going to be a big event. Once again it was a steep learning curve. Of course, during such lengthy negotiations there were Irish media leaks, as well as that leak to *The Times*, so a thumbnail sketch of the content was already in the public domain: a power-sharing administration between unionists and nationalists in the North; a North–South body or bodies, including members of both the new Northern administration and the Republic's government; and a new, strengthened relationship between Dublin and London. The belief that the two states would continue to be members of the EU was so taken for granted that it was invisible.

4

JOINT FRAMEWORK DOCUMENTS LAUNCHED

On the evening of 21 February the taoiseach's party left Baldonnel on the government jet to fly to Aldergrove airport, Belfast. Among those travelling were the taoiseach's wife, Finola; Paddy Teahon, the secretary general of the Department of the Taoiseach, who would play a larger role in Northern Ireland affairs in the future; Seán Donlon, who had a dual role as programme manager and adviser on Northern matters; the taoiseach's private secretary George Shaw, and myself. We were met at Aldergrove by Michael Ancram, the Northern Ireland minister, who guided us in the cold clammy evening darkness to a waiting military helicopter which was to fly us to Hillsborough. At moments like this the excitement of being on the inside was intense. Instead of waiting in Belfast to report on events the next day, as I would have done in my previous career, I had a close-up view as a participant. The noise of the helicopter soon brought me back to reality. We had to wear large headphones to protect our ears and through which we could hear the pilot's instructions, and we sat on cold metal seats along the bare superstructure of the chopper. Michael Ancram was sitting between the taoiseach and myself, but all I could do was smile wanly amid the din. We took off with the door open, a soldier hanging out of it keeping watch. When we were in the air, he closed the door – stopping the cold

February twilight draught – and smiled grimly at us. I wondered if he had taken part in other more unpleasant missions across the Irish countryside, but before I could conjure up any imaginings, we were already descending from the ten-minute journey, and he was opening the door again.

I saw the outline of the grey stone of the stately house as we dropped down to the helicopter pad in the growing darkness. Out we bundled and into the house for our room assignments. Seán Donlon and myself were sent to the coach house, a short walk from the main building. Because of the shortage of space – Dick Spring's foreign affairs team were also being accommodated – Seán and I had to share a fairly spartan room. After dumping our bags, we headed back to the house for supper. The meal for the officials was in two rooms that opened on to each other. Some of the Liaison Group, most of whom I was only barely familiar with still, sat together in one room, while George Shaw, myself, Chris Meyer and some of his team sat in another room. The meal was fairly rushed because we still had a fair bit of work to do making arrangements for the joint press conference to be held at the Balmoral Conference Centre after the summit the following day.

Major, Bruton, Spring and Mayhew were in the main dining room with the key Anglo-Irish officials discussing the principle Framework Document and its likely impact, as well as the questions and answers required for the news conference. After I'd eaten, I wandered into the spacious, comfortable drawing room, which was empty, and tried to look at the pictures, but I found it difficult to relax. The fact that the taoiseach had no speech yet for the launch of the document the next day was weighing on my mind. It may seem strange that there was no polished and double-checked speech, but I was discovering that, by necessity, government business is sometimes done on the run, and it takes time for a new administration to oil the wheels. At the time, I thought this was coming close to the edge. George Shaw spotted me in the drawing room, and he came in to confer. He outlined to me the secretariat arrangements he had in place, with a typist, a computer, a printer and the works all set up and ready to go. I was impressed and relieved. Soon we were joined by Seán Donlon and Paddy Teahon. The latter had not been heavily involved in Northern Ireland affairs previously but was now fully intent on playing a serious role. Donlon was the dominant player then as the taoiseach's adviser on the North. He also had a wealth of experience as a former foreign affairs official working in Northern Ireland, where he had developed a close relationship with John Hume, then was promoted to secretary general of the Department of Foreign Affairs, and afterwards, Ireland's ambassador to Washington. Seán, as the taoiseach's programme manager, also had to keep on top of the whole range of cabinet business and the work of every department. We started discussing the taoiseach's speech and were preparing to set to work.

Unfortunately for us, but perhaps fortunately for the sense of occasion, the prime minister and the taoiseach finished their dinner, and, with Patrick Mayhew and Dick Spring, joined us in the drawing room for after-dinner drinks. The mood was one of celebration and the rest of the Liaison Group from foreign affairs joined the party as well. I was too worried about the speech to enjoy it fully, and though I joined Bruton and Major, while the British PM regaled us with political stories, my mind was elsewhere. Eventually people drifted off to bed, or to other parts of the house, Fergus Finlay with Sir Patrick Mayhew to drink a bottle of fine port, and Seán, Paddy, George and myself were left alone once again to concentrate on the speech. We sat down with a few drinks and worked until nearly one o'clock, each of us contributing to and refining, page by page, a handwritten speech, which was then taken away by George for typing. Bruton was waiting with his wife, Finola, in their suite upstairs, so in the middle of the work we went to join them for a nightcap. We sat in comfortable chairs around an open fire, and Dick Spring joined us.

Spring was very relaxed, chatting about Major and Mayhew's buoyant mood over dinner. Then, in a rare moment of personal reflection in a group outside his own inner circle, he mused about the irony of how in the previous administration he played a role that was seen as 'on the side of the unionists', sympathetic to their case, while now there was a switch of roles and he was the 'nationalist' one, while Bruton was now seen as the key administration figure who was sympathetic to unionist concerns. Spring said he felt it struck a balance and sometimes this was necessary. I was a bit uncomfortable with the sort of 'hard man/soft man' routine that seemed behind his remarks, and the potential for a cynical interpretation. Unionist perception of Dick Spring's change of position, from guardian of their rights to support for the nationalist side, was later to blight his relations with unionist politicians. However, my main concern at the time was that Bruton should not be painted into a pro-unionist position. That was a straightforward reaction coming from my background, which made me a strong supporter of the constitutional nationalism that underpinned the peace process. I did not know then how deep and visceral some of Bruton's political and emotional sentiments were about the IRA, and thus Sinn Féin, which made a change of attitude related to the peace process complicated and difficult, though he worked night and day to sustain peace.

Anyway, it was getting late, so when Dick and John turned in, Seán, Paddy, George and I returned to our task. We finally completed the script and took to our beds at close to half past two. We all met again with Dick and the foreign affairs team at breakfast some hours later to fine-tune the speech and run through some of the Q&As – the agreed approach to answers by the two governments for anticipated questions from journalists at the launch of the Framework Documents. Apart from the Framework negotiations, the Q&A itself had required close negotiation since the interpretation of the complex language of the text would be crucial.

There was a photo call outside Hillsborough for the two leaders as they left for the characterless Balmoral Centre in Belfast for the press launch. I was fascinated that there were so few protesters on the way as we drove there, remembering what had happened after the signing of the Anglo-Irish Agreement in 1985. Ian Paisley, unionists and loyalists had mustered more than 100,000 demonstrators, packing the streets and grounds outside Stormont. My RTÉ *This Week* radio team and I were in Belfast to cover the Paisley/unionist rally at Stormont, staying in the famous Europa Hotel. In the evening we were enjoying a break from a tough, busy day with a few pre-dinner drinks in Robinson's bar opposite the Europa when loyalist paramilitaries smashed in the plate glass window and door, sending a cloud of glass shards flying around us as we dived to the floor. The hooded paramilitaries shouted to the staff and customers to get out immediately. When we did manage to crawl out, luckily unhurt, we hurried to a basement Chinese restaurant some distance away, thinking this would be safe, but after giving our orders, the loyalist paramilitaries arrived to close it up as well, giving us five minutes to leave.

Now, as the motorcade passed through the streets, we passed only one small group of three people shouting at the cars. Even outside the Balmoral Centre there were only a handful of protesters. I was surprised, given the significance of what had been agreed by the two governments – the detailed draft of what would be the foundations of the Belfast Agreement. Its potential dynamic for the future of Northern Ireland was far-reaching. The British government signed up to a radical approach on the 'Northern problem' not seen since the Sunningdale Agreement in 1973, so it was an encouraging sign that no major protest took place. The key text was 'A New Framework for Agreement', described as 'a shared understanding between the British and Irish Governments to assist discussion and negotiation involving the Northern Ireland parties'. I was stunned when I first studied the text as agreed. The Irish side in the Anglo-Irish Liaison Group of officials had achieved extraordinary success in the negotiations, acknowledged by John Major in his memoirs. The second document, 'A Framework for Accountable Government in Northern Ireland', from the British government, set out proposals for a new power-sharing governance structure for Northern Ireland after 22 years of direct rule from Westminster. Direct rule was introduced in 1972, suspending the Stormont parliament, when the British government was finally shamed internationally about the deliberately unionist/loyalist-dominated Northern Ireland area they had created with a gerrymandered six counties carved out of the ancient nine-county province of Ulster in 1920. The aim then had been to ensure a long-term Protestant unionist majority. When he was awarded the joint Nobel Peace Prize in 1998 with John Hume, the late former Unionist Party leader David

Trimble, first minister in the first power-sharing Executive formed after the Belfast Agreement, admitted that Northern Ireland was 'a cold house' for Catholic nationalists. That was putting it mildly.

It must be said as well that Protestant denunciation of the Irish Free State established by the Anglo-Irish Treaty in 1922 as a papist, priest-ridden place was true. Even if the Irregulars, as the anti-Treaty republican forces were known, had prevailed in the civil war, it is very unlikely that the priest-ridden nature of the south would have been different. De Valera was still the political, not military, leader of the anti-Treaty side, and his 1937 constitution as taoiseach of Saorstát Éireann, naming the state Éire, was a constitutional endorsement of the Catholic nature of the southern state, recognising the 'special position' of the Catholic Church as the religion of the majority of the people. Thankfully that was deleted in the early years of the Troubles. However, there is still much more to be done to fillet out the remains of theocratic doctrine that mar Ireland's constitution.

The power of the Catholic Church was finally broken as a result of the exposure in recent years of the appalling clerical sexual and physical abuse of children and teenagers, unmarried mothers, adoptive children and others at schools and in institutions. This, combined with direct interference in political life and legislation – telling taoisigh and ministers what to do; supporting a dangerously worded and divisive constitutional ban on abortion that contributed to the death from sepsis of Savita Halappanavar; famously bringing down an inter-party coalition government in 1951 when its Minister for Health, Noël Browne, sought to provide free health services to mothers and children – broke the grip of the Catholic Church on society. Now, with the legalisation of abortion, divorce, homosexuality and same-sex marriage (divorce, as we shall see, was made legal by the Rainbow government), the Republic is a far more enlightened and liberal place, while the North is still in large part imbued with a severe, illiberal, dissenting Protestantism.

In May 1974, to my surprise, a newly elected British Labour government disgracefully allowed the North's first power-sharing administration to fall by refusing to stand up to loyalist intimidation. Under the banner of the 'Ulster Workers' Council' (UWC), loyalist paramilitaries barricaded streets, cut off electricity and forced businesses to close. The enlightened power-sharing government including the UUP and nationalists from the SDLP was established after the Sunningdale Agreement in 1973 between Ted Heath's Conservative British government and Liam Cosgrave's National Coalition Irish government of Fine Gael and the Irish Labour Party. That agreement also included a Council of Ireland for cross-border co-operation, recognising the all-Ireland dimension, just as the key Framework Document proposed a North–South Body for the same purpose. The Sunningdale Agreement was opposed by Sinn Féin and the IRA, as well as by Ian Paisley's DUP and other unionist and loyalist organisations and paramilitaries, so violence continued, including, in May 1974, a series of loyalist paramilitary bombings in Dublin and Monaghan that killed 33 people and injured nearly 300.

I was on Dublin's O'Connell Street when the bombs started going off, awaiting my then wife at a prearranged location near the GPO; she was heavily pregnant at the time, and shopping in town with my brother and sister-in-law. I spent a frantic time waiting anxiously at the meeting place; then, when they didn't turn up, apprehensively searching for them for some time in the streets before discovering on the phone that they had managed to escape home safely to Donnybrook. They were all in a state of shock. I then called the editor of RTÉ's *7 Days*, for which I worked, to offer my services as a man on the spot in central Dublin, but the programme was already well covered, he said, so, feeling useless, but calm now that I knew my family members were safe, I went to join them.

Garret FitzGerald, who was foreign minister at the time, played a central role in the Sunningdale negotiations. In his 1991 memoirs *All in a Life*, he lambasted Harold Wilson's Labour government for allowing the loyalist paramilitaries in the UWC, which he saw as a potential 'proto-fascist movement', to bring down a hard-won power-sharing democratic government. He wrote that he and all parties in the Republic held the view that if the British government had quickly used the British Army to clear the barricades and support the operation of the electricity stations that were knocked out, the power-sharing government could have survived. But the Wilson government did not act.

JOINT FRAMEWORK DOCUMENTS LAUNCHED

With heavy irony, in the 1990s' peace process Sinn Féin beat hard on the door to all-party talks in order to conclude the similar Belfast Agreement in 1998. The late Seamus Mallon, who was the SDLP's deputy first minister in the initial Executive under the Agreement, wryly commented at the time that the 1998 Belfast Agreement was 'Sunningdale for slow learners'. His remark did not go down well with some. The core elements of the Belfast Agreement were very similar to Sunningdale, as well as the 1995 Framework formulas: a power-sharing administration in Belfast including representatives of the unionist and nationalist communities; a North–South Council with members from both the Dublin government and the Northern administration; and new Dublin–London arrangements. The Frameworks proposed that the Northern administration would be based on a 90-seat assembly elected by proportional representation, the same system used in the Republic and very different from the Westminster first-past-the-post system, a deeply unfair method that leaves millions of voters in the UK without adequate national parliamentary representation.

The key Framework for Agreement now being laid out in 1995 by Bruton and Major contained the guiding principles for achieving co-operation in the search for an overall agreement. I outline the use of the Framework principles in the Belfast Agreement here:

> The principle of self-determination as set out in the Joint Frameworks, that is the consent of both parts of Ireland, recorded separately.

This was adopted in the Belfast Good Friday Agreement, with Sinn Féin dropping its demand for self-determination of the Irish people, as a whole, on the island of Ireland.

> That the consent of the governed is an essential ingredient for stability in any political arrangement.

This was adopted in the Belfast Good Friday Agreement.

> That agreement must be pursued and established by exclusively democratic, peaceful means.

This was achieved through US Senator George Mitchell's International Body on Decommissioning's 'Six Principles', a signed-up requirement for parties to enter into all-party talks. Both the International Body and the all-party talks were established by the Bruton Rainbow coalition and Major's British government.

> That any new political arrangements must be based on full respect for, and protection and expression of, the rights and identities of both traditions in Ireland and even-handedly afford both communities in Northern Ireland parity of esteem and treatment, including equality of opportunity and advantage.

This Framework text became central to the Belfast Agreement.

The new North–South institutions were an essential part of the drive in the Framework Documents to sustain peace and the six-month-old IRA ceasefire, recognising the importance of the all-Ireland dimension. John Major appealed to people in Northern Ireland to 'carefully and calmly' consider the documents; they would see that their 'fears about it are illusory'. John Bruton said the purpose was a 'new dispensation' in which both communities could feel at home. In their remarks, and their answers to the Balmoral press conference questions, both leaders stressed time and again that 'consent' and 'agreement' were central to everything. The documents were a 'landmark event in the affairs of this island' and they were 'fair and balanced, threatening no one', Bruton said.

The North–South body was spelt out in considerable detail over 58 paragraphs in the Framework. It would have the power to create other bodies by agreement to deal with specific topics 'on an all-island or cross-border basis'. This North–South institution would bring together members of the Irish government and the new administration in Northern Ireland to deal with functions under the headings Executive, Harmonising or Consultative over a range of matters, including those involving the EU. Activities of potential 'harmonisation' included: agriculture and fisheries; industrial development; consumer affairs; transport; energy; trade; health; social welfare; education; and economic policy. It was a lot wider than *The Times* had reported. Meetings were expected to be regular and frequent. Envisaging further North–South bodies to cover the range of government business, the document said they should 'cater adequately for the present and future political, social and economic inter-connections on the island of Ireland, enabling representatives of the main traditions, North and South, to enter agreed dynamic, new, co-operative and constructive relationships'. The remit of the overarching North–South body 'should be dynamic, enabling progressive extension by agreement of its functions to new areas', keeping pace with 'harmonisation' and 'greater integration between the two economies'. This language could hardly be stronger and testifies to the intelligence and negotiating ability of the officials.

While the media reported that Sinn Féin welcomed the Framework, it led Gerry Adams to declare at the Sinn Féin ard fheis that year, as reported by the *Irish Times*: 'It is undeniable that the document embraces an all-Ireland character and that it deals with the general notion of one-island social, economic and political structures.' In his updated testamentary book published shortly afterwards, he wrote that the 'ethos' of the main Framework Document 'and the political framework envisaged is clearly an all-Ireland one. It deals with the general concept of one-island social, economic and political structures, and moves the situation closer to an all-Ireland settlement.' While the Framework Documents were for discussion, Adams wrote, 'its publication by the two governments was a clear recognition that partition has failed, that British rule in Ireland has failed, and that there is no going back to the failed policies and structures of the past.' Under the terms of the main Framework Document, he continued, 'the British must remove all anti-nationalist symbols and appearances from the Six-County statelet in order to provide parity of esteem in the North ... they are obliged under the Framework to bring about legislative change to improve the position of nationalists while protecting the rights of other citizens.' Until now,

British policy had labelled nationalists as inferior, second class; but 'parity of esteem' implies an 'equality of respect, an equality of opportunity' and, as Adams preferred to express it, 'equality of respect and treatment for nationalists in the North'.

Gerry Adams and Sinn Féin appeared satisfied to some degree and supportive of the Framework Documents, but the unionist parties were outraged. Paisley declared it was 'a one-way street to Dublin' (i.e. a united Ireland). William Ross, deputy leader of the UUP, said it was 'a manifesto leading to the creation of a united Ireland'. Peter Robinson, later leader of the DUP and a first minister of the Northern Ireland Executive, said the main document was 'an eviction notice' for unionists to leave the UK. He said it established an all-Ireland executive power-sharing structure in which unionists would be in a permanent minority, and this was the 'embryo of a United Ireland. Northern Ireland [is] the only detachable part of the UK.' Ironically, this document included a pledge by the Irish government to introduce changes to Articles 2 and 3 of the Irish Constitution, which claimed that Ireland's national territory included Northern Ireland; and said that the changes 'will fully reflect the principle of consent in Northern Ireland and demonstrably be such that no territorial claim of right to jurisdiction over Northern Ireland contrary to the will of a majority of its people is asserted'.

Frank Millar, London editor of the *Irish Times*, and formerly an adviser to the UUP, wrote: 'Few in London will deny that the terms for the Union have changed. John Major, embattled, with a falling majority, appears determined to reconcile unionists to that fact – yesterday was a defining moment.' This was the moment when the basis of the deal that had to be done between the two traditions in Northern Ireland was revealed. It was a defining moment, but significant important hurdles still had to be crossed. The Framework Documents were truly remarkable, historic in their scope and their depth of understanding of the nature of Northern Ireland problems and their resolution. Greeted by unionist denunciation and rejection, they were followed three years later by the Belfast Agreement in 1998, and the election of the first minister and deputy first minister from the biggest unionist and nationalist parties. David Trimble of the UUP and the SDLP's Seamus Mallon were both formally appointed on 1 July and the Executive took office on 2 December 1999. There were many suspensions of devolution, including one for nearly five years from 2002 to 2007. Then the lead roles passed to the extremes: to the radical Protestant DUP and its leader, the former firebrand cleric Rev. Ian Paisley as first minister; Sinn Féin overtook the SDLP, and Martin McGuinness, a former IRA leader, became deputy first minister, an unlikely pairing of formerly deadly enemies. Extraordinarily, they got on very well and came to be known as the 'chuckle brothers' because in public they were always smiling and laughing together.

I first met Martin McGuinness at a 1995 lunch at the Forum for Peace and Reconciliation in Dublin Castle with Bruton, Adams and Paddy Teahon. I was sitting close to Martin at the round table, so I got a chance to chat to him more personally. I told him about my Donegal background, my friends in Belfast whom I visited as a teenager, and a scrape I'd had with the B Specials in the North. I asked him what he did to relax, and he said that he really enjoyed fishing, which he had taken up for that very reason. He then launched into a story about his first time fishing for salmon on Derry's Foyle River. He got a tug on his line close to the bank and, feeling pleased with himself, started reeling it in, with the big fish leaping and struggling in the water to get free of the hook. He played it a bit and then all of a sudden his reel jammed – he could reel out but not in. So he handed the rod and reel to his companion, jumped into the river, and waded through the water to the fish, took it into his hands and literally threw it onto the river bank. I have to admit I roared with laughter, he told the story with such drama and delight. I said, 'I see where your determination comes from.' He laughed and said, 'There was no way I was going to let that great catch get away!' The story did reveal the man's willpower, but it also showed how, apart from being tough, he could be charming. Years later, that warm sense of humour would win over Ian Paisley. Despite his background and high profile, Paisley was no exception to the MacNaughton rule. For half a century he was the foremost vitriolic purveyor of the 'no surrender, not an inch' faith, but he was pushed out of the DUP, the party he founded, because of his compromises with Sinn Féin, and alienated from the DUP until his death. Remarkably, even after the death of Ian Paisley and then Martin McGuinness, the families retained some friendly relations, a harbinger perhaps of better general relationships across the divide in the future.

In annexes to the 1995 Joint Frameworks, the British government set out in a statesmanlike manner its objectives and role in relation to Northern Ireland, and Ireland as a whole:

> The Government's primary interest is to see peace, stability and reconciliation established by agreement among all the people who inhabit the island of Ireland and it has committed itself, in the Joint Declaration, to working with the Irish Government to achieve such an agreement, which will embrace the totality of relationships. The Government has defined its role as being to encourage, facilitate and enable the achievement of agreement over a period through a process of dialogue and co-operation based on full respect for the rights and identities of both traditions in Ireland.

This statement is both forthright and conciliatory on peace and co-operation, in contrast to the scant regard for international law shown in post-Brexit confrontations.

Finally, a key section of the British documents was an important declaration from the British government about law and order, which sounded the death knell for the RUC. Major changes had to be made in the policing of the North.

> The Government wish to see the maintenance and development of a police service in Northern Ireland that is effective, operationally independent and accountable to the community which it serves. It must be capable of maintaining law and order, and of responding to any renewed terrorist threat should that prove necessary. Subject to these requirements, the Government are open to the consideration of proposals designed to enhance the

extent to which the community at large in Northern Ireland can identify with and give full support to the police service.

This is the foundational text that led to the establishment of the Police Service of Northern Ireland (PSNI). There was so much in the Framework Documents for the media that the significance of this strong declaration by the British government about policing was overshadowed. Ultimately, not least because of this commitment, the RUC followed the fate of its infamous B Specials, abolished in 1970 after their attacks on peaceful civil rights marchers in the late sixties, and their replacement, the also infamous UDR, which was quietly folded into the British Army in the early nineteen nineties. After the Belfast Agreement, an Independent Commission on Policing for Northern Ireland was established. Chris Patten, a distinguished Conservative Party minister under Thatcher and Major, also a chairman of the Tory Party and the last Governor of Hong Kong, became the chairman of this commission, which recommended a new policing body, the PSNI, to replace the RUC. The RUC was in effect a unionist paramilitary group, involved in attacks on civil rights demonstrations, leaking information to loyalist paramilitaries to aid murderous attacks on Catholics, and was generally heavy-handed and biased against nationalists. There were of course many officers, and some Catholics in the force, who wanted to work on behalf of both communities, but they were overshadowed by those who were biased against or contemptuous of nationalists. This Framework Document sought a police service 'which the community at large in Northern Ireland could identify with and give full support to'.

It is worth quoting Professor Tom Garvin's comparison of the RUC with the establishment of the Civic Guards in the Free State after partition. Courageously, he says, in the throes of a civil war, it was totally unarmed, 'and contrasted starkly with the emergence of an armed gendarmerie [the RUC] augmented by the occasionally murderous armed part-time constabulary recruited from the ranks of the Protestant community.' This was of course the B Specials, with whom I had a brush myself in 1964 when I was visiting friends in Belfast. One of my friends took me on a journey around the city pointing out the sports clubs, facilities and places they could not join or go to because they were Catholic. Then four of us were stopped in a car driving to Dublin, ordered out and lined up on the side of the road by heavily armed B Special thugs, toting their guns threateningly. They asked my friends what school they attended – their way of confirming they were dealing with 'Taigs' – while sneering at me because I was from the South. When they finished this intimidation and had stolen a pack of beers we had in the boot, they shunted us back into the car. One growled, 'When ye get South, stay there.' We were all a bit shaken after this menacing experience, though it was not new for my friends.

The launch of the Framework Documents in February 1995 and the subsequent news conference were both successful. By lunchtime the taoiseach had completed all the necessary television and radio interviews and we were ready to leave. John Bruton had to speak that afternoon in the Dáil, while John Major was to address the House of Commons. Again, the speech had to be put together on the run; the taoiseach was dictating paragraphs over the phone as he was driven from Baldonnel aerodrome to the Dáil. He was greeted with a standing ovation from all parties when he arrived in the chamber to formally present the Framework Documents to the House. In his address he paid full tribute to the input of Tánaiste Dick Spring and former Taoiseach Albert Reynolds, 'without whose vision and considerable courage' the peace process would not have been possible.

One of Bruton's own ideas, which he was to use repeatedly to sell the Framework Documents, was incorporated in his Dáil speech. It was the 'beginning of a new form of expression of traditional aspirations focusing on individuals and communities, rather than on *territory*. By expressing aspirations in this way, we hope the two otherwise irreconcilable sets of aspirations can be reconciled.' In the Commons John Major tried to reassure unionists by saying there was a 'triple lock against any proposals being imposed on Northern Ireland'. First, proposals had to secure the support of the political parties in the North; second, proposals must be approved by the people of the North in a referendum; and third, the

JOINT FRAMEWORK DOCUMENTS LAUNCHED

legislation to implement them had to be passed by Parliament. UUP MP Ken Maginnis wasn't impressed, denouncing the Framework as 'this dishonourable blueprint for a united Ireland'. The Sinn Féin leader Gerry Adams said the documents should clear the way for inclusive peace talks 'with everyone at the table and everything on the table'. The SDLP was very positive, so that meant the nationalist side were on board. I expected then that the all-party talks would be called in the relatively near future, certainly some time that year.

The UUP leader Jim Molyneaux expressed his disappointment. But that was a mild response compared to what other unionists, including his own party, had said. The UUP published its own proposal, 'A Practical Approach to Problem-Solving in Northern Ireland', which envisaged a 'time-limited' interim Northern Ireland Assembly to facilitate the development of trust between the parties and to prepare the way for bilateral and trilateral negotiations involving the parties and the governments. Their preference for an elected assembly was later to be used effectively to help lever unionists into all-party talks, but there was fierce opposition to an election from John Hume and Gerry Adams. DUP leader Ian Paisley, as expected, continued to denounce the Framework Documents, saying that they indicated that the British government had lost the will to maintain Northern Ireland as part of the United Kingdom. In the Republic there was support from all parties for the documents, and they were warmly received in the media. Another milestone had been passed on a rocky road, but united unionist opposition was a hurdle that was going to be difficult to overcome.

Tánaiste Dick Spring went to Washington after the launch of the Framework Documents to brief the US administration on them. The US secretary of state, Warren Christopher, speaking to reporters with Spring before their meeting at the State Department, made a very strong appeal, 'clearly directed at the IRA' as Conor O'Clery reported for the *Irish Times*: 'We continue to call on all parties to refrain from violence. We particularly urge those who laid down their arms to take the next essential step and that is to begin the process of decommissioning, or perhaps more accurately stated, disarming.' Christopher said that he and President Clinton regarded Northern Ireland as 'one of our highest foreign policy priorities'. The British government had been pressing the US to maintain a ban on Sinn Féin fundraising as leverage on them 'to force the start of negotiations on the decommissioning of arms', O'Clery wrote. It was certainly a strong message from Christopher. During this visit to Washington, Spring suggested that a third country or party could assist in the decommissioning of paramilitary arms in Northern Ireland, such as one of the Nordic countries or the Organization for Security and Co-operation in Europe. Later, he warned that the arms issue should not be a 'roadblock' to all-party talks.

Meanwhile, back home, both the taoiseach and Gerry Adams welcomed a speech by Mayhew in the North which appeared to indicate a break in the ice over British ministerial meetings with Sinn Féin that had not taken place yet, six months after the IRA ceasefire. Mayhew said that if there was 'substantial progress' towards the decommissioning of IRA arms, and it was clear that the process would be accelerated by British ministers talking to Sinn Féin, that would be considered. Bruton responded, through me, to a query from the *Irish Times*, saying he hoped the ministerial meetings would take place soon and deal constructively with the arms issue. He said that Mayhew's statement was an important move towards 'normalisation of the political situation in Northern Ireland'. Adams welcomed what seemed a more 'sensible approach' to ministerial talks with Sinn Féin. 'Of course we recognise the importance of the decommissioning of weapons issue. Our commitment on this is clear, the whole question of arms and decommissioning of arms will have to be dealt with as part of the peace process,' he said. But he pointed out that it was 'bizarre' and a 'nonsense' that Mayhew, speaking at Craigavon Borough Council, met two Sinn Féin councillors on local issues, but refused to meet party leaders about peace.

On 6 March the UUP published *its* policy paper, which the party had already given to Major, recommending a seven-member international commission on arms decommissioning. Then, on 9 March, in Washington, Secretary of State for Northern Ireland Patrick Mayhew made a speech that would contribute in great measure to the breakdown of the IRA ceasefire a year later. The speech laid down the tests or conditions the British government wanted Sinn Féin and the IRA to meet before the party could take part in all-party talks. The British wanted Sinn Féin to discuss the issue seriously: that did not pose a major problem. Sinn Féin had to examine with them the modalities of how decommissioning was to be carried out: thorny, but not insuperable. But then came what was later infamously called 'Washington 3' in official circles. This third condition required the IRA to begin the process of disarmament, 'the actual decommissioning of some arms' for Sinn Féin to gain access to round-table talks. Sir Patrick defended it as a tangible confidence-building measure, but it proved later to be fatal for the ceasefire. Irish officials involved in the process knew how sensitive this issue was; how the IRA would resist anything, even symbolic, that could smack of surrender. My own view was that the ceasefire had held now for nearly seven months, clearly indicating that Sinn Féin and the IRA were serious about peace and about making an agreement, and that was the essential element. Decommissioning could come later, after trust had been built on the possibility of agreement during inclusive all-party talks.

5

BRUTON MEETS CLINTON IN THE US

I WAS SERIOUSLY CONCERNED, WITH others, about this Mayhew development, which ran counter to the British agreement with us at Christmas that the peace process was not a 'single-item' agenda. It was about to turn into just that. This issue had to be overcome before anything else could happen. But while this was a shock for some, it was in fact well flagged to the previous administration that decommissioning was a rock that could sink the ship.

A review summit was held in October 1994 between Albert Reynolds and John Major at Chequers, the British prime minister's retreat northwest of London. Dick Spring, Patrick Mayhew and the Anglo-Irish Liaison Group personnel attended. Fergus Finlay wrote, 'It was the first experience we had of the British obsession with decommissioning of arms. Most of that meeting was taken up with a discussion of the subject, and there was no doubt in our minds that the British prime minister attached great importance to it.' The meeting ended with an agreement to set up a group of officials from both governments called the Dalton–Chilcot Group, which would be led by Tim Dalton of Ireland's Department of Justice, and Sir John Chilcot, the head of the UK Northern Ireland Office. The group would provide a report on arms, but it would also play a 'wider role' in the peace process. Finlay continues: 'Later assertions that the

Fianna Fáil and Labour government never got involved in decommissioning were essentially untrue. It was an issue from the beginning, and we always knew it was going to be a difficult one to resolve.'

For some commentators and political opponents, as we'll see, the decommissioning issue became, falsely, 'a difficult one to resolve' only after Bruton spoke on the issue at the time of his St Patrick's Day visit to the US in March 1995. It was an absurd and inaccurate claim. This Washington 3 development, requiring a start to decommissioning weapons before Sinn Féin could enter into all-party talks caused much trouble for the taoiseach. Bruton had a deep antipathy to violence and to the IRA campaign, and he felt that Irish democratic governments and their leaders had to be in favour of decommissioning illegal paramilitary weapons, not least because it was a constitutional imperative that there be no secret private armies. Initially, he was attracted to the idea that some evidence of good faith should be provided by republicans. After all, he reasoned, there was a ceasefire in place, which, according to Martin McGuinness, would hold 'in all circumstances', so why the need for weapons stockpiles? The war was over and democratic discussions would be given a great impetus if this evidence of good faith could be provided.

Within days the taoiseach himself was due to fly to the US for the annual St Patrick's Day festivities, which had become even more significant because of President Clinton's involvement in the peace process. Complicating matters, on 9 March Clinton announced the lifting of a ban on Sinn Féin fundraising in the US and also invited Gerry Adams, and all the Northern Ireland party leaders, to the White House St Patrick's Day reception in honour of the taoiseach. So Adams was going to be in the US at the same time and at many of the same events as John Bruton, on his first visit as taoiseach. That meant the scene was set for intensive media scrutiny of the peace process, and after Mayhew had turned Washington into a political decommissioning minefield it would, I felt, shine an unwanted light on the arms issue. The timing of Sir Patrick Mayhew's Washington 3 speech had to be deliberate. The British were very annoyed with Clinton's agreement to allow another visa for Gerry Adams, and with his inviting him to the White House for the St Patrick's Day festivities just days later.

I had a sense of foreboding that there could be a public clash, and that is just what happened, though both the taoiseach and Adams kept their differences under control. I had arranged well in advance for the taoiseach to brief political correspondents before his visit to the US. During the briefing, Bruton expressed his view that the IRA should put its weapons out of commission. But he stressed that he was not laying down how this was to be done; the details were entirely a matter for them. In an interview with Joe Little of RTÉ, broadcast on *Morning Ireland* on 13 March, he went a bit further. He said that in forthcoming talks between the British and Sinn Féin, he wanted to see proposals on prisoners (remission and early releases) and ideas about policing from the British side, and 'from Sinn Féin I'd like concrete commitments and proposals in regard to putting arms, Semtex, rocket launchers and things like that out of commission.'

> Little: All arms, all Semtex?
> Bruton: Let them put forward solid proposals. It's for them to put forward proposals. I'm not going to be prescriptive about detail. It's important that there be a sense of movement on both sides towards one another's positions.

Then on 14 March 1995, at Dublin airport, on his way to the US, he spoke to reporters, including RTÉ's Charlie Bird, in the press centre attached to the VIP lounge. In response to questions based on reports of his 'pol corrs' briefing and his *Morning Ireland* interview, he denied that he had used the words 'give up' weapons. 'I think get rid of, put them out of commission is the word that I would prefer to use,' he said. In answer to a further question – 'You're saying to Sinn Féin that they must do something?' – Bruton said:

> Yes, they must do something, and they must show that they're going to do more. I think it's very important that there should be a clear political signal from them on this issue. This is an important issue concerning America as well. You won't see Ian Paisley

or Jim Molyneaux sitting down with Gerry Adams until this issue is dealt with. If you're pursuing the democratic road, you don't have the need for arms. Arms are not part of your method of operation and these arms are now redundant.

He went on to stress that he would not be drawn into exactly 'how, why, by whom, to whom, where, the precise dates that all this is going to happen', but enough had been said to be interpreted by Sinn Féin and the British government as support for Washington 3. Gerry Adams, in contacts with Irish government officials thereafter, frequently referred to this exchange as John Bruton backing the British position. The British used it with both Sinn Féin and the Department of Foreign Affairs to confirm the taoiseach's support for their position.

Bruton had left himself a small escape route by talking of a 'clear political signal' from Sinn Féin, and his refusal to say 'how, why, by whom, to whom, where, the precise dates that all this is going to happen', but, given the context of his words, it was a narrow enough path to tread. Before we left the airport press centre a few of the journalists asked me if this meant that Bruton wanted Sinn Féin to get the IRA to decommission some weapons, as Mayhew had asked. Happily, I was able to stress repeatedly that he'd spoken of a 'political signal' on the decommissioning issue. Paddy Teahon, Seán Donlon, Seán Ó hUiginn and I all advised him to avoid anything that could be seen as direct support for Washington 3. While instinctively he would have liked to see some movement on decommissioning, Bruton quickly assimilated the advice that this was not a hook on which he should impale himself. The issue of decommissioning was now on everyone's agenda, and it dogged the taoiseach wherever he went. It was raised at every news conference and in every interview.

John Bruton constantly reiterated that there was a need for some 'political demonstration' of good faith on decommissioning (later adequately met by the Mitchell Principles), but that nuance was invariably lost. He came across as reiterating the need for decommissioning. The waters had been muddied, and Bruton had to live with the consequences for some time to come. Part of the background to all this is Bruton's briefing by Martin Mansergh about the peace process. In his biography of Mansergh, Kevin Rafter quoted Bruton's contemporaneous written note of the meeting with Mansergh on 13 December 1994, a week before I joined the Department. Bruton wrote:

> The distinction between peace and Sinn Féin ideology should not be forced. Too quick a move on arms could break the Sinn Féin leadership. It was psychological. They might surrender them to the Irish Government but don't use the term 'surrender'. They don't contest the process of decommissioning. There was little real disagreement on the shape of a political settlement. Adams agreed that a united Ireland was impossible without unionist support. Fifty per cent plus one was not enough. The talks–arms deadlock might be broken by the loyalists moving on arms first. Archbishop Eames [Robin Eames, the Anglican Primate of All Ireland and Archbishop of Armagh] was an important conduit to Molyneaux. The Framework Documents were a Department of Foreign Affairs operation. A good formula had been worked out for solving the constitutional problem involving Section 75 of the Government of Ireland Act and the papers were with the attorney general.

In an interview with Rafter, Bruton further recollected what Mansergh had told him:

> He also told me that there was a clear understanding that there would be decommissioning, that that was understood by Sinn Féin, but that too quick a move on decommissioning could break the leadership of Sinn Féin. But there was no question that decommissioning was part of the deal. Now he cautioned against the use of the term 'surrender of weapons' which is entirely understandable … but it was made quite clear by him to me at our meeting on the 13 December 1994 that the understanding was on the part of Sinn Féin that in the context of the ceasefire there would be decommissioning by the IRA.

Bruton frequently told me that in his briefing by Mansergh he was reassured that decommissioning was recognised and accepted by Adams as an important issue in the peace process. But I was not made aware of the warning that 'too quick a move' on the issue might break the Sinn Féin leadership.

The latent tensions were soon exposed in the US. In New York, the taoiseach and his party attended Niall O'Dowd's Top 100 Awards for leading Irish Americans, sponsored by his (then Smurfit-owned) magazine, *Irish America*. The US ambassador to Ireland, Jean Kennedy Smith, was to receive the top award, a hand-made Waterford Glass dove of peace, to mark her efforts for the peace process. I was looking forward to the occasion, which was to be held in a famous New York night spot, the Tavern on the Green. The awards had been going for ten years and brought together a glittering array of Irish Americans who had succeeded in every aspect of American society. The event frequently threw up interesting and sometimes surprising members of the Irish-American community – that year the list included Republican House Speaker Newt Gingrich, who could trace his mother's Daugherty roots to Donegal and Derry; and the legendary actor Marlon Brando, who was a great-grandson of a Dublin physician, Francis Gahan.

Gerry Adams was at the event as well, along with senior figures such as Irish-American businessman Bill Flynn, the chairman of Mutual of America; and Don Keough, former chairman of Coca-Cola Enterprises, the first Catholic to reach the top in the company – I had interviewed him for *Moneymakers*, a series of RTÉ radio programmes I presented. Don and Bill had been previous winners of the Top 100 Award. Former Congressman Bruce Morrison, who was deeply involved in Irish-American affairs, was also present. Bruton and Adams both spoke at the event, but Adams went on for some time, to the annoyance of the taoiseach, who was forced to sit and listen to his lengthy contribution. Then, before the presentation, too many people got up on the stage. The audience watched in horror as someone bumped into the dove of peace, which was resting on a stand. It rocked and then fell on the floor, shattering into pieces. There was a moment of total shock, but Don Keough, in a quick-witted attempt to rescue the disastrous situation, said it was 'the first time anyone had been presented with literally thousands of pieces of Waterford glass!' There was a ripple of nervous laughter, but the event had turned into a shambolic mess. The taoiseach left as quickly as he could. I stayed to brief a number of British and American correspondents and give them information on our itinerary, while Niall O'Dowd hunted around for another piece of glass to give to Jean Kennedy Smith. They had immediately contacted the maker's senior executive in New York, who had a fine decorative piece in his apartment, and he raced with it to the Tavern on the Green as a replacement.

Still at the Tavern, I got a phone call from our ambassador to Washington, the late Dermot Gallagher, a superb diplomat. He had taken the taoiseach, Seán Donlon and Paddy Teahon to an excellent Japanese restaurant – would I join them? We had a most enjoyable remainder of the evening. What happened at the 1995 award was out of the ordinary, the event was a brilliant marketing idea and a great success for Niall O'Dowd.

After some media interviews the next day, we moved on to Washington to attend the Speaker's lunch, and the famous US social calendar item – Bill Clinton's Irish-American bash in the White House. The St Patrick's Day lunch, held by the Speaker of the US House of Representatives, is a set piece started during the reign of Speaker Thomas Phillip 'Tip' O'Neill. This is the official account from the Congress records of the establishment of the Speaker's lunch on 17 March 1983:

> Speaker Thomas P. 'Tip' O'Neill of Massachusetts hosted the first St Patrick's Day lunch. President Ronald W. Reagan and other House and Senate Members attended the event. The House arranged the festivities to ease tension between the two Irish-American leaders, who embodied distinctive conservative and liberal political persuasions. By excluding the press for most of the event, O'Neill fostered the feel of an informal bipartisan celebration rather than a political summit. 'I'm going to cook you some Boston corned beef and I'm going to have an Irish storyteller there,' O'Neill promised Reagan. 'I'll have to polish up some

new Irish jokes,' the President quipped. The luncheon became an annual event on Capitol Hill for people of all political affiliations and ethnicities. It did not, however, mark the first celebration of St Patrick's Day at the Capitol. In 1884, Members donned green ribbons – distributed on the floor by Representative John O'Neill of Missouri – in honour of the Irish holiday.

It's worth noting that Reagan had been a Democrat, but left the party, ultimately for the Republicans, during his Hollywood years. John Hume told me in Derry later that year that he had the honour of being Tip O'Neill's first guest in 1983, and later the main guest would be the taoiseach. The lunch is held in a dining room on Capitol Hill, attended by invited members of Congress, and it ends with the taoiseach, speaker and president being led out of the building by a bagpiper. My first visit was to the second lunch, in 1984, when as an RTÉ journalist I was covering Taoiseach Garret FitzGerald's visit. It's an off-the-record occasion, so the media aren't let in until a later stage, and then they're fenced off from the dining area, to take pictures or make diary and sketch notes about attenders. FitzGerald was also given the rare honour of addressing a joint session of Congress, both the Senate and the House of Representatives, which was broadcast live by RTÉ radio, a programme I introduced and summarised. Bruton was to have this honour as well in September 1996.

The FitzGerald visit to the US was the first time I had entered the Oval Office. I brushed shoulders with President Ronald Reagan after the bowl of shamrock was presented to him, an extraordinary experience simply to be there. I didn't like Reagan's right-wing politics, which he shared with Margaret Thatcher, though at that time it was hard for non-Americans to see a really substantial difference between the Republicans and the Democrats. In an RTÉ interview afterwards with Tip O'Neill, I asked him that question. He leaned back in his chair and said, in his Massachusetts–Kennedy-style drawl, just one word, which sounded like a sentence: 'Fair–ness!'

I was presenting the St Patrick's Day bank holiday *News at One-Thirty* programme on 17 March 1977, when the so-called 'Four Horsemen' of leading Irish-American politicians, Tip himself, Senators Edward Kennedy and Daniel Patrick Moynihan, and New York Governor Hugh Carey, issued their first powerful joint statement together against the use of violence to resolve the problems of Northern Ireland. The statement was heavily influenced by John Hume, Seán Donlon, then Irish US ambassador, and the Fine Gael–Labour coalition government. It called on Irish Americans not to take any action that 'provides support or encouragement for organisations engaged in violence' (i.e. the IRA).

They stressed that the Northern Ireland question should be resolved by peaceful means. Assisted by the Department of Foreign Affairs, I managed to get Tip O'Neill in Washington to record a phone interview very early in the morning about this important landmark statement. He discussed the urgent need for Irish Americans not to support or donate to a violent approach to the Northern Ireland problem, and instead support those working for a peaceful solution; then I prefaced a question in the middle of the interview with the words: 'This is a difficult question to ask an Irish-American politician signed up to this statement ...' Quick as a flash Tip interjected, 'Don't ask it, then!' I was taken aback, but ploughed on, asking him if he 'still wanted to see a United Ireland'. He hedged a bit at first, but then said that practically every Irish American wanted to see a united Ireland, but it should be achieved 'by peaceful means'. Seán Donlon played a key role in briefing the Irish-American politically aware community that guns were not the route to a Northern Irish settlement and were strongly opposed by the Irish government.

President Jimmy Carter had made a statement on Northern Ireland during his election campaign in 1976, influenced by a meeting with the pro-Sinn Féin Irish National Caucus in Congress. He said to the gathering, 'It is a mistake for our country's government to stand quiet on the struggle of the Irish for peace, for the respect of human rights and for unifying Ireland.' The Irish government was concerned that this statement could be misinterpreted as support for the IRA's violent campaign, so there were immediate official contacts with Carter's team. The following day Carter sent a telegram of clarification to then Irish Foreign Minister Garret FitzGerald saying he was informed of media misrepresentations of his views. He stated clearly: 'I do not favour violence as part of a solution to the Irish question.' Today, almost everyone is on that same page.

This visit with the taoiseach to the Speaker's lunch was my first time on the inside, getting to mix with the guests before we sat down to eat a plate of bacon and cabbage. I talked briefly before we ate with Bill Clinton, who told me how impressed he was with the schoolgirls from Derry who had sung at his White House party the year before. Then I chatted with former Democrat House Speaker Tom Foley, whom I'd known for years. He had lost his seat in the House of Representatives the previous autumn. The loss of position and power had given him a look of the bereaved, and I felt sorry for him.

Republican Newt Gingrich was now the speaker – the first Republican to hold the office in fifty years. I felt that there was some chemistry between himself and Bruton as the new boys on the block. The lunch is an odd affair because the members keep getting called for votes in the House of Representatives or the Senate, so they disappear from the tables and reappear afterwards for another few hurried mouthfuls. Bruton spoke passionately about peace, the terrific support from the US and Bill Clinton in particular, and the prospects for Ireland in a new peaceful era, receiving a standing ovation at the end. There had been a minor smattering of applause from guests at Gerry Adams's table when he was acknowledged by President Clinton. Afterwards I got caught in a briefing battle with Republican Congressman Peter King when I discovered that he was saying to reporters that the only 'spontaneous' applause at the event was for Adams. On any reckoning, this gave a misleading impression because the reception for Bruton's speech was genuine, not merely polite. In his speech, Newt Gingrich referred to his mother's Irish roots.

The next day was White House Day, the first Bruton Oval Office meeting with Clinton, and my second time in the room. The American media's concern that morning was a Latin American issue, with reporters questioning Clinton. Bruton got support from Clinton on the decommissioning issue. During the news conference after the traditional presentation of shamrock, President Clinton asked 'those who had laid down their arms to take the next step and begin to seriously discuss getting rid of these weapons so that they may never be used again and violence may never again return to the land'. The taoiseach said he did not want to put deadlines on decommissioning; this was a decision Sinn Féin must take 'in their own time, in their own way and with their own modalities'. It was clear that he did not embrace the British precondition to all-party talks, but neither did he support a Sinn Féin stonewall on this issue.

The White House party had a wonderful array of foods for self-service, but there were waiters offering hot plates and wine as well. None of this was available to John Bruton and Finola, who were with the Clintons at the welcoming line, and were then taken straight into the main auditorium to listen to and make speeches. So Bruton was both exhausted and hungry, and he tried to ad-lib his speech. It wasn't good and overflowed with improvised compliments and thanks. 'Thank you very much, Mr President.' He said that repeatedly. Geraldine Kennedy of the *Irish Times* told me she found it embarrassing. It was a low point. Donal Kelly of RTÉ had difficulty getting a sound bite for RTÉ TV news. There would have been plenty if the taoiseach had read Ambassador Dermot Gallagher's draft, which I thought was perfectly attuned to the occasion. This was an early warning of the effects of fatigue on John Bruton, and the dangers of ad-libbing. When I discussed it with him, he said he felt much more able to connect with the audience by addressing them directly, rather than via a script. He could be a fine direct speaker. But, as taoiseach, there are times when you have to use a script. The next illustration of that fact was the St Patrick's Day celebrations in the US the following year.

Between the speeches and music, Gerry Adams had a brief conversation with me. He was quite agitated, and said Bruton was causing him difficulties with what he had said about decommissioning. I told him that everywhere we went journalists had raised the decommissioning issue. Bruton had no option but to address the questions, and since whatever he said appeared in print or was broadcast, it would inevitably seem that he was talking about decommissioning all the time. We were in the middle of a crowded room in front of the podium, and I should have drawn Adams out of that space to somewhere we could talk more privately. I was too new to the job, and too cautious.

Bruton and Finola ended up standing in the receiving line for two hours. He and Finola had a courteous relationship with Bill and Hillary, but there was no real empathy. They were very different couples. Did Clinton respect John? He realised John was not a wheeler-dealer like himself; he was bemused, I think, by Bruton's 'straight bat'.

The last notable part of the end of the evening was John Hume and Gerry Adams joining on the podium to sing Derry's anthem, 'The Town I Loved so Well', by another famous Derryman, Phil Coulter. It's a moving tribute to the city of his boyhood years that became enveloped by the violence of the Troubles. The Brutons were long gone, only the hardcore revellers were still about, but it was quite emotional to see the two giants of the nationalist community in the North, formerly bitter rival political leaders, singing the Derry anthem. To coin a phrase, it was 'the singers and the song'.

John Bruton's US line on decommissioning came essentially from four sources. First, he explained to me, he was 'strongly of the opinion that Articles 15.6.1 and 15.6.2 of the Constitution had to be respected. The right to raise an armed force is vested exclusively in the Oireachtas.' Private armies corrode democracy – he gave the example of the Freikorps in Germany after the First World War assisting the rise of fascism and Hitler. Secondly, as taoiseach, he said he 'was obliged by word and deed to uphold these Articles of the Constitution to the limits of [his] ability'. Thirdly, he felt that the best chance of an IRA move on decommissioning was with the leverage of the US. It failed and he did not return to it. And fourth, his good friend and political ally, TD, and later senator, Billy Fox, a Protestant, was murdered by the IRA when they came to his fiancé's house near the border seeking weapons in a preposterous belief that some were being stored for loyalist paramilitaries. Finding none, they brutally shot him dead as he tried to escape.

When we returned to Ireland, Bruton's visit was considered a success by the ministers I spoke with, though some unfavourable comparisons were made by government backbenchers with the amount of coverage devoted to Gerry Adams. But that was always going to be a problem since Bruton was a relatively obscure political figure in the US. Gerry Adams, with a whiff of cordite surrounding him, was more broadly seen there as a colourful bearded leader of armed revolutionaries who were now seeking peace. Ironically, the arms issue ensured that Bruton had maintained a higher profile in the US than might otherwise have been the case, though that was never the rationale. Raising decommissioning was a political mistake, despite the constitutional imperative, and gave Bruton's opponents political ammunition.

While Northern Ireland was always the dominant issue, there were other matters to deal with. Back in Ireland, I became aware of rumblings among some of Bruton's backbenchers about the quality of his choice of government colleagues. While Michael Lowry, then Minister for Transport, Energy and Communications, and Hugh Coveney, Minister for the Marine, were most often cited as lacking experience, the second-line junior ministers were considered far from the best and the brightest in the party. It was a tricky subject, but I felt it myself – heavyweights like Alan Dukes and Alan Shatter were sitting on the back benches – so I brought it up with the taoiseach. He had a very clear view of the matter. He had faced a heave against his leadership just nine months before he took office. He won the battle, but it left the Fine Gael party divided; some key talent had opposed his continued leadership. He accepted that selecting politicians from one side of a divided party limited his choice, but he told me it was an 'iron law' of politics that you reward those who stand with you in difficult times. Those who had resigned from his front bench in February 1994 had made a 'massive political error in attempting to overturn the decision of the party on its leadership – and they have to pay the price'. While he was crystal clear about this, he was also clear about the future. The aim was to win another term in office, and after that all bets were off. There was only minor media interest in the whispers of the disgruntled, since everyone knew that John Bruton was secure. However, in a few months that inexperience, and the trial of new people, was to plunge the government into a further crisis.

The main domestic political battle now shaping up as a milestone for the first one hundred days was over one of the most dangerous issues in Irish public life – abortion. The Minister for Health, Michael Noonan, was charged with disposing of an outstanding problem left over from the X case – providing legal protection for those who wanted to publish and access information about abortion and its availability. The right had been formally established in a referendum in 1992, but the minister in the previous government, Labour's Brendan Howlin, had not got around to legislating, and Howlin had moved to Environment. Despite the fact that legislation for abortion information was part of the previous Fianna Fáil–Labour programme for government, Fianna Fáil in opposition mistakenly decided to U-turn and make political capital out of the issue.

To make matters worse, the Archbishop of Dublin, Desmond Connell, made a public statement challenging the taoiseach directly. Bruton publicly said the Abortion Information Bill was not about abortion itself but about information. Connell issued a statement saying this was 'incorrect and misleading'. The terms of the bill, he said, amounted to knowing (that girls and women were going to have abortions) and assisting them in obtaining these abortions (by permitting the publication and access to information about abortion and its availability), and that was 'a grave offence'. Our legislators, he went on, 'have a serious obligation in relation to this bill which not merely accepts that abortion is permissible, but will facilitate its procurement.' I was called by a journalist from RTÉ who read the text of the statement to me before it was broadcast. I rang the taoiseach at home immediately, and his first reaction was to shrug it off. He said Connell was 'entitled to his views – but he's not entitled to *direct* members of the Dáil'.

Our public response was to brush off Connell in a non-confrontational manner. Happily for the government, the issue divided Fianna Fáil, with the progressive wing deeply unhappy at the attempt to exploit what had been agreed by the previous administration. The media were very critical of what they saw as Bertie Ahern's failure to lead the party on the issue, and Michael Noonan lived up to his reputation as a shrewd operator, coming up with a masterly political strategy to push it through. He came to my office in Government Buildings beforehand to discuss it. He would tell party TDs it was obligatory legislation since the fundamental right had already been established by the people in the 1992 referendum; that this was a 'critical test' for Fine Gael in office and it would be a 'defining moment' for the party's left-wing partners, whom they would need in order to win a further term in office at the next election. 'They'll know they can trust Fine Gael on the social agenda, with divorce on the way.' I also told him that I thought it would be important for John Bruton's credentials, given his own deeply held religious views, which were opposed to abortion, and party members should be reminded that he will demonstrate in the vote that he strongly supported the national will on this issue. Despite the party's well-known group of conservatives, the only Fine Gael defector was Donegal's Paddy Harte, and everybody inside government believed that that had more to do with anger at being denied office than principle, despite Paddy's repeated statements to the contrary. In any case, that loss could be absorbed. Paddy lost the whip but the government won the day. It was seen as an important milestone, widely complimented by the media.

But the euphoria was short-lived and Michael Noonan, now receiving bouquets, was to be on the receiving end of brickbats as soon as the scandal of hepatitis C arose once again. Women infected by this potentially deadly disease were getting it from blood products. On 3 April, shortly after the abortion information success, Noonan briefed his party colleagues in government on the controversy, saying that in phase one, he intended to publish the first hepatitis C report. He told them that negligence would be exposed, and he anticipated that there could be public service difficulties. Phase two he saw as replacing the top people at the Blood Bank with two highly respected professionals: Liam Dunbar, the senior administrator at St James's Hospital, and Professor Seán McCann, a specialist in leukaemia, also from St James's. I knew Seán McCann well at the time because of his treatment of my teenage nephew, Ronan, who had tragically died of leukaemia. He had been cared for well in St James's

Hospital, and given every possible treatment, including a bone marrow transplant. I held Professor McCann in high regard. Phase three was the speedy establishment of a compensation tribunal like that which dealt with the 1981 Stardust tragedy (a fire in the Artane dance hall in north Dublin, where many young victims were unable to get out because of locked exit doors, causing 48 deaths and 214 injured) combined with an overhaul of the Drugs Advisory Board.

It was the Noonan touch again; everything seemed perfectly under control. But the execution was to misfire badly. At the same meeting of Fine Gael ministers, Michael Lowry, Minister for Transport, Energy and Communications, gave an indication of his gung-ho approach. This would eventually land him in hot water and destroy his political credibility – his eventual ministerial demise came over the funding of an extension to his Tipperary house. He told his colleagues that there were ten state-sponsored bodies either 'in trouble or recuperating', adding that appointments made in the state transport company CIÉ were causing difficulties. The taoiseach quickly told him that the board of CIÉ should take the difficult decisions. Lowry responded, 'Every board is ninety per cent Fianna Fáil, so I have to take a hands-on approach.'

I didn't know Michael Lowry very well before becoming press secretary. I first met him in the Dáil bar during the collapse of the Reynolds administration. He had played a pivotal role in fighting off the attempt to unseat Bruton as leader of Fine Gael, and we talked about that and the prospects of Fine Gael and Labour forming the next government. That night I was convinced from our conversation that the party would be willing to do a deal with Labour on a rotating taoiseach in order to form a government. That was before the Labour swing to Ahern, and away again. Afterwards with John's brother, Richard Bruton, Lowry was central to the negotiations to put the Rainbow coalition together, and from what I had heard, he made it patently clear that he wanted a deal. In my first week in Government Buildings, Bruton asked me to listen to Lowry on political matters and he even mused that he could be the next leader of the party. Lowry himself came into my office after a meeting with the taoiseach to discuss the problem state companies under his control. Now, after the first 100 days, he seemed even more like the coming man; he was a kingmaker in Fine Gael and a high-flyer on his way. He had featured as the cover story in *Business and Finance* magazine. The thrust of his own personal public relations campaign was that he was a fast mover and out to do things. The trouble was that he appeared like a man in a hurry, and he hadn't done anything of substance yet. Emily O'Reilly, writing about him in the *Sunday Business Post* around this time, noted that the jury on Michael was still out. My colleague John Foley told me he was well thought of in Labour circles, where he had impressed during the negotiations to form a government. He also had a certain boyish charm. It helped to cover a hard-edged approach to politics and a determination to get his own way.

On 5 April 1995 Lowry asked to see me in his office. I felt some foreboding, but bearing in mind what John Bruton had said, I went to see him. It was a bizarre meeting. Lowry went on about the need for a 'proactive' PR policy. He was quite candid that he was pushing himself as the man on the move, the man who was going places, the man with a strategy: 'They're printing it – saying that I mean business, and I'm doing a good job.' There was an instant answer to most problems. He railed about the *Sunday Business Post*'s repeated attacks on John Bruton's handling of the peace process. Lowry felt this could be seen off with a letter. I found it hard to suppress a belly laugh. I said no – a letter would be a drop in the ocean. The newspaper had a fundamentally 'green' nationalist editorial line in politics at the time and its opposition to Bruton was based on this political standpoint. My view was that it would remain so – and so it did. We just had to deal with the issues as they arose; success would bring its own PR reward. That was the PR strategy John Bruton himself had outlined to me.

Lowry also wanted Bruton to stop making Phil Hogan the hero of his stump speeches for resigning and taking responsibility for the budget press release debacle; and to stop praising Albert Reynolds for his contribution to the peace process. This I agreed with – both themes were worn out. Lowry was keen that the government should be projected as in it for the long haul – for another two and half years, followed by re-election for a further five. This was fairly unoriginal and commonplace in Fine

Gael. His next thought, however, had some merit. He felt the government should be presented as a form of national government, or national movement straddling left, right and centre. John Bruton picked up this theme and used it in his speeches, and it did strike a chord from time to time with his audiences. But to be fully exploited it needed cross-party emphasis, which it never really got until the end, when the parties fought the election together as a government.

Then Lowry told me about a recent meeting he'd had with Dick Spring in the tánaiste's office, when he'd complained bitterly about leaks from government. He said he told Spring it was like 'a tap full on', that the leaks came from Labour, that they were 'deeply corrosive', and that they could divide the government if they didn't stop. Lowry said he believed that Ruairí Quinn was coming round to the Rainbow, but that Brendan Howlin was still a problem. These two were considered the main players who had favoured another deal with Fianna Fáil after Reynolds was gone. He also said that he had told Spring that he could identify four to five potential scandals in his own Department which could be attributed to Fianna Fáil. In fact, he told me, 'there were two'. The purpose of the exaggeration was to 'frighten Labour about any future alliances with Fianna Fáil'. His battles with CIÉ over the chairman's spending on a visit to New York, and the 'cosy cartels' of business people he spoke openly about some months later, together with his allegations that they spied on his activities, were all explained by this conversation. Far from doing damage to Fianna Fáil, these outbursts gave wonderful ammunition to the opposition to damage the government, and they fatally wounded Lowry's own credibility with the media and with Labour. He survived an autumn Dáil battle over his cosy cartel allegations, for which he could not put forward very much hard evidence, but Fergus Finlay, with a laugh, told me he considered it a 'pyrrhic victory'. The emperor had no clothes, and his credibility was gone.

Lowry also said Spring had told him he was happy with Bruton as taoiseach for the next two and a half years. It was in Labour's 'interests', he reported the party leader as saying. I left Lowry's office fairly sure that Bruton would have nothing to do with this kind of proactive PR strategy, which was laying the groundwork for Lowry's fall. However, I had to follow it through, so I drafted a lengthy memo setting out what I thought it would involve for the taoiseach: many more current affairs interviews; fireside chat family photo interviews; briefings of hand-picked key journalists and so on; modern and better clothes for improved presentation. I sent that to John Bruton and put the matter on the agenda for the taoiseach's strategy group, which met every Monday morning in the briefing room next to his office. It came up at the next meeting, which I always attended with Seán Donlon, the taoiseach's programme manager; Roy Dooney, political adviser; George Shaw, Bruton's private secretary; and Seán Barrett, government chief whip; as well as Paddy Teahon, and Frank Murray, secretary to the government. There was a very brief discussion, and no one voiced support for this proactive PR approach. I did tentatively raise the issue of better presentation. The taoiseach said with a smile, 'Can you not make a virtue of my scruffiness?' Everyone laughed. That was the end of that.

A public relations issue of a different dimension was shortly to erupt. I had escaped for my first break over Easter to a wonderful guest house in the Nire Valley, Mary and Seamus Wall's Hanora's Cottage, to walk for a few days in the wonderful Comeragh mountains. I had no sooner arrived and was enjoying a gin and tonic when the phone rang. Emily O'Reilly had got hold of a story about an angry exchange between the taoiseach and a Cork radio reporter. Immediately after his American visit, thoroughly exhausted, Bruton had gone straight on to a party tour of the south-west. Because it was strictly party business, I did not go with him, and I felt it was asking too much of him. Against his express wishes, Bruton told me, after the conclusion of some party business, he was pushed into giving an interview to this young reporter by one of the Cork Fine Gael TDs, Liam Burke, who ambushed him by ushering him into a room with the journalist. Bruton strictly stipulated that he would give the interview only about local Cork issues. But the interviewer ignored this and turned to Northern Ireland. The taoiseach exploded in frustration, saying, 'I'm sick and tired being asked about the fucking peace process.' Hardly diplomatic, but not that unusual from some politicians, particularly if the ground rules are ignored. John Bruton quickly apologised at the time and the matter seemed to be resolved.

Now, weeks later, the *Sunday Business Post* had this story, and given their editorial bias and spin, it was likely to be splashed on the front page, which it duly was. I returned to Dublin on Easter Sunday to help deal with the aftermath. John Foley had advised the taoiseach to explain to all comers what had happened – and I agreed with that. Happily, other journalists showed deep annoyance that this perfectly human response had been turned into an issue, and the affair died before the bank holiday was over. But it left a handy stick for Bruton's critics on the North to beat him with – they claimed it was a revealing glimpse of his 'real' feelings about the peace process.

The story had a bizarre, farcical postscript during the 1997 election campaign, when practically the entire *Last Word* programme on the fledgling Radio Ireland was devoted to discussing a tape recording of John Bruton making a joke about this affair, implying that this was further 'evidence' of his disregard for the peace process. Later in the peace process, when Sinn Féin was under pressure, Gerry Adams, frustrated by a journalist's questions, said, 'I'm totally pissed off trying to keep this thing [the peace process] going'. This was reported in the *Irish Times*. It was Adams's 'fucking peace process' moment. The double standards and bias involved ensured that there was no mention of this entirely human outburst on the *Last Word* or in the *Sunday Business Post*. The truth is that Bruton toiled with an embattled and increasingly paralysed British government to get them to do the right thing and drop their insistence on a 'gesture' of decommissioning as a precondition for entry into all-party talks, which Bruton wanted to be launched in 1995.

Bruton's commitment to supporting the peace process was one hundred per cent and he left no stone unturned to sustain it, as Fergus Finlay said in his memoirs. The British doggedly and impassively resisted, led by a fatally weakened, if well-disposed, prime minister. If Bruton appeared to also demand evidence of good faith from republicans, it was because of his principled and democratic rejection of political violence. But he even dropped that to advance the peace process, after the US visit.

All this time, during the ceasefire, British government officials had been meeting key figures from Sinn Féin – but they were refusing to allow Sinn Féin delegates to meet government ministers on the same basis as other Northern parties. Given the previous year's revelations of secret British government contacts with Sinn Féin and the IRA, when there was no ceasefire, it was an inexplicable and hypocritical position to adopt. Later I was to learn of a diplomatic report about a key Tory-leaning journalist contact in London, saying that Mayhew and Major intended to keep the pace of the peace process just short of collapse. That journalist was Boris Johnson of the *Daily Telegraph*. Whether it was simply analysis, or based on something more direct, I do not know, but it explained a lot about how events would unfold.

At Easter 1995, John Bruton was determined to commemorate the end of the Second World War in Europe. The Nazis surrendered unconditionally to the Americans and the British on 8 May 1945; and in Berlin on 9 May, at Stalin's insistence, they surrendered to Marshal Georgy Zhukov and senior figures from the Allies. Bruton's commemoration at Lutyens's First World War Memorial Park at Islandbridge, built for the 50,000 Irish dead in the Great War, was both quixotic and fascinating. It was extraordinary that the event actually took place, and it was very well attended. It had several objectives: to remember the 10,000 Irish from North and South who died fighting in the British Army in the Second World War; then, because of sensitivities about any positive sentiment towards the British armed forces, it was more formally described as marking the liberation of Belsen concentration camp by British troops, a commemoration of the millions who died in the Holocaust; and finally a salute to all the Allied forces who defeated Nazi Germany.

I accompanied the taoiseach on a visit to the synagogue in Terenure, south Dublin, for a Jewish Holocaust commemoration, at which we heard the story of an Irish survivor. The sheer barbaric horror of Hitler's Final Solution is really brought home when you hear victims speak of the unspeakable. The day picked by officials was Easter Saturday, and arrangements were made. Shortly before the event, representatives of the Jewish community complained that this day was the first day of the

Jewish Passover and was therefore unsuitable. John Bruton was deeply annoyed that this faux pas had not been picked up by the civil servants organising the event. A fresh date two weeks later was hastily agreed and the ceremony was a success. Tom Hartley from Sinn Féin took his seat at the memorial, alongside the diplomatic corps, ministers, TDs, Sir Patrick Mayhew, senior officers of the Irish Army, leading figures of political parties, North and South, and representatives of the Jewish community. It was the first official event in the history of the Irish state that positively marked, even in an oblique manner, the efforts of Irish soldiers in British uniform who had fought in the First and Second World Wars. It was a small victory for John Bruton's respect for the Parnell/Redmond parliamentary Home Rule struggle, and a healthy indication of Sinn Féin's ability to do unpalatable things to bolster the peace process.

On 12 April 1995 we travelled North to attend an official event for the first time. The taoiseach was to address a gathering of the Northern branch of the Confederation of British Industry with Sir Patrick Mayhew. At my suggestion, the taoiseach's speech included a declaration that the Irish government would now seek to open talks with all the Northern parties as a means of putting pressure on the British to end their ban on ministerial contacts with Sinn Féin. This would have been the main story from the speech, if the British had not tried to engage in another piece of backsliding. We got a copy of Sir Patrick's speech only at about the same time that it had been given to a number of key political journalists. There was consternation among the Irish group – already ensconced in the picturesque Culloden Hotel overlooking Belfast Lough, halfway between Belfast and Bangor – when we saw what Sir Patrick was going to say. The script indicated that the British government was going to exclude Sinn Féin from a series of bilateral meetings that were to take place with the Northern parties, and it put the onus on Sinn Féin to change that situation.

A brief impromptu news conference by Bruton and Mayhew was planned for when Sir Patrick arrived – but we quickly scrapped this idea, with about a dozen journalists and cameramen waiting. Instead, when the secretary of state for Northern Ireland arrived, the taoiseach insisted on an immediate meeting in a room away from the entrance. For forty minutes it was hot and heavy going. John Bruton told Mayhew he would not tolerate the impossible situation into which he was being put. If Sir Patrick didn't change his text, he would have to tell the audience that night that there was a clear rift between the two governments. The implications of saying that – in the North – were immense. Eventually, Mayhew relented and agreed to change his speech along the lines suggested by the taoiseach, saying instead that he hoped that 'intensive and ongoing communications with Sinn Féin will shortly make it possible to add them to the numbers'. It was now up to the British to make this possible.

The media had no idea of the drama that was unfolding within. The Northern Ireland Office press officer was nonplussed when he was told about the changes. He rushed off to get the new version of the speech printed. Before the dinner, Sir Patrick and John Bruton gave brief comments to the waiting journalists, but nobody raised the reason for the delay. When I briefed, by phone, political correspondents in Dublin about what had happened, I was initially met with some scepticism – the awful 'spin doctor' effect. Luckily the *Irish Times* had received a copy of the earlier text and comparisons proved what I was saying. The paper's front-page story was headlined, 'Bruton Persuades Mayhew to Adopt New Line on Sinn Féin', while the *Irish Press* headlined 'Bruton Secures a Breakthrough'.

In his Culloden speech to the assembled businessmen and their partners that evening, a relaxed John Bruton ironically referred to the meeting before dinner where the 'secretary of state and I were *entirely at one* on the need to maintain momentum towards comprehensive dialogue'. He also made a passionate reference to the Islandbridge Memorial Commemoration of the Irish dead in the Second World War. He spoke about the British liberation of Belsen death camp and the horror of the Nazi Holocaust. To an enthusiastic response, he said his generation – on the fiftieth anniversary of the end of the Second World War – could 'acknowledge the heroic role played by ten thousand Irish people from both parts of the island who joined the British Army in an effort to free Europe from the tyranny of Nazism'. Bruton told of successfully seeking attendance from all the major parties, North and South, including Sinn Féin. It went down very well with his audience. I was besieged by people afterwards who were complimentary about Bruton's address, saying they never expected anything like that from a 'Southern prime minister'.

It was a successful mission, which was rounded off the next morning with a visit to the Ulster Folk Museum. Afterwards, in the taoiseach's suite at the Culloden, before we set off to return to Dublin, we were looking out at the beautiful Lagan estuary, which was bathed in sunshine, and commenting on how beautiful it was. I said: 'It's the fourth green field and we want it back!' The taoiseach swiftly grated, half-jokingly, 'We do not!'

At the Culloden, Mayhew had also given an indication of a different approach with different treatment of Sinn Féin, concentrating only on decommissioning in ministerial meetings, but he backed down in the discussion with Bruton. The first meeting took place in Belfast shortly afterwards, on 10 May. The Sinn Féin delegation was led by Martin McGuinness with Gerry Kelly, and the British minister Michael Ancram was present. A range of issues, including prisoner releases, were discussed. A few days later, on 16 May, Martin McGuinness and Pat Doherty of Sinn Féin came to Dublin to meet the taoiseach and tánaiste. Afterwards McGuinness told reporters it was 'a good meeting'. A few days later the Northern Ireland Office announced that a first private meeting between Secretary of State, Sir Patrick Mayhew, and Gerry Adams would be held while both were attending the Irish-American economic conference in Washington, which was being held by President Clinton. Bruton made a statement welcoming the meeting at the Clinton conference: 'As I agreed with the British prime minister in Moscow, the intention of the British and Irish governments is to move to a situation in which Sinn Féin are *fully involved* in political talks on the same basis as other parties in Northern Ireland.' This meeting, he said, represented 'a further step on the road to achieving that objective'. Adams said afterwards that it had been 'a frank and friendly, positive exchange of views' that helped to bridge the gap between Sinn Féin and the British government. Mayhew said he had stressed the government's position on decommissioning.

Press coverage of the first 100 days had been very favourable. Denis Coughlan wrote in the *Irish Times*:

> Within his own party dissatisfaction with his leadership has shrunk ... while, in Leinster House, he is seen as a man reborn, bringing unexpected strengths and conviction to the toughest political job around. He has stamped his authority on parliament, preparing carefully for Question Time and displaying a cool and relaxed poise on Northern Ireland issues.

In the *Sunday Tribune*, Stephen Collins wrote:

> Mr Bruton has confounded his critics, some of them within his own party, by his sure handling to date of the issues which have confronted [him] since he moved into Government Buildings. In the Dáil he has demonstrated an ability to handle almost everything that the Opposition has been able to throw at him on the order of business and during Question Time ... some of those in the North and in the Republic who were worried about Mr Bruton taking over have been pleasantly surprised by his deep commitment to the peace process.

Bruton did do well in the Dáil at Taoiseach's Questions when he gave answers to written questions. But then TDs are able to pursue supplementaries, which inevitably raise current issues sometimes far removed from the original question. So civil servants prepare for potential supplementaries, researching and drafting answers that might be needed. This was not a function of the press secretary, but Bruton asked me to join the civil servants to question him closely about potential supplementary pitfalls. He was using my years of expertise as an interviewer very well from his point of view, but it took hours out of my time twice a week and frequently when I got back to the office there would be a list of political correspondents and others who had been calling me. It did not endear me to the journalists that for long periods twice a week I was not in my office. I raised it with John, but he was very pleased with what I was doing in the Q&A sessions, and he saw it as more important. I often gave him a tougher time than he ever got from deputies, so I guess it did pay off. Attorney General Dermot Gleeson was particularly complimentary after a Q&A session he joined. John Bruton's star had risen sharply in the opinion polls after languishing for years. All seemed well in a sunny world. But this was politics. And a double crisis was about to strike.

6

HUGH COVENEY'S PHONE CALL

On the morning of Saturday 20 May 1995, I drove to the taoiseach's home town of Dunboyne, County Meath. John Bruton was recording an interview with the Australian Channel 9 television station for their *Today* programme. They wanted a folksy setting, so it was shot in the cosy bar of Brady's pub. It all went well and I was expecting to get away immediately, but instead the taoiseach asked me to come for a walk with him. As we strolled around the church in Dunboyne, he told me that he'd had a call that morning from Hugh Coveney, Minister for the Marine and Minister for Defence. Coveney had told him that in a recent phone conversation with Michael Conlon, the chairman of Bord Gáis Éireann (BGÉ), he had asked that his own family company of quantity surveyors be considered if the company was going out to tender for the contract to develop new offices in Cork. Coveney had said the *Sunday Business Post* had now contacted him about this phone conversation and they were going to run a story about it.

Bruton was deeply shocked at what he heard and told Hugh they would have to meet. The appointment was fixed for the taoiseach's house the next morning, because Coveney thought it was too dramatic to go to Government Buildings. He felt that his phone conversation was simply a casual reference, stating the obvious, and he did not intend in any way to seek a special favour or put pressure on the BGÉ chairman. If the contract had gone to tender, which it ultimately did not, it would have been inconceivable that Coveney's family firm would not be invited to tender since they were among the top half-dozen in their field. But that did not matter to Bruton. It was the political principle – do nothing in office that could enrich yourself – which mattered here.

As the taoiseach told me about the conversation on that unseasonably grey May morning, I felt an awful sinking feeling. I found it hard to understand how Hugh, whom I greatly respected, had made such a blunder without knowing or suspecting that it was dangerously off-limits. As a minister he could not make any representation through which he could profit, directly or indirectly. Although Hugh Coveney had properly cut his official ties with his quantity surveying business, it was nonetheless the family firm. The taoiseach asked for my opinion. Grimly, I said I thought Hugh would have to resign his cabinet post. Bruton said that was the attorney general's reaction as well. It was clear that he shared this view, and he was both amazed at what had happened and distraught at its consequences. I said it would be a big story, and coming on top of Phil Hogan's resignation, it would revive comments about the naivety and inexperience of some of his Fine Gael ministerial appointments. He was aware of that. We gloomily trudged back around the church. He would have to talk to his colleagues and the other party leaders, Spring and De Rossa. I had to return to the pub then for a promised drink with the television crew, but my interest was gone, and I got away quickly.

At 3.30 p.m. that same day, the taoiseach, Minister for Justice Nora Owen, Attorney General Dermot Gleeson and I met in Gleeson's office. Other ministers had been contacted and were due to arrive later in the day. From there Bruton called Dick Spring and Proinsias De Rossa. Dick Spring listened, and then said it was the taoiseach's call, and he'd back whatever decision he took. Proinsias wondered whether an apology would suffice – but again it was left to the taoiseach to decide. Bruton was clearly distressed. Hugh Coveney's narrow victory over Fianna Fáil in the Cork South Central by-election had come on the day the Labour Party walked out of Albert Reynolds's cabinet, while Kathleen Lynch of Democratic Left had taken a seat from Labour in the Cork North Central by-election on the same day, making the Rainbow coalition a realistic possibility. It had been difficult to persuade Hugh to stand. His promotion to the cabinet was enormously popular in Cork. A sacking or a resignation would be a devastating blow. But there seemed to be no other course. The Department of the Taoiseach's secretary general and his private secretary, Paddy Teahon and George Shaw, were both called in. Paddy Teahon had one of his officials draft a memo on the formalities of resignation and sacking while the secretary himself drew up the options for staying or going. At dinnertime, I went out for some food with Teahon and Shaw – I had not eaten since breakfast – and when we returned at about 10.30 p.m. I found Gleeson, Minister for Agriculture Ivan Yates, Nora Owen, Michael Lowry and Richard Bruton, Minister for Enterprise and Employment, sitting in my office. We trooped in a depressed mood down to the taoiseach's conference room.

The background facts were that Ted Harding of the *Sunday Business Post* had phoned Hugh the previous day and put to him that he had sought favour for his firm in a conversation with Michael Conlon. Hugh then told Harding what had transpired. He had phoned Michael Conlon, whom he'd known for three decades, about five weeks before on an unrelated issue. When they finished discussing the subject of the call, he made a reference to BGÉ's recently published intention to develop its headquarters at the offices of the Cork Gas Company on Victoria Road rather than go ahead with the earlier plan to extend the company's offices at Inchera, Little Island, in Cork. A design team had already been appointed for the Little Island project – including a quantity surveyor – but those premises had now been sold. Coveney said to Michael Conlon: 'I asked that if they were considering inviting a number of firms to tender and apply for the work, that Coveney's might be considered for inclusion on the list together with others. I made it quite clear that I was not asking for the work for Coveney's, merely that they be given an opportunity to compete.' Michael Conlon had said he would look into the matter and come back to Hugh. About three weeks later, Conlon told him that BGÉ had simply reappointed the Little Island team for the Victoria Road project. That was 'the end of the matter', as far as Hugh was concerned. But it wasn't. The Sunday paper account of this affair was going to cause a serious crisis, even if Hugh felt that he had done nothing improper; and Michael Conlon had told Hugh that 'he did not believe there was any impropriety, or any attempt to compromise him or pressurise him to deliver a favour'.

The Coveney crisis meeting at Government Buildings was a dismal affair: John Bruton opened by saying that this 'event' had taken place against the background of the 'Beef Tribunal, the Masri affair granting passports for investments in Ireland, and the Father Brendan Smyth affair, which had led to the formation of the government – and since then I've spoken repeatedly around the country about the need for the highest standards in politics.' Looking at it from the other side, he said that if Hugh Coveney had to go 'it would be a blow to Fine Gael and a blow to the government'. However, it was a matter of principle. Some might see arguments for conflicting principles – like 'survival'. Bruton indicated that he would listen to views put forward. He let the meeting know that the other party leaders felt it was his call but they would back his decision. At this point, his controlled emotion began to show. He said Hugh Coveney was present on occasions in Cork when he had spoken about standards in politics. He could not understand what had happened.

Michael Lowry made a passionate plea to 'batten down the hatches'. Resignation or sacking would be a 'near fatal' blow to the government, devastating to the Fine Gael organisation generally, but particularly in Cork where the organisation would be demoralised. Fine Gael would be seen as incompetent. 'Who would work with them in government – losing two ministers in five months?' Richard Bruton said he saw it differently – the organisation would respond supportively to the defence of a matter of principle. Ivan Yates was clear in his approach: the 'position was not defensible', but there would be a big problem if Hugh Coveney had to be sacked – it would be better if he resigned. Michael Noonan, Minister for Health, who had joined the meeting, took the view that if Coveney was defended, and the taoiseach was then forced to drop him, it would be the worst of all worlds, and that could happen through media and opposition pressure. I contributed my tuppence-worth, questioning Michael Lowry about how we might defend Coveney if we did batten down the hatches. I said it would be difficult to come up with a plausible and sustainable defence. I agreed with Noonan that it would be worse to be forced to sack Coveney under pressure. But the bottom line was that Hugh 'had made a representation, which had been followed up and responded to'. Lowry said in response that the taoiseach might suffer, but he could take it. 'If Hugh Coveney goes, Cork will be devastated,' he said. 'Fine Gael can at times elevate a crisis, overreact.' The taoiseach said the principle was very clear: in political office you do not do anything which could 'potentially enrich yourself – and in this case there was a potential benefit to Hugh Coveney through his family company'.

After the meeting, I rang John Foley to get a sense of how Labour were taking it. He told me that Dick Spring had called him and said, 'When you've left a company, you've gone.' It was cryptic but clear. John said he saw merit in making a clean cut. Then I spoke to assistant press secretary Tony Heffernan. He said that when Proinsias had told him first he thought Hugh had no choice but to go. However, he softened a bit when he saw the actual story; and then he thought of the dangers of Hugh having to go under pressure. It wasn't all over by a long shot.

On his way to meet the taoiseach the following day, Coveney was doorstepped by reporters and demonstrated a bit of the steel that had made him a successful businessman. He said his approach to the chairman of BGÉ was 'not a resigning matter'; and a request for his resignation would be 'disproportionate punishment for an unfortunate but not a major error'. He revealed that the conversation had taken place six weeks before, after he'd read in the paper that BGÉ was to develop its headquarters at a new site. It was 'not an unnatural thing' for him to ask to be on the list for tenders. In retrospect, he regretted what he had said – it was an 'error of judgement' in a casual conversation with a person he'd known for over twenty years. He denied that it was the 'Old Pals Act' at work.

When I spoke to the taoiseach on the phone about this, he wasn't pleased, but he accepted that Hugh would have to give some account of himself; he couldn't be seen to be furtive. However, the first meeting in Dunboyne did not go well. Hugh initially told the taoiseach that if he had to resign from cabinet, he would have to resign his Dáil seat as well.

He felt that after resigning, he would not be able to stay on in public life, because he would have no reason for continuing. This would mean an untimely by-election for the government in the worst of circumstances. Bruton was now far from happy and considered Coveney's position to be self-indulgent.

After an hour and a half with the taoiseach, Hugh then saw the attorney general. That meeting clarified for Hugh the seriousness of what he had done in regard to the proprieties of office, which he had not fully appreciated. In the afternoon, Coveney had to attend a family function at Clongowes Wood College, which gave everyone space for reflection. While the opposition was getting ready for attack, there was a sense in the language they used that there was no real appetite for Hugh's blood. Bertie Ahern spoke about this 'worrying incident' and the 'rules and codes' of government ministerial behaviour. But he went on, 'The public knows full well what Mr Bruton would demand if this were a Fianna Fáil minister.' That was fair enough. I was getting besieged by journalists as the evening approached, but I had to hold them off with the promise of a statement later.

Democratic Left became even more supportive of Coveney. Pat Rabbitte said publicly that a phone call doesn't prove anything, and Proinsias De Rossa phoned the taoiseach at home to say that he agreed that resignation would be a 'disproportionate punishment'. He made a very strong plea for an alternative. Michael Noonan also called the taoiseach to say that the issue was no longer clear-cut – he was leaning towards battening down the hatches. In the resumed meeting with Hugh, the taoiseach maintained his view that the issue was one of principle, but he proposed an ingenious solution. Hugh would recognise the course he must take, and offer his resignation, and then Bruton would offer him an appointment as minister of state in the Department of Finance with responsibility for both public expenditure and the Office of Public Works, which comes with a seat at the cabinet table. This was Phil Hogan's old job. The changes the taoiseach had in mind to follow this would be: Seán Barrett would become Minister for the Marine, then Jim Higgins would be promoted from the finance role to take Seán's job at the Whip's office, leaving the finance responsibility for Hugh.

At first Hugh was not enthusiastic about this formula – he would prefer a clean break. He questioned whether he would have any authority as a 'demoted man', but the formula had its attractions. He was not being dismissed from cabinet. He would resign over his mistake, so his integrity would not be an issue. The two men discussed the serious consequences for the government if he did resign as a minister and a Dáil deputy. Hugh's view eventually was that it would be throwing Cork and Munster to the winds, and, additionally, the taoiseach would be under scrutiny for a 'holier-than-thou' attitude. About tea-time on Sunday, Hugh agreed, but not without misgivings. It was an honourable compromise, though I was strictly forbidden to use that description at the time. There was a lot of anger in Cork because of a feeling that Coveney had been politically targeted in an unfair manner. I got a phone call from a high-profile Fianna Fáil linked contact, Frank Dunlop, long before he was jailed for bribing councillors. Dunlop said Coveney was a gentleman, naive about politics, who was deliberately and disgracefully targeted by a Fianna Fáil figure in Cork who leaked information about the call. Tragically, three years later Hugh Coveney lost his life when he fell from a cliff into the sea at Roberts' Cove near his home while walking his three dogs.

That month there were a couple of other media stories that illustrated the power of RTÉ's morning item 'It Says in the Papers', which had been made clear to me in the 1980s by Garret FitzGerald's 'handlers', who complained about bias. Now it was phoney stories. On 16 May the *Irish Independent* carried a front-page lead story – 'Minister approves abortion price list'. At about seven-thirty that morning I saw the story in the papers delivered to my home, and almost at the same time Minister for Health Michael Noonan rang me. He was livid. He said the story was 'outrageous and false'. It claimed that he had 'cleared the way for doctors to supply an abortion price list to women in crisis pregnancies'. Noonan assured me, and I knew, that he had nothing to do with any list. The story was really referring to an information pack compiled by the Irish College of General Practitioners. As minister, he had no role whatsoever in this matter. He asked me if I could call RTÉ before the eight o'clock news to tell them and whoever was compiling 'It Says in the Papers' that this story was 'false and libellous'.

A spokesperson for Michael Noonan was quoted in the *Independent* story as saying that the minister would not 'interfere' with the general practitioners' information work – and that was the underhand ploy used to drag him into the headline about approving an 'abortion price list'. So I called the RTÉ news desk to pass on the minister's remarks and then spoke to John S. Doyle, who was reviewing the papers. The story wasn't carried in the review.

A week later, with the taoiseach facing into the Dáil debate on the Hugh Coveney affair, Sam Smyth wrote in the *Irish Independent* that John Bruton, 'like many in Cork, had known of Mr Coveney's phone call to Mr Michael Conlon since last week'. The article claimed he acted only because the story was going to appear in the *Sunday Business Post*. This claim was included in 'It Says in the Papers'. Bruton was incensed. He feared that this inaccurate distortion, if unchallenged, would feed into the debate on Hugh Coveney's demotion. So the taoiseach rang *Morning Ireland*, the programme in which the paper review is broadcast. Not getting any satisfaction, he then rang me at home. He was so angry, demanding a correction of this 'falsehood and misrepresentation', that he didn't tell me he had already rung the station himself. I duly called the editor, my old colleague Shane McElhatton. I told him the taoiseach said that the assertion was false and he wanted a correction. A correction was not forthcoming, but they would carry a statement.

The taoiseach was very upset to hear this response. In his view the story was untrue and it was up to the programme to correct this misinformation. He wanted me to call again, which I did – but the answer was still the same. The item was broadcast unchanged on the nine o'clock news. By now the taoiseach was furious. He wanted me to call again. I said the only point in doing that would be to make a statement. So he finally agreed to let me make a 'government spokesman' comment. In the event, the rebuttal statement broadcast in the eleven o'clock headlines was attributed to the taoiseach himself, which was not factually accurate. When I met the taoiseach in the office, before that broadcast, he wanted to tackle this matter in his speech during the Coveney debate. So I suggested to him that he should directly quote the Smyth article and his criticisms of it. Somebody said, 'you can't criticise journalists'. Being one, I didn't believe that.

At the end of May, because of improved Anglo-Irish relations during the peace process, with a 'complete cessation' of IRA violent armed actions against the British presence, Prince Charles (now King Charles III) made a semi-official visit to Ireland, invited by Bruton. I met him almost by accident when he was being shown around Government Buildings by an official. I was alone in the Sycamore Room after a meeting, and was about to leave, when the door opened and he came in. The official introduced me to him as the government press secretary, and we shook hands. The official mentioned that I was a well-known news and current affairs broadcaster with RTÉ. The prince was quick off the mark, asking me how that was working out now I was the 'poacher turned gamekeeper, as it were'. I said it was tough at times. I had discovered that the media 'could not swallow their own medicine – criticism', and he laughed. I said it was a great insight to work on the other side of the fence, and invaluable to see up close how government worked. 'Yes, indeed', he said. Then we said our goodbyes as his guide ushered him to the taoiseach's office.

Later that evening I attended the state reception and dinner in Dublin Castle in the prince's honour. Bruton read a fine, balanced speech, sticking to the text all the way through, at which I was relieved; then he unnecessarily ad-libbed a comment that Charles's visit had 'done more in symbolic and psychological terms to sweep away the legacy of fear and suspicion that has lain between our two peoples than any other event in my lifetime'. It was a gratuitous and exaggerated remark for which Bruton was inevitably criticised in some quarters. I wondered what Michael Collins would have said – this was the first visit to Ireland by a member of the British royal family since he got Dublin Castle from them in 1922. Dick Spring accompanied Charles at the airport and on a walkabout in Dublin city, while the Minister for Finance, Ruairí Quinn, met the prince, with a group of three-year-olds, at a crèche in his constituency. A further planned visit for the following year was called off because, by then, the IRA ceasefire had broken down.

The strained relations with the *Irish Independent* were on my mind in my brief chat with Prince Charles, and now were to play into a more 'sensational' story from a media perspective. I got a call from the *Independent* political reporter Brian Dowling. He told me he was in possession of some very important information which he wanted me to confirm. I told him noncommittally that I would listen. He then said that he believed that the attorney general, Dermot Gleeson, had acted as legal adviser to Matt Russell, the senior legal assistant in the attorney general's office, during the controversy over the Father Brendan Smyth extradition case, which had brought down the previous government – and that John Bruton had known this before he appointed Gleeson as attorney general. He said he believed he alone had this story, and he would be faxing me through a letter containing these points and seeking a response. I told him I would bring the letter to the attention of the relevant people but obviously I could make no commitment. This was the result of yet another mindless leak from the Labour side to curry favour with the media about a 'shock-horror' story which was in reality much ado about very little.

Bruton had prepared a parliamentary reply dealing with this very issue for Taoiseach's Questions that day – but his official and legal advice was not to use it in the Dáil unless he was specifically asked why he had sought 'formal and independent legal advice' about what action might have to be taken in relation to the Father Smyth case in the attorney general's office. Matt Russell was the senior official who had dealt with the Father Smyth case, and during the controversy the previous year, before the Rainbow government was formed, he spoke several times to Dermot Gleeson, whom he knew as a Senior Counsel, about the position he was placed in and his response to any possible disciplinary matters that might arise. I never met Matt Russell in Government Buildings, but nearly thirty years earlier I had attended his lectures in Trinity College while studying law. The senior officials in the Department of the Taoiseach were warning that this was a sensitive personnel matter and nothing about it should be said in public for fear of prejudicing a fair resolution of the matter.

It meant that Dermot Gleeson, as attorney general, was conflicted in dealing with any personnel issues that might arise from the affair. The normal procedure in such conflicts, which can arise in the busy practice of any successful barrister who later becomes attorney general, is that he/she would not advise on the conflicted matter, and independent legal advice would be sought. A similar procedure was taken concerning Larry Goodman, for whom Dermot Gleeson had acted during the Beef Tribunal. That had already been made public. Both the other coalition party leaders, Spring and De Rossa, had been informed of the Gleeson conflict in the Smyth extradition affair, and how it would be dealt with, before Gleeson was appointed the previous year. So this matter was in one sense routine, but because of the nature of this particular conflict it could be portrayed as sensational, particularly if it was presented as a 'secret' forced out of the government. My Labour colleague John Foley told me much later he believed the leaker was a Labour ministerial adviser with failed political ambitions who had access to the prepared Dáil answer or the information contained in it.

It was gravely damaging. It was also pointless, because Bruton was to reveal this matter within the next two days, when all the proper legal and personnel steps had been taken to deal with the aftermath of the Father Smyth affair in the attorney general's office, without prejudicing the constitutional and legal rights of anybody involved. So this leaker inflicted self-harm on the Rainbow government. It was an irresponsible and shameful act of vanity – preening about possession of short shelf-life 'inside' information – which plunged the government into a three-week-long political imbroglio instead of a three-day wonder. As a journalist, I am not against leaks from government. Sometimes they are the only way the truth of what's going on can be brought into the public domain. There are notable national and international examples. In this case the offender was simply grabbing the opportunity to falsely pose with an 'exposé'. To demonstrate the sensitivity of the situation, I was called by a reporter from the *Sunday Independent* in the midst of the negotiations. I told him I could not comment. He asked me how long before a settlement. I said I hoped it would be soon. To my surprise that was the lead in the paper next day and it was interpreted in the negotiations as placing undue pressure on the client for an outcome.

Glumly, I hastened to tell the taoiseach about this leak to Brian Dowling. He was dumbfounded. Then I returned quickly with Brian's letter. Bruton was galvanised into action. He called Paddy Teahon and instructed him to bring forward immediately the necessary legal steps that were being prepared. That night the taoiseach signed a formal legal instrument revoking personnel powers delegated in 1957 to the attorney general under the Civil Service Regulations Act. This meant that the taoiseach himself, rather than the attorney general, had the power to deal with personnel issues in the attorney general's office, acting on the basis of independent legal advice.

This dealt with Dermot Gleeson's conflict. It was a complex issue that senior officials in the Department had been working on for some time, so Bruton had the secretary prepare a statement to be issued that night. I warned him that the *Irish Independent* would be sore about the loss of their 'exclusive', but the taoiseach was adamant. He had no choice but to make a pre-emptive statement – otherwise everything he did to deal with this issue would be portrayed as simply a response to the sensational revelations, rather than something he had already been planning. It was impossible to argue with that logic – it was exactly the way the *Irish Independent* would have played it – but I told him that there would be consequences.

I had no idea how badly the *Irish Independent* would behave, or how I would be targeted for doing my job. I was to get a salutary lesson in how Upper Abbey Street could wield its power if you got on the wrong side of them. I rang the political correspondents to alert them that an important statement was on the way. The revocation document was brought to the taoiseach to sign about nine-thirty in the evening, along with a draft statement. There was little time left to meet the newspaper deadlines. It was finalised and copies printed within a half an hour, and then I raced up to the political correspondents' room to give it to them, fully expecting to see Brian Dowling. But he wasn't there. The senior correspondent, Chris Glennon, was the only one there from the *Irish Independent*. I spoke to him, as well as the few others there, about the background to the statement. I thought that Chris would tell Brian, who I presumed was just out of the room for a moment.

I then spent about two hours on the phone talking to the correspondents who had left for home, briefing them on the statement and the background to it. I spoke twice to the news editor of the *Irish Independent*, Philip Molloy, explaining to him the taoiseach's attitude to the leaked information, and I returned a call to Sam Smyth after midnight. He said I was too late – for what, he didn't explain. The response of the *Irish Independent* the following day and over the next week or so was extraordinary. The paper splashed the story on its front page in a 'shock-horror' manner, and then clamoured in its editorial and news features that an ethical code had been broken by the government in issuing a full statement to all media on the story about which they had a partial leak; a number of nasty personal attacks on me were made along these lines. In essence, the position the *Irish Independent* adopted was that the taoiseach had no right to act to defend the government's interests once the newspaper was in possession of partial leaked information. Bruton was expected by them to behave like a rabbit caught in the headlights. I spoke to my predecessor Seán Duignan about this. He was amazed at what was happening. He told me that on two occasions – on behalf of then taoiseach Albert Reynolds – he had done the same, responding to 'exclusive' information with a general statement, and there had been no inflammatory reaction.

John Cooney, the then political correspondent of the *Irish Press*, speaking on RTÉ television, called for my resignation over a 'fundamental breach of principle' and said he would be asking the political correspondents to 'sever' relations with me. Given the fact that I carried out my duties on behalf of the taoiseach and the government, and I was specifically following the taoiseach's instructions, I found this a bit rich. If I refused to do my job, I could be fired. Also, after a quarter of a century in journalism – with two years of investigative reporting on RTÉ television – I knew well that one of the risks you take in asking for a story to be confirmed is that the parties informed can take action after being alerted. In response to the libellous attacks, I set out the facts in letters to the *Irish Independent* and RTÉ's current affairs department, seeking an apology. RTÉ thoroughly investigated the claims of principle and the bogus alleged 'ethical issue'. The editor, Peter Feeney, told me that senior media figures they spoke to dismissed these false claims; RTÉ also took legal advice, and made a full apology on air for John Cooney's remarks and those of my old *7 Days* colleague Brian Farrell, who, foolishly, had joined the libel brigade. The *Independent* never replied to my letter. That is the kind of operation it was at that time. I considered taking legal action and I privately consulted some journalist friends and Dermot Gleeson. I was advised that if I did, the government would likely be victimised in retaliation, so I dropped the idea. I did not want to expose the government to more abuse.

When the cabinet met for its final session before the summer break after this prolonged phoney controversy, Pat Rabbitte, super junior Democratic Left minister, said he was 'worried that the government would get caught in the crossfire between Shane Kenny and the political correspondents'. When I heard of this I went straight to John Bruton's office and offered my resignation, telling him that I did not want to become a burden or a problem for the government. Bruton would not hear of it, and he told me what he'd said in response to Rabbitte: 'I told him that in fact you are a lightning conductor for the government, safeguarding it from criticism. You deflect it!' That was the last I heard of the matter.

Ultimately, I got what I wanted from the *Irish Independent*. After returning to RTÉ when the Rainbow lost the election, I developed business news broadcasting, a neglected field at the time. As a result, I was courted by the newspaper's managing editor, who offered me the job of business editor. We had a number of lunches to discuss the offer over some months. One of my requirements was that the *Irish Independent* would print an apology. The newspaper printed a general apology based on a more recent gutter press item about me emphatically stating that I was 'an ethical journalist' with the highest standards. I had no interest in working for the paper, but I had strung the process out over three or four months because of the apology, and I was also negotiating within RTÉ about the launch of an internet business news service, of which I would be the managing editor. Taoiseach Bertie Ahern came to an event in RTÉ's huge *Late Late Show* studio in 2001 to launch the new service and was very complimentary, which I appreciated. We had always got on well, and met occasionally for lunch. He had been very helpful when I was writing a book about the first-ever Fianna Fáil coalition government formed by Taoiseach Charles Haughey with his deadly enemies, the Progressive Democrats – *Go Dance on Somebody Else's Grave*. In 1991 I helped Bertie, then Minister for Labour, by making a dramatic breakthrough on the *News at One* live on air which delivered an end to a week-long national electricity strike, causing serious countrywide blackouts for homes and businesses. All the national industrial relations institutions had failed. In widespread media coverage Bertie told one paper he'd offer me a job. I thought he was joking. A senior member of Fianna Fáil told me on my first day in Government Buildings that if Bertie had become taoiseach, word in the party was that I would have been offered the press secretary job as well.

There was an amusing footnote to the attorney general affair on RTÉ radio's *Ryan Tubridy Show*, when the 'controversy' was resurrected live on air with me and Brian Dowling, who was then working for RTÉ. I explained the facts and the background. It was crystal clear that there was nothing 'sensational' in the story. It had been whipped into vindictive, unethical journalistic hysteria by the *Irish Independent*, and had spilled into other media. I concluded on air that 'the whole thing was a bottle of smoke'. Ryan exclaimed, 'Brian, he's calling your story a bottle of smoke!' I knew Brian, whom I respected, had nothing to do with the hype. His response was muted; he was clearly not going to be drawn into a defence of this unseemly affair.

7
MOSCOW, PARIS AND CANNES

WE RETURN NOW TO THE peace process via the unlikely route of the Russian capital, Moscow. On 8 May 1995, the taoiseach and his official party flew to the city to take part in the Russian ceremonies held by Boris Yeltsin marking the 50th anniversary of the defeat of Hitler's Nazi Germany in the Second World War. We had two Northern engagements on the agenda: a bilateral meeting with John Major at the British embassy in Moscow; and a secret meeting with Jim Molyneaux in London on the way back. En route to Moscow from the airport, we stopped for a TV interview beside enormous sculptures representing tank traps, commemorating the spot where the German advance in 1941 was halted by the Red Army, in view of the spires of the city. It was suitably bleak, a grey afternoon with swirling sleety rain on the wind.

The next morning John Bruton attended the official ceremonies at the Kremlin, and talked to Bill Clinton about his planned visit to Ireland that was being considered for the autumn. He chatted with the chairman of the Chinese Communist Party, Jiang Zemin, who fondly remembered a visit he had made to Shannon; and he discussed, in French, his own forthcoming visit to Canada with Canadian Prime Minister Jean Chrétien. These international gatherings are used by top politicians just like people use cocktail parties. Networking goes on all the time. That afternoon, following colourful commemoration ceremonies within the Kremlin's walls, there was a huge military parade. We watched it from the same Kremlin platform where, in 1941, on the 24th anniversary of the Bolshevik communist revolution, Stalin had reviewed the marching troops, tanks and artillery, who continued on out of the city to the German front line. Marshal Georgy Zhukov was preparing a counter-attack that pressed the Nazis back 130 kilometres from the capital in December 1941. Yeltsin also unveiled a very new statue of Zhukov on horseback near the eternal flame at the Kremlin walls commemorating the fallen in the Great Patriotic War, as the Second World War is known in Russia. One of the Russian officials told me that Stalin had the popular Zhukov deleted from history books about the war. I journeyed to Moscow again in 2003, this time also visiting St Petersburg (formerly Leningrad), and Strelkovka, Zhukov's birthplace, to make a documentary about this extraordinary military man, which was broadcast on RTÉ radio for the 60th anniversary of the end of the Great Patriotic War in 2005. Those were very different times in Russia; it was still a relatively open society after the collapse of the Soviet Union, with some free media and hopes of developing a strong democracy.

The Irish official party went to the British embassy, across the Moskva River from the Kremlin, for Bruton's meeting with John Major over lunch. The embassy then was an elaborate old palace, with wood-panelled rooms, gilt decoration, and a life-sized portrait of a bushily bearded King Edward VII in the reception room where we met. One of the British officials said this caused some suspicion among their former Soviet guests from time to time because they thought it was a picture of Tsar Nicholas II! He was Edward's cousin. It was on the tip of my tongue to say that all those pompous asses looked the same – but I bit my lip. We moved into the dining room for a four-course lunch with rich claret and white wines.

John Major spoke of his recent visit to Derry, when he had been met by a noisy, aggressive Sinn Féin demonstration. Bruton told him he regretted that, but Major didn't seem particularly perturbed. Major was glowing about the Islandbridge Second World War ceremony, and said he had received 'warm' reports. With both governments now inviting all the parties for talks, Bruton wanted to tease out what progress could be made. We got the clearest insight yet into Major's thinking at that juncture.

Sinn Féin and himself, he indicated, had quite a different understanding about how matters would unfold. 'Sinn Féin think exploratory talks can proceed quite quickly into bilaterals with other parties. I have never seen it that way, and I doubt it'll be that way. I doubt if progress will be easy to produce. I haven't high hopes.' It would be easier for Sinn Féin and the British, as the dialogue went on, he said, but 'there will be no miraculous breakthrough'. So the peace process was condemned to grind on slowly. Then came an even more depressing revelation. Major said there was a belief among Sinn Féin that the British thought 'decommissioning is the rock to sink the ship. But that's not true. The reality is that without agreement on modalities and a practical demonstration of decommissioning neither unionist parties or the Alliance Party will sit down with them in talks.' He said they were trying to persuade Sinn Féin of this – that it was not simply 'game playing' but he wasn't entirely sure the message was believed. However, he said, there would be no sudden breakdowns on their side; they would have the 'patience of Job'.

Bruton said he didn't fully understand Sinn Féin's thinking either. He told Major he had asked Gerry Adams the previous week what Sinn Féin would say to Michael Ancram about decommissioning. The answer was unclear, but Adams had told him that 'on a contingency basis' they'd be willing to discuss the subject, among other issues, such as prisoners, the most emotional issue in the republican community. Then Bruton tackled the Washington 3 issue, the British precondition of some IRA arms decommissioning before all-party talks. Picking up the language that Major had used, he said bluntly he was 'worried' about the British pursuing the 'practical demonstration of decommissioning; the peace process could be derailed.' There was an awkward silence around the table. One of the Irish officials broke it, saying that the British government had a 'full presentation' from the Irish side on this issue. The IRA would not decommission any weapons before talks.

Then Major, ignoring the challenge to Washington 3, launched into a diversion. First he said that the initial talks would move into detailed private discussions and the less 'megaphone' from the British and Sinn Féin, the better. Then he switched again, claiming that Mitchel McLaughlin, the chairman of Sinn Féin, had been saying the IRA would 'never give up arms. It's not in the press yet, but it will emerge ... then there'll be questions to me in the House about why I'm talking to them.' The less said the better, Major said: 'Masking tape after meetings! No detailed statements!' But he added that he wanted Sinn Féin in the 'full process' and some decommissioning would make getting into the talks easier.

Another Irish official asked if it was not a 'chicken and egg' situation. Which came first? Agreement and then decommissioning, or the reverse? If anybody walked from the table over this issue, everyone would be impaled on a hook. Sinn Féin wanted recognition of their representative mandate. They did not feel they were being treated fairly.

Major turned philosophical. He said that he spent a lot of time trying to put himself 'in Sinn Féin's mind'. He was aware of these points – and that there 'must be a degree of parallelism. I was going to meet one of their members in Derry – and what do they do? I just wish I could see more clearly into the Sinn Féin mind.' Bruton told Major that republicans make a distinction between peace now and the wishes of the next generation. 'They're committed to peace now – but they want a settlement which will hold off violence in the future.' Republicans, he made clear, could not commit the next generations. Major answered crisply, 'They're not dreamers!' He clearly meant a united Ireland.

The taoiseach mentioned the reaction of unionists to the main Framework Document, telling Major of his planned second secret meeting with Molyneaux in London the next day, after his foray across the border to meet the unionist leader last February. 'What bothers them is not so much a settlement in embryo – but a staging post en route with one destination [a united Ireland]. We don't see it like that. The Framework Document could be for as long as anyone can see.' Then the taoiseach surprised me and the rest of his team by saying, 'The Framework Document does allow for further movement. If the unionists were given small modifications, they might accept it on the basis that it'll be the last that is asked of them.' John Major quickly knocked down this idea; he wasn't 'keen' to make concessions, because there would then be a demand to make counter-concessions and the 'whole document could unravel'. Major was quite right. It was one of Bruton's impetuous ideas, which members of the official team, including myself, took issue with later.

The taoiseach continued, on the unionists: 'Some of their worries are just plain wrong. They are genuinely angry about cross-border structures, and they read too much into it. They think the British will take them by the scruff of the neck and push them where they don't want to go.' Major responded, 'I'm inclined to leave the Framework Document there.' It wasn't until after Bruton's visit to Molyneaux at his flat in London that the 'modifications' became clear. He suggested to Molyneaux that a condition might be included in some context, which would guarantee that a simple majority vote would not change the constitutional status of Northern Ireland – some figure in excess of 50 per cent plus one would be required. Molyneaux politely noted the idea.

Officials opposed this notion, and when I found out about it – I was not at the Molyneaux meeting – I said to Bruton that it was not on. While I and others recognised the majority size issue, and Bruton was told that Gerry Adams also believed that 50 per cent plus one would not be enough, it would be unhelpful to put this on the table now. It was an issue for the all-party talks that we were seeking. The idea was quietly dropped. But in 2021 Bruton returned to this proposition in an article in the unionist Belfast *News Letter* saying that a simple majority or a 51/49 per cent vote would be unlikely to achieve the peaceful unity of Ireland 'without coercion or violence' as agreed by the British and Irish governments in the Downing Street Declaration. Writing that he personally favoured unity, Bruton compared a small majority for a united Ireland to the deeply divisive Brexit referendum, with a 51.89 per cent win. The December 2022 opinion poll in the *Irish Times* on unity in Northern Ireland showed that persuaders for unity still have a job of work on their hands, particularly within their own natural constituency. There was a decisive majority against unity, 50 per cent, and that included 21 per cent of those from a Catholic background. Just over a quarter, 26 per cent, would vote for unity, and there were 19 per cent don't knows.

The conversation in Moscow turned to republican prisoners, particularly the issue of 50 per cent remission of sentences in Britain, which Bruton was pushing hard. Major said legislation would be needed for that. On relations with the unionists, Major said the damage caused by the 'malicious' leak of the main Framework Document had been substantially repaired. On the international level, a discussion followed about Russian fears of an expanding NATO. Interestingly, one of Major's ideas was to draw the Russians into NATO's Partnership for Peace, a project aimed at undertaking peacekeeping and humanitarian missions, but that never happened. Major also understood Russian fears about EU expansion – because, he said, if a member of the Union were attacked, it would be 'inconceivable' that others would not support a member state. Two of his officials who had served in Moscow said the Russian attitude to EU enlargement 'would not be at all so strong'. Time has proved Major right, and his officials wrong. Those live contemporary issues discussed back in 1995 finally exploded with the brutal aggression of the Russian invasion of Ukraine in February 2022 and, ironically, President Putin behaving like Hitler, the murderous dictator overthrown by his fellow countryman Marshal Zhukov in the Battle of Berlin. In Moscow, at the end of the conversation, they agreed to make a focus on the battle against illegal drugs across the EU a key element of their media briefing. Bruton had been pushing this in Europe and at home, and Major agreed.

A month later the atmosphere between Bruton and Major at their next meeting was not so gracious. Jacques Chirac had won the French presidential election, ending 14 years of socialist rule at the Élysée Palace, and had invited the EU heads of government to a working dinner in Paris on 9 June 1995. In Paris we got wind of a British plan to release paratrooper Lee Clegg, who was in prison for the murder of teenager Karen Reilly in Northern Ireland in September 1990. She had been in the passenger seat of a stolen car when she was shot dead at an army checkpoint. Clegg was now just four years into a life sentence. With the British side endlessly dragging their feet on the peace process, and difficulties over the early release of republican prisoners in Britain and Northern Ireland, this was going to raise the temperature on the nationalist side.

Before the dinner there was little time to talk privately, but Bruton took Major aside to warn him of the serious consequences of such an unequal move, with many republicans serving long sentences without remission. The prime minister did not respond verbally – but appeared to take the point on board. The British were still insisting on the IRA making a gesture of decommissioning as a condition for entering all-party talks. Bruton warned Major again that on the arms issue, while the Irish government wished it were possible, he did not think that any disposal of arms would take place. Major immediately said there would *have* to be some decommissioning.

John Bruton spelt out his position on the Clegg case for the broadcast and print media before and after the dinner. Such a move would 'create a sense of one law for members of the security forces and another law for everybody else,' he said. As I waited in the cobbled courtyard of the Élysée Palace for the dinner to end, watching the twinkling lights in the growing darkness, I was aware of a gathering storm. The British and Irish media were very keen on the story. We heard the following day that Major was annoyed at the wide publicity given to the taoiseach's statements on the BBC and elsewhere. This was one of a series of 'annoyances' Bruton was to cause for Major and his government as he continuously pressed the British to drop the demand for an IRA arms 'gesture'; he demanded respect for nationalists during the North's Orange Order marching season, and recognition of historic wrongs visited on nationalists; and he wanted equality of treatment for republican prisoners, with early releases. The taoiseach's interviews were borne out when Clegg was finally released about three weeks later, sparking violent demonstrations in the North. Bruton's public comments in Paris delayed the Clegg release, which had been expected within days. In the Republic at this juncture, 20 IRA prisoners had already been released early as a result of the ceasefire. In the Dáil on 4 July 1995, the taoiseach had this to say about the release of Private Clegg:

> It is of critical importance that the issue of prisoners should be treated in an even-handed and balanced way. History tells us

that in the Northern Ireland context, symbols are often matters of substance and perception is frequently as important as reality. It is crucially important, therefore, that equality of treatment is seen to be applied. Yesterday's decision to release Private Lee Clegg, who had a life sentence, should be set in the wider context of prisoner issues. The criteria for that decision should be applied to republican and loyalist prisoners as well.

Notwithstanding the disturbances in Belfast, he said, the 50 per cent remission rate should be restored in Britain as a first step. There should be a review of life sentences, and the regime for prisoners in Britain should be as flexible and humane as possible. In particular, contact with prisoners, including by families, should be facilitated, and he would continue to raise these matters with the British authorities. He also spelt out the need to take into account the sensitivities of the victims of violence of the past 25 years. 'The family of Karen Reilly are at present being forced to revisit the agony of their loss. Many other families will face the same trauma in the event of further prisoner releases ... we can only hope that they can find it in themselves to forgive the perpetrators of violence and to help us to build a better future for all.' He referred to the 20 IRA prisoners who had been released in the Republic since the ceasefire, after serving substantial portions of their sentences. 'The decision to make these releases, clearly signalling to prisoners, their families and their paramilitary comrades that the pursuit of political goals, through exclusively peaceful means, holds an immediate dividend for them as well as everyone else.' On the street rioting, Bruton said, it was important to ensure that there was no slippage back into the vortex of violence and suffering.

John Ware, presenter of the then BBC programme *Rough Justice*, wrote a courageous article for the British conservative *Spectator* magazine in the middle of this controversy. He said the British government should listen to what John Bruton said because of his moderate outreach to unionists, when he had said in Paris that Clegg's release 'would create a sense of one law for the security forces and another law for everyone else'. Major's response denied that political considerations would apply to Clegg's release, but 'by choosing to grant special favours to Private Clegg, Mr Major's own ministers have, in fact, already tarnished the criminal justice system with politics'. A British prisoners' release package with 50 per cent remission was at last announced by Sir Patrick Mayhew in mid-August 1995. Bruton had got his way. 'Vintage humbug' was how John Ware described Major's assertion that 'the British legal system was untainted by politics'.

The Clegg affair was the backdrop to the main business that would occupy us just a few weeks later – a big push to get John Major to move seriously towards all-party talks. While the taoiseach was engaged at the Élysée with European business and talking to Major, elsewhere in the palace, Department secretary Paddy Teahon was talking to Major's private secretary Rod Lyne about the plan to get the British off the arms precondition hook. The proposal was to establish an international commission to deal with the illegal weapons issue, getting rid of the demand for a start of IRA arms disposal before Sinn Féin could enter all-party talks. Then those talks, including Sinn Féin, could get under way, negotiating the political issues about a settlement. We called it the twin-track policy. Lyne's initial response was not favourable, indicating that Major needed a beginning of decommissioning to satisfy parliament. That issue had to be overcome – it was already ten months since the IRA ceasefire.

Major's precarious situation in the House of Commons was worsened a great deal by the Tory right wing, which could rebel on Northern Ireland policy. But Sinn Féin did not appear to appreciate Major's political dilemma or place any relevance or importance on it. Just a few weeks later he was to face his party critics down when he himself initiated a Tory leadership contest, effectively calling for a vote on him as prime minister. He survived, but without materially weakening the 'bastards', his enemies in the Conservative Party. In fact, the 'bastards'' hold on his Northern Irish policy strengthened as the Tory majority was eroded. His description of his party opponents like this came from unguarded comments he made to an ITV correspondent after he won the vote on the Maastricht European Act 1993 by just one vote. He was unaware that a live BBC 'feed' cable was still running to a studio and the comment was overheard.

The next key opportunity to advance the twin-track proposal, not yet public, was the French EU Presidency Summit held in the Côte d'Azur capital, Cannes, towards the end of June 1995. Bathed in sunshine, the famous French Riviera resort was a marvellous location for a summit. Understandably it was a destination that attracted officials from every Department who could possibly justify a presence. There were nearly forty in the Irish official party – and that drew sharp criticism in one newspaper, leading John Bruton to lay down strict guidelines for attendance at summits.

The important event for us was the Anglo-Irish summit held on the margins. It was attended by Tánaiste Dick Spring and British Foreign Secretary Douglas Hurd, as well as the taoiseach and the prime minister. The usual 'margin' meeting is between the leaders only, and rarely goes on for more than half an hour. This was a serious engagement which lasted for nearly an hour and a half and had been well prepared on the Irish side, with documents furnished to the British well in advance. The meeting substantially advanced the twin-track strategy with the British side showing considerable interest more quickly than we anticipated. It was decided that no media briefing would take place afterwards. Bruton refused to talk to RTÉ's Éamonn Lawlor about the meeting afterwards. I was a bit upset about that.

About a week or so later an unusual interview took place. Paddy Teahon, who had been present at the Cannes talks, demonstrated that he wasn't as sensitive as his boss about talking about the outcome. We both accompanied Bruton to Tralee, where he was speaking to the Irish Congress of Trade Unions. Unbeknownst to me, Teahon, who is from Kerry, was buttonholed by local reporter Conor Keane, son of the writer John B. Keane, both of whom I knew well. The temptation to appear in the local paper proved too much for Paddy. He went on the record to Conor with an extremely optimistic projection: 'I would hope that we could move to the decommissioning of arms within a year in conjunction with round-table talks engaging all the parties involved,' he was quoted as saying in the *Kerryman*, with the story headlined: 'Top Kerry Civil Servants Play Crucial Role in Deal on Weapons'.

Paddy Teahon's role was linked in the paper to that of Tim Dalton, secretary general of the Department of Justice, who worked with the then Northern Ireland Office under-secretary, Sir John Chilcot, on justice-related issues in the peace process. This was known as the Dalton–Chilcot Group. Both Teahon and Dalton, the report said, had been in the same class at St Brendan's College in Killarney. The story went on to say that another Kerryman, Tánaiste Dick Spring, was also playing a crucial role in the peace process: his 'proposal that a third country could provide the mechanisms for the decommissioning of arms, first floated in the White House five months ago, is central to the present talks'. The story speculated that Nordic personnel could be involved (former Finland Prime Minister Harri Holkeri became a member of the international team on the arms issue) and it was 'understood that a positive reaction has been received from soundings taken in these quarters'.

This was the first public reference to any of the real substance of the summit. Second secretary of the Department of Foreign Affairs Seán Ó hUiginn, who was also in Cannes, demonstrated that nothing escaped his eyes, and sent Paddy Teahon and Tim Dalton a photocopy of the *Kerryman* story after it appeared, noting on it, 'I haven't been to the school, but I met the scholars!' I was sent a copy too. Bruton said nothing to me about this publicity. The national media had not been briefed at all about the twin-track strategy yet. Emboldened by this, I decided to brief Geraldine Kennedy of the *Irish Times*, along Teahon's lines, about the twin-track formula that the two governments were now pursuing. At a prearranged meeting with her in the National Gallery I was dumbfounded to be told over tea that she was writing an article about the Rainbow government being secretive, 'the most closed and least transparent administration for more than twenty years' with an 'iron curtain around the operations of government'. All she wanted to do was talk about this article. Geraldine told me she was writing that I was probably the best-informed press secretary ever on Northern Ireland affairs, but Bruton would not allow me to brief journalists. All my efforts to focus her attention on the important new information I wanted to give her about the government's twin-track policy were to no avail; she wanted to talk through the article in detail. The *Irish Times* missed a good story on the peace process, while condemning the government for not telling them enough about what was going on. It was a surreal moment.

Throughout July 1995, Bruton was focused on the need to get movement in the peace process, with civil servants working away on the twin-track policy. He was conscious that people in both administrations would be away on holiday during the month of August, and this would be a critical lead-in to the first anniversary of the ceasefire. Consequently two weekends were given over to meetings at Bruton's house in Dunboyne to brainstorm the issues. Those in attendance included Paddy Teahon, Dermot Gleeson, Seán Donlon, Roy Dooney and me. Every conceivable outcome was considered, and John Bruton himself contributed a series of papers that he had either written himself or had had drawn up on his behalf.

One paper dealt with his idea of an election as a gateway to talks. It had the advantage of delivering on the Sinn Féin call for a date for the start of talks and drew on the unionist idea of an elected assembly or convention, in order to get them to buy into the process. This thinking proved prophetic. We discussed it as a way out of the impasse. But an election was to become a highly controversial issue, even demonised as another delaying tactic, when it was proposed by the new Unionist leader David Trimble in September. However, there was a reason for nationalist concern. In an elected assembly, the unionists would have a majority and might seek majoritarian rule; but the Framework Documents absolutely ruled that out. Mayhew, Major and Bruton individually ruled it out, but the dark shadow of the old 'Protestant Parliament for a Protestant people' was hard to completely dispel. Bruton was also seized by a recent comment from Brian Feeney in the *Irish News*: 'It will be 1997 after both British general and Northern Irish local government elections before unionists begin to talk about the future. But when they do, they know it will be about the shape as described in the Framework.' This provoked further worries about having to think longer term – and concern about sustaining the peace process if the unionists refused to come to the negotiating table. It should also have acted as a warning about the date of an election in the Republic as well, but sadly it did not.

John Bruton's concern about unionists brought him no rewards from them during his term of office, as John Major rightly said in his autobiography. It also led to criticism from Sinn Féin that he cared too much about unionists, and neglected nationalist concerns and needs. That issue seriously worried me, going back to the fireside chat with Dick Spring at Hillsborough. I often tried to get Bruton to speak out on important nationalist issues while doing my job of supporting him and explaining his policies. An event on 14 July 1995 brought matters to a head. Together with the tánaiste, Dick Spring, he held a summit meeting at Dublin Castle with the two Northern nationalist and republican leaders, John Hume and Gerry Adams. The joint statement issued after the meeting later caused John Bruton some anxiety. It was only two paragraphs:

> We reiterate our total and absolute commitment to democratic and peaceful methods of resolving political problems and our objective of an equitable and lasting agreement that can command the consent and allegiance of all.
>
> The current impasse in the Peace Process is a concern to all who share that objective. It must be overcome. Accordingly, we are seeking a commencement, as soon as possible, of the inclusive, all-party talks necessary to the achievement of our objective.

Pressure for this meeting had come from the Northern leaders, and this text had support among Irish officials, including myself. John Bruton was so concerned that he gave me, and all other officials involved, a detailed outline of his approach to policy and his worries, and he asked that they 'underpin' all our work. His main worry was that the Irish government was becoming a hostage to Sinn Féin's line on the shape of the peace process – and that Sinn Féin and the IRA 'held all the cards'. Bruton warned civil servants that they should not use 'Sinn Féin-speak' about decommissioning. He was concerned that the IRA could switch on violence at any time, with little or no concern for public opinion, given that unpopularity never bothered them in the past. The length of a ceasefire was no barrier, he thought, to a renewed campaign – a prophetic insight. The immediate wave of condemnation would not last long. He had been warned recently by a senior official that if the peace process broke down, that would probably be the 'end of the government'. So he felt his freedom of action, and the independence of the government, was being badly eroded. He was, at the same time, acutely aware that, unlike the IRA, the government needed the support of the public.

Now that he had signed up to a joint statement with Sinn Féin, Bruton felt he would be open to criticism for any perceived departure from the 'agreed line' as being unhelpful or even damaging the peace process. If the IRA restarted violence, then he felt his comments, or the position he took on particular issues, would be cast by Sinn Féin, Fianna Fáil and their media friends as a cause of the end of the ceasefire, a fear that became a reality, no matter how bogus were the grounds for such a claim. I saw it another way. If he continued a peace process 'consensus' with the Northern nationalist and republican leadership, occasionally meeting with Hume and Adams together, he would have some insurance against blame if the ceasefire broke down. He was doing all that was within his power. However, as taoiseach, he would not want them 'dictating' policy to him.

Ironically, Bruton was the one who relentlessly pressed John Major to drop the demand for an instalment of decommissioning and to allow the proposed international commission to decide the matter, with all-party talks as quickly as possible. Both Hume and Adams made the point that if round-table talks were started, the unionists would eventually come in to defend their interests, and if they didn't, the British government would represent their views. In fact it turned out to be the other way round: the all-party talks were started without Sinn Féin and eventually they joined to conclude a deal.

In early August, we got a warning of trouble on the domestic front in the Republic which would spiral for some time. The day before Bruton left with his family to holiday in northern France, I got a call from the *Sunday Times* about a 'surveillance' story. Was the taoiseach aware of the fact that Michael Lowry thought he was being followed? Shortly beforehand, I'd had a call from Michael Lowry, who wanted the taoiseach to make a very strong statement about the alleged surveillance. I was very uneasy about the whole business, and in that frame of mind, I called Bruton. Lowry had already made him aware of his suspicions. Whatever the truth, Bruton was instinctively wary of this being hyped up in the media, and I cautioned against anything other than a purely factual response – that the taoiseach was aware of the allegations. That was where we left it. Bruton departed the next day, and I left for the south of France a few days later; by the middle of the month, Michael Lowry had the entire media on his trail seeking proof of his claims that there was a 'cosy cartel' who got state contracts, and his alleged 'surveillance'.

Hill-walking was my sport, and I was doing just that in the Alpes-Maritimes north of Cannes, between France and Italy. My mobile phone didn't work in the mountains, so in the evenings I checked the home front from my hotel. I had a couple of worrying conversations with Tony Heffernan about Michael Lowry's allegations of being spied on. Lowry had gone public a lot about this and the media wanted details. He was to survive this 'spying' affair, which exploded in the Dáil in October, but his reputation was left in tatters. In his defence he produced evidence of some questionable procedures in the sale of CIÉ property in Cork to developer Owen O'Callaghan and apparently excessive expenses for an outing to New York by the chairman of CIÉ, but these fell way short of what was needed to swing opinion in his favour. The following year he was forced to resign in circumstances that I'll describe later. Lowry's scrapes worried me most because he was known to be close to John Bruton.

I was briefed by Paddy Teahon on developments with the British when I returned from holiday. He was sanguine about the prospect of a deal, with a summit to endorse it at the beginning of September. He always stayed at work during August, preferring to holiday at another time of the year. The secure fax had been whirring away to the taoiseach in France, and to Downing Street officials, who were in touch with John Major, also on holiday in France. Major seemed to be on board; in one conversation he remarked to John Bruton that together they were going to take the 'next big step' in the peace process. All Teahon's work hung on Sinn Féin accepting the proposed international commission on the arms issue that John Bruton saw initially as running in parallel with an all-party talks process. But at his meeting with Gerry Adams and John Hume at Dublin Castle on Bastille Day, 14 July, before the holidays, Bruton had been surprised to discover that the international commission formula was not acceptable to Sinn Féin. The party just wanted an immediate round-table conference to launch the process, and a date set as quickly as possible for September. John Hume supported this approach.

It was as if there was a magic formula by which the taoiseach could entrance John Major to do their bidding. Major was both adamant and stubborn on the decommissioning of arms. In early summer, Martin McGuinness had given an ominous warning in the *Sunday Business Post* that the ceasefire was in peril if there was no progress by the first anniversary. Everyone wanted that, but the only way to get progress with the British was the twin-track, establishing an international group of eminent persons who could carve a path around Major on the arms issue, forcing him to drop the precondition for talks. At the start of the last week in August, John Bruton remained dubious about Sinn Féin's co-operation with an international 'body', renamed because of Sinn Féin objections to a 'commission'. Paddy Teahon was in daily contact with Major's adviser Rod Lyne, and each day when he briefed me he was more confident.

A formula was finally agreed to set up an international body on the arms issue – to report quickly, with an all-party talks process to start in the autumn. On 28 August, three days before the anniversary of the ceasefire, Bruton, Spring and De Rossa, together with key officials, met Adams, Martin McGuinness and Lucilita Bhreatnach, and briefed them about the deal. The government side came away believing that Sinn Féin, albeit reluctantly, accepted the arms body formula, so it was publicly announced that a summit would take place on 6 September at Chequers, the British prime minister's retreat. But some days before the summit date, Sinn Féin had a meeting with the British side as well and that changed their approach. Two senior civil servants set off for Belfast to meet Adams. They intended to go over the text of the communiqué and discuss the follow-up after the summit. The meeting took place in a monastery, and Father Alec Reid was present.

The government officials were left in no doubt that a return to IRA violence would happen if the proposed text was agreed in the summit communiqué. Father Alec Reid piled on huge pressure for the government to do as Sinn Féin wanted and not agree to the document. Gerry Adams and Martin McGuinness strongly and repeatedly warned that this would be a breaking point that would put the peace process in danger; the IRA would abandon the ceasefire if this communiqué went ahead. If the IRA ended the ceasefire, innocent people were likely to die, as they did when the IRA exploded a giant bomb in the London Docklands on 9 February the following year. There was an inexcusable failure in communicating to me the substance of this meeting immediately so that I could plan for media coverage. It was only by luck that the British reaction to the failed summit didn't erupt immediately after it was cancelled. A week later, the *Sunday Business Post* splashed the story when we were in Canada, saying that if the summit went ahead 'there would be blood in the streets'. I was furious. This appalling lapse hamstrung our response to the British, who attacked us over the cancelled summit, briefing the British media that a communiqué was agreed but 'the rats had got at the text'.

I learned that Sinn Féin would only co-operate with an international body if the British made it explicit that they would no longer insist on a start to arms destruction or disposal before all-party talks. Despite the best efforts of John Bruton, Dick Spring, Paddy Teahon and Seán Ó hUiginn, the British had not given this guarantee. The communiqué was a fudge that, it was hoped, would allow time for the British to quietly drop the demand for a pre-talks instalment of arms disposal, or the International Body would get the British off the arms hook – which came to pass when it was established three months later. Bruton spoke to John Major on the phone several times before the summit was cancelled, but Major was not to be moved; he wanted to keep the precondition of some decommissioning of arms. Bruton got all the Northern Ireland officials team to write to him on the question of a cancellation. The general view was that there was no alternative. Fergus Finlay published the full text of his letter arguing that case for cancellation in his memoir, *Snakes and Ladders*.

Finally, on 5 September, it was decided that the next day's summit would be postponed, despite Major's last-minute attempts on the phone to press Bruton to go ahead. It was the worst crisis for the taoiseach since he took up office, and he was visibly upset and shaken. Remarkably, that day, British Labour Party leader Tony Blair and Alistair Campbell, his adviser and press officer, had come to see the taoiseach. Campbell, in his book *The Irish Diaries*, noted that Bruton seemed in a 'really bad way, he was twitching, rubbing his eyes then letting his head fall into his hands. Bruton said the UK government had got themselves on the decommissioning hook, it was a mistake, the IRA would never do it, and it meant a logjam.' There would be no weapons 'gesture' and 'Gerry Adams was coming under pressure' from republicans saying 'told you so'. Bruton said the governments were 'heading for deadlock'. Tony Blair blurted out, 'God, this is difficult politics.' Blair said their basic position was support for the peace process and that meant support for the UK government. But 'privately' he agreed that getting firmly on the pre-condition hook seeking some decommissioning was a mistake. Campbell wrote, 'Bruton had looked physically ill with it all. You could see the pressure he was under.'

The taoiseach might be seen as bowing to the threat of violence from the IRA; on the other hand, if he went ahead, he would be attacked by Sinn Féin, Fianna Fáil, John Hume and media supporters for wrecking the peace process. The British would not agree a joint statement on the cancellation, and that rang alarm bells for me. I found it impossible until late in the day to concentrate minds, or even get access to the taoiseach to deal with the presentation of this cancelled summit. Around five o'clock he called me to his office. He wanted a two-sentence statement: 'The taoiseach, Mr John Bruton TD, has suggested the postponement of tomorrow's Anglo-Irish summit, and the British prime minister, Mr John Major, has agreed to this. The purpose is to allow some more time to attempt to resolve outstanding differences.' Not very enlightening when there was an intergovernmental disagreement. The agreed on-the-record briefing notes for the political correspondents were also an attempt to minimise the conflict. I said I wanted them in writing because of the seriousness of what had happened and the sensitivity of the issues. They could also be faxed to all press officers who had to deal with press queries. The taoiseach was due to travel to Canada on an official visit the following week, but that was now in doubt. These were the main points from the briefing notes:

> The Taoiseach has suggested a short postponement of the summit. He is now reviewing his Canadian schedule. The Irish government is not interested in setting preconditions for all-party talks. Nor is the government interested in artificially postponing difficult questions. The government objective is early round-table talks, and talks that will work. We want all of the relevant people there. All-party talks without full participation could prove to be little more than a cosmetic gesture. The government wishes to establish trust in relation to arms.

There was more of that nature – attempting to tread softly and avoiding the core issues with the British prime minister, Sinn Féin and the IRA. John Bruton asked me to co-ordinate with Fergus Finlay at the Department of Foreign Affairs. Finlay's view was that we should stress that this 'was not a row between two governments, we are trying to get two protagonists together – and we should resist apportioning blame'. If there was a ceasefire breakdown, Bruton felt the government's best position would be holding the middle ground, able to criticise both the IRA and the British.

When I went with my colleagues to the political correspondents' room there was some mild puzzlement about the cancellation, but it wasn't a contentious affair. However, next morning, the British papers were full of reports based on a British government briefing that 'the rats had got at the text' of the agreed communiqué, accusing the Irish government of bowing to threats from Sinn Féin and the IRA by calling off the summit. Furthermore, John Major had written a strong letter to John Bruton implying that the Irish had breached an agreed position on decommissioning reached in the Dalton–Chilcot report. Everybody was shocked at Downing Street's behaviour. Paddy Teahon, who had worked hard with the British over the text, was particularly upset at the 'rats' reference. Who were the rats? Nationalist-minded officials or Sinn Féin? He wrote a letter of complaint to the chief UK official, Sir Robin Butler, saying the press briefers had engaged in activity 'that is entirely destructive in its effect in both personal and political terms'. Downing Street press secretary Chris Meyer later personally apologised to me about this briefing, which, he said, had come from 'somewhere in the system' – which stretched credulity. He sent me a Christmas card that year signed 'Christopher Meyer (without fur!).'

The gloves had to come off, so in briefing I attacked John Major's letter for containing a 'fundamental misconception' about the status of the Dalton–Chilcot report. In the official contacts between Dublin and London during this stand-off, the British finally accepted there was no 'agreed' report on decommissioning. During discussions on the draft of this report, the Irish side had insisted that paramilitaries would have to 'buy into' any proposals for decommissioning. So if Sinn Féin didn't accept a particular decommissioning proposal, under the terms of the draft Dalton–Chilcot report it was consistent to defer the summit for further consideration. However, there was a sense that the government had sailed too close to disaster. It made John Bruton more determined than ever to free himself of having to continuously defer to Sinn Féin on the peace process. In a carefully drafted speech given two days later to the American multimillionaires' club, the Warren Buffett group, at Dublin Castle, he sent a deliberate message to Sinn Féin.

In the speech he stressed that he had made an 'act of faith' that the government accepted that the 'cessation of violence by the IRA is irreversible'. As leader of the opposition on the day of the ceasefire in 1994, he had told the Dáil he believed it was 'permanent and total'. The people of Ireland, he said, had placed their trust in Sinn Féin that the IRA will never again use or threaten to use arms to achieve a political objective. Sinn Féin's references to a 'crisis in the peace process' are interpreted, not least by unionists, as threatening a return to violence unless certain things are done their way. However, he stressed that there was an obligation on the two governments to move forward 'while seeking to bring the maximum number of people' along with them. In some cases political parties might be 'unwilling, on principle, to give a commitment' to a proposal. But the two governments 'must act together, as governments, when the time is right'. Bruton needed some flexibility from Major to get things done.

When this speech was reported in the media, in the context of the cancelled summit, as a warning to Sinn Féin that Bruton would not allow himself to be placed in the same situation again, Gerry Adams expressed annoyance through official channels, saying I was putting a 'spin' on the speech.

8

ARMS DISPOSAL CRISIS

We left almost immediately on the taoiseach's now shortened official visit to Canada, and it proved a good antidote to the tense atmosphere in Government Buildings around the failed summit. We went first on Aer Lingus to the US, and then took a commercial flight to the country's capital, Ottawa. We couldn't use the government jet because it had developed a fault on a return journey from official business abroad, with the tánaiste on board, and had been diverted to Shannon for repairs. We were put up in the comfortable and attractive surroundings of the government guest house after arriving in the afternoon. Later, we were entertained to dinner at the guest house by Canada's then prime minister, Jean Chrétien, a French Canadian who had been in power for nearly two years after his Liberal Party won the election in 1993.

Chrétien came alone and spent the evening telling us story after story about Canadian politics and the separatist push of his fellow Quebecois. He kept the taoiseach, me, Roy Dooney and his private secretary, George Shaw, in stitches with laughter. Chrétien recounted how he began his campaign for the leadership of the Liberals by making fun of his own disability, a youthful attack of Bell's palsy that had left the entire left side of his face paralysed. He declared that he was 'one politician who didn't speak out of both sides of his mouth'. Despite being mocked by a journalist as looking like 'the driver of a getaway car', he was a wily and highly intelligent political street fighter, whom I warmed to immediately, and not surprisingly he went on to serve two further terms in office, finally resigning after a decade at the top in 2003. One of the legacies he left was his insights about politics with which he entertained us that night. Two examples stand out:

> A successful politician must not only be able to read the mood of the public, he must have the skill to get the public on his side. The public is moved by mood more than logic, by instinct more than reason, and that is something that every politician must make use of, or guard against.

There's a lot of truth in that insight, and in this one: 'The art of politics is learning to walk with your back to the wall, your elbows high, and a smile on your face. It's a survival game played under the glare of lights.'

While we were in Ottawa, Chrétien agreed to Bruton's formal request for a Canadian to take part in the International Body on Decommissioning. It was very helpful to the peace process, not alone then, but over many years ahead.

The peace process wasn't dominating the headlines then. They were more concerned with none other than Michael Lowry, whose claims of a 'cosy cartel' of people receiving lucrative semi-state company contracts were followed by his allegations that he was the object of a spying operation; 'under surveillance' in his public life as well as his commercial and private affairs. This heady brew was all coming to a head. Lowry insisted he would not be deflected in his plans to reform the semi-state companies' tendering system, which was not a bad idea on its own merits.

But a much more significant event took place in Lowry's Department in October 1995. There was a rushed announcement that the competition for the coveted second Irish mobile phone licence (points having been awarded for the detailed elements of proposals), had been won by Denis O'Brien's Esat Digifone submission. That was a surprise to many. A number of high-profile consortiums with international and Irish partners had submitted proposals, and Anderson Management International,

Danish consultants, had carried out the evaluation process. Esat Digifone was a consortium made up of Denis O'Brien's Communicorp and the Norwegian state company Telenor, which each owned 40 per cent, the remainder was expected to be taken up by independent institutional shareholders. Esat Digifone was then able to enter into exclusive negotiations with Lowry's Department for the formal award of the licence the following year. During those negotiations, it emerged that financier Dermot Desmond's International Investment and Underwriting Ltd, an investment company, was taking a 25 per cent share of the mobile company. That was not accepted by the Department, which insisted on a return to the original share allocation.

Lowry told Bruton, Spring and De Rossa about Esat Digifone winning the competition for the licence before he had the final report on the competition. Martin Brennan, the chairman of the departmental committee supervising the process, told the Moriarty Tribunal, investigating the licence affair in 2003, that it was not unusual for a minister to take that course of action, as reported in the *Irish Times* on 29 January 2003. Lowry did not immediately take the Esat Digifone win before the full cabinet, but later the approval of the licence award was made by the government. I recall receiving an elaborate invitation card to an extravagant victory party hosted by O'Brien at the Point Depot on the Dublin quays, to launch his new mobile service the following year, which I didn't attend.

O'Brien later first publicly said on my RTÉ radio *Moneymakers* programme in autumn 1999 that his radio and telecoms business was in financial stress when he got the news from one of his 98FM radio reporters that his company had won the mobile competition. He was so ecstatic that he leapt up, punching his fist so high in the air that it went through the ceiling in his office. That night he was so excited he could not sleep. At 4 a.m. he got up and went back to the office. On his fax machine, he told me, he found an offer from a British bank for a loan of many millions to roll out the new mobile service network. During the programme he reflected on the irony of the fact that, at that time, they were sending out couriers every day with final demand notices to desperately get money in to keep the business going. O'Brien knew the value of the licence he had just won better than any member of the cabinet – including the taoiseach and tánaiste – except for Lowry himself. I cannot recall the taoiseach ever broaching the matter with me; the only aspect that I was briefed on was the explanation of the extraordinarily low fee for the licence – just £15 million.

I was told that initially a fee of £60 million was proposed, but under European Community rules this fee would also have to be demanded from Telecom Éireann for its mobile unit. Telecom was being prepared for privatisation at the time and this figure was considered to be too big a financial burden for the company, so the licence fee was reduced to £15 million. I was also briefed that there was a clawback clause in the licence terms to ensure that the state would get a share in profits if the licence was sold. Esat Telecom, including landlines and Digifone, was sold to British Telecom in 2000 for £1.8 billion (€2.25 billion). With hindsight, including what I subsequently learned as a business editor for RTÉ, the licence fee explanation seems pitifully inadequate now.

The story wasn't really on the radar for political correspondents – it was being handled mainly by media business staff – so it wasn't on my agenda. It should have been splashed regularly on the front pages, but it did frequently feature on the business pages. One night I returned to my office in Government Buildings from the usual evening briefing for the political correspondents in their rooms at Leinster House, to find a small group waiting in my office – an official from Lowry's Transport, Energy and Communications (TEC) Department and two others. The TEC official, whom I'd not met before or since, explained that the process of awarding the licence included an evaluation of the submissions outside Ireland, and that was managed by officials in TEC, and completely insulated from the minister. But, he said, they weren't getting that across in the media. I told him that the best way to explain it would be for those officials to hold a news conference themselves, to outline this procedure, and answer journalists' questions about it. The TEC official was content with that advice, so they left. I believe a news conference was held by officials, but it didn't end media scrutiny of the process. The licence award was formally made to Digifone in 1996, but the controversy continued, and it was investigated by the Moriarty Tribunal, established in 1997. It concluded 14 years later in 2011.

RTÉ News reported the findings in detail in March of 2011. It was 'beyond doubt' that Mr Lowry gave what the tribunal termed 'substantive information to Denis O'Brien, of significant value and assistance to him in securing the licence'. Mr Lowry, it said, bypassed consideration by his cabinet colleagues and thereby not only influenced, but delivered the result that Esat Digifone had won the evaluation process, and that ultimately led to the licensing award. The tribunal report described these matters as elements of Mr Lowry's 'insidious and pervasive influence' on the process. The 'most pervasive and abusive instance' of Mr Lowry's influence on the awarding of the licence was his action in withdrawing time from the Project Group, which had requested an extension to its work to reconsider the Esat Digifone nomination as the winner. The group had wanted an opportunity to revisit and review the evaluation. The report summarised payments to Michael Lowry:

> In aggregating the known payments from Mr Denis O'Brien to Mr Michael Lowry, it is apposite to note that, between the granting of the second GSM licence to Esat Digifone in May 1996 and the transmission of £420,000 sterling to complete the purchase of the latter of Mr Lowry's English properties in December 1999, Mr O'Brien had made or facilitated payments to Mr Lowry of £147,000 sterling, £300,000 sterling and a benefit equivalent to a payment in the form of Mr O'Brien's support for a loan of £420,000 sterling.

It added that in 2011, when the report was published, the value of the sums was 'obviously well in excess of the amounts transferred at the various times mentioned in this Report'. During the period of the competition for the second mobile (GSM) licence and subsequent licensing negotiations, Mr O'Brien or his companies supported 14 Fine Gael fundraising events, contributing a total of £22,140 in donations to the party's funds, the tribunal report found.

Both Denis O'Brien and Michael Lowry rejected the tribunal's findings. O'Brien said it was 'fundamentally flawed ... based on the opinions and theories' of Mr Justice Moriarty and his legal team. He insisted that he had never made any payment to Mr Lowry as a government minister, a public representative or a private citizen. Lowry said Justice Moriarty had 'outrageously abused the Tribunal's ability to form opinions which are not substantiated by evidence or fact'. The tribunal report also found that in relation to the state-sponsored company Telecom Éireann, 'Mr Lowry sought to procure unwarranted rent increases, that over a seven-year period would have improperly enriched businessman Ben Dunne. The matter was 'profoundly corrupt to a degree that was nothing short of breathtaking'. Mr Dunne strongly rejected the findings. We'll hear more about Lowry's interactions with Ben Dunne, which forced him to resign from the Rainbow government the following year.

In Government Buildings, there was continuing anxiety about the peace process and the lack of any sense of urgency for movement on the British side, despite the fact that nearly two months had passed since the cancelled summit. On 27 October 1995, John Bruton became the first taoiseach to visit Derry, including one of the main Protestant areas of the city. It was my second time in the city; my first visit had been to cover an election in the 1970s. At the count, I was approached by an older RUC man who, to my surprise, wanted to chat. I remember well a story he told me of attending a County Antrim meeting in the 1950s where a young Reverend Ian Paisley denounced the Irish government led by de Valera as 'that Spanish onion in the Irish stew'.

John Bruton fared a good deal better than John Major in this wonderful historic city. The visit, at the invitation of the SDLP leader John Hume, was a great success. Everywhere, people were welcoming, and local community leaders were happy to show off their city highlights. Derry of course produced two important leaders on the nationalist and republican side, now both dead, John Hume and Martin McGuinness, who made history as Sinn Féin's deputy first minister of the Northern Executive, serving with first minister Ian Paisley, founder of the DUP. The first stop of the visit was at the city's famous Guildhall, where the taoiseach was greeted by John Hume and Derry SDLP mayor John Kerr, and introduced to the four attending Derry church leaders, Catholic and Protestant. Also attending the event were local officials and councillors. Bruton used the occasion to play down media speculation about an early Anglo-Irish summit. He said that he couldn't predict when it would take place: 'There are difficulties to be sorted out.' There was agreement about the twin-track approach of an international group – one track to deal with the arms issue, and the other for political talks. One of the issues was 'the status of those who would deal with the international group – would they be able to speak with authority for the paramilitaries about arms?' I thought then that the taoiseach would soon need to use strong critical language in public about the British stonewalling the peace process.

With general awareness now of US President Bill Clinton's plan to visit Ireland at the end of November, Bruton said he agreed with Gerry Adams that 'the visit would add a dynamic to the peace process'. But he did not want the visit to put pressure on the summit timetable. As it happened, Clinton's visit did build that pressure – largely generated by the taoiseach himself. When the rest of the notables were speaking, John Hume, whom I knew well and had met frequently as a journalist, motioned for me to follow him, and we slipped out of the room. He brought me to a chamber nearby where we sat down to talk. We discussed the stubborn British demand for a start to decommissioning. In the past week, John Major, under pressure from his backbenchers in parliament, had assured them that there had been 'absolutely no change' in the British government position of seeking an IRA start to disposal of arms before round-table talks, to demonstrate their commitment to peace.

I assured Hume that Bruton was totally opposed to this precondition, and he hoped that Major would come around to the idea that the international group on weapons was the route out of the stalemate. I explained his visceral detestation of the IRA because his friend, Fine Gael TD and later Senator Billy Fox, a Protestant, had been murdered by the IRA; there was his conviction that 1916 was a mistake, and his regard for the Home Rule Irish parliamentary party leader John Redmond – he had a picture of him on his office wall. John Hume then completely surprised me by saying, 'I too think 1916 was a mistake, and at some stage I'll say that publicly.' I was so flabbergasted that words failed me. All I could say was 'Really?' but just then we heard a lot of movement in the room when the speeches had ended, and John said we had better go back to join the others.

I never got the chance to follow up this conversation with Hume, but thinking it over, he was so opposed to the gun in politics, and so intent on peaceful means of resolving differences, it was not surprising. For him, however, the timing of speaking his mind on 1916 in public would have been crucial. I understood the deep alienation of Northern nationalists who had been oppressed as 'second-class' citizens in what was effectively a one-party dictatorship in a heavily armed police state. There were pogroms against Catholics, with appalling discrimination in jobs, housing and government supports of many kinds. They were treated like unwanted outsiders in their own country. I had experienced it myself. Many people in the Republic who never visited the North, with no friends or connections there, did not understand Northern nationalist feelings and had no real empathy with their fellow Irish men and women in the Six Counties.

In the North during the late 1960s and early 1970s, the civil rights movement was making huge progress in internationalising the fifty-year proto-fascist nature of Northern Ireland, a 'Protestant state for a Protestant people'. However, the shameful, violent, loyalist sectarian attacks on Catholic areas and civil rights demonstrations, often assisted by the RUC and B Specials in 1968–9, provided an opportunity for the Provisional IRA to emerge as the defenders of the Catholic nationalist people. The failure of the Irish government to identify with nationalists and properly support them, in some manner, with weapons to protect themselves from armed attack has been identified in *The Arms Crisis of 1970*, a deeply researched book by former RTÉ producer Michael Heney, as a possible cause of assisting the IRA to occupy that space.

After the church leaders had left the Guildhall, I joined the taoiseach at a lunch with nationalist and unionist councillors. As expected, DUP councillors did not attend, but we were shortly to meet one DUP member. After lunch there was a walkabout up Shipquay Street, Bruton shaking hands with people out shopping, tourists and shop owners. It was all very casual and friendly. As part of the programme, the Church of Ireland Dean, Reverend Cecil Orr, took Bruton into St Columb's Cathedral and showed him around its historic features, after which Bruton signed the visitors' book. Then the Dean took us to a nearby part of the famous city walls which had withstood the siege by James II and his army. Now it struck me: We're not outside the walls, but inside ...

We continued the tour with Reverend Orr, who led the way to a new school in the nearby Protestant Fountain Estate. On the way, the DUP turned up in the guise of councillor Gregory Campbell, who had some notoriety in matters like this. He handed the taoiseach a letter of protest and said, 'Your country must respect the right of our country to exist.' Bruton took it in his stride, smiling benevolently as we swept on to the school, where he was greeted by the chairman of the Fountain Area Partnership, George Glenn; inside he spoke briefly to a happy and warm gathering of pupils and staff full of enthusiasm for this interruption in their daily routine by the 'prime minister' from Dublin.

Then we were whizzed off to the Bogside and Free Derry Corner, where we viewed the striking revolutionary murals, and the taoiseach went to chat with some of the afternoon customers of the Bogside Inn. The next stop was a meeting with community leaders in the Creggan and to see the extraordinary, attractive Ráth Mór, a community enterprise centre with a cathedral effect: a long, curved glass atrium supported by a façade of brick and stone, and internal walls all built by local professionals. 'An Creagán' is a 'stony place' in Irish, and there was an echo of that in the stone façade. A large ancient circular earthwork known as the rath lies on the western edge of Creggan. Finally we reached the end of the tour, meeting with Derry business people at the Chamber of Commerce. John Hume's last words capped the day. He said the visit was a historic event: 'Who would have dreamt of such a visit a year ago?'

That same day, there were other events in the peace process in both Dublin and the US. In Dublin, the Alliance Party leader John Alderdice announced that he was withdrawing temporarily from the Forum for Peace and Reconciliation, which sat in Dublin Castle. He criticised Sinn Féin and SDLP leaders for not taking the forum more seriously. It had been set up as part of the peace process with an open invitation to all parties to take part; the criticism was of course rejected by both parties. Around the same time, at the White House in Washington, Ian Paisley and Peter Robinson of the DUP met US Vice-President Al Gore and National Security Advisor Anthony Lake. Paisley and Robinson accused the Clinton administration of 'a gross imbalance in favour of the minority point of view'. A White House official later rejected this, emphasising the neutrality of the US in the peace process.

A couple of days later, on 31 October, Minister Michael Ancram and Martin McGuinness held a three-hour meeting, after which McGuinness said there were major difficulties preventing agreement on decommissioning and all-party talks, but that Sinn Féin was attempting 'to salvage the peace process'. The next day, in Washington, the newly elected leader of the Unionist Party, David Trimble, met President Clinton at the White House for talks. White House press secretary Mike McCurry later told journalists that the peace process was 'at a fairly critical stage'.

In the North, Gerry Adams warned that talks between Sinn Féin and the UK government have 'failed or are at the point of failure'. On 2 November, John Bruton met Adams for talks in Dublin about the state of the peace process. Adams warned even more starkly of the cliff edge that the process had reached. The taoiseach told Adams that John Major would have to compromise. Unfortunately, the taoiseach had earlier refused to have another joint meeting with John Hume and Gerry Adams at the forum, though he was open to meeting them separately. I thought that was an unnecessary mistake, damaging to him, upsetting both Hume and Adams, laying himself open to criticism – which duly arrived. Fianna Fáil leader Bertie Ahern accused him of 'abdicating' the leadership of Irish nationalism, and he was criticised by Adams. Because John Bruton was the leader of a sovereign state, my view was that he could encourage everyone to follow the path of peace and democracy, alone or together.

In Washington, after his White House meeting, David Trimble made a pitch that was bound to land on stony ground, calling on loyalist paramilitaries to 'take the courageous first step and the moral high ground by beginning the process of disarmament as quickly as possible'. The following day, writing in the *Belfast Telegraph*, Gary McMichael, an Ulster Democratic Party (UDP) councillor, replied to Trimble (the UDP was associated with the loyalist paramilitary organisation the Ulster Defence Association (UDA)): 'I do not believe that a physical hand over of guns is a solution or at this stage even possible. But I am convinced that there will be no movement until republicans address the fears which exist within my community.'

On 3 November, British minister Michael Ancram and Martin McGuinness met again to discuss the issues of all-party talks and arms decommissioning, but they failed to resolve the deadlock. The British government rejected the latest Hume–Adams formula that all-party talks should be convened and the arms issue resolved when the talks reached a settlement. McGuinness said afterwards that an appeal had to be made to the international community, in reality the White House, to convince the British government that the peace process must not be squandered. The same day, the Northern Ireland Office released a document already circulated to all political parties and to the US and Irish governments. Known as the 'Building Blocks', it was to facilitate a shared understanding of the steps for a 'twin-track approach to the way forward'. It proposed:

1. 'Preparatory' bilateral talks with the parties, and an independent International Body to consider the decommissioning issue, to be convened in parallel by the two governments.
2. A target date for all-party negotiations might be announced, but it would depend on success in creating the necessary conditions (the IRA arms 'gesture', of course).
3. The International Body would be asked to 'ascertain and advise on how unauthorised arms and other material which had been used to advance political ends could forever be removed from the political equation'.

The DUP deputy leader, Peter Robinson, later attacked the proposals, saying that the governments' jointly managed preparatory talks meant that 'from now on there is effectively joint authority, that is totally unacceptable'. Two days later, on 5 November, Gerry Adams said the British government had subverted the peace process to the point that it no longer existed. Bew and Gillespie recorded his response in their 1996 book: 'What we have now are two cessations of violence: one by the IRA, which is a complete military cessation which is now totally unanchored, and we have a conditional, qualified loyalist cessation.' Later he went even further: 'The British government has subverted the peace process to the point that it no longer exists.'

On 8 November, the SDLP put forward a proposed statement to be made by both governments, similar to that given to Michael Ancram by Martin McGuinness. It suggested starting the preparatory phase of the talks no later than 30 November and sought Senator George Mitchell to head an international body advising the governments on the arms question. This body would report on whether there was a clear commitment on the part of the respective parties to an agreed political settlement, through democratic negotiations, and to the 'satisfactory resolution of the question on arms'. These proposals were rejected by the UUP and the DUP. At a Sinn Féin rally in Belfast's Ulster Hall on the same day, Martin McGuinness said that any formula 'which republicans could live with would require a date as soon as possible for all-party talks, the dropping of the precondition for Sinn Féin participation, and a project on the arms issue which resolved the matter to everyone's satisfaction'. David Trimble that day said the government's twin-track proposals were 'not acceptable in their current form'. On the arms question, he said 'in any event, there is no question of any negotiations without decommissioning'.

So as we got deep into autumn, the need for some progress on the peace process became critical, with a lot of pressure from both Hume and Adams, but the word from our side of the regular Anglo-Irish Liaison Group meetings was very bleak. There was no sign of any movement from the British; and, worse, there didn't seem to be any sense of hurry. The colder weather and the effects of the intense pressure over the first ten months of the job finally caught up with me and I was hit by a severe flu that put me in bed. On 9 November the taoiseach confirmed in the Dáil that he had put forward ideas to the British government in a private letter to John Major. He wanted to move forward urgently towards all-party talks. The letter was another attempt to urge Major to allow the international group to deal with the arms issue, and get all-party talks going as quickly as possible. He knew that time was running out, and British obduracy could wreck the peace process. But Major would not move. Bruton's view was that: 'The Washington 3 condition would never have been raised if the IRA used the word *permanent* about the ceasefire, as required in the Downing Street Declaration. If they did not like that approach there was an obligation on republicans to come up with their own form of reassurance on the arms issue. But like unionists they preferred to let others do the work – and they say NO!' Nevertheless, he had to do that work and try to get the British off the hook.

On 11 November, Bruton headed for London to make an important address to the Meath Association, emigrants from his county. I was unable to accompany him because of the flu. However, I worked on part of his script at home, interacting with Paddy Teahon in the office, stressing the urgent need to agree that the International Body would deal with the decommissioning issue, and the semantics of an arms 'gesture' should be abandoned. I was concerned that the ceasefire was now 14 months old, much longer than any other. In 1921 the British government had ignored the demands from some political quarters that republicans disarm before the Treaty talks. Now we had to do something quickly.

At the opening of Bruton's speech to the Meath Association, after commending John Major's genuine engagement and real interest in a settlement of the North's problems, he got down to the key message: a British compromise was required. He dismissed the 'gesture' of arms: 'The issues that are now stopping us from starting the talks are small, and, in historical terms, little more than semantic.' The issue should be given to the International Body, clearing the way for the next step to all-party talks. Bruton's speech was wide-ranging. He noted that for five years he had reached out to unionists to understand their fears, concerns, and wishes, but also setting out why the Irish government 'must perform the role of clear and truthful articulation of long-held nationalist concerns'. He recalled the violent role of the RUC in Derry in 1968, then in Derry and Belfast in 1969; British Army paratroopers in Derry on Bloody Sunday 1972 killing 14 innocent people in a civil rights anti-internment march, all this and more without any adequate official response or expressions of regret. He said that one side was asked to show 'moral responsibility' through decommissioning, while 'officialdom is not willing to accept a moral responsibility for injustices for which its forces may have been responsible'. He then attacked Northern Ireland over cultural and symbolic grievances:

> The attitude towards the use of the Irish language, the flying of the Union flag in a provocative or excessive manner, the design of official publications, are all examples of ways in which the Northern Ireland official system fails to give adequate recognition to the existence and legitimacy of Irish nationalism as an inherent part of Northern life.

Bruton gave it all he could, even enlisting President Clinton that November by phone to try to get the 'gesture' dropped, to no avail. He spoke with Major and Clinton about it in Israel when they attended the funeral of the assassinated prime minister, Yitzhak Rabin. In the coming years Bruton was proved right about the 'semantics'.

Decommissioning would not even begin until three and a half years after the Belfast Agreement was reached in 1998, and it would be eleven years after their first ceasefire in 1994 before all IRA arms were put beyond use.

We expected the speech to upset the British, but we did not reckon on a carefully constructed speech being seriously misreported by RTÉ on its main TV news, radio and Aertel bulletins (text news on TV), chiming with the Sinn Féin slogan 'All-Party Talks Now!' These bald, inaccurate headlines were carried on the *Six One News*, which reported that 'the taoiseach has called on the British government to convene all-party talks on the North now'. This was repeated on radio's *News at Six Thirty* and on Aertel text on TV. I had offered to brief the RTÉ news desk on the speech three hours before the broadcast, but my offer was not taken up. I rang the news desk to point out the falsity of the claim, clear from any serious reading of the text. All other significant media accurately reported the speech. No RTÉ action was taken. In retrospect, I'm sorry that I persuaded the London correspondent of the *Irish Times*, Frank Millar, not to write a story he proposed on how the British initial overreaction to Bruton's speech was caused by misreporting on RTÉ. The Northern Ireland secretary, Sir Patrick Mayhew, had responded: 'This is an extraordinary speech at an extraordinary time – the eve of Remembrance Sunday and delivered in Britain through a megaphone.' This was wildly over the top and that was made clear to an embarrassed Mayhew. Our Maryfield secretariat reported that even the Northern Ireland Office thought it too much, and, talking to journalists, Mayhew clearly backed off his 'extraordinary' remarks, first refusing to answer, then retreating to 'some surprising things'.

John Major, attending a Commonwealth gathering in New Zealand, was doorstepped at Auckland airport. A Reuters report carried in the *Irish Times* quoted Major accusing the Irish government of causing delays by cancelling the September summit under pressure from Sinn Féin and threats of a return to violence. He said that 'Mr Bruton is under heavy domestic pressure to make progress', but he insisted that Britain was not at fault:

> The problem lies with Sinn Féin, and Sinn Féin's complete reluctance to tackle the question, even with an International Body, of how their arsenal of weapons and explosives are going to be taken out of commission. Unionist parties would simply not agree to talks until the IRA handed in its arms. The blockage is theirs and no weasel words to the contrary will change that hard reality … What is not a starter is for people to make it clear that they would resort to violence if they don't get their way in talks, and then expect to be admitted to talks. That isn't on.

John Major wrote in his autobiography that the taoiseach, under pressure from his coalition partners and John Hume to take a more aggressive line against British ideas, 'let off steam' in an uncharacteristic speech, attacking British governments past and present and playing to his nationalist audience. This provoked crisis headlines in the press, he wrote.

> If the 'twin-track' was going to work, I knew that the Irish government would have to take the Provisionals [IRA] on, and ignore their objections. I understood John Bruton's speech; he needed to buttress his support and show sympathy to hallowed nationalist dogma. I regretted only that I was marooned in New Zealand and unable to help him out.

If Major really wanted to help out, he could have dropped the arms disposal precondition to talks.

Major's reference to 'hallowed nationalist dogma' and letting off steam was indeed uncharacteristic language, patronising and clichéd about Irish sentiment, unworthy of a truly decent man like him. The film of the RUC bludgeoning of unarmed Derry civil rights protesters in 1968 is there for the world to see, as well as the burning of Catholic houses in Belfast during the sectarian attacks of 1969. Then there was a vicious and bloody attack by loyalists, aided by off-duty RUC B Specials, on a peaceful civil rights march from Belfast to Derry at Burntollet Bridge in 1969, and the 11 civilians shot dead by British paratroopers in Ballymurphy, Belfast, in 1971 and then 14 ultimately at the Derry Bloody Sunday march in 1972 that aroused nationalist anger throughout the island of Ireland, provoking the burning of the British embassy in Dublin. It took many decades before the innocence of the Bloody Sunday victims was finally admitted in Britain with an apology by Prime Minister David Cameron in 2010. In a formal state apology he told the House of Commons, 'What happened on Bloody Sunday was both unjustified and unjustifiable. It was wrong.' Later we will learn of the turbulence caused in Major's Downing Street on the 25th anniversary of Bloody Sunday in 1997, and Bruton's work on seeking a new Inquiry.

It was also inaccurate to say that the speech was made under pressure from the coalition partners or others; it came entirely from the taoiseach's own utter frustration, and that of his team, with the British government's hardline inflexibility on Washington 3, something that would make no difference to the armed capabilities of the IRA. Bruton and his team knew where this blockage could end – innocent lives were at stake. The *Irish Times* recognised the seminal importance of Bruton's London speech by printing it in full and covering all the responses. Commenting on the speech and the reaction, Sinn Féin's vice-president, Pat Doherty, accused the British government of doing a 'deal' with the unionists because its majority in the House of Commons was disappearing. It was 'more concerned about its own survival at Westminster than with the peace process'. John Hume expressed a similar view in the House of Commons, and in his autobiography Major expresses dismay that Hume would embrace such a notion. Politicians understand political reality, so nobody could understand Major's fierce adherence to this roadblock, which had no security value, without looking at his fragile situation in the House of Commons. Gerry Adams rejected John Major's assertion that Sinn Féin was responsible for the impasse in the peace process. He said that every issue raised by the British government, including decommissioning, had been addressed.

I went to the VIP reception area at Dublin airport to meet the taoiseach when he returned from London. Paddy Teahon was also there. When Bruton came into the room, I was preparing for the worst. He looked at me and said, 'So you're the one who got me into this controversy.' But his eyes and his broad smile told the story. He was not displeased that we had caused waves, and in fact the speech worked, spurring renewed intense negotiation for the next Irish–British agreement. It took place on the phone between the two leaders, about sixteen long calls in total, as Bruton and Major ironed out issues in the twin-track strategy to finally set up the International Body on arms, combined with political talks.

9

VICTORY IN THE DIVORCE REFERENDUM

IN THE MIDDLE OF ALL of this intense work on the peace process, we also had the divorce referendum on Friday 24 November to remove the constitutional ban on divorce. This was a second run at this issue. The first referendum, held in 1986 by the Fine Gael–Labour coalition led by Dr Garret FitzGerald, failed by a 25 per cent margin.

The Minister for Justice, Labour's Mervyn Taylor, handled the issue with a special team. He toured the country early in the campaign talking to local media and radio. But the government campaign was hampered by the decision of Mr Justice McKenna in the High Court that public money could not be spent in pursuit of government policy in a referendum, after legal action was taken by the No campaign and others. This meant that materials commissioned from an advertising agency (Quinn Mc Donnell Pattison) had to be scrapped, and even their placing of advertisements for the government was stopped. There were some grumblings in the media about the choice of agency, since the brother of Minister for Finance Ruairí Quinn was involved, but the agency had been chosen in a political hands-off manner. All to no avail. The early polls showed a commanding lead in favour of divorce, which led to some complacency; but towards the last week nervousness took hold as those numbers tumbled. The Labour-led campaign, derailed by the court ruling on state money, was losing support fast.

Meanwhile, the No campaign ruthlessly exploited people's emotions, featuring children and young couples on their poster campaign hoardings with the slogans: 'Hello Divorce – Bye Bye Daddy' and 'If this was your daughter ... would you destroy their marriage?' On media outings by the No campaign, predictions were made of a flood of Irishmen deserting their wives. (The divorce statistics later showed that did not happen.)

RTÉ's outstanding and fair-minded journalist Gerald Barry sought an interview with the taoiseach for the flagship radio *This Week* programme on the Sunday before the referendum. I felt that John's appearance arguing the case for permitting divorce would be quite compelling for Catholic voters, since it was well known that he and his wife Finola were committed Catholics. He readily agreed to do the programme, thinking it was proper for Ireland to show tolerance towards those of any religion whose marriages had failed and broken up. The issue could also have an impact on sentiment in Northern Ireland if the state voted a second time against divorce, with the Catholic bishops and clergy waging a strong campaign of opposition. His performance on the *This Week* interview was widely praised. Fergus Finlay, in his memoir published in 1998, after the government left office, referred to it as 'a brilliant interview ... and undoubtably swung some undecided voters our way'. Fergus wasn't aware that I had also organised a campaign of similar lengthy interviews on the major local radio stations throughout the country over the next two days, getting the taoiseach to stay in his office and follow a schedule of interviews at prime time for these stations on Monday 20 and Tuesday 21 November (working around his phone call with John Major on that Tuesday). This was a sure way of talking directly to conservative Catholic Ireland outside Dublin, to rural Ireland, farms, villages and small towns, as well as the cities beyond Dublin. In the course of his interviews, these were some of the important points he made:

> The essence of the Catholic faith is particularly that it shows forgiveness. It would be very wrong not to allow our law to express forgiveness to those whose consciences allow them to remarry. The case I'm making in regard to Northern Ireland is that we

must have a way of governing that includes both communities, that includes the minority community. If we don't show tolerance for minorities here, we'll find it harder to argue for tolerance elsewhere.

Is it the Ireland we like to present to the world as a place that has very strong beliefs but doesn't need to enforce them by law, that welcomes people with a different point of view and treats them well? Or an Ireland that's so afraid, it has to use the criminal and civil law to enforce a particular set of beliefs?

He took on the bishops, who maintained that 'any undermining of the meaning of the marriage promise would profoundly damage the stability of society', responding that broken marriage was 'a growing reality in Ireland ... which the Catholic Church, despite its extensive influence on the opinions of many, has not so far been able to reverse'. The Catholic Church's position was 'unproductive' he said. The number of broken marriages in Ireland at the time was estimated to be about 80,000.

Getting the taoiseach to stay in his office and do those prearranged interviews one after the other over these two days was a challenge, particularly with his work on the summit, but it proved critical. I have no doubt that this local radio campaign, along with his *This Week* interview, were decisive factors in the divorce referendum, stalling the fall in support, and convincing enough wavering Catholic voters, as well as some of the undecided, throughout the length and breadth of the country to vote in favour of permitting divorce. The result was paper thin: 50.28 per cent Yes, and 49.72 per cent No. My colleague from Democratic Left, Tony Heffernan, agreed that Bruton's series of interviews carried the referendum over the line. I was with the taoiseach at the RTÉ TV referendum studio as the countdown to a result was approaching. He joined John Bowman, who was presenting the programme, just a short time before the count ended, and while the Yes vote was just a little ahead, the gap was dwindling dangerously.

These were moments of high drama. I was quite nervous; and it was a close-run thing, ending with a tiny majority of just 9,000 votes.

The taoiseach was visibly relieved and happy as he told John Bowman he was pleased with the result: it was 'a very important decision for the country'. And so it was. It was the beginning of a turn in the tide for Irish society on the way towards a modern liberal republic. This result was a critical benchmark of a different kind of Ireland, the first great crack in the moral and political power of the Catholic Church, which was defied by a majority, slender though it was, of the people. It was a signal victory for John Bruton.

After the intense radio intervention, and a few days before the referendum, I met Bride Rosney, President Mary Robinson's highly talented adviser and media chief, at an event in Dublin Castle. Bride and I had a lengthy discussion about the vote and its outcome. She was sure the referendum would be defeated, because of the collapsing polls. I was adamant that it was going to pass. Neither of us could convince the other of the validity of our positions, so we agreed to bet a bottle of the expensive but wonderful malt whiskey Tullamore Dew on the outcome. Shortly after the victory, Bride's package with the whiskey arrived at my office in Government Buildings, with a note that I still have: 'I've never had such delight in paying a lost bet!' I was shocked and sorry to learn belatedly that Bride died suddenly in September 2023 – the loss of a great woman.

10

PEACE DEAL AS CLINTON ARRIVES

DIVORCE FINALLY ACHIEVED, WE WERE then back quickly to the peace process. There were sharp exchanges between Sir Patrick Mayhew and John Bruton after a phone call with John Major on 22 November. The taoiseach was still insisting in the negotiations with Major that the British side needed to drop the arms precondition. But Mayhew, while visiting Derry, defended it, saying that Sinn Féin and loyalist parties were 'welcome to participate' in political life; 'What they cannot expect to do is keep a foot in both camps, to sign up as it were to democracy à la carte.' On RTÉ, Bruton said it would be a 'waste of time' to begin the twin-track approach on this basis: 'A twin-track approach is useless unless it removes all preconditions.' He went on: 'You can't lay down the sort of immutable position that I felt that Sir Patrick was laying down today and expect that there is going to be a compromise. There must be mutability, not immutability, in this area.'

While this torturous political struggle with the British government to get them to drop the arms precondition for all-party talks was going on, at the very same time, in November 1995, Ronnie Flanagan, then an acting deputy chief constable of the RUC, soon to be chief constable, told David Donoghue, Irish head of the Maryfield Anglo-Irish Secretariat, that the British government had 'foolishly impaled itself on a hook' with its Washington conditions. He said, 'There was never any hope of the paramilitaries agreeing to hand over even a small quantity of arms in advance of political negotiations.' He told Donoghue that 'the ability to develop and manufacture new types of explosives and weaponry is of much greater concern than the material currently hidden in IRA caches'. The demand for the gesture of decommissioning was, he said, 'geared more to symbolism and unionist sensitivities than to the practical needs of the situation'. He was also critical of the British government's grindingly slow response to the IRA ceasefire, which was 'too little and usually too late'. There was, he concluded, a risk of destabilising the situation. Prophetic indeed.

Meanwhile, also talking to Donoghue, the general officer commanding the British Army in Northern Ireland, Sir Roger Wheeler, said: 'The security forces neither expect, nor are they particularly pressing for, the handover of any weapons in advance of political talks … the ability of the paramilitaries to manufacture their own weapons and explosives is at least as important as the actual weaponry in their possession.' The demand for decommissioning, he said, 'makes sense only at the level of symbolism'. These views are damning evidence that this ultimately deadly arms 'gesture' pantomime was all for the unionist parties' benefit, with the added benefit, from Major's point of view, that his government might see out its term of office.

Over the six days between 21 and 28 November there were nine extensive Bruton phone negotiations and discussions, eight with Major and one between Bill Clinton and Bruton. Major and Bruton negotiated a communiqué to finally launch the twin-track policy and find a way around their differences on the arms disposal precondition for all-party talks. Bruton wanted it in the remit of the International Body, but even the softest Irish proposal about submissions made to the Body was condemned by Major as 'dynamite over here' and 'inflammatory in the extreme'. On the very last day there were two important calls, morning and evening, and between them a negotiation between Sir Robin Butler, British cabinet secretary, and Paddy Teahon to fix fine wording differences in the communiqué. Bruton wanted language to allow political parties to 'get things off their chests in a way that's not unduly constrained' in submissions to an International Body, and governments to 'consider constructively practical suggestions'. Major agreed. 'I have no objection to their making representations.'

President Clinton was soon to be airborne on his way to London, and then to the North and the Republic, so on Tuesday 28 November, the last call brought a breakthrough, with Major able to agree the 'deal' on the text. Bruton had been pressing to have the summit that evening in Downing Street while the British suggested issuing a Joint Statement, and a summit after Clinton's visit. Bruton feared a joint statement could be picked apart to unravel the agreement. Major expressed his concern that a late-night meeting would bring accusations of 'cobbling together' a deal before Clinton arrived, when it was in fact the result of extensive negotiation, and he was worried about a 'threesome' meeting with Clinton in London the next day, which he believed would make unionists very angry, there would be 'dangers', it would 'absolutely kill the position with the unionists'. Bruton assured him that he would not stay in London overnight, and he already had a plan to be in Downing Street by 10.30 p.m. Major said, 'You're keen to come? Okay, far be it from me to spoil a good party.' It was to be a unique summit, the two leaders agreed to publicly disagree about the arms precondition, but they agreed on the essential establishment of the International Body on Decommissioning to make an 'independent' report on the issue, with former US Senate leader George Mitchell in the chair, and General John de Chastelain, the Canadian military chief, as a member of the team. It was a dark, cold winter's night as we set out for this historic rendezvous in London.

I went with the taoiseach in his car to the Irish Air Corps' Baldonnel airfield to the west of Dublin, where the government's G4 jet was already waiting. Other members of the team followed, and in minutes the plane took off for London. I remember looking at the cities and towns all lit up as we crossed into Wales and then England and wondering if this piece of the jigsaw would fit. Would it bring everyone on board? On this flight, as on others in less pressured circumstances, I thought of the people in those lit-up properties below and wondered about their lives and worries. Would what we were engaged in that night make a real difference to their lives?

After an hour we descended rapidly to Northolt RAF airfield and landed gently – the Air Corp pilots were the best at their job. There was a fleet of cars at Northolt ready to whisk us to 10 Downing Street, escorted by police outriders on their motorbikes with sirens they weren't afraid to use. We were greeted by John Major, his advisers and staff at Number 10. Tánaiste Dick Spring arrived separately from Spain, having cut short a visit to Barcelona. Spring and Bruton, with their officials, went to a room they were given to prepare for the news conference, which was to take place in the upstairs state dining room, where journalists were already gathered. There had been differences between their officials in the run-up to the summit. Paddy Teahon had gone to London earlier in the month to meet his opposite number and iron out some issues in the text; subsequently a team from the Department of Foreign Affairs went to London to review the text again, 'unpicking all that had been agreed', according to Major in his autobiography. The same problem from September loomed over any communiqué: although Sinn Féin had come to accept the International Body, there was no explicit dumping of the arms instalment – which they wanted. In fact, it would be the exact reverse, with the British publicly trying to exclude the new body from even considering the arms disposal demand.

Bruton was determined, despite this disagreement, to do a deal on the establishment of the International Body because he believed it would address the IRA arms disposal precondition to round-table talks and allow, perhaps force, the British off that hook. He also had great confidence in Senator George Mitchell, appointed as chairman of the International Body, to be even-handed in his work on the issues, as well as bringing the US president more closely into the peace process. All this was proved correct over the years ahead. Senator Mitchell ended up chairing the all-party talks until the Belfast Agreement was reached in 1998, and General de Chastelain, the Canadian military chief, presided over the decommissioning issue until it finally began for the IRA five years after the start of the talks. Further delays in establishing the International Body could have led to a change in the US presidency – an election was coming up in November 1996 – or different personnel, since these eminent people could be in different jobs.

Bruton deserves more credit for taking the risks involved. Like him, I expected the International Body would deal with the decommissioning precondition, and supported him in every way I could in the difficult and stressful negotiations leading to the agreed communiqué formula, recognised by Bruton in a personal letter of thanks afterwards. The International Body remit was about the totality of the weapons issue, no matter what John Major said, or tried to exclude. Bruton hoped that a deal done on the eve of President Clinton's visit would get a favourable political and public wind behind it, and that proved to be the case, but not with Sinn Féin or Fianna Fáil. Neither wanted Bruton to be popular. Sinn Féin could not be briefed beforehand on the deal because of the late-night summit, but they did co-operate and made a good submission to the International Body.

Dick Spring was concerned, as we all were, about the impact on the ceasefire of the continued British insistence on the Washington 3 precondition for all-party talks. This was unresolved when Bruton and Spring sat down in the Downing Street room set aside for them to discuss the final communiqué and the handling of the news conference. I was busy in the state dining room providing background on the late-night summit for journalists gathering there, and preparing them for the unusual presentation on the way. The Spring–Bruton meeting was a worried, angst-driven session on the text and the outcome. Spring hadn't been present in Dublin when the final deal was done on the phone. No one was happy about Major's point-blank refusal to drop a useless and dangerous precondition, and Spring was determined to confront Major about it. President Clinton and Hillary were already on Air Force One and would arrive in London in hours, but Spring was going to make his displeasure with Major clear in the cabinet room. In his autobiography, Major claims 'this was less of a negotiation between London and Dublin than between the coalition partners in the Irish government. John Bruton was determined to get the initiative launched before the imminent visit by President Clinton. His deputy Dick Spring, the Labour leader, was not keen to make the necessary compromises.'

Major wrote that this showed the downside of 'coalition' governments, which was somewhat ironic, given that the public divisions in his own party were far worse than any differences in the coalition; he had to deal with his Tory right-wing 'bastards', as he had called them. Spring, Major said in his 2000 autobiography, 'had unmade the previous Irish government ... and that evening he looked ready to do the same to its successor'. There was no sense that this was going to fracture the government, so Major's claim was wide of the mark. His remarks, I believe, reflected his irritation with Dick Spring's criticism, in his own house, in front of his ministers and officials, and possibly his understanding that both Spring and Bruton were right, but he couldn't agree.

Spring sat directly opposite him at the cabinet table to confront him about his position. This is how Major described it: 'An unhappy Spring began to interrogate me over the text,' he writes; 'he didn't like our position on decommissioning (although it had once been his) and warned that differences between London and Dublin could lead to disaster.' Douglas Hurd, the foreign secretary, and Sir Patrick Mayhew were at the table witnessing this attack. Major continued: 'British and Irish officials hovered around the fringes, like spectators watching a street brawl.' Spring was simply expressing what we all felt. Major makes clear in his autobiography that he knew the peace process was stretched to breaking point, and his own intelligence was saying the IRA was preparing the troops for a return to war. He must have been aware of the consequences of the IRA ending the ceasefire with a likely 'spectacular'; lives could be lost, and others maimed. I'm sure the precondition roadblock to talks would have been long abandoned, or perhaps never have arisen, if Major had had a secure majority in the House of Commons.

During the many phone conversations between Major and Bruton over those weeks this issue came up repeatedly. On the call to President Clinton in Washington the previous Thursday, 23 November, Bruton had sought the president's assistance in getting Major to drop the decommissioning precondition, but even the Americans could not move Major. In the end,

Bruton got Major to agree to a press conference with open disagreement on the issue, but to implement the twin-track policy and proceed with the establishment of the Mitchell Body. These decisions were key to the peace process over subsequent years. After the scenes in the cabinet room, it was nearing midnight, so the taoiseach and the prime minister headed for the state dining room to make the formal announcement.

Major opened the presentation. The communiqué, he said, was 'an agreement that, in our judgement, is going to generate further momentum in the peace process and help us address some of the difficult issues that lie ahead ... to take us closer to negotiations on a lasting settlement involving all the political parties.' He also said that the British government view of Washington 3 hadn't changed; it was needed to create confidence for other parties who would not join all-party talks unless decommissioning had started. He added that the International Body would be advisory.

Bruton countered, stressing that paragraph 5 of the communiqué made it clear that the International Body would be 'making an *independent* assessment of the decommissioning issue'. It would be consulting widely and receiving submissions from all 'relevant parties'. He went on: 'Just as the British government has not changed their view of Washington 3, the Irish government hasn't changed its view either.' The physical handover or disposal of weapons was, he said, 'not attainable'. The International Body was part of 'a process aimed at solving a problem, overcoming and transcending an impasse'. He made it crystal clear that the International Body did not have all the terms of reference that he wanted, but he thought its work, chaired by Mitchell, would be an important part of the peace process. It would assist in getting all the parties – unionist, nationalist and republican – to realise that they needed to begin talking seriously to one another.

Journalists were not used to news conferences announcing an agreement in which the proponents disagreed about its terms. A new institution on arms decommissioning had been agreed, but Major and Bruton disagreed on the interpretation of its mandate. Major excluded its consideration of Washington 3, while Bruton looked to the International Body for an independent assessment of decommissioning 'overcoming and transcending an impasse'. I had explained this to journalists before the news conference. They needed the earlier briefing to absorb and appreciate the subtlety of what was going on here, and most were good at it. When the two leaders finished with questions, it was already late and journalists had to rush off to meet deadlines.

The communiqué required the Mitchell Body to report in mid-January, which was a tall order given that the Christmas and New Year holidays intervened, but they achieved it. In the run-up to the summit there had been some stiff resistance to Senator George Mitchell as chairman; the unionists were against him. But, fortuitously, he had been President Clinton's special adviser for economic initiatives in Northern Ireland for some time, and, in this role, Major felt he had begun to win over the unionists who generally feared Irish-American influence in the US Democratic Party.

The communiqué promised: 'Both governments reaffirmed their commitment to securing the early launch of all-party negotiations. By way of the twin tracks, the two governments have the firm aim of achieving this by the end of February 1996 ... that objective should prove achievable.' They also agreed they would 'consider carefully' any recommendations the International Body made: 'to this end and to review progress in preparatory talks for all-party negotiations, the two governments plan to meet again by mid-February 1996.' These texts make clear the falsehood of claims that this summit on arrangements for all-party talks happened only because the IRA broke the ceasefire. The Docklands bombing ensured that there would be a delay for an election in advance of the talks.

Major's attempt to exclude Washington 3 from the remit of the International Body was taken to the extreme with a separate British government handout for journalists at the news conference, alongside the communiqué. This handout, headed 'Remit of International Body to Washington 3 Test', said:

> AS FROM HMG We will not be asking the Body to question our position on the third Washington criterion. The International

> Body was not established to make recommendations on when decommissioning should start. That is properly a matter for discussion in the preparatory talks and for Governmental decision.

This heavy-handed document backfired since it was not part of the communiqué, and was overruled by Article 5, which empowered the International Body 'to provide an independent assessment of the decommissioning issue'. In its findings announced just seven weeks later, the International Body said that there would be no decommissioning of weapons prior to all-party talks. That reality was based on the evidence they had gathered from the submissions and their own investigations. Gerry Adams and Sinn Féin prudently kept under the radar because of Clinton's arrival in London the next day, 29 November. However, Gerry Adams did phone into an RTÉ *Primetime* programme to say he had not been briefed about the details of the communiqué. John Bruton wanted all parties, including Sinn Féin and the unionists, to be involved in the talks from the start; hence he wanted the 'intense preparatory talks' proposed in the communiqué to clear the way. Major was not going to agree to calling all-party talks, no matter what Sinn Féin, Fianna Fáil or the Irish government wanted, without at least a UUP buy-in.

What we did not know then was that the IRA was already making preparations for an end of the ceasefire. In his memoir, John Major revealed that he took President Clinton into the cabinet room at Downing Street alone, 'for fear of leaks', to share with him – and only with him – his secret intelligence that the IRA was making active preparations for a return to violent operations. *The Times* had reported in late November that the IRA had warned its members to prepare for a 'return to war' if efforts to break the current impasse in political talks failed. Gerry Adams made many comments about the peace process 'no longer existing', and that what existed was an 'unanchored ceasefire'. Eamonn Mallie and David McKittrick claimed in their book *The Fight for Peace* that the lorry used in the Docklands bombing 'was being prepared as early as late November'. If this is correct, then during the drama of the late-night summit in Downing Street and the extraordinary, joy-filled scenes of the first US presidential visit to Belfast and Derry, 'an IRA team was working on the vehicle' that caused many millions of pounds in damage and took the lives of two innocent civilians in the Docklands, seriously maiming others. Major also told Clinton that since the 1994 ceasefire the IRA had carried out 148 'punishment' attacks and the loyalists 75.

In London, Clinton got strongly behind the communiqué and the leaders, saying, 'Ireland is closer to true peace than at any time in a generation and the risks taken by the prime minister and the Irish prime minister are the reasons why.' Addressing the Provisionals, he said, 'My message to the IRA is that the twin-track process has provided a mechanism for all the parties honourably now to bring their concerns to the table and be heard. In the end, peace means peace and we are all going to have to support that.' It had emerged, mildly embarrassingly for Major, that he wanted to be part of Clinton's visit to Northern Ireland to host or attend some event, but civil servants were strongly opposed. In released British State Papers, this is how Robert Crawford of the Northern Ireland Office put it: 'Sinn Féin will almost certainly be invited to the reception. We cannot see a way of the prime minister avoiding Gerry Adams without reverting to the undignified hiding-behind-potted-plants scenario, which creates almost as valuable a news story as the first handshake.'

Mayhew and other government figures were also concerned. The prime minister's private secretary for foreign affairs, Edward Oakden, consulted Major on concerns about an event:

> This would inevitably include Adams, and the prime minister does not think that Clinton's visit is the right occasion or context for him to meet Adams for the first time ... On Northern Ireland, there will be a tendency for Clinton to seek the limelight as an Irish peacemaker.

After a briefing from the Americans, Oakden concluded: 'What he wants is a demonstration that the peace process which he (according to the Clinton gospel) helped to launch is still in being.' A bit catty, to say the least. They finally came up with a late-night dinner for Clinton and Major, but Clinton's packed schedule made that unrealistic. The idea of Major appearing in the North was dropped.

Media coverage of the summit and the communiqué was favourable in the UK and Ireland. Reporters recounted the drama of the late-night pre-Clinton meeting and the news conference in Downing Street just hours before the US President arrived. Reports included the differences between Major and Bruton on the decommissioning precondition. The main news points highlighted were the establishment of the International Body and Senator George Mitchell's role, together with the 'firm aim' of all-party talks at the end of February, and the 'intense' preparatory talks before the round table. The other two members of the International Body were the Canadian chief of defence staff, who had grown up in England, General John de Chastelain; and Harri Holkeri, former prime minister of Finland. The *Irish Times* 'Drapier' political column was glowing about Bruton's 'breakthrough' in the peace process.

> He was totally in control and determined that the British were not going to put any spin or twist on what had been agreed ... in fact, it was Bruton who dominated the press conference and sent out a clear signal that he and Dick Spring were the driving forces.

Geraldine Kennedy, the paper's political correspondent, had this to say about Bruton:

> He also must be commended for salvaging the peace process with the joint communiqué with John Major launching the twin-track political and decommissioning initiative ... it is now clear the British demand for a symbolic handover of IRA arms as a precondition to all-party talks, the so-called Washington 3 test, can be considered by former Senator George Mitchell's decommissioning body.

My old colleague from RTÉ Eoghan Harris, in his *Sunday Independent* column, wrote that Bruton had now 'got Sinn Féin where he wanted them'. I appreciated Eoghan's political nous and super-fast intellect, but the triumphalism jarred. He detested Sinn Féin and the IRA, and that was reciprocated. As he was an occasional adviser to Bruton, I was concerned that Eoghan's comment played to strong emotional rather than rational responses, at a time when the ceasefire was on a cliff edge. Political analysis by the London correspondent of the *Irish Times*, Frank Millar, and the paper's political editor, Denis Coughlan, was very positive.

Professor Paul Bew and Gordon Gillespie, of Queen's University Belfast, concluded in their book that while the late-night summit at Downing Street looked at first like a panic reaction to President Clinton's arrival, it appeared that the two premiers had fudged the issue 'and yet pulled off a coup', getting the support of the most powerful man in the world, President Clinton. They likened the peace process negotiations going back to 1993 to a 'game of poker', at which Major 'excelled'. They give the balance of advantage in the Downing Street Declaration of December 1993 to Major. But then in the Framework Documents of February 1995, 'the British side palpably lost'. Major concedes as much in his autobiography.

Meanwhile President Clinton's visit to Northern Ireland, the first ever by a US President, was an unparalleled triumph. He was rapturously greeted by huge joyous crowds wherever he went in Belfast and Derry, in both nationalist and unionist areas. During a major speech given at Mackie's factory in west Belfast, he once again gave strong backing to Bruton and Major, but this time his speech also included a roll call of all the other actors. Albert Reynolds, Foreign Minister Spring, Sir Patrick Mayhew, Unionist leader David Trimble and the SDLP's John Hume had all, he said, 'laboured to realise the promise of peace'. And, he added, Gerry Adams, along with loyalist leaders such as David Ervine and Gary McMichael, 'helped to silence the guns'. Clinton's message to the people of Northern Ireland was powerful: 'You must stand firm against terror. You must say to those who would still use violence for political objectives – you are the past; your day is over.'

On 1 December President and Hillary Clinton left the famous Europa Hotel to fly to Dublin on Air Force One. Greeted at the airport by the taoiseach and President Mary Robinson, Clinton later paid his respects to the president at Áras an Uachtaráin, and went on to address the Dáil. Afterwards, he came to Government Buildings for a meeting in the taoiseach's office. After their talks, the cameras came in for shots with RTÉ, who were covering most of the visit live. The taoiseach and president spoke briefly, seated in the sofas by the fireplace. President Clinton was asked if he was encouraged by the summit outcome.

> Yes I was encouraged. I think Mr Bruton and Mr Major came up with a brilliant formulation that enables them to continue to have dialogue with each other without giving up their positions. It seems to me that is the genius, and then asking Senator Mitchell along with two very distinguished people on this arms decommissioning work, so that it can proceed in parallel, I think it was a great formulation, obviously none of the people with whom I spoke yesterday changed their positions, in their brief meetings with me, the point I tried to make to them is that the two prime ministers had given them an honourable way to continue to engage in peace talks without giving up any of their previous positions. And if they look in the streets of Belfast and Derry they could see that the young people of their country, without regard to whether they were Protestant or Catholic, they desperately want this to be resolved, they want to live together, they want to live on equal and honourable terms and they want to live in peace. Those were the only points I could make and I made them as forcefully as I could.

It was an extraordinarily strong statement of support; he got the strategy and liked it very much. Bruton was beaming.

The two went downstairs to the courtyard of Government Buildings for a short official press conference on a wonderfully sunny but cold winter's day. The taoiseach thanked the president for all he was doing to bring peace to the country. The president again praised the summit formula, adding that he was 'gratified that my good friend George Mitchell is going to lead the International Body, which is going to deal with that issue [decommissioning], he is seizing this opportunity, already he has begun to organise the effort with other members.' To finish, he pointed to the sky and said, 'The sun is shining, I hope it's a good omen for peace in Northern Ireland!'

Meanwhile Finola Bruton accompanied Hillary Clinton to an event organised by the Women's National Council, introducing her address to the gathering. Afterwards lunch was provided for the president and his wife in the old Irish Parliament Building on Dame Street, now a Bank of Ireland branch, while a huge crowd, eventually numbering 80,000, gathered around College Green to hear Clinton's keynote speech on this bright, sunny day. There was a carnival atmosphere, with the traditional group The Cassidys playing favourite tunes on the specially constructed stage – Clinton's Irish link, through his mother, is the Cassidy clan. The stage backdrop was a giant picture of the Star-Spangled Banner, curved as if floating in the wind, accompanied along the majestic classical pillars of the bank portico by a similar display of the Republic's tricolour of green, white and orange.

Hosted first on the stage before the bank's portico was the Dublin mayoral party, including Lord Mayor Seán Dublin Bay Rockall Loftus and City Manager Frank Feeley. With great pomp and ceremony, the city's sword and mace were carried onto the stage by two gardaí to formally present the president with the Freedom of the City. Pat Kenny was master of ceremonies for live RTÉ TV coverage of this major event. The massed audience was in terrific form, thrilled and happy on this sunny December day, out to enjoy the spectacle. Just before the taoiseach, Finola, President Clinton and First Lady Hillary were due to take the stand from the right-hand side of the portico, I was in the open doorway of an almost empty corridor on the left-hand side, taking in this extraordinary heightened, emotional scene, when out of nowhere President Clinton strode up and greeted me, saying, 'What a great day, the people seem to be enjoying it all.' Though we'd met quite a few times by then, I was amazed that he'd stop to say a few words, taking it all in such a casual, friendly, easy-going way. 'Say,' he said, 'can you tell me the Irish for long life and health?' I had a momentary panic as my mind went blank – I am far from a Gaeilge scholar – but if the President of the United States wanted a few words in Irish I had to do it. My brain focused tightly on the words and what came out was '*fada ... saol ... agus ... sláinte!*' Before I could grammatically reorganise, he thanked me, whirled off, and was gone through the door. My panic turned to shock and worry. I ran through the door after him, but he'd vanished into the throng of officials and security personnel. I thought anxiously, 'There'll be angry letters to the papers asking *who* advised the president about the phrase, and taking the government to task.' Then, I comforted myself, how could he even remember it?

Clinton got a rapturous reception from the audience in College Green when he took the stage, looking out over a sea of waving hand-held stars and stripes and tricolours. He had to wait some time for the rapturous cheering to die down before he could speak. He told the people he had been in College Green before; 'in 1968, when I was almost as young as the young people over there!' he said, pointing towards Trinity. (I was there as a student that year, and I wondered if our paths had crossed unawares.) Wild cheering again greeted his words. 'I never dreamed I would be back here in College Green in this capacity, but I am delighted to be here, and I thank you.' It was clear he was enjoying himself and revelling in the adoration of his audience. 'To look at this sea of Irish faces, on this beautiful Irish day, I feel like a real Dub today! Is that what I'm supposed to say?' That brought the house down with a massive wave of cheering, whistling, shouting and flag-waving all the way from College Green down Dame Street. 'Not only that, I know we have a handy football team!' – a well-chosen nod to the Dubs taking home the Sam Maguire trophy.

He apologised that he had to cut short his trip to Ireland because of the Bosnian peace talks, but responding to raised posters of Ballybunion in the crowd he vowed: 'I will return to Ballybunion to have my golf game!' He would keep that promise, but it would be in May 2001, when his second term as president was over, and his golf partner Dick Spring was no longer tánaiste. Clinton then singled out for honourable mention the US ambassador to Ireland, Jean Kennedy Smith, who was seated with Senator George Mitchell. He reminded the audience that 32 years before, she was with her elder brother President John Fitzgerald Kennedy when he made the historic first visit to Ireland by a US President in the early summer of 1963, five months before his brutal assassination in Dallas.

President Clinton's visit was the next outstanding historic visit by a US President. Nixon and Reagan had both come on the election trail, seeking votes from the Irish-American community. Kennedy came to honour his Irish ancestry and simply because he wanted to make the visit; Clinton to copper-fasten the peace process which he had already helped, to celebrate his Irish roots, and as a memorial to Kennedy – extraordinarily, he had met JFK at the White House as a teenager in a group specially chosen to visit the president because of their accomplishments. That meeting was the source of a dramatic moment at the US Democrat Convention in New York in 1992, three years earlier, which I covered for RTÉ. Just before the nomination of the then governor of Arkansas as the Democrats' candidate for the presidency, on the giant screen behind the podium we were shown old film of a teenage Clinton stepping forward in the White House Rose Garden to shake hands with JFK – a master-stroke that sent a palpable thrill through the assembled delegates.

The President, after recognising Ireland's contemporary contribution to international culture through its writers, poets, musicians and filmmakers, citing, among many others, Roddy Doyle, Paula Meehan, U2 and Neil Jordan, he went on to speak of his Irish ties. 'My mother was a Cassidy – how I wish she were alive to be here with me today; she would have loved the small towns, she would have loved Dublin, and most of all she would have loved that you have almost 300 racing days a year – she loved the horses!' To a delighted Cassidy clan in the audience, he said: 'In my best Arkansas accent, *céad míle fáilte, fada saol agus sláinte!*' My clanger was faithfully repeated. Sorry, Bill! But the audience lapped it up. The error was never mentioned in public until now, a tribute to those who knew and kept mum.

Addressing the peace process, he said, pointing at John Bruton, 'I ask all of you to think about the next steps we must take, stand with

PEACE DEAL AS CLINTON ARRIVES

the taoiseach as he takes risks for peace.' He quoted Seamus Heaney: 'We're living in a moment where hope and history rhyme.' He evoked the memory of JFK's visit in 1963, and described how he was 'moved the most on that extraordinary day in Northern Ireland' by the young people he met, both Catholic and Protestant, who made it clear to him that 'they want peace and decency – among all people'. He ended with this tribute: 'For the risk you must now continue to take for peace, for inspiring the nations of the world by your example, and for giving so much to make America great, America says thank you, Ireland, and God bless you all!' The people in College Green and Dame Street – and the army band – gave Clinton a rousing, emotional sendoff as he shook hands with the Lord Mayor and the taoiseach. It was a magnificent occasion and a fitting set piece to end the formal events of his visit.

Later that evening we assembled in Cassidy's fine old pub on Camden Street. There was standing room only for the obligatory pint of stout and the photos that went with it. It was an entirely relaxed occasion where Bill and Hillary could really wind down after a whirlwind, triumphant visit, North and South. Certainly it gave the twin-track strategy as much momentum as was possible, but the hard men of the IRA, Sinn Féin, the UK and the unionists, were not moved. The IRA's message for the British government and the International Body a week later was blunt but not unexpected: 'There is no question of the IRA meeting the ludicrous demand for a surrender of IRA weapons either through the front door or the back door.' So the peace process would not exist if the British government did not change its policy. In January it did change, but in a way that unfortunately inflamed anger not only among republicans, but in Government Buildings as well. Christmas and the New Year provided a respite for all involved except the International Body. Senator Mitchell, John de Chastelain and Harri Holkeri were hard at work to meet the January deadline for its report.

Sinn Féin was quick to deliver its submission on 18 December, just over two weeks after the summit setting up the International Body and President Clinton's visit. The document was presented in Dublin by a delegation of Gerry Adams, Martin McGuinness, Pat Doherty, Lucilita

Bhreatnach and Rita O'Hare. They also made an oral submission, which included a formal request to the Body to ask the British government for the Stalker, Samson and Stevens reports and all other reports 'which the British government has suppressed and which have accumulated over the years on issues like shoot-to-kill; collusion; Brian Nelson (UDA loyalist and British Army spy); and torture in interrogation centres'.

The foreword of the printed document produced in January 1996 said: 'The stated objective of the twin-track approach is to remove the preconditions to all-party talks which have been erected by the British government.' That indeed was the stated objective of the *Irish* government. The submission included this: 'We agree with the Taoiseach John Bruton who said that "a twin-track approach is useless unless it removes all preconditions."' Their submission was a strong document, compelling as a concise account of the peace initiative against the background of '25 years of conflict, and the wider context of 75 years of oppression of nationalists in the six counties since Ireland was partitioned by the British government'.

In a summary, the party said that all the armed groups made it clear that they would not surrender their weapons, and there was no expectation among any of the opposing groups that the issue of arms would be settled except in the context of a negotiated settlement:

> The demand for an arms surrender from the IRA, a native guerrilla army which has not been defeated, by an occupying power which has not been victorious, raises many questions about the British government's actual agenda and real intentions. Thankfully the guns have been silent for 16 months now. The critical first step has been made. It must be consolidated by being underpinned by a negotiated and agreed political settlement.

Bruton maintained that the Sinn Féin reference to a 'surrender' was wrong; 'putting some weapons beyond use' was preferable.

The Sinn Féin document said a clear and absolute objective of a lasting peace settlement was the permanent removal of the gun from the political equation in Ireland. That meant, it said, agreement on six points: the transitional role and deployment of the British Army and the RUC, pending the establishment of acceptable law and order forces; a withdrawal of British troops, and the creation of an unarmed police service must be part of the general demilitarisation of the situation – the document said no one seriously expected the IRA to surrender their weapons; a review of the proliferation of licensed weapons in the hands mainly of unionists; the removal of all repressive laws and a review of the performance and independence of the judiciary; the release of all political prisoners; and the disarmament of all armed groups.

And then, at last, a prophetic endorsement of the International Body: 'An independent third party could prove to be of assistance here. This would, of course, have to be agreed by those in possession of weapons.' Little did General de Chastelain know that he would still be labouring on this issue many years later. It was a belated recognition of the value of an international presence on the decommissioning issue. Sinn Féin had rejected the idea when it was first put to them, and the IRA threatened war. As a new year began, our hopes rested on a report from the International Body that would give John Major an opportunity to drop the precondition 'gesture' of decommissioning without too much political flak from his disgruntled right-wing backbenchers and former ministers known colloquially as 'the has beens and never beens' – and of course, the unionists.

While the Mitchell Body was doing its work, John Major and his wife Norma paid a visit to Northern Ireland and the Republic just before Christmas, his 13th to the North as prime minister. It was balanced between Protestant Ballymena where he was greeted 'warmly' in sleet and freezing rain by Ian Paisley and his wife Eileen, with a large crowd of his constituents; then, after a carol service, they went to visit the predominantly nationalist town of Downpatrick, after which he and his wife flew to Dublin. 'I wanted a chance to relax with the Brutons after the tension of the twin-track negotiation,' he wrote. The short summit talks in the Sycamore Room at Government Buildings were just diplomatic; there was no appetite for reopening the torturous and lengthy negotiations. Afterwards there was a joint press conference on the steps of Government Buildings.

I saw the visit as a bit of plastering over the cracks at a time of seasonal hospitality while we awaited the arms report. As we know now, there was no IRA decommissioning until three years after the Belfast Agreement in 2001. But the fourth and final act of IRA decommissioning did not take place until September 2005, *eight years* after Sinn Féin entered the all-party talks. In his memoir, *A Shared Home Place*, Seamus Mallon was a harsh critic of Bertie Ahern and Tony Blair over their handling of the arms issue after the 1998 Belfast Agreement. He said they had 'fudged this issue with obfuscatory language' about Sinn Féin and the loyalist parties, using 'any influence they may have' to get full paramilitary decommissioning within two years. 'In the end it took the Provos eleven years after their first ceasefire to put their arms beyond use, and that led to huge mistrust and misunderstanding which has beggared the practice of politics ever since.' Most shocking of all was Mallon's 'vivid memory' of the dinner conversation he had with Tony Blair in Hillsborough, complaining to him about their pandering to Sinn Féin while the SDLP was the largest nationalist party in Northern Ireland. 'His answer was breathtaking' said Mallon: 'The trouble with you fellows, Seamus, is that you have no guns.'

He blamed the two governments' lack of action in support of the more moderate constitutional parties for Ian Paisley's 'more extreme DUP' taking over from David Trimble's UUP and the 'more extreme Sinn Féin' replacing the SDLP as the main nationalist party: 'I saw the way in which the decommissioning issue – and the cynical way in which the Provisionals dragged it out – destroyed middle unionism, and did enormous damage to the SDLP.' He said Blair, Ahern and Clinton should have come together to get rid of all arms, either when the Northern Ireland Executive was set up in December 1999, or 'after the Good Friday Agreement's proposed decommissioning deadline of May 2000'. Mallon courageously stood up to the IRA over decades, and he had deep experience of Northern politics throughout the Troubles, so we must pay some attention to his words. Politics in Ireland is still paying a price for what he saw as serious mismanagement by the government leaders.

After the pro forma summit between Bruton and Major at Government Buildings, we all went round to a pub just a few steps away on the corner of Merrion Row for another obligatory pint of Guinness and for Major to have a brief chat with the clientele. I was surprised to see in the State Papers for 1996 that some of the staff in the Department were rounded up to ensure that the hostelry would be busy! Roy Dooney and I lingered with some of the officials as Bruton and Major went for dinner with their wives, and none of them said anything about having been 'recruited' to enjoy a drink with the British prime minister. Bruton also got some cricketers to attend because Major likes the game. After their meal the two couples went for a scheduled visit to the National Concert Hall for the second half of a performance of Handel's *Messiah*. 'To my astonishment,' John Major recalled, 'the audience rose in a standing ovation as we entered. They and the cast gave us a second ovation at the end, and cheered us through the foyer ... the warmth of the Irish people was up-lifting.' After Clinton's visit and this limited, but encouraging, event at the Concert Hall, it seemed that people strongly supported both Bruton and Major in the peace process, but there were still hurdles to be crossed.

Early in January 1996, the UUP leader David Trimble sought a meeting with the taoiseach. John Bruton told him that if they were to meet, it would have to be within the context of the twin-track approach. Trimble would not accept that approach, so Bruton refused the request. It was not only Adams and Hume seeking a meeting who were turned down. For a taoiseach of the Republic who reached out to unionists, this was stern stuff and obviously not expected by Trimble. The request for the meeting had come to Paddy Teahon through Jeffrey Donaldson, who was then a senior figure in Trimble's party. In a notebook covering Sunday 14 January 1996, I recorded what happened:

> The Taoiseach faxed the Paddy Teahon report outlining his meeting with Donaldson to Dick Spring with the request to meet the Taoiseach, combined with a meeting with Dick Spring afterwards ... The response came on Sunday. Not Good. Dick Spring was displeased – he says this is a 'dangerous backchannel'. [This refers to Paddy Teahon's contact with Donaldson. Spring had already invited the Northern parties for talks, as agreed

in the summit, and was sensitive about unionist criticisms of him.] Written messages are exchanged. Paddy Teahon says the Taoiseach's first reaction is to tell him to 'go jump in a lake'. But the second reaction is 'the interests of the Government ... he [Bruton] is very exercised about this today, he is still troubled.' In the evening, Paddy Teahon says I should call him. I do so. It's a mistake. He's very angry that I know about the exchanges [Donaldson/Trimble] with the 'South' as I put it. I shouldn't have been told, he said. I told him that it would not go further and he knew that. He agreed. But, he said, it's widening the circle.

It was a mistake to call Bruton, because his secretive reaction about 'widening the circle' inhibited Paddy from sharing information, making my life more difficult. As press secretary I had to know what was going on, so that I could make sense of issues and developments when I was to brief about them, or had to deal with issues coming at me from elsewhere, like the 'rats had got at the text' smear after the cancelled summit in September 1995. All politicians have to be discreet from time to time, but this was frustrating to say the least. Peter Prendergast told me that during his time as press secretary, Garret FitzGerald nominated a cabinet minister to keep him briefed on the debate or discussions, not just decisions, which were what we got weekly from the secretary general to the government, Frank Murray. John Bruton kept this role for himself, and it was rolled up into a meeting with all three press officers. I should have asked for the FitzGerald system.

Over the next two weeks, as we awaited the Mitchell report and then dealt with reactions to it after it was published, an evolving drama was playing out on two fields of play – the Forum for Peace and Reconciliation in Dublin Castle and Dáil Éireann; and between Government Buildings, 10 Downing Street and the House of Commons. To begin, there was a bizarre coincidence – 'a funny thing happened on the way to the Forum' as the saying goes. I was going to a lunch at the Forum on Friday 19 January, five days before the Mitchell report was to be published, and I met Rita O'Hare of Sinn Féin, a bright, strong woman who was later to represent the party in Washington. We talked about the forthcoming report and about Trimble's election proposal. She told me there was a fear of the Irish government accepting a Northern Assembly (which would have a numerical unionist majority) as an internal settlement. In my notebook for January 1996 I wrote that I had assured her that the Irish government was:

> Rock solid on any arrangements having to be linked to the three-stranded process, internal power sharing, North–South arrangements, and Dublin–London institutions. I said the challenge for nationalists was to use unionist proposals to deliver on their own agenda in talks and possibly get unionists into discussions with other parties to take part in elections. I mentioned the British Labour Party position which was broadly supportive of Major and added: 'A blanket Sinn Féin NO! was seen as just as intransigent as unionists' NO! Better to say yes with qualifications!' She said she was aware of how it was seen, but she said there were no circumstances etc.' [re prior decommissioning]. She was very dismissive of Tony Blair and Mo Mowlam [shadow Northern Ireland secretary] but, prophetically, said they might be different in government 'like others'. The latter was a firm belief of mine. There were no votes in the UK worth having a row about Northern Ireland policy, people just didn't want to know. But I strongly believed that a Labour government with a majority would be very different handling the peace process. I asked her about the Sinn Féin National Chairman, Mitchel McLaughlin's comment on Trimble's election proposal, that Sinn Féin would give it 'very serious consideration'. She said it was an attempt to 'demonstrate that all proposals would be considered'. I noted that she did not appear to be totally absolutist. She advised me to talk to Mitchel McLaughlin about it. I said I would and she promised to get me a number for him. Within a few days the George Mitchell report would be out, and Major's response would change everything. I never got the number from Rita so the Mitchel McLaughlin conversation never happened.

I went on to the lunch and found myself at a table with Martin Mansergh, previously an adviser to Charles Haughey and Albert Reynolds, and now an adviser to the Fianna Fáil leader, Bertie Ahern. He raised the issue of elections in the North immediately, and these are my notes of the occasion:

> Martin Mansergh: strongly opposed to any elected body, any elections. If the Mitchell Body proposes this, they [Fianna Fáil] will say it is outside his remit. He and John Hume had to 'stiffen' Sinn Féin's back on this issue after Mitchel McLaughlin. Brit Govt (Mayhew, Major) in speeches before ceasefire indicated that talks would take place within a short time of permanent peace. They (SF) didn't accept the Downing Street Declaration but 'implicitly' there was a 'deal' with the Irish Government and now the terms were being changed. He seemed to be taking the Father Alec Reid line. He said the 'deal' is implicit in Paras 4/10 of the Downing Street Declaration. His reasons against elections: they would polarise – a DUP/UUP [unionist majority] Assembly, a resonance of Stormont, an internal settlement excluding Dublin and the North–South dimension, a delaying tactic. Acceptance of elections is acceptance of this agenda. He wouldn't listen to any qualifications – he dismissed British Labour ideas (cosying to unionists). He said Fergus Finlay tried for 18 months of the last government wining and dining unionists, he'd spent a lot of money and got nowhere (indicating about a quarter of an inch with his fingers).

This episode was raised in the Dáil by Fianna Fáil after the Mitchell report was published. It came up during the opposition leader's questions to the taoiseach after the publication of the Mitchell report, and Major's presentation of an elective process in the North as an either/or precondition for entry into all-party talks – either an instalment of decommissioning, or an election.

> Bertie Ahern's Questions – Official Dáil Report
> Were the Taoiseach's office aware, as far back as last Friday, that the British would go for an elected body?

Taoiseach: No. Apart from the various public indications of serious interest, we had no specific, direct information on the British Government's approach.

Did a member of your staff approach members of Sinn Féin and Fianna Fáil at the Forum last Friday expressing support for the elective body idea?

Taoiseach: No. A member of my staff was approached by a member of SF and a FF adviser, separately, in the normal course of such contacts at the Forum. During his conversation he gave assurances that the Government's view was that such a proposal should be considered in the political track, under the terms of the November Communiqué. He also said the Government would insist that any such proposal would have to be firmly anchored in the three-stranded approach. The Irish Government would not countenance the return of a Stormont-type assembly.

He expressed the view that we should be open to discussion of the proposal since it was put forward by Unionist Parties – and this was specifically provided for in the terms of the Communiqué. The Fianna Fáil adviser made it clear that his party would reject the Mitchell Body report if it proposed such an elective body, as being outside the International Body's remit. These conversations, exchanges of views, for which the Forum is most useful, were not based on anything other than publicly known information. I regret that what should be private, confidential, exchanges, have been used for political purposes.

I was surprised at this use of informal discussions at the Forum. I sent a copy of my notes to the taoiseach's office for use in the Dáil reply and spoke to the taoiseach directly about my encounters at the Forum. I simply discussed a very current topic in the peace process, and expressed my views, which were in line with those of the Sinn Féin chairman Mitchel McLaughlin that the Unionist Party proposal of an election should be seriously considered. I could see advantages to a discussion on an election: Trimble had already agreed that there would be no legislative or administrative role for the elected body; and he had accepted that Sinn Féin would be in the subsequent all-party talks, albeit that real negotiations would require decommissioning.

I saw Trimble's ambition and felt that could be developed, exactly what happened in the 1998 Belfast Agreement. The British government was not alone in digging trenches. I was a bit shocked at Mansergh's comment that he and John Hume had to 'stiffen' Sinn Féin's back after Mitchel McLaughlin's statement that the UUP proposal would be given 'very serious consideration'. John Hume could have had a politically justifiable reason for opposing an election – that Sinn Féin could gain ground on the SDLP because of the peace process. But the old bogeyman of a return to a majority unionist Stormont would not be tolerated by the Irish or British governments and was ruled out by the Framework Documents. The UUP deputy leader John Taylor had publicly strongly rejected such an idea, while Trimble accepted that the assembly of elected members would have no powers – the British government had made that very clear. When the election came anyway, Sinn Féin took part and did very well. Heightened emotions about an election 'gateway' to talks were unproductive and contributed to republican tensions.

Meanwhile, the International Body delivered its report on time to the two governments before its publication on 24 January 1996, an amazing feat given the complexity of the issues and the number of submissions it had to absorb and analyse. It accepted that there was a commitment by those in possession of illegal arms to make full and verifiable decommissioning, but, significantly, it concluded that the paramilitary organisations would not decommission any arms before all-party talks. It said, 'The parties should consider an approach under which some decommissioning would take place during the process of all-party negotiations, rather than before or after as the parties now urge.' It also put forward what came to be known as the 'Mitchell six principles of democracy and non-violence' to which all parties in the talks process must subscribe. Parties should affirm their commitment to:

> Democratic and exclusively peaceful means of resolving political issues.

The total disarmament of all paramilitary organisations.
That such disarmament must be verifiable to the satisfaction of an independent commission.
Renounce for themselves, and to oppose any efforts by others, to use force, or threaten to use force, to influence the course or the outcome of All-Party negotiations.
Agree to abide to any agreement reached in All-Party negotiations and to resort to democratic and exclusively peaceful methods in trying to alter any aspect of that outcome with which they may disagree.
Urge that punishment killings and beatings stop and take effective steps to prevent such actions.

The report listed a number of possible confidence-building measures, including that an elected body might be set up, but with conditions: 'if it were broadly acceptable, with an appropriate mandate and within the three-strand structure'. If an election met these conditions, the report concluded, 'an elective process could contribute to the building of confidence'. The British government put strong pressure on Mitchell to include the proposal for an election to strengthen party mandates and provide negotiators for all-party talks in his report, as he revealed in his book *Making Peace*. Trimble's proposal four months before did not include the conditionality added by Mitchell, and had already been rejected by the SDLP and Sinn Féin – fiercely so by John Hume. Just days before the International Body report was published, Trimble publicly said a new elected body was needed to establish the 'mandate and authority' of parties. The body would have no administrative or legislative powers; it could discuss matters about negotiations, but actual negotiations could happen only after decommissioning was resolved. The latter point was clearly not acceptable to the Irish government, Sinn Féin or the SDLP. The three-strand structure is, as we have seen: internal to Northern Ireland; the North–South dimension; and east–west arrangements between London and Dublin. The unionists were contemptuous of the last two, and opposed the Anglo-Irish Agreement, under which the Irish government had an advisory role in Northern Ireland policy, with Irish diplomats in the Belfast Maryfield office operating very effectively for ten years. But to unionist chagrin, the two governments were resolutely committed to the three-strand structure for an agreement.

The report presented a dilemma for John Major, ruling out prior decommissioning before talks, as we had expected and predicted. The *Irish Independent* speculated on a 'climbdown'. In *Making Peace*, George Mitchell said 'it wasn't just the Irish government and the SDLP who insisted that there would never be decommissioning prior to negotiations. Other parties north and south, religious leaders, business leaders and community activists, nationalist and unionist, repeated the argument.' Members of the International Body were told that the British government had got itself on the hook of prior decommissioning, 'and we had been brought in to get them off'. The 'clinching argument', Mitchell wrote, came from the top British police officer in Northern Ireland, RUC Chief Constable Hugh Annesley, an 'intelligent, thoughtful man'. Asked whether, if Gerry Adams wanted to, could he 'persuade the IRA to decommission prior to negotiations', Annesley replied flatly, 'No, he couldn't do it even if he wanted to. He doesn't have that much control over them.' In a later meeting, Irish police and security figures expressed the same opinion in even stronger terms. 'That seemed to us to make the case against prior decommissioning convincing,' wrote Mitchell. It was 'unworkable'.

However, the arms team were taken aback when they met British government officials who 'expressed concern' after Mitchell outlined the evidence they had gathered about prior decommissioning. The officials, to the arms team's 'surprise', believed that members of the Body 'were simply going to reaffirm their position' on the arms issue. John Major wanted a meeting, at which he bluntly told them that if they recommended parallel decommissioning, he would reject their report. They were getting a lesson in Major's tactics in the poker game. This was followed up by an invitation to dinner from minister Michael Ancram, at which he 'stressed the importance of an election [in the North] from which delegates to the negotiations would be drawn', and Major wanted a reference to an election idea in their report. Later in the evening, Ancram suggested that if the International Body was going to propose parallel decommissioning, could it be done in a separate section of the report, not as a recommendation, but as a suggestion to the governments? Mitchell had no problem about taking these ideas on board, and Major had constructed his escape hatch from prior decommissioning.

John Bruton spoke to John Major by phone very late, at about 10.30 p.m., on Tuesday 23 January – Mitchell's document was to be published the next day. The late hour was the only time Major was available – he was obviously still struggling with his response to a document which ignored all his declarations at the November summit about the inviolability of prior arms disposal, and the British government's handout telling the International Body to keep their hands off the infamous instalment of weapons. Bruton wanted to co-ordinate the two governments' response to the report, but he found Major elusive, and still defensive about the validity of the British demand for some arms decommissioning before all-party talks. The Mitchell Body had no mandate to review it, he insisted, and the unionists would not take part in such talks without it. The taoiseach reiterated his view that it wasn't going to happen, and it was wrong to seek it as a precondition.

Bruton told me that Major mentioned Trimble's proposed election as a 'mandate for the parties' to engage in talks, and he elucidated to Major John Hume's strongly held antipathy; and that there was no party consensus on the idea of an election – that was the consistent Irish position. Bruton could not get Major to agree on a co-ordinated response, but there was agreement from the British that they would 'take us through' Major's speech for the Westminster debate on the International Body report the next day, probably by Sir Patrick Mayhew or his deputy, Michael Ancram. It was a bit fraught in Government Buildings after the phone conversation, with a fear that Major would just bluntly reject the report's conclusion on arms, effectively wrecking the peace process.

I rang my opposite number in Downing Street, Christopher Meyer, after the phone call, to see if there was any way we could put together a formula of words about the two governments' approach to the Mitchell report for a joint statement. It was a bit of a try-on, since Major had rejected a joint response, but I proposed we could at least say in a statement that we 'welcomed the report and complimented the work of the three members who had delivered a comprehensive document which no doubt interfered with their Christmas and New Year celebrations, meeting the deadline set by the November summit. The report's findings would help to underpin the peace process.'

They were my suggestions, but Meyer was having none of it. There would be no joint statement. We went on to talk about the logistics of the government statements, Major to the Commons, Bruton to the Dáil. Meyer did say there would be a positive response to the Mitchell report and that he would make it plain in his briefing that it was going to help all-party talks by the end of February. There was no other content in this very brief conversation. Overall it was not encouraging, and within 24 hours that phone call was to be grotesquely misrepresented.

Three Irish government secretaries general, Paddy Teahon from the Department of the Taoiseach, Seán Ó hUiginn from foreign affairs, and Tim Dalton from justice, had flown to London on that same Tuesday morning to talk to their British counterparts, but were told on arrival that the British side had no instructions from Major's office, and his cabinet sub-committee was not meeting until 5 p.m. The British, however, indicated that they wanted it to be 'as positive as possible' about the findings. Questions to the British about a proposed election in the North provided no enlightenment. They returned to Dublin in the late afternoon. The very vague, almost tight-lipped, response by the British officials and a refusal to have any kind of joint statement were ominous signs.

After publication on 24 January 1996, Tánaiste Dick Spring welcomed the report in the Dáil. He said it 'replaces the polemics which had sprung up around the so-called "Washington 3" debate' – the British demand for an instalment of arms. The next step, he said, was 'to intensify still further the round of preparatory talks so as to achieve the launch of inclusive negotiations' at the end of February. We anxiously awaited Major's text for the Commons and the promised briefing, but the full text arrived only some minutes before Major spoke, and there was no briefing. It was a serious breach of good faith. As Gerry Adams said, Major 'ambushed' the Irish government, but he also ambushed his own backbenchers and everyone else. He told the House of Commons that he accepted the report without mentioning its crucial finding that there would be no decommissioning before all-party talks and a suggestion that it take place during the all-party talks, rather than before or after.

He then slapped down his trump card – there were now *two* ways to enter all-party talks: 'The first is for the paramilitaries to make a start to decommissioning before all-party negotiations. They can – if they will. If not, the second is to secure a democratic mandate for all-party negotiations through elections specially for that purpose.' His loyal troops in the Commons did their usual loud braying and cheering at this denouement. The *Irish Times* called it the 'rabbit out of the hat'. He had unilaterally created another precondition to all-party talks, which happened to be the unionist proposal. That was the way it was provocatively presented and received.

The shock waves were so intense on the nationalist side after this stunt that it was a game-stopper, not a winner. Gerry Adams accused Major of 'unilaterally dumping' the International Body's report. In *Making Peace*, Mitchell disputes this reaction; 'it wasn't support, but it wasn't exactly a dumping', he said. The substance – an election as a gateway to all-party talks – had potential but was incinerated for now by this poker game presentation. That made it clear to me why Major was silent about his 'either/or' preconditions; he needed the surprise factor to sell it to his backbenchers. Paul Bew and Gordon Gillespie concluded that Major's manoeuvring was 'all about buying time', but if the Mitchell report had given the chance to stave off a breach of the ceasefire, it was destroyed by this play-acting theatre in the Commons.

Major didn't even mention the communiqué commitment of a 'fixed aim' of all-party talks at the end of February, but said his government stood ready to introduce legislation for this proposed election. It was a crafty way of sliding away from the arms instalment, but at a very high price, paying only lip service to the principle of 'widespread acceptability' of an election. He avoided the embarrassment of having to climb down on Washington 3 in the House of Commons, but he shredded trust with the Northern nationalist parties who opposed an election, and almost immediately the Westminster 'rats' got to work on a misinformation campaign to deflect the breach of faith. There was a palpable frisson of shock in the Department of the Taoiseach when Major made his 'either/or' declaration. The tánaiste's adviser, Fergus Finlay, noted in his memoirs that he watched that part of Major's speech on TV with some colleagues in a state of disbelief. 'I thought, and said aloud, that's it. That's the end of the peace process.' It put the 17-month-old ceasefire in very serious doubt – though there was a lingering hope that Martin McGuinness's assurance, 'it would hold in all circumstances', would still carry the day.

In the Commons, John Hume strongly attacked the election proposal, saying it would be 'utterly irresponsible' for any party to play politics with the lives of people in the North. 'It would be particularly irresponsible for a government to try to buy votes to keep themselves in power.' Major quickly rejected the imputation that he was buying the votes of unionists by adopting their election proposal, but it hung heavily in the political atmosphere.

In this fraught and fragile political situation, the Downing Street briefing machine started claiming that Major had informed the taoiseach fully in the Tuesday phone call about what he was going to propose, and they tried to drag me into it, saying that the British press secretary, Christopher Meyer, had also briefed me about the election proposal that night during our phone call. I was completely shocked by these untruths – Meyer and I had not discussed the election proposal at all! But against the background of the September episode, I wasn't surprised by the underhand tactics. However, I was taken aback that the British account was reported in the *Irish Independent* and the *Irish Times*. Thankfully, I had evidence to prove that the British side was not telling the truth. At lunchtime on the day of Major's speech, I heard RTÉ's London correspondent reporting speculation that Major would announce procedures for an elected body. I was alarmed and immediately rang Christopher Meyer, who denied there would be anything specific. I quickly emailed the taoiseach about my call. He was awaiting the speech text and briefing. So I had this note, dated and timestamped, in my departmental desktop computer. 'Chris Meyer tells me that is wrong. There will be no specific proposals. But the Prime Minister will say in general terms that the elected body could produce a way forward, it may work, it's a matter for the parties.' I rang Geraldine Kennedy, the *Irish Times* political correspondent, and gave her a copy of the internal email. It spoke for itself – if I had been briefed by Meyer, as Downing Street was spinning, on Major's speech, just as they maintained the taoiseach was, why on earth would I be ringing Meyer in a state of alarm about this election report?

Kennedy's front-page lead story in the *Irish Times* on Saturday 27 January began:

> New information came to light yesterday revealing the scale of the breach of faith surrounding Mr Major's speech to the House of Commons. At 1.20 p.m. on Wednesday, one hour before Mr Major's speech was faxed to the Taoiseach's office, his press secretary, Mr Mayer. stated that there would be no specific proposals for an elected body.

The British claim of taking me 'through the terms of Major's intended statement' was pure invention. In fact, Major was very specific about an election, and this would make it impossible to open all-party talks at the end of February.

The government waited fruitlessly that Wednesday for contact from Mayhew or Ancram about Major's speech. Liaison Group officials were in touch with the British again before lunch, but they said the speech was not finished. It was repeated that the taoiseach had to answer questions on Northern Ireland in the Dáil at 2.30 p.m. Major's speech did not start arriving by fax until 2.21. Bruton did not see it before he went to the Dáil. After that he headed to Donnybrook for an RTÉ interview on the Mitchell report. He had still not seen Major's speech and had to be briefed by officials in the car en route. Major's political abuse of the election proposal, rhetorically making it another alternative 'precondition' to talks, made an election even more toxic for nationalists in Northern Ireland and made an IRA ceasefire breakdown a stronger possibility.

The late Mary Holland was an independent and highly respected reporter and commentator on Northern affairs. Her professionalism was outstanding. If there was any underlying sympathy, it would have been with the nationalist side. Just before the Mitchell report was published she had written about why nationalists were suspicious, and rejected the unionist idea of an election leading to talks. She wrote in the *Irish Times*: 'They see it as an attempt to shift the whole basis of negotiations about the future of Northern Ireland back to a six-county setting, undermining the joint approach of the two governments which was first enshrined in the Anglo-Irish Agreement of 1985.'

After the Mitchell report was published, again in the *Irish Times*, Holland praised its balance and political sensitivity, but saw the conclusion that there would be no decommissioning before talks effectively coming down on the side of Sinn Féin and the Irish government. However, she added that Senator Mitchell's formula for an elective process – 'broadly acceptable, with an appropriate mandate and within the three-stranded structure [which] could contribute to the building of confidence' – was a challenge to Sinn Féin.

> It was always on the cards that if the British Government were to swallow the recommendation that Washington 3 should be quietly dropped, there would have to be some quid pro quo to make this very distasteful medicine palatable for unionists. Increasingly, it is becoming clear that simple rejection of an elected assembly is not an adequate reaction.

Since David Trimble first put forward the idea of an elected body as a way around the decommissioning impasse, she continued, 'he and his colleagues in the UUP have tried to reassure nationalists that this is not a cunning plan to resurrect Stormont.' Holland drew attention to the words of Trimble's deputy, John Taylor. Giving an 'important' speech in Newtownards just a week before, Taylor had told his unionist audience:

> If Northern Ireland ever was a Protestant state for a Protestant people, it certainly is not today. For the leader of a major party [referring to Ian Paisley and the DUP] to promise the return of Stormont is not to address the issues seriously. It is not something that can be delivered to unionists, and it only serves to revive the worst fears of nationalists.

Despite the angry rejection of the idea by John Hume and others, she concluded that the unionists were entitled to a hearing on the issue. 'Otherwise we are doomed to return to the dialogue of the deaf from which the Mitchell report was meant to help us escape.' I thought Mary Holland's analysis was brilliant, both informed and insightful, and I fruitlessly hoped it would be read and pondered by Fianna Fáil and Sinn Féin. The main political problem now was that Major's presentation of the election in the provocative 'take that!' manner to provide himself with cover for dropping the misguided Washington 3 demand, meant that he had elevated the election process to the status of another precondition.

If Major had been willing – and, more importantly, able – to graciously bow out from Washington 3, making an appeal for much closer attention to the election proposals, solemnly pledging they would not be allowed in any way to bring a 'return to Stormont', there might have been a chance for agreement. The dropping of the arms instalment would have bought some good will. Major's theatrical confrontation was engineered to keep the right-wing Tory backbenchers on side and the unionists happy, but it inflamed anger among nationalists. The dialogue of the deaf had taken over.

11

LONDON DOCKLANDS IRA BOMB

It is a particular irony of the Docklands bombing that on that very morning the taoiseach was meeting a group of the right-wing Conservative MPs that Major depended on for his majority in parliament. They were led by Andrew Hunter, the chairman of the House of Commons Conservative Committee on Northern Ireland. Nine years later, in 2005, he became a member of the Orange Order and, later still, a member of Paisley's DUP. He opposed the Belfast Agreement in 1998.

Bruton began with a criticism of Major's presentation of an election in Northern Ireland as an alternative precondition to a decommissioning gesture for entry into all-party talks, which was 'seen as a victory of unionists over nationalists'. He asked them, 'how reasonable is it of the unionist parties to refuse even to talk to Sinn Féin after a ceasefire of 17 months? Particularly when every other party has agreed to no change in the status of Northern Ireland without the consent of a majority? What can they fear from talking to Sinn Féin?' He pointed out that the timetable was agreed in the November summit with an early launch of all-party talks at the end of February. 'There's only a short number of days,' he said. Hunter responded, 'I support the statement that it is unreasonable of the unionists not to speak to Sinn Féin and the [Irish] government … It may be helpful if we try to encourage the UUP in particular on that … It was unfortunate, the reaction to the prime minister's statement, an unfortunate wording was selected.' He wanted the UUP to take part in all-party talks with Sinn Féin, accepting that the DUP would not.

James Cran MP, a member of the group, interjected: 'John Major had to keep an alignment with his backbenchers, the prime minister has always got in his mind there are three of his MPs who've voted against his government a hundred times ... the government does tend to be looking at the unionists.' He was doubtful about unionists taking part in talks. Bruton was critical of this negativity: 'The violent past was immoral, but they've stopped for 17 months now, we must do everything to stop them going back. If they're willing to go back ...' That question was answered a few hours later. 'The only thing the unionists have to fear is the return to violence. They have an institutional responsibility to talk.' Bruton said there was no time for 'treading slowly, treading slowly is the past'.

Olga Maitland MP supported Andrew Hunter on unionists talking to Sinn Féin: 'I join with him. We must explore this more.' Maitland asked, 'Is Gerry Adams able to look at things from a unionist point of view?' Bruton replied, 'My view is not yet. Unionist views explained by a [southern] Irish accent help.' Then he continued: 'By asking for decommissioning, it's seen as a surrender – a symbol of surrender. There are practical internal problems – only three or four know where the arms are. If Gerry Adams said "do this" he could be told "No – and you're going to meet your end."' He reminded them again that the ceasefire had now lasted for 17 months. The group trooped out of Government Buildings, going North to continue their fact-finding mission, little knowing that all would change a few hours later, no doubt including Hunter and Maitland's extraordinary pledges to Bruton about urging the UUP to talk to Sinn Féin.

At about 6 p.m. on Friday 9 February 1996, just over two weeks after the Mitchell report was published, the phone rang in my office in Government Buildings. It was Peter Cluskey, a fine journalist from RTÉ who was working on the news desk. He told me they had just got a statement from the IRA (Óglaidh na hÉireann) that the ceasefire was ending at 6 p.m. that day. The *Irish News*, a Northern nationalist newspaper, had received a message at 5.45 p.m. that there was a bomb planted in the London Docklands; my noted record says, 'South Quay Station, Isle of

Dogs: evacuate immediately.' Shaken and alarmed, I asked Cluskey if it was serious. He said it had come in the usual way of such IRA warnings and he believed it was real. I thanked him, said I'd be back to him and then rushed to the taoiseach's office, just a few steps away.

I barged in. The taoiseach was meeting with Pat Rabbitte, the super junior Democratic Left minister. I hurriedly told the taoiseach about the ceasefire ending right now and that there was a London bomb warning from the IRA. He was clearly shocked, as was Pat Rabbitte. Bruton asked me if it could be a false alert, and I told him what Peter Cluskey had said about the statement and about the *Irish News* warning. We could expect an explosion anytime soon. The taoiseach lifted the phone to ring Dick Spring, and I returned to my office to call back RTÉ. Then my notes record the next moments:

> 6.15 p.m.: Gerry Adams phones Paddy Teahon to say that a contact had called to say that the ceasefire was ending. He was going to check but there was some substance in it. He said hold your nerve but tell the Taoiseach and Tánaiste there is some substance in this. Channel 4 was reporting rumour about the ceasefire ending and a bomb warning.
>
> 6.40 p.m.: Rita O'Hare called – looking for Paddy Teahon – but saying they are even more concerned than they were 20 minutes ago.

My note says, '17 months and nine days.' It's poignant to look at it now. That was the length of time the ceasefire had lasted. My next note is what an angry Joe Hendron, an SDLP MP, said:

> Blame bombers, but also foot dragging by the British Government and Unionists, British Government pussyfooting around because of the House of Commons (Major's loss of a clear working majority) playing with fire and people's lives.

The ceasefire was over. The IRA had decided more human sacrifice was required. News came at about 7 p.m. that a massive explosion had taken place at South Quay, Canary Wharf, in the London Docklands, an area that had been redeveloped and had expensive multi-storey office blocks. I rang RTÉ and spoke briefly to Edward Mulhall, a TV news programme editor. We were all a bit stunned, and depressed. We knew that the ceasefire was endangered, due to the lack of progress on round-table talks over more than a year and half, but it was still a shock when the end of the ceasefire came. My notes say that Sinn Féin in Dublin and Belfast were indicating that they knew nothing beforehand.

The IRA's truck bomb had exploded with an estimated 3,000 pounds of explosives, mixed with ten pounds of Semtex, believed to have come from Libya's Muammar Gaddafi. An eyewitness said 'a tower shook, all the buildings were totally destroyed – windows gone front and back just after seven p.m. Six were taken to hospital, many walking wounded.'

That was just the early story. Later it emerged from the emergency teams at the site, and from the police, that a number of innocent victims had been killed. Inam Ul-Haq Bashir (aged 29), who ran a small newspaper shop that also sold sweets and snacks at the South Quay station in Canary Wharf, and his friend and assistant John Jeffries (31) were killed. More than one hundred people were injured in the rain of flying glass, masonry and metal, some very seriously, including a young woman, Barbara Osei, who had a glass shard buried in one eye, and was in danger of losing her sight.

The two dead men were well known to hundreds of office workers at Canary Wharf who bought papers, sweets and snacks from them on their commutes to and from work. The small kiosk shop took the full blast of the bomb, and Mr Jeffries's body was found inside. For nearly 24 hours, his widowed father – also named John – had double- and triple-checked the lists of injured people taken to the Royal London Hospital in Whitechapel after the Friday bombing. Early the following day, the search of the rubble covering the South Quay station newsagent's site was called off when his son's body was found. The body of John's colleague and friend, Inam Ul-Haq Bashir, was also dug from the rubble near the underground car park. Both men lived at home with their parents. Mr Zaoui Berezag, a 55-year-old Moroccan, was still in a 'critical condition' in intensive care the following week and a hospital spokeswoman said he had extensive head and chest injuries and would remain in intensive care until he could breathe for himself. 'His condition remains very worrying.' The ceasefire had ended in a bloody tragedy for the innocent dead and wounded in February 1996.

Jonathan Ganesh, a 23-year-old student who was working as a bank security guard at South Quay on that day, was injured in the bombing. More than twenty years later, as president of the Docklands Victims Association, he gave a painfully vivid account to the *Sunday Express* on 23 December 2018 of what happened to innocent people that evening:

> I was on patrol on that Friday night and remember thinking something was going on because I saw a lot of police cars around. As I walked towards South Quay Plaza at 7pm the bomb went off. I didn't hear it. All I saw was a flash of light. Then all hell broke loose. I saw an energy wave coming towards me. Then I heard a deafening noise. The whole thing was over in seconds but it lasted forever in my mind. Buildings started to collapse. Concrete, girders and bits of iron fell all around. As it hit my body I didn't feel pain. I just thought: 'I'm going to die, now.' I passed out and when I came to, everything was on top of me. Somehow I managed to dig through it. My radio light was flashing, because they were trying to contact me. But I couldn't hear anything.
>
> I saw Barbara Osei, a cleaner, from Ghana. She had a shard of glass in her eye. Zaoui Berezag was in a car. A piece of concrete had flattened it and smashed in his skull. Everyone thought he was dead. I didn't think I was badly injured. I was covered in blood and dust, and my clothes were badly ripped, but I was walking normally. As I crossed the road I fell over Farid, Zaoui's son. He'd been in the car with his dad and was thrown out. He had a piece of metal in his neck and was in a terrible state. I tried to reassure people that help was coming but I remember thinking that it was taking a long time. I looked at the newsagent's shop where my two friends Inam Bashir and John Jeffries worked. Later I learned that they'd died. They were lovely people …
> It was like some meteor had landed, destroying everything. It is

something I will never be able to forget. I lost the hearing in one ear and my body is badly scarred from flying metal and where the girder hit my chest. But I was one of the lucky ones.

There are continuing efforts by victims of terrorist bombings to get some compensation from the estimated €69 billion Gaddafi secreted in accounts in Europe and elsewhere, frozen by the UN after his death in 2011. The 25th anniversary of the Docklands bombing was marked in 2021 by a small gathering of victims and their relatives at the site – the numbers were limited by Covid-19 rules. Jonathan Ganesh and others released doves to mark the day and called once more for compensation from the frozen Libyan funds. Just over a month later, on 23 March 2021, the BBC reported that frozen Libyan assets in Britain would not be used to compensate IRA Semtex victims. That was confirmed by James Cleverly, then British minister of state for the Middle East and North Africa, later foreign secretary. In the Belfast *News Letter* UUP member of the British House of Lords, Lord Reg Empey, said: 'It's disgusting … I just cannot understand the attitude of our government towards the Semtex victims.' Jonathan Ganesh told the *Sunday Express*:

> We have been campaigning for more than 10 years for justice and for 10 years the British government has done nothing while other nations have secured compensation for victims. Just this year Zaoui Berezag, who was left blind and permanently brain damaged when his car was crushed, passed away. Two years ago his wife Gemma, who was desperate for help in caring for him, took her own life. Victims are in desperate need.

Britain's share of Gaddafi's wealth is estimated at about €13 billion, potentially producing over €3 billion in interest or dividends. The figure to compensate victims and relatives of IRA bombs is estimated at around €2.5 billion.

Back to the evening of the Docklands bomb. The taoiseach had reached Tánaiste Dick Spring on the phone in the government jet – he was returning from Washington after what his team felt was a very successful meeting with President Clinton and Anthony Lake, chief of the National Security Council, as part of the campaign to get all-party talks started. Fergus Finlay, who was with Spring on the plane, said they were devastated by the news because they felt that US pressure would have made a breakthrough likely with the British. While the search for the victims in South Quay was continuing, an emergency meeting of some ministers and advisers took place on the evening of 9 February, attended by Garda Commissioner Patrick Culligan. The mood was sombre. Ministers were upset and surprised that the IRA ceasefire had ended and stunned by the Docklands bombing. Afterwards the taoiseach, while condemning the bombing, said that he would work in every possible way to get the peace process back on track, insisting that the setback would be overcome 'if we are determined enough and apply sufficient dedication and imagination to it'. He called on 'all who may have any influence on those responsible for this appalling act' to use it publicly as well as privately, to ensure no further acts of violence would take place.

President Clinton rang both Major and Bruton to express his dismay, sorrow and regret about what had happened. 'It's bad news, really bad news,' John Major told him. Speaking to Bruton, Clinton said he had met Adams just a few days earlier and had no 'inkling' of the bomb attack. He didn't see it coming, though he had noticed the Sinn Féin leader seemed 'ill at ease' and he felt 'badly' having met Adams. Bruton said the bombing was 'dreadful – it was completely sudden and unexpected'. Clinton dealt harshly with the IRA statement that blamed Major and his government for the ceasefire breakdown: 'Blaming the British under these circumstances is pretty gutless,' he said. Bruton told him it appeared that 'a lot of Sinn Féin's leadership was taken by surprise'. He commended the president for his statement on the bombing, saying, 'The terrorists who perpetrated today's attack cannot be allowed to derail the effort to bring peace to the people of Northern Ireland – a peace they overwhelmingly support.'

Speaking to Major about his meeting with Adams, Clinton said 'he [Adams] was grousing' and I told him he could say what he wants about

Major, 'but the fact remains – he [Major] found a way to at least offer you an alternative: the possible permutations of the election proposal'. With a forthcoming Anglo-Irish summit, agreed at the late-night November meeting, Major felt that the two governments could act together and 'lock arms' to keep the peace process alive. Bruton told Clinton that the three governments should move with caution. 'We don't want to rush into it, but we can't reverse the course. We have to keep hope alive.' Clinton agreed: 'We don't want to overreact. It is sad and troubling.' (The details of this conversation are contained within the US National Archives transcript released to the William J. Clinton Presidential Library in Arkansas and were reported by the *Irish Times* on 6 September 2019.) The following day there was a further emergency meeting of ministers and advisers with Taoiseach John Bruton, Tánaiste Dick Spring, Minister for Social Welfare and leader of Democratic Left Proinsias De Rossa, Minister for Justice Nora Owen, and Attorney General Dermot Gleeson. It evolved into a broader meeting, including more ministers and key officials and advisers. I was there. It was a solemn and tense gathering. The taoiseach said there would be a party leaders' meeting later, and his view was they should not 'rush' on Sinn Féin.

Paddy Teahon spoke about a phone conversation he'd had with Rita O'Hare. He said she was emotional, and said she hadn't known about the Docklands bomb. He quoted her saying 'We'll be working to see what we can do to pull this back.' There were a few doubtful remarks from officials, ranging from 'It's been blown to bits' to one key official saying she 'wouldn't be looking forward to a further meeting'. There were expressions of controlled anger and frustration. Everyone had worked so hard to keep the peace process going, in the context of a British prime minister who was increasingly a prisoner of unionists and his right-wing backbench MPs, whom we had encountered that very morning of the bomb. Bruton's achievement swinging two key hostile figures to press the ulster Unionists to speak to Sinn Féin was blown up by the bomb.

Seán Ó hUiginn said there would be a united front in the Dáil, but the basic situation was that 'non-violence must be returned to, there is a clear distinction, the ceasefire being on – allowing risks – or off, leaving us hostage to the next bomb.' Fergus Finlay suggested that the government should have one 'face-to-face' meeting with Sinn Féin to demand that the ceasefire be reinstated, while Seán Ó hUiginn added that there must be a 'formal statement of reinstatement from the IRA'. I thought that one last meeting was a good idea, but it was not adopted. There was a tense, frustrated discussion around the strong belief that the British government could have done much more, and testy resentment that the unionists had 'screwed it'. Dermot Gleeson spoke about both the British government with Washington 3, and the unionists supporting it – they carried a *moral* responsibility, but 'we'll all try again,' he said. 'It's a matter of record there were different views on how we should proceed. I believe the Irish government had charted the correct way forward. There were totally legitimate frustrations with the passage of seventeen months without unionists taking part in talks, but *nothing* justifies the killing of innocent people.'

A number of Fine Gael ministers agreed that whatever the government said about the ceasefire ending, they 'must not exonerate the British'. They felt that, while the taoiseach had reached out to unionists, 'they would have been better off supporting the taoiseach earlier'. This was the moment for the taoiseach to 'ward off' the unionists, one minister said angrily. Meanwhile, the Minister for Justice, Nora Owen, halted the planned release of a further nine republican prisoners. A senior official involved deeply in the peace process was very sceptical about the lack of knowledge in Sinn Féin about the ceasefire ending and the Docklands bombing. 'Don't tell me nobody knew,' he said. The government had been given no indication by Sinn Féin of the ceasefire ending, at a regular meeting with Gerry Adams and a party delegation just two days before the bomb.

The government meeting agreed a statement on the end of the ceasefire and the bombing:

> The Government note with profound regret the statement announcing the ending of the IRA's complete cessation of hostilities. They unreservedly condemn last night's bombing in London

and express their deep sympathy, on behalf of the Irish people, to
the victims of that act of violence and to their families.

It reiterated the government's fundamental position:

> Violence, and the threat of violence, have no place in democratic
> negotiation. Nothing can justify a resort to violence in an attempt
> to override the democratic political process.

The statement pointed out that the government's search for an 'inclusive process of negotiation was based on a clear commitment by the IRA to a total cessation of violence. The fact that this commitment has now been revoked alters the situation fundamentally.' It stated: 'Only those who take no part in violence, in the threat of violence, or in support of violence, can take part in a democratic negotiation.' It underscored the fact that the ceasefire enabled a whole range of top-level political contacts and developments to take place; it noted that Gerry Adams had requested a meeting and said: 'The Government wants the IRA ceasefire to be restored immediately.' The basis for previous government meetings with Sinn Féin was that a total cessation was in place and 'any meeting with Sinn Féin should be consistent with that long-standing policy'. So there would be no taoiseach's or ministerial meetings with Gerry Adams, or other personnel from the party, until the ceasefire was restored. But contact with officials would be maintained.

In his 13 February speech to the Dáil, Bruton raised some important questions. Inam Bashir and John Jeffries died because of republican violence; 'What did these two young men ever do to Ireland, or do against Irish republicans, to deserve such a death? Who has a right to decide that Inam Bashir and John Jeffries should die for Ireland?' He also asked: 'Who authorised it? When did they decide? Who knew in advance that it was going to happen? Who knew that it would happen but was not told the exact date?' We still do not know the answers to these questions, decades later. There are no Provisional IRA records available, unlike the old IRA during the civil war. The bombing was shocking in both timing and context. We were on the cusp of achieving a fixed date for all-party talks – in less than two weeks. The UUP leader David Trimble had committed to sitting down with Sinn Féin and the other parties after an election. Trimble put a reserve on the key political settlement negotiations until the decommissioning issue was dealt with, but now we had Senator Mitchell's report saying this could be considered during the negotiations, so he would find it impossible to stick to that line, and it would not be accepted by either the British or Irish governments. Bruton said to the Dáil:

> I believe the British Government did make a mistake in its response to the Mitchell Report. I believe Unionist Parties made a mistake in not sitting down with Sinn Féin and asking them the hard questions face to face. But I do not believe that any comparison can be drawn between political mistakes, and a response to those mistakes that took human life ... The blame for the suffering and deaths of innocent people rests solely on the shoulders of those who agreed to, who knew about, and those who planned and planted the bomb at Canary Wharf. Let us not become so lost in a moral fog that we cannot see this much clearly.

Dick Spring told the Dáil how he had heard about the bomb, which disrupted progress being made with President Clinton towards all-party talks:

> I was actually flying over the Atlantic, last Friday, one hour after a very productive visit to Washington which I believe had significantly advanced the prospect of talks, when I was informed of the IRA statement and when the bomb exploded in London. Progress, slow, torturous, but real, was put at risk by a murderous, but ultimately futile, gesture of frustration.

Why did the ceasefire end? There is no doubt that there was tension and frustration that everyone shared because talks had not taken place

17 months after the ceasefire. In his autobiography, John Major quotes an IRA spokesman putting the blame directly on him: 'The IRA leadership delivered a complete cessation of military operations; on a clear, unambiguous and shared understanding that inclusive negotiations would rapidly commence to bring about political agreement and a peace settlement ... John Major reneged on these commitments.' The IRA spokesman he quoted said Bruton had known 'the basis upon which we agreed a complete cessation of military operations in August 1994. It was a quid pro quo understanding that all-party talks would commence rapidly ... which the previous taoiseach was clear about and which John Bruton was informed of when he assumed office.'

When this notion first appeared shortly after he took office, John Bruton directly checked with Albert Reynolds if there was any 'quid pro quo understanding' in relation to the ceasefire reached with the IRA, and Albert Reynolds told him there was no such understanding. Bruton also sent Department secretary Paddy Teahon to check with Martin Mansergh, and he came back with the same message – there was no 'understanding'. Mansergh's later comment to me that it was 'implicit' in the Downing Street Declaration that all-party talks would come about quickly, after a ceasefire, was an interpretation, and is clearly of a very different nature to a 'clear, unambiguous and shared understanding'. But it was possible that this 'implicit' interpretation of the Downing Street Declaration that the talks would commence quickly fuelled Sinn Féin and IRA anger. In fact, the Declaration said: 'The British and Irish Governments reiterate that the achievement of peace must involve a *permanent* end to the use of, or support for, paramilitary violence.' The British were suspicious right from the start because the IRA did not use the word 'permanent' or the other terminology, slowing their response as Major's government became hostage to parliamentary numbers.

In his autobiography Major states bluntly, on the claim of an understanding, 'I was certainly not party to one' and he goes on to say, 'It was a weak attempt at ex-post facto justification by the IRA.' He said it was made weaker by the fact that the British and Irish governments were working intensively to launch all-party talks by the end of February.

In the wake of the bombing, Bruton continued to strongly press Major that any election proposal made by him had to meet Senator Mitchell's terms, 'broadly acceptable, with an appropriate mandate and within the three-stranded structure'. An election would have to be accepted by the Northern Ireland political parties and he insisted Major had to agree a date for all-party talks. Clinton, meanwhile, called on the IRA to reinstate the ceasefire. The IRA had been involved in a lengthy backchannel exchange with the British government and John Major, which ended in November 1993, according to Eamonn Mallie and David McKittrick. They write in their book *The Fight for Peace* that the IRA received a 'lengthy British document' with a copy of the communiqué from a Major–Reynolds summit in Brussels in 1993 attached. The British document said:

> There can be no departure from what is said there [in the Brussels communiqué] and in particular its statement that there could be no secret agreements or understandings between governments and organisations supporting violence, as a price for its cessation … It is the public and consistent position of the British Government that any dialogue could only follow a *permanent* end to violent activity.

There is no evidence that there was any 'clear, unambiguous and shared understanding'; in fact, the evidence is to the contrary. But it was reasonable for there to be frustration and anger about the 17 months without talks. The unionists and the British government had to accept the blame for that. The ceasefire was publicly taken to be permanent by Bruton and other politicians so that they could explain their interactions with Sinn Féin to their own constituencies. The word 'complete' was chosen very carefully by the IRA for its ambiguous nature – it could be interpreted just as an order to all units, no matter where they were. It left the door ajar for a return to violence. John Major was even more suspicious of Sinn Féin and the IRA in consequence. I believe that the delay in talks had

Taoiseach John Bruton and Tánaiste Dick Spring welcomed at the door of 10 Downing Street by Prime Minister John Major – a familiar event during the Rainbow years. (© PA Images / Alamy Stock Photo)

The first Rainbow meeting with Sinn Féin leader Gerry Adams and general secretary Lucilita Bhreatnach with the taoiseach and tánaiste in early 1995. (© PA Images / Alamy Stock Photo)

A peace settlement in Northern Ireland came closer as Bruton and Major launched the Joint Framework Documents in Belfast. (© RollingNews.ie)

Taking notes as Clinton and Bruton meet in the White House Oval Office.

I was delighted to meet Vice-President Al Gore, later denied the presidency in 2000 when the US Supreme Court stopped democracy, ending a vital recount in Florida.

I told Clinton that I predicted he would win the presidency in Ireland's *Sunday Press* – when he was third in the polls!

Finola joins her husband as he briefs the White House media, and I record it.

Former House Speaker Tom Foley (left) was a great friend of Ireland.

After the first 100 days, a cartoon of the inside team appeared. From left: Paddy Teahon, Dermot Gleeson, John Bruton, Roy Dooney, Seán Donlon and me. (© Patrick Brocklebank)

A blazing truck on the nationalist Falls Road, Belfast, after Paisley and Trimble led an Orange march down the Catholic Garvaghy Road in July 1995. (© PA Images / Alamy Stock Photo)

The winning vote in the divorce referendum! The taoiseach has a busy day ahead as Ireland votes YES. (© PA Images / Alamy Stock Photo)

Bruton and Major bring former US Senate leader George Mitchell into the peace process at a dramatic late-night summit in London. (© Trinity Mirror / Mirrorpix / Alamy Stock Photo)

Mission accomplished – establishing Mitchell's International Body on arms decommissioning. A midnight goodbye as Bruton and Spring head for home.
(© Trinity Mirror / Mirrorpix / Alamy Stock Photo)

Laughter is the best medicine. John Bruton and former Taoiseach Albert Reynolds share a joke. (© Stephen Barnes / Politics / Alamy Stock Photo)

Clinton with Bruton in the taoiseach's office during his historic visit to Ireland. Clinton hails the summit a success with George Mitchell in the peace process. (© PA Images / Alamy Stock Photo)

Clinton was thrilled by the huge welcome and sheer joy of the over eighty thousand people who packed College Green and Dame Street for his address. (© Reuters)

The devastation caused by the massive IRA London Docklands bomb, which ended the ceasefire with two dead and many more injured. (© Richard Baker / Alamy Stock Photo)

Ihsan Bashir (left), brother of Inam Bashir, one of two killed by the Docklands bomb, and Jonathan Ganesh, head of the victims' campaign group. (© PA Images / Alamy Stock Photo)

Bruton is met by German Chancellor Helmut Kohl and his German Army guard of honour on an official visit to his chancellery in Bonn. (© dpa picture alliance / Alamy Stock Photo)

All-party talks at Stormont begin on 10 June 1996. From left: General de Chastelain, George Mitchell, Spring, Bruton, Major and Patrick Mayhew. (© PA Images / Alamy Stock Photo)

A stab in the back. Another huge IRA bomb destroys the centre of Manchester just days after the all-party talks started in Belfast. (© PA Images / Alamy Stock Photo)

The British Army was deployed with the RUC to stop the Drumcree Orange march in 1996. (© PA Images / Alamy Stock Photo)

David Trimble squeezes through the RUC blocking the banned Orange march in 1996, but a shock British reversal lets the march down the Catholic Garvaghy Road. (© PA Images / Alamy Stock Photo)

Taoiseach Bruton addresses a joint session of Congress – the House of Representatives and the Senate – in September 1996, a great honour. (© Richard Ellis / Staff / Getty Images)

John and I enjoying a drink in the government jet on the way home from our extraordinary adventure in Ireland's western outpost of Newfoundland.

Bruton is the first foreign leader to meet Prime Minister Tony Blair a week after his election. (© Allstar Picture Library Ltd / Alamy Stock Photo)

Bruton tells the media in Downing Street that Tony Blair will greatly improve British–Irish relations and progress on the peace process. (© PA Images / Alamy Stock Photo)

Denis O'Brien arriving at the Moriarty Tribunal investigating the award of the second mobile licence to his consortium. (© Albert Gonzalez / RollingNews.ie)

Bertie Ahern and John Bruton shake hands before the RTÉ Election '97 TV debate. The media said Bruton won the debate, but Ahern won the election. (© PA Images / Alamy Stock Photo)

The former taoiseach's state funeral was held at his local St Peter and Paul's Church, Dunboyne, on 10 February 2024, with burial at nearby Rooske Cemetery. (© Julian Behal / RollingNews.ie)

split the IRA Army Council, and the decision to end the ceasefire was carried by a majority; the peace process supporters accepted that decision.

The most virulent immediate critic of Bruton after the bombing was a journalist who became a politician, and then returned to journalism. Geraldine Kennedy became a Progressive Democrat TD in 1987, then lost her seat in 1989. She later joined the staff of the *Irish Times*, becoming political correspondent in the early 1990s. A week after the South Quay bombing, she published an article that shocked me; I found it unreasonable and unfair. Because it was published in the highly respected *Irish Times*, in my view it had significant potential to further inflame already angry republicans and undermine efforts to get the ceasefire restored. She also contradicted herself in a litany of blame. None of my opinions will be a surprise to Geraldine Kennedy, I had a vigorous conversation with her on the phone after her piece was published. I greatly admired her work as an exceptional journalist – she had broken important stories, particularly about the scandals during Charles Haughey's time as leader of Fianna Fáil – and I had been on friendly terms with her for a number of years. I was both dismayed and disappointed with what I saw as an unbalanced view of events, with no mention of Major's perilous limitations in parliament. This extract includes some of the points she made about whether John Bruton was 'the man', as she put it, to get the ceasefire restored:

> The first, and most irreparable, mistake was made by Mr Bruton last March when he implicitly accepted the Washington 3 test, the precondition imposed by the British government for Sinn Féin's entry into all-party talks … either inadvertently or worse, knowingly, Mr Bruton underwrote the British demand for Washington 3, a decommissioning gesture prior to talks. He helped place it at the top of the Anglo-Irish agenda. It has dominated the agenda at heads of government, ministerial and official level ever since. On the eve of his departure to the US on March 13th for St Patrick's Day ceremonies in the White House, Mr Bruton said he would be telling President Clinton that they had to see some movement

on the arms question so that talks could begin between British ministers and Sinn Féin.

He made statement after statement implicitly supporting Sir Patrick's position on decommissioning, in the US and at home, for the remainder of the month ... This ... approach [by Sir Patrick Mayhew in Washington on 7 March 1995] was seen by the Taoiseach the following day, March 8th, in the Dáil as 'a serious statement' of its position by the British government. It deserved, he said, an equally serious response.

Accepting that it could not be delivered three months later, Mr Bruton, on the advice of Anglo-Irish officials, tried to extricate himself from Washington 3. He sold the idea of the twin-track initiative, separate preparatory talks and decommissioning tracks, to Mr Major at the EU summit in Cannes in June. Officials worked out proposals for the initiative throughout the summer. Mr Bruton was exposed again when he took the unprecedented step of postponing, at 6 p.m. the night before, the planned Anglo-Irish summit with Mr Major for September 6th. The joint communiqué for the summit, launching the twin-track strategy of political talks and an international decommissioning body, had been agreed on Friday but, by the following Monday, the understandings with Sinn Féin and Mr Major underpinning it had fallen apart.

The twin-track initiative, to surmount the Washington 3 hurdle, was eventually launched by Mr Bruton and Mr Major at the most hastily convened summit at 10.30 p.m. in Downing Street on November 28th, the night of the British budget. The two leaders had to agree to disagree publicly on Washington 3 so that the summit could be held on the eve of President Clinton's visit. Mr Bruton did not seem to comprehend the British government's position on Washington 3, the arms gesture, at that meeting. Both he, and Government sources, openly professed that Senator George Mitchell's independent assessment would surmount it. Mr Major was assumed to be morally bound to accept the Mitchell recommendations, although it was described in the communiqué as an advisory body.

The most catastrophic turn in Anglo-Irish relations and the intergovernmental partnership on which the peace process was based came on January 16th, the day the Mitchell report was published. The humiliating breach of faith between Mr Major and Mr Bruton, following their controversial 35-minute telephone conversation to co-ordinate their responses the previous night, was followed by Mr Major's unilateral announcement that an elective process was now to be the alternative precondition to decommissioning for Sinn Féin's entry into all-party talks.

It was simply wrong to imply that Washington 3 would never have been on the significant agenda if John Bruton had not spoken about decommissioning before and during his US visit for the 1995 St Patrick's Day celebrations. In his autobiography John Major provides evidence from speeches, messages and comments that he, Patrick Mayhew and Albert Reynolds made during 1993 and 1994, underlining that arms and equipment was one of the issues to be dealt with 'expeditiously once public confidence in peace had been established'. As we've heard, most of a UK Chequers Anglo-Irish summit between Albert Reynolds and John Major in October 1994 after the IRA ceasefire in August, before Bruton became taoiseach, was *devoted* to Major and his chief lieutenants insisting that IRA decommissioning had to take place before any talks, or even ministerial meetings. Ms Kennedy appeared unaware of this. Fergus Finlay said the British were so seized by this issue, it was going to be difficult to resolve. The late Dr Éamon Phoenix, analysing the British December 1994 Northern Ireland papers for the BBC about the first meeting of Martin McGuinness and the senior Northern Ireland Office civil servant Quentin Thomas, wrote that decommissioning was the 'key issue of the time'.

International assistance on the decommissioning issue was suggested by Dick Spring as far back as early March 1995 in the US and the idea was also mooted independently at the same time by unionist Ken Maginnis, who published a paper on the proposal. In Moscow, Bruton told Major he was 'worried' that his demand for prior IRA decommissioning could 'derail the peace process'. There was no lapse of 'three months' on the arms issue until 'officials intervened'. This political meme was subsequently taken up and repeated by Gerry Adams and other republicans. Bruton embraced the international dimension put forward by Spring. Officials at the time were working on the 'twin-track' strategy and trying to identify the best occasion for successfully presenting it to Major and Mayhew.

I spoke at length with Bruton about Kennedy's charges the day her article was published, and noted his responses:

> I called on the IRA in early March 1995 to make a move on decommissioning [on] the eve of the visit to Washington. Was there a risk? Yes – that they wouldn't do it. Was it a risk worth taking? My contention is that it was. Sinn Féin had committed themselves to peace, so there was no need for arms ... Timing was the best way of getting a small gesture, of no military significance – through the US. It was entirely reasonable. Furthermore, potential downsides were hard to identify in March '95, I asked them then, *and not since*. Does that justify a bomb? What would have happened if there was a gesture? Sinn Féin would be in all-party talks. I also knew Loyalists would have done so [dispose of some arms] if the IRA did. It could be argued that what happened in March was really significant in that, in a sense, they hadn't bought into the peace process at all. What was the problem with asking? I just asked them to do it – not a precondition.

Unionist leaders were insisting on some decommissioning before talks. Bruton again:

> Obviously, if we hadn't asked them [the IRA], the Irish Government could be seen by loyalists and unionists as condoning the holding of arms as a political bargaining counter. The fact that we asked at least gave us insurance from that quarter [loyalist paramilitaries],

which as Geraldine Kennedy knows, people on this side of the border have most to worry about in terms of their own safety.

Five days after the Docklands bomb there had been a meeting of the Combined Loyalist Military Command (CLMC), where representatives of the main loyalist paramilitaries joined together to co-ordinate their activities. In my daybook I noted that the taoiseach had received intelligence of threats to Dublin from the Ulster Volunteer Force (UVF) and the UDA after the bomb.

Then, Ms Kennedy went on, Bruton was 'exposed' by the 'unprecedented' postponement of the September 1995 summit. This was extremely pejorative language, but Ms Kennedy neglected to explain just *how* this so-called 'exposure' took place. The government party leaders, Bruton, Spring and De Rossa, met with Sinn Féin a week before the planned September summit, where it appeared to all the government leaders that Sinn Féin accepted the idea of an international body on the arms issue. Then they dramatically opposed it after a meeting with the British shortly before the planned summit. Senior Irish officials were warned in Belfast that the ceasefire would end if the summit and communiqué went ahead. All the key Irish officials felt the summit had to be delayed. Fergus Finlay, who was a member of the Anglo-Irish Liaison Group, wrote a detailed letter to the taoiseach passionately advising cancellation. It is in his book *Snakes and Ladders*. The taoiseach had requested that all the officials write to him on this serious issue. Bruton said:

> In this case we got explicit warnings from the IRA that they would resume violence if we went ahead with the summit. We could be exposed to more serious charges if we'd gone ahead. There's a real question for Sinn Féin, they accepted in November 1995 what they didn't accept in September – under US pressure. The question really arises – US pressure can get them to do things they otherwise won't do?

The most serious 'exposure' here, it appeared to me, were the judgements of Ms Kennedy.

Then she tackled the late-night November London summit, while President Clinton was airborne, already en route to his visit to London and Ireland. Laughably – there is no other appropriate word – she wrote that Bruton 'did not seem to comprehend the British government's position on Washington 3 at that meeting'. This contradicted what she accurately wrote in the *Irish Times* about Bruton at the time:

> He also must be commended for salvaging the peace process with the joint communiqué with John Major launching the twin-track political and decommissioning initiative ... it is now clear the British demand for a symbolic handover of IRA arms as a precondition to all-party talks, the so-called Washington 3 test, can be considered by former Senator George Mitchell's decommissioning body.

It was breathtaking that she binned her contemporaneous praise.

This is what Bruton said at the summit news conference in Downing Street in November 1995:

> Just as the British government has not changed their view on Washington 3, the Irish government hasn't changed its view either. I'm not asking the prime minister, on this occasion, to change his position, nor is he asking me to change mine. What we have agreed upon however is on a process whereby we can move forward. This is a process aimed at solving a problem, overcoming and transcending an impasse.

Bruton's reaction to Kennedy's comments, at the time, was: 'First, it's totally untrue, we publicly disagreed, and said so beforehand. Second, the strategy worked, Washington 3 has been quietly dropped under the brouhaha about the election.'

The International Body's report was called 'advisory', but that was a Major mirage. It was independent, it would hear all sides, and have overwhelming moral standing and authority – these were the correct opinions and predictions that night in Downing Street, with which Ms

Kennedy agreed in December, and then dumped now. The twin-track and the appointment of George Mitchell to chair the International Body on arms were part of an important pillar in the peace process with long-term benefits. They survived Major's bluffing trick in the Commons, and the IRA's murderous wrecking bomb in the London Docklands. It was a significant risk taken by Bruton without the endorsement of Sinn Féin, ultimately working to their advantage leading to the all-party talks which Sinn Féin wanted and eventually joined to agree a peace settlement. But there was no thanks for that.

Senator Mitchell and General de Chastelain were brought into the Irish peace process by Bruton at that November 1995 summit, and continued to provide invaluable service for years to come in the all-party talks and on arms issues. Senator Mitchell went on to chair the all-party talks with great intelligence and skill while the General dealt with the arms issue. President Clinton recognised what he called the 'beauty' of the summit agreement, where the two sides could differ and move the peace process forward.

Finally there was Kennedy's so-called 'catastrophic turn' in Anglo-Irish relations over the publication of the International Body's report. John Bruton was to be blamed for the multiple deceptions by Downing Street as Major concealed his manoeuvring of an election to the status of an alternative precondition, with the arms 'gesture' binned thereafter. Ms Kennedy herself had been given proof of Downing Street deceptions and she wrote the story for the front page of the *Irish Times*. Major also broke a commitment to have the Irish side taken through his Commons speech beforehand. Bruton's response to Kennedy in 1996: 'There's no problem about canvassing the merits of an election, but the formulation was NOT on – as an alternative precondition to talks. I asked for Major's speech in advance, what more could I have done?'

What was 'catastrophic' in my view, were the misjudgements, unfairness and contradiction of Kennedy's own work in this article, and its potential to inflame and justify angry republicans. It was extraordinary that in such an article, there was no reference to the dire British parliamentary context which imposed limitations on John Major and made him dependent on the UUP MPs; and no awareness of the 'balance' of the peace process that Mary Holland had analysed with depth and perception a few weeks before in Ms Kennedy's newspaper. If the gesture of arms were to be dropped to suit nationalists, the unionist proposal of an election would have to be considered.

Before Bruton became taoiseach, the chief under-secretary of the Northern Ireland Office, Sir John Chilcot, gave an early warning in 1994 to Declan O'Donovan, Irish secretary at Maryfield, Belfast, that John Major was 'walking on egg shells, risking a unionist backlash after any concessions to republicans. The prime minister would not be deflected from a determinedly cautious response, even if that were to put our two systems (British and Irish) at loggerheads and cause a rift with the Clinton administration.' This interaction was recorded in the UK State Papers and was later reported in the *Irish Times* in 2021.

John Hume had accused John Major of sacrificing the peace process for votes, and so had Pat Doherty of Sinn Féin. The canker that had taken a grip on nationalist responses to an election as a gateway to all-party talks was unfortunately supercharged by Major elevating it to a precondition. This was seen as giving in to the unionists, with Adams claiming that Major was 'binning' the Mitchell report, as we've seen, dismissed by Mitchell himself. Deaglán de Bréadún says in *The Far Side of Revenge*:

> With hindsight, this looks like an overheated and politically unwise reaction: the view that elections were Major's device for getting off the hook of prior decommissioning seems plausible in retrospect ... Bruton had told Major the previous September that the election idea had potential on the basis that this created a unionist cart onto which you could put nationalist baggage.

Bruton was not mentioned in the statement by the IRA about the end of the ceasefire. They attacked John Major. Bruton is mentioned with Major in another IRA statement in the republican newspaper *An Phoblacht* that resurrected the 'understanding' issue of swift all-party talks after the ceasefire in late August 1994 as a quid pro quo – which was denied by all the key parties involved. The Fianna Fáil leader Bertie

Ahern emphatically rejected this IRA claim in the Dáil – 'There was no secret deal, understanding or quid pro quo agreement between the Irish Government and Sinn Féin in August 1994' before the IRA ceasefire – and urged Bruton to confirm his statement.

Gerry Adams, in an article in the *Irish Times* on 12 February, wrote: 'It was the absence of negotiations and the consequent failure to address and resolve the causes of conflict which made the reoccurrence of conflict inevitable.' Adams also wrote about Bruton's 'flawed' management of the peace process, that he took a 'neutral' position between the British government and republicans and allowed Major to dominate and dictate in negotiations. All these points were seriously wrong; the greatest 'flaw' was that Sinn Féin allowed the republican hardliners to 'dominate and dictate' that the murder of innocents would resume. Bruton was never 'neutral' on the peace process. After Washington in 1995, he tried everything to get Major to drop the arms precondition, but Major would not move because he would have lost office. Far from allowing Major to dominate and dictate, Bruton cancelled a summit, to Major's great annoyance. He wore Major down on the twin-track and got it done with a public disagreement on Washington 3 while Bruton was in Sinn Féin's corner. And despite the Docklands bomb, he got Major to agree to an all-party talks date. He also had one of the most intense and outspoken conflicts that a taoiseach ever had with a British prime minister over the Orange march down Garvaghy Road later in 1996. The facts, not opinions or propaganda, tell the story about Bruton's role in the peace process. Adams and republicans simply ignored the political reality in London. Bruton's outreach to unionists riled many of them. I myself thought it was a bit overdone, and ultimately won nothing from them directly for him, but I do believe it was relevant in the context of Trimble supporting the Belfast Agreement.

Bruton tried everything in his power to bring about inclusive talks. I don't believe any other taoiseach would have succeeded any better with Major at the time, because of the *realpolitik* of the House of Commons. Deaglán de Bréadún records a republican argument that Major's positive actions in the peace process came on the watch of Albert Reynolds, and after him there was no one with the same influence on the Irish government side. But de Bréadún correctly says: 'Doubt must remain, though, over Major's capacity to bring his party and the unionists with him even if Reynolds had remained at the helm in Dublin.' He adds that 'many believed only a British government with a clear majority of 30 seats (some said 50) would feel strong enough to resist unionist anger, and pro-unionist sentiment in the Commons – giving the republican movement the guarantees it was seeking'.

Later we'll see how Bruton, together with Tony Blair, as a prime minister commanding a huge majority, could agree in just two months all that was necessary for a ceasefire and getting Sinn Féin into the talks, after two years of stressful wrangling with Major. All this before Bertie Ahern arrived into the taoiseach's office. Fergus Finlay, more than a year after the government had lost office, and with the independence to speak his mind, said in his memoir:

> Those who have criticised John Bruton's role in the peace process since then seem to me to have forgotten how hard he struggled to hold onto the peace. In so far as things were in his control, there was no stone left unturned, no effort left unmade, to keep the process alive. The failure in the end was not his.

Sinn Féin wore blinkers at that time about the importance of getting unionists to do a deal and were not able to see that the new UUP leader, David Trimble, and his deputy, John Taylor, were publicly demonstrating an interest in playing a role to get to talks, as Mary Holland observed. The years of bloody conflict dulled political sensibility. Bruton was a proud descendant and defender of the pro-Treaty party that founded the state, and an opponent of the physical force tradition in Irish politics. This meant that he was hardly likely to be a poster boy for Sinn Féin or the IRA; they wanted someone more malleable, and the SDLP leaned very much towards Fianna Fáil. In the context of a renewed bombing campaign by the IRA, with lives at stake, it was very important that commentators seeking to influence public opinion about those events should take care to avoid a one-sided blame game. Bruton had his faults, as we all do, but he did not create or detonate the London Docklands bomb and he had worked long and hard, in the difficult political context prevailing in London, to deliver for Sinn Féin.

My notes of the period just after the cabinet meeting of 13 February 1996, at which the taoiseach, tánaiste and Minister for Justice gave a detailed briefing about the Docklands bomb and its consequences, include a record of an opinion poll on 16 February – *after the bomb* – showing that 85 per cent in the Republic and 56 per cent in Northern Ireland wanted all-party talks immediately. My deputy, John Foley, was able to get a preview of the second part of the poll to be published the next day, evaluating the public approval, in Northern Ireland and the Republic, of the main Irish political actors in the peace process. The results were: John Hume 85 per cent (Republic), 72 per cent (North); Dick Spring 78 per cent (Republic), 50 per cent (North); John Bruton 77 per cent (Republic), 50 per cent (North); and Gerry Adams 76 per cent (Republic), 40 per cent (North). The result, not surprisingly, put John Hume clearly in the lead. Just one point separated Bruton and Spring with very strong approval ratings in the Republic, and the same 50 per cent result in the North. Both Bruton and Spring could take great comfort in their results.

A cabinet meeting held on 20 February endorsed the continued pursuit of a fixed date for round-table talks by the taoiseach and the tánaiste. President Clinton called Bruton from Air Force One just five days before the London summit on 28 February 1996 for an update and to see if he could help. In a conversation recorded in the US National Archives and reported by the *Irish Times* in 2019, the taoiseach told him that there needed to be a definite date for all-party talks and that he felt he could convince John Hume and reluctant SDLP members to accept some form of election, 'so long as the transition to talks is absolutely direct and there would be no delay and no further conditions'. Bruton said that a fixed date for the talks was the 'best and only chance' to get the IRA ceasefire restored. Clinton said he'd stay in touch with Adams and help to persuade Hume on the election proposal. Bruton appreciated his support and Clinton ended with this pledge: 'Call me at any time.

I am heartsick about this, but I believe we still have a shot at getting this back on track, so if there is anything I can do, I'll do it.'

Sinn Féin's national chairman, Mitchel McLaughlin, an astute and intelligent Derry figure in the party, said UUP leader David Trimble's election proposal would be given 'very serious consideration' by the party, until he was silenced by Fianna Fáil's Martin Mansergh and John Hume or whomever else; and while Bruton wasn't a pan-nationalist, his door was always open (while there was a ceasefire), as Adams knew. Adams's disposition really was that he and the IRA didn't like Taoiseach Bruton's strong antipathy towards violent paramilitarism. Bruton did not want to be governed solely by the Sinn Féin and IRA agenda, but on the key points of peace process policy, getting the British to drop the decommissioning precondition to talks, and establishing all-party talks as quickly as possible, he was absolutely at one with Adams and the IRA – he pressed Major relentlessly on the issue. His US approach in March 1995 was a once-off miscalculation on arms disposal.

12

SUMMIT SETS TALKS DATE

The Anglo-Irish summit of 28 February 1996, setting the new date for all-party talks, had to take Major's election into account. There are those who think it was the Docklands bomb which moved the governments; but serious analysis of the events as they unfolded, which I've revealed here, shows that idea was nonsense. After Major's election ruse to get off the 'gesture' hook, Bruton had continued to publicly repeat the November communiqué's end of February target for all-party talks; but it soon became clear that Major was determined to push the Northern parties into an election mandate for joining talks, and that meant a delay. On 26 February 1996, a couple of days before the summit, John Major met David Trimble. I noted in my diary, 'There was a stand-up row at No. 10, Trimble went in, there was an almighty row – looking for concessions the PM was not willing to give. Sir Patrick Mayhew accused the UUP of trying to make a clandestine deal with the government over elections.' The row came before a House of Commons vote on a controversial report about sales of British arms to Iraq. Major also met with John Hume, who said positively after the meeting that Major made it very clear that 'his objective is to set a very firm date for all-party negotiations, that's what the two prime ministers are working towards at the moment'. President Clinton had made a very strong statement on the resumption of violence by the IRA a few days before: 'These cowardly acts of terrorism are the work of individuals determined to thwart the will of the people of Northern Ireland.' The response from Sinn Féin's Martin McGuinness on 24 February was that if a guaranteed date for all-party talks was given there would be a major onus on Sinn Féin to give a political analysis to the IRA which would recognise the need for 'an imaginative initiative to be taken' (according to Bew and Gillespie). In fact, no such 'imaginative initiative' was taken by the IRA.

On 28 February the Anglo-Irish summit took place in London, fulfilling the pledge in the November communiqué. The Docklands bombing had delayed the summit by a week. Bruton and Major announced a fixed date for the all-party negotiations to begin on 10 June, allowing time for the election, and the communiqué made it crystal clear that Sinn Féin could take part in the talks if there was a restoration of the ceasefire. There was widespread welcome for the announcement and the details of the communiqué. The *Irish Times* gave the summit extensive coverage. Other media also splashed the story, and the deputy leader of the SDLP, Seamus Mallon, said this was 'the moment of truth for all paramilitary terrorist groupings in Northern Ireland'. The summit text also included the proposal that referendums, North and South, could be held on the same day to endorse an agreement in the all-party talks. The IRA Docklands bombing delivered only death, injury and destruction.

Sir Patrick Mayhew and Tánaiste Dick Spring were to start talks with each of the Northern Ireland qualifying parties, now called 'intensive multilateral consultations', at Stormont the following Monday, 4 March, about the election process and other issues. The main unionist parties, however, would meet only with Mayhew; the process would last just ten days, ending on 13 March. Major had committed to an immediate review of the outcome after that. My belief is that the summit communiqué took Sinn Féin and the IRA by surprise, so soon after the Docklands bomb. But this summit had been promised in the November communiqué with a 'firm aim' of all-party talks at the end of February. Two things made that outcome impossible: the IRA bomb; and Major's definitive switch from the arms instalment to an election as the gateway to talks. The earliest an election could be held was the end of May. Major's manoeuvres were designed to keep his administration going, while the IRA suspected it was a plot by the 'securocrats' – a republican description of a mix of hostile British intelligence officers, UK officials and politicians in the British government who wanted to break the IRA. During one phone conversation in November 1995, with Bruton pressing him to drop the arms precondition, Major said he would be 'eaten alive in the Commons' if he did this. Parliament was the real problem.

John Hume in his response carefully outlined the gains of the summit. The British and Irish governments had 'solemnly agreed' that an elective process would lead to all-party talks, he said, 'without preconditions' on 10 June, and Sinn Féin would be involved in those talks if the IRA restored its ceasefire. The communiqué also had strong support from the Clinton administration. Denis Coughlan, chief political correspondent of the *Irish Times*, gave this assessment: 'Now that the two governments have fixed a date for all-party negotiations and swept aside all decommissioning preconditions, Sinn Féin stands exposed as the arbiter of peace or violence. If the IRA continues with its campaign then blame for the bombing cannot be laid at Britain's door.' Gerry Adams welcomed the communiqué, but once again he was seeking 'clarifications'. Both Adams and McGuinness were critical of the fact that Sinn Féin was being treated differently to the other parties, without ministerial meetings, in the 'intensive multilateral consultations' which would discuss the election and talks. Sinn Féin could talk only to officials because the ceasefire had ended.

In one of history's unfortunate coincidences, it appeared that John Hume and Gerry Adams met with representatives of the IRA the same day as the London summit, a clash of events that was to cause deep confusion about the IRA reaction to the communiqué, and remarks being made that would not have been made if this coincidence had been avoided. The IRA issued a statement the next day confirming the Hume–Adams meeting with representatives of the Army Council and reiterated their 9 February position 'stressing that a resolution of the conflict in our country demands justice and an inclusive negotiated settlement without preconditions'. They accused the British government of being responsible for the failure 'thus far' of the Irish peace process without 'inclusive negotiations free from preconditions', and an abuse of the peace process over the last 18 months. They also criticised 'an absence of an effective and democratic approach capable of providing an irrevocable momentum' to just and lasting peace in Ireland. However, the statement ended with: 'We repeat that we are prepared to face up to our responsibilities. Others need to do likewise.'

The media and the governments thought this was the IRA's response to the summit outcome. Some took heart from that latter statement, seeing it as a hopeful sign of a renewal of the ceasefire. Tánaiste Dick Spring responded, saying the two governments had faced up to their responsibilities by setting the date for all-party talks. Adams is quoted in the *Irish Times*, not very prominently – down near the end of an inside page – as saying the IRA claimed at the meeting that Bruton spent three months on the decommissioning issue, which was untrue, repeating the inaccuracy in Geraldine Kennedy's *Irish Times* article just over a week before, a sign of its negative impact. David Trimble said that if the ceasefire was restored, he would talk to Sinn Féin about the International Body's principles for those taking part in political talks and what they said about decommissioning. It's worth recalling the exact words of the communiqué: 'The Prime Minister and the taoiseach agreed that an elective process would have to be broadly acceptable and lead immediately and without further preconditions to the convening of all-party negotiations with a comprehensive agenda.' The communiqué ended with the two governments calling on Sinn Féin and the IRA to make possible Sinn Féin's participation in the process of such negotiations.

Deaglán de Bréadún, in *The Far Side of Revenge*, deals with the attitude of the republicans after the Docklands bombing: 'All along the republican side was eager and even anxious to restore the ceasefire: Canary Wharf was meant to be part of a short, sustained campaign which would come to an end quickly when Major invited Sinn Féin into talks. The invitation never came, and the delay was causing concern on the Republican side.' In fact, the February summit communiqué was both Major and Bruton's clear invitation to the all-party talks 'with no preconditions' if the ceasefire was restored, and that was repeated publicly many times. If the republicans were 'eager and even anxious to restore the ceasefire', the IRA would have given a positive response to this summit communiqué, because the door to the all-party talks was thrown wide open to Sinn Féin by both governments if the cessation was restored. The real reason why the IRA didn't renew the ceasefire was more likely to have been that another bomb in Britain was already being planned.

Republicans speaking to de Bréadún said they felt they had missed a significant opportunity by being absent from the talks when ground rules were being agreed because these turned out to be very important when terms for agreement were being worked out. To see who was to blame for that, all they had to do was look in a mirror. John Major was so disappointed with the IRA statement that he called it 'pathetic' and a 'sick joke', thinking, like all of us, that this statement was their response to the communiqué, but in fact they were locked in a room secretly with Hume and Adams; they hadn't read it, or seen any of it. The timing of the Hume–Adams meeting with the IRA on the same day as the London summit was a grave mistake. (Another source claims it had been held a week earlier.) It was followed by a strange event. Gerry Adams had a meeting with officials, and their report of the meeting was astounding. I copied it into my 1996 daybook:

> Adams made it clear in our meeting tonight that the IRA statement was solely a response to the meeting with John Hume and Adams himself. It specifically did not take account of Wednesday's Communiqué. Adams will clarify this publicly tomorrow.
>
> Adams asked that we ask the British to confirm that the restoration of the 1994 ceasefire will mean that Sinn Féin can participate in both (party) consultations and All-Party negotiations. There was comment to the contrary from Sir Patrick Mayhew, Adams claimed. Adams did not ask for a Ministerial meeting.
>
> Adams did raise the Paddy Kelly case, who is terminally ill. Adams said a humanitarian gesture of transfer to Portlaoise would be a confidence-building measure. (The taoiseach made this request to John Major in a telephone call and he was to look into it.)
>
> Adams said 'I would recommend that in any comment tomorrow – you say something on the lines of "I understand

that it is now becoming clear that yesterday's IRA statement did not take account of Wednesday's Communiqué. That is unfortunate and understandably frustrating. While recognising that legitimate frustration, the Irish government will persevere in working for the outcome all of us seeking peace wish to see – the restoration of the 1994 ceasefire and fully inclusive All-Party negotiations on the 10th of June."

'You might also say to PM Major that his "sick joke" and "pathetic response" public references have in the circumstances not been helpful to achieving the restoration.' On the US front Tony Lake (National Security Council Chief) has spoken to Adams and is 'on the optimistic side'. Adams said 'Clearly you should not be publicly optimistic. But my own judgement is that a restoration of the ceasefire at mid/end next week remains credible.'

The official summary after that closing remark was: 'Our judgement having spoken to Adams.' I noted in my daybook that the 'Hume–Adams/IRA meeting took place on the morning [of the Downing Street summit] – same story from Hume. There were 10 people H+A+8 including note-taker. IRA did not have the communiqué at the meeting with H/Adams.'

So the reception of this historic communiqué, meeting the demands of Sinn Féin and the IRA, was blighted by the accidental coincidence of a Hume–Adams meeting with the IRA, and the latter publishing a statement, without any knowledge of the communiqué. Then things were said – also without knowledge – which queered the pitch and created bad feeling. I felt very sad about this. The meeting between Hume and Adams with the IRA – in the Republic, I believe – was secret, so the governments were not aware of it. And the negotiations on the communiqué were not totally completed, including setting the date, until the Downing Street meeting took place, hence there were no leaks. The result ultimately was a missed opportunity. However, Sinn Féin and the IRA now had the full details from the widespread coverage of the summit and Sinn Féin had a copy of the communiqué, so the opportunity did not need to be missed. Whatever about Adams's viewpoint as seen in the above account of his meeting, it did not prove to be accurate, but it demonstrated that Adams was quite positive about the contents of the communiqué. Clearly Adams saw the opportunity and wanted to exploit it, but the vigorously stirred animosities, and Major's harsh words in the confusion caused by the IRA statement, triumphed over Adams's optimism and the peace process.

Some insights can be gained from the summit discussions of the teams in Downing Street. The principals on the British side were John Major, Sir Patrick Mayhew, Sir John Chilcot, chief under-secretary at the Northern Ireland Office, and ministers of state Michael Ancram and Sir John Wheeler; and on the Irish side, Taoiseach John Bruton, Tánaiste Dick Spring and the Minister for Justice, Nora Owen. The date was decided in the discussion. These are my cryptic notes on the meeting held in the Downing Street cabinet room:

> Major said he will 'take some flak' about making decisions on the electoral process. Fixing the date for all-party talks had to take into account legislative drafting difficulties, there are constitutional and legislative novelties if the election is on a list system (with ballots cast for parties not individuals). It needs more time. The list could be very long administratively, it could be open to legal challenge which could throw the date – there is a need for precision. Time is needed for postal vote applications regardless of the system. So he said the best they could do is June 14th. There was a Parliamentary recess to mid-April, then coming back from mid-June would be giving Parliament no more than two weeks for delays etc. There is the possibility of a judicial review.
>
> The Tánaiste Dick Spring said, 'if the governments agree, the British Labour Party would be very supportive' (in terms of the legislative progress).
>
> The Taoiseach John Bruton, who wanted the earliest date possible, suggested Wednesday 29 May or Thursday 30 May. Then he adjusted with election day on Wednesday May 22; all-party talks on Friday 31 May. Bruton made it explicit: 'Doors open, everyone walks in.'

Mayhew commented 'Depends on maximum good will – the days could be counted on the fingers of a badly mutilated hand.' [He was referring to potential walkouts.]

The taoiseach then countered: 'Better to accept a June date rather than having escape routes.'

Tánaiste Spring suggested 7 June, 'before the marching season …'

Bruton summed up: If the election day was Thursday 30 May, then we 'credibly start negotiations on Monday June 10th.'

The Prime Minister ending the discussion on that date, and said to officials we better 'check the diary, not to clash with some ghastly anniversary of a battle etc.'

Bruton then raised the Mitchell Principles of non-violence, and how they are dealt with in the negotiations. He was 'anxious that it didn't form a basis for aborting negotiations. Meaningful negotiations are important – there's no excuse for people to use Mitchell to prevent meaningful negotiations.'

John Major responded saying 'the constitutional parties have no arms for decommissioning – all the constitutional parties have an interest. It's one of the disadvantages of going ahead without the Building Blocks, and a 4th Strand.'

The 'Building Blocks' was a British document sent to all the parties, and US and Irish governments, the previous November. The fourth strand would be about decommissioning. The British wanted discussions with all the parties in the proposed bilateral meetings to achieve a 'shared understanding' on these issues. There had been talks with parties after the November summit, continuing into the New Year until the Docklands bombing, but no building blocks of a 'shared understanding' were achieved, principally with the unionist parties and Sinn Féin, on a decommissioning 4th strand. This summit announced another series of multilateral talks with all the parties in the period up to the election, on the 'Building Blocks' and issues the parties might raise.

Major continued: He was 'not sure how to determine (this issue of a decommissioning blockage) until the building blocks discussion has finished. We can't chain them to their seats.'

Mayhew interjected, 'This is a 'tender issue for unionists …'

Major said: 'There is a problem if there's no clarity about commitments on decommissioning.'

Bruton responded quoting the Mitchell Report suggestion: 'There is a principle of dealing with this matter in parallel. Could we agree to a mechanism that this matter will be progressed in parallel with negotiations, so that it's not a rocket launcher question interfering with other matters?'

Major: 'I'm not sure we can give that this morning.' He cited the discussions to take place on the Building Blocks paper. 'If we push too far it could raise such concerns …'

The Taoiseach took another tack asking for an 'understanding on best endeavours'.

Major: 'I don't know how that contingency will arise. I hope you take our good faith …'

Bruton: 'Truth is a matter not dealt with in the Building Blocks paper.'

Major: 'Don't nail something down until you can commit yourself to it.'

Mayhew interjected saying confidence was needed.

Major: 'We got into a dispute about private deals on the Scott report [on the sale of arms to Iraq] – there weren't any. If there's a Parliamentary Question about a private deal with the Irish government, I cannot lie to the House of Commons.'

Tánaiste Spring said there will be people using decommissioning to block the talks.

Major: 'We are going to have to deal with it at the beginning of the talks. You can take a donkey to water, but you can't make it drink. We're going to have to suck it and see.'

Bruton: 'We should understand one another's minds. I accept you want to listen to the parties to test the degree of resistance.

The problem is going to arise in one shape or another, we need to understand your mind, not an agreement you can't expose. There have been misunderstandings and exaggerations. We're anxious to see how you think, how you see yourselves overcoming the problem of the injection of a category of a (political) weapon that disrupts the proceedings. How can chairs deal with it? We need to know your mind – not compromising you – what's in your heart?'

Major: 'We don't want blockages. How do you think we should deal with it if one of the parties says they're not going to decommission at all? Or demands for complete decommissioning, or to no decommissioning until the final settlement? We take the view that we don't want blockage – we'll try and persuade those we have influence with not to create it.'

The date was fixed and at least we had Major's mind on any attempts to disrupt or block the negotiations. They did not want blockages, and *effectively* there was another strand to the talks for decommissioning. Mayhew said we could 'refer it to the fourth strand', so that the issue could not be used to block progress on the other strands. There was a sense of achievement in the cabinet room when the agenda was finished, and a friendly atmosphere, calm in the circumstances, given the stormy exchanges since the previous September. But nobody was in a mood to open the champagne. Major and the taoiseach went off to lunch with their ministers, while we lesser mortals went upstairs in the prime minister's house to another room, where we were treated to beef Wellington, washed down with a French claret. The mood was relaxed and relieved. That wouldn't last long.

The following year, at a press conference in Belfast, Martin McGuinness criticised Bruton, claiming that the Framework Documents 'had not been advocated or pushed forward by the two governments since its publication two years before', as recorded in *The Far Side of Revenge*. This was jaw-dropping ignorance, totally untrue, and McGuinness would have known that if he had read the summit communiqué where Bruton succeeded in having this article agreed with the British:

> The taoiseach and the prime minister reaffirmed their commitment to work for a lasting peace and a comprehensive settlement on the basis of the fundamental principles shared by their two governments and set out in the Downing Street Declaration and in the Joint Framework Documents.

Bruton brought the Frameworks up with President Clinton at the 'Peacemakers Summit' in Sinai, Egypt, two weeks later, and he quoted the Framework Documents twice in his opening speech at the all-party talks. In September 1996, when he went to the US to address a joint session of the Senate in the Capitol, Bruton seized every opportunity to emphasise the importance of the Joint Framework Documents. How could Sinn Féin's chief negotiator make such a sweepingly false statement? It was revealing and damning evidence of a preference to nurse prejudices rather than seek the facts; there's none so blind as those who will not see.

The republicans didn't like Bruton because he wasn't enamoured of Sinn Féin or the IRA. But that did not stop him working hard to deliver for them in the interests of the peace process in which he believed deeply, despite his detestation of those who use violence in politics. Deaglán de Bréadún captures another aspect of this poisonous political atmosphere: 'There was a cynical element in Fianna Fáil which wanted the IRA to hold back the ceasefire until after the general election in the Republic,' due the following year. Bruton also told me he knew that that was happening. The deadly cynicism of this attitude was sickening, and it appeared the IRA went along with the approach the 'Fianna Fáil element' wanted – of which the IRA was no doubt aware. It is hard to avoid a conclusion that the IRA was, among other objectives, using its campaign of bombs and murder to influence the 1997 election in the Republic.

Back in Dublin, we were trying to unscramble the misunderstandings created by the Hume–Adams meeting with the IRA, and the subsequent IRA statement, taken by the media as well as politicians as the answer to the summit communiqué. Adams had told officials he would clarify the following day, but if he did so it made little impression without a further statement from the IRA. Was it the umbrage they took at Major's 'sick joke' and 'pathetic' remarks? These sharp comments merited a pass – surely they were understandable in the circumstances. Everyone knew when the summit of the two governments was taking place, so why on earth was the Hume–Adams meeting with the IRA scheduled on the same day, and why issue a press release that was obviously going to cause confusion? It appears that IRA policy thereafter was at least in part decided negatively, because Major did not know the IRA statement was *not* a response to the communiqué. There's something pathetic in the real sense of the word about that – it was in fact pure pathos.

Geraldine Kennedy pulled back a bit from her attack on Bruton just eleven days before, now writing in the *Irish Times* on the summit outcome:

> The Taoiseach John Bruton can be satisfied that he has fulfilled his government's obligation to consolidate the peace process after Wednesday's Summit in Downing Street. In the joint communiqué he has presented the Sinn Féin leadership with a stark choice: to get on the democratic bus leading to all-party negotiations with a restoration [of the ceasefire] or to remain with the IRA in the trenches.

She said it was the 'best joint communiqué since he assumed office', adding that it was 'precise and unambiguous'. The mood in the cabinet room 'was reminiscent of the Downing Street Declaration'. The two governments had met all Sinn Féin's demands for advancing the peace process and reinstating the ceasefire, she wrote, with an agreed 'broadly acceptable' elective process that would 'lead immediately and without further preconditions to the convening of all-party negotiations with a comprehensive agenda'. Unfortunately, her thrashing of Bruton just days before didn't help republicans to grasp or respect what had been achieved.

It wasn't only the entire constitutional republican and nationalist community, and their political leaders, who were sickened by the IRA's decision to return to violence. There were also a number of critical voices in *An Phoblacht*, chief among them the 44-year-old IRA man

Joe O'Connell, a member of the London Balcombe Street IRA active service unit, arrested after a week-long siege in 1975. He had already served more than 21 years in jail, out of a sentence of at least 30 years. He wrote:

> For the IRA to order a resumption of war until it is promised a date for all-party negotiations – something which is achievable under the now binned peace process anyway – must surely go down as the most stupid, blinkered and ill-conceived decision ever made by a revolutionary body anywhere ever before in history.

Reported in the *Irish Times* on 1 March 1996, the Clare man said he was 'saddened and disappointed' by the IRA decision and did not believe 'returning to the armed struggle can be justified in any way in the light of the past 18 months of peace'. That was his message for the IRA, but he had another message for the British government. In O'Connell's speech from the dock in his 1977 trial he said this: 'We have instructed our lawyers to draw the attention of the court to the fact that four totally innocent people – Carole Richardson, Gerry Conlon, Paul Hill and Paddy Armstrong – are serving massive sentences for three bombings, two in Guildford and one in Woolwich, which three of us and another man now imprisoned, have admitted that we did.' In yet another chilling revelation about British justice, the innocent Guildford Four spent a further 12 years in jail until their release in 1989, with all charges against them dismissed. O'Connell's forthright and brave words were ignored by both the IRA Army Council and the British government.

13

CLINTON'S MIDDLE EAST PEACE SUMMIT

European duties called immediately after the London summit. Ireland was taking over the EU presidency in July, so the taoiseach had to leave hastily for Bangkok to attend the Asia–Europe Meeting, ASEM, on the first two days of March. It was a quick turnaround from London, pack fresh clothes and get to Baldonnel for this long round-trip journey with an overnight stop in Dubai. Just over a week after our return to Dublin, we were in the Middle East, on Egypt's Sinai Peninsula. President Bill Clinton had called the 'Summit of the Peacemakers' at short notice after the latest suicide bombing in Israel; there had been a series of these bloody attacks on ordinary people, leaving many dead and injured. The summit was co-chaired by the Egyptian President Hosni Mubarak at the fine resort town of Sharm El-Sheikh at the end of the peninsula on the coast of the Red Sea. Ireland was invited because we were part of the EU presidency troika. On the margins we got our latest opportunity to meet with Clinton, as well as Vice-President Al Gore, Secretary of State Warren Christopher and National Security Advisor Tony Lake, to review the crisis in the Irish peace process, and discuss the achievement of a fixed date for inclusive all-party negotiations.

The summit was held on Wednesday 13 March 1996 on the campus of a vast lodge hotel, with high-quality mini-villas dotted over the substantial grounds, beautifully laid out with flowers and shrubs circled by pathways from the villas to the main buildings. An indelible memory is the huge German Chancellor Helmut Kohl squeezed into a golf buggy being driven from his villa on the winding pathway around the flowers and shrubbery to the conference centre. Many key world leaders joined those of the Middle East countries (apart from Syria and Lebanon), including Palestinian leader Yasser Arafat and Shimon Peres, the prime minister of Israel, who were both heavily involved in peace negotiations.

President Mubarak opened the conference of kings, sheikhs, presidents and prime ministers by saying the enemies of peace must be stopped in their efforts 'to abort our peace process'; while the Palestinian Assembly President Yasser Arafat, wearing his signature black and white keffiyeh, said that the 'dream of freedom and independence can never prosper in the middle of a sea of blood and tears'. While he asserted that Palestinians would support the uprooting of violent extremist factions, he wanted Israel to end the policy of closing off the West Bank and Gaza so his people would not be 'collectively punished', prevented from reaching jobs across the border, which created a 'hotbed for extremism and violence'. Shimon Peres demanded strong action from the Palestinians, emotionally recalling the children murdered in the series of bombings that had killed 62 people in just nine days: 'Terrorism knows no borders, so borders must not restrain action to smash the terrorist snake.' Boris Yeltsin, president of Russia, similarly condemned the bombings, saying that 'terrorism is terrorism anywhere and the struggle against it should be universal'. Clinton praised the character and strength of the leaders, who had gathered at short notice, saying it was proof that the region had changed for good. 'Peace will prevail,' he said. This optimism was genuine, but in the Middle East violence has endured and grown.

Representatives of the 27 countries and two multi-state institutions (the United Nations and the European Union) attended the summit, an extraordinary success. After the primary addresses by Presidents Clinton, Mubarak and Yeltsin and the principals of the Middle East peace process, Shimon Peres and Yasser Arafat, the summit heard from speakers from Jordan, Morocco, Turkey, France, the UN, Bahrain, Italy, Norway, Germany, Spain, the United Kingdom, Ireland, Mauritania, Canada, Saudi Arabia, Kuwait, Yemen, Qatar, Oman, the United Arab Emirates, Tunisia, Algeria, Japan and the EU.

The concluding statement of the peacemakers' summit could have applied equally to the peace process in the North. It was read out by President Mubarak, who said the peacemakers:

> Express their full support for the Middle East peace process and their determination that this process continue in order to accomplish a just, lasting and comprehensive peace in the region.
>
> Affirm their determination to promote security and stability and to prevent the enemies of peace from achieving their ultimate objective of destroying the real opportunity for peace in the Middle East.
>
> Re-emphasise their strong condemnation of all acts of terror in all its abhorrent forms, whatever its motivation and whoever its perpetrator, including recent terrorist attacks in Israel; they consider them alien to the moral and spiritual values shared by all the peoples of the region and reaffirm their intention to stand staunchly against all such acts and to urge all governments to join them in this condemnation and opposition.

The following is my record of the conversations I had mainly with senior American figures during the conference, but I'll begin with my attempt to press a British official about the case of the terminally ill IRA man Paddy Kelly imprisoned in Britain. Bruton had already asked Major to transfer Kelly to Ireland on humanitarian grounds so he could be closer to his family. These are my diary notes:

> I spoke to Jonathan Haslam [John Major's new press secretary] inside the Orangerie Conference Centre. Well into our discussion about the transfer of Paddy Kelly, the US Secretary of State, Warren Christopher, came to join us. Haslam said they were

going to separate the humanitarian issue from the transfer issue [in the Paddy Kelly case]. This was being looked at he said – but the Prime Minister already had problems with backbenchers on Northern Ireland [over the summit communiqué]. He cited David Wilshire, a right-wing MP [who would go on to oppose the Belfast Agreement, and who was already infamous for a 1988 clause in a local government act that was considered homophobic. Britain did not get rid of it until 2003 under a Labour government]. He said the prime minister had done a lot, gone a long way. I said that was recognised, but this transfer of a man seriously ill, probably dying, would involve little risk for a possible substantial gain [in good will]. He said they had to be careful in a situation where bombs were being planted in London. So the discussion was inconclusive when Warren Christopher joined us. He enquired of Haslam how the elective process was going, and got a non-committal vague answer about the timetable of the multilateral consultative process [with the Northern parties] which was finished that week, and a decision awaited. I returned to the Paddy Kelly issue for Warren Christopher's benefit. I said this transfer could send the right signals. Haslam once again demurred. Christopher, who was standing in a narrow pathway with people constantly asking him to move, finally said he seemed to be 'standing in a thoroughfare' and took his leave of us as the opening event was approaching. Haslam and I went to sit in Ireland/EU seats while the proceedings began.

Later I met Warren Christopher again at the post conference press conference. Since Haslam had told him nothing, I said that my understanding about the elective process was a decision would be made the following Monday and the prime minister would speak in the House of Commons on Tuesday. He said he knew it was arising about now – then he spotted Tony Lake nearby and went to say something to him, then Lake came to speak with me. I had been joined by Simon Hare [an official in the taoiseach's office]. Lake said he would be speaking to Trimble,

Hume and Paisley, if Paisley came to Washington, on Friday 15th of March. [They were invited as part of the St Patrick's Day celebrations at the White House, which of course we would be attending as well, travelling to the US immediately after the peacemakers' summit was over.] Tony Lake said Adams would be seeking a meeting, but he thought he should just call him – what was my view? [Lake was at ministerial rank or higher in the administration as National Security chief; after the Docklands bombing, access was only to Irish officials.]

I said he should call him – not meet. Lake said he would be pressing him to accept that the date for talks was now fixed – something we had been seeking for nearly two years. He had to do the business with the IRA and not be excluded. He was sure Adams really wanted to be in and this was the time. He said he understood the talks would go ahead anyway. I indicated that I shared that view. He said he was puzzled by their reaction [to the summit agreement of a date for all-party talks without preconditions]. I replied that there was an element of shifting the goalposts – they had demanded a fixed date without preconditions – now the date was fixed unconditionally and they claimed the preconditions were at the outset of the talks, on the Mitchell report and decommissioning. I told him that the Taoiseach had spoken to President Clinton about the possibility of getting Senator Mitchell to reassure or guarantee that decommissioning would not halt the talks at the start. Lake said that it was hard to see how a guarantee could be provided – he thought the word 'address' was very good – we would have to see how the issue could be 'parked'. I said our suggestion was a sub-committee to deal with the issue [the fourth strand raised during the London summit negotiations].

I mentioned to him that I thought Gerry Adams would find the US a different place from last St Patrick's week. He agreed and indicated that this would send its own message. He asked me how Sen. Mitchell was perceived by Sinn Féin now? I told him

I had not heard anything negative, though I knew the British were reluctant to see him in any role which could 'internationalise' the problem. I also told him about the Combined Loyalist Military Command [CLMC] statement threatening 'blow for blow' and he was surprised – he'd not heard it. His last contact with McMichael and Ervine [leaders of the UDP and the Progressive Unionist Party (PUP), political parties linked to the UDA and UVF paramilitary organisations] reassured him that the loyalist ceasefire was holding. I said the statement had come in the wake of the IRA admission of responsibility for a London litter bin bomb [the latest of several smaller explosive incidences in London after the Docklands bomb, one of which killed its carrier on a bus, also injuring six people]. He asked me if we feared that the South would be a target. I said that was the expectation – 'proxy' attacks in London and Dublin, but the tit for tat could go nowhere.

I said he should stress to Gerry Adams that the fixed date was vital – the talks would start – there could be many 'alarums and excursions' but the two governments would be there to hold it together. Gerry Adams should be there, and not miss the historic opportunity. Like in South Africa where the talks were held together by de Klerk and Mandela with many walkouts.

I asked him why Sen. Mitchell left politics, since he was so good at it. He said he wasn't sure, and thought he had felt it 'heavy', he had a young wife and wanted to spend more time working on that. He said Sen. Mitchell was a baseball fanatic, he thought that it was because he wanted to be Baseball Commissioner, and he was perplexed to find that that was not the case. I mentioned that it might be useful in the near future for the Senator to return to explain why the Six Principles [of non-violence and totally accepting democratic methods in his report] were so important for all involved in the talks. He thought it an interesting idea, but queried whether this might cause a problem with Sinn Féin because of his suggestion of parallel decommissioning.

Lake said he would be telling them he didn't care what kind of elective process – just do it. He said he didn't understand the problem about the election. He found their own [US] system difficult enough. I quoted John Chilcot at the Summit saying that 'if it was a list of candidates, the ballot paper would stretch from one end of the cabinet room to the other!' However, I agreed with him on the election. Lake said he might say to Gerry Adams – did he want to be the Syria of the peace process? Syria was absent from the Sharm El-Sheik Summit.

He asked me what role did we see for the US after the negotiations started? I said continue to show goodwill and encourage everybody to stay in the talks (including Sinn Féin with a restored ceasefire). Tony Lake agreed and commented that this would mean he'd be clocking up further phone bills! He said if Adams was excluded it would be a 'nasty' exclusion but it would be their own fault. He offered some technical equipment for attacks (re the CLMC threat) that they'd also offered to the Israelis. I thanked him and said it would be passed into the system, but we hoped it wouldn't be necessary, and that concluded our conversation, saying we'd probably meet again in Washington.

The Summit of the Peacemakers was an extraordinary event. At coffee breaks or at lunch outside the conference centre the leaders would gather informally around tables. I saw Clinton chatting with Jacques Chirac over a meal, John Major, Helmut Kohl, Al Gore and others all sipping tea or coffee in a very relaxed manner with other prime ministers and heads of state. I wondered how many other issues they could resolve there and then. From my own experience covering the Middle East in Israel, Egypt and Syria, it would be worth working a little on something else, because whatever about Ireland, it appeared to me that the Middle East was very nearly insoluble, and indeed the peace process in the Middle East did later fail, despite the efforts of Clinton, Rabin, who was assassinated, Peres and Arafat.

We managed to get time with President Clinton after the main Middle East peace process event was over for a meeting in some depth about the Irish peace process. The meeting went well. He was as supportive as he could be about the restoration of the IRA ceasefire and the need for the all-party talks not to get bogged down at the start over decommissioning. The following are my notes:

> The Taoiseach thanked the President for Senator Mitchell's work and the support of Democrats standing against violence. 'Restoring the ceasefire is essential, Gerry Adams and others are working for that. Having achieved a date for all-party talks, perhaps some don't know how important that is.'
>
> He explained how the Mitchell report's six principles of non-violent politics for those who take part in the talks, and the suggestion of decommissioning during the talks might be abused by unionists to prevent the talks proceeding to other matters. 'There must be confidence given to the parties that other issues are dealt with as well,' he said. 'It may be helpful for some American involvement as an external guarantor of the integrity of the process, to say "hold on!" to parties, don't allow a bog-down on this item ... external reassurance not to have a logjam.' He told the President he had not broached this idea with John Major. It could help to 'bring over that crucial segment of the republican movement'.
>
> He also explained that to get to the 10th of June talks, the parties have to agree an electoral system; he was worried that the British may make a call on this issue that John Hume doesn't like and establish a Forum that he doesn't want. 'It's important that the British make a call on this issue which allows John Hume to come into this process.'
>
> President Clinton asked if John Hume would accept a Forum with no role?
>
> The Taoiseach replied that he might, but at this stage he didn't know. He was worried that the 'most important' election

proposals brought to the House of Commons could be amended to move further in the unionist direction. 'I would prefer no Forum at all, ideally no election, but it'll do something to bring the unionists in'.

Seán Ó hUiginn, Second Secretary in the Department of Foreign Affairs, said: 'A Forum with *any* administrative role is off the screen for nationalists.'

President Clinton asked, on the decommissioning issue, if we didn't want the British to take the position that they want a resolution at the start? But simultaneously ...

The Taoiseach said yes, perhaps in the 'Fourth Strand' idea, decommissioning discussions in that track.

The President said: 'I'm convinced one of the things in the Middle East peace process that is "explosive" is the issue of Jerusalem, it's being kicked to the end – and it could take on a life of its own. There's a problem with talking about it, then leaving it aside ... you have to have that 4th track.'

The taoiseach said the fundamental aim was a system for the talks which will preserve the unionists on board, but takes account of the Nationalist position. He said he discerns some movement in the unionist attitude.

He then raised the issue of the terminally ill IRA prisoner Paddy Kelly in jail in Britain, and his efforts to get the British to transfer him to Ireland on humanitarian grounds. 'It would have a disproportionate effect, a move on Kelly would be great. A funeral [in Britain] would do a lot of damage for the restoration of the ceasefire.'

In response to the National Security chief Tony Lake raising the issue of the future of Northern Ireland, the Taoiseach first returned to the all-party talks to say forcefully: 'The Irish government will not allow the talks to be bogged down because of decommissioning.' The talks will have to address that question of the Framework document on the future governance of the North – and he pointed out that the (main) Joint Framework Document which he and John Major launched in Belfast the previous year, with the proposed North–South institutional bodies and structures for East–West relations between London and Dublin, 'the end point of the talks is already sketched out'. And as it happened with the Belfast Agreement, he was right.

The Unionists, he said, wanted JFD [Joint Framework Documents] minus, and the Nationalists wanted JFD plus. 'The differences are not going to be big.'

The President then asked: 'Do you believe, if those differences are resolved – can they resolve the decommissioning issue?'

The Taoiseach said: 'If Sinn Féin are satisfied with the agreement, then decommissioning doesn't matter.'

The President: 'Will Sinn Féin address decommissioning as the talks go on?'

Bruton's equivocal view was they'll 'possibly address it' (his tone was the same as above, 'it doesn't matter' if the parties can reach a political agreement). He went on to say that the President's interest was 'crucial' in restoring the ceasefire, and to stress that the only qualification for any party to the all-party talks was not to support a campaign of violence. Full Sinn Féin participation required an IRA ceasefire. 'Sinn Féin is unique and deserved a part in the negotiations on the 10th of June. I want to say that the Irish government will not allow any one item to prevent progress on other issues. The goal is truly ambitious, a comprehensive settlement, not an internal settlement, but the North–South bodies, East–West arrangements, justice and fairness in Northern Ireland, a system of government with both communities' allegiance, no one community to be dominant, a system where both communities feel equal – that deserves to happen in this generation.' He referred to the Dark Ages when 'Ireland preserved civilisation'. We have a capacity to do something which [will] affect the whole world. If we have imagination, spirit and confidence for the talks on the 10th of June – Ireland will be contributing a model which will be a beacon to the world.'

President Clinton referred to the 'one quarter roots' he had in Ireland, and he was thankful for Ireland's willingness to stand for peace, not only in Ireland. The London Summit Communiqué was a 'milestone achievement, the 10th of June date for all-party talks – that's what we've been working for. The ceasefire must be restored, that's the way the talks can be inclusive, otherwise talks can't go forward. We can't allow anyone to hijack the future of peace in Northern Ireland. I'll do anything I can to support the peace process.'

He said he'd had a good meeting with the prime minister John Major, and they were 'together' on the way forward. And he thanked the Irish leadership for taking on the demanding issues. Referring to the Taoiseach's suggestion of a role for the US on the 'integrity' of the talks, and 'external reassurance not to have a logjam', the President said: 'I'm not sure how we could guarantee things. Senator Mitchell is still on the case – and we'll do whatever we can. My own view is, if we can start all-party talks with a restoration of the ceasefire, the chances of a successful outcome are pretty good. The gaps are not too difficult to bridge,' though he acknowledged it would be overcoming enormous ancient distrust and emotional states that are the 'baggage of the past'. The Taoiseach had a meeting with Major on the margins as well, where the main topic was the multilateral talks with the Northern parties which were ending. There was no consensus among the parties about the elections, and the British Government would be deciding on the process four days later as agreed at the Summit and addressing the House of Commons the next day.

The President gave advice – you don't have to trust – 'take these things as they come ... show up at the start, go to work' – and republicans can finally reach agreement with unionists 'in good faith'. The United States placed good faith in the ultimate outcome of the peace process, he said. He had confidence about the outcome: 'What's happened in the past hasn't worked. People prefer peace ... how to assure everybody is treated with dignity and fairly, these issues can be resolved, with a leap of faith it can happen. It's in no one's interest to keep a foot on the brake.'

On Sinn Féin he said, the US had worked hard 'at the appropriate level' (on the restoration of the ceasefire) and that included with Gerry Adams. The appropriate level meant through officials.

When the summit was over, we made a fast exit to get on the G4 at Sharm El-Sheikh airport because the intention was to travel to Ireland first for a brief overnight and then immediately go on to Washington for the annual St Patrick's Day celebrations. I canvassed a little to just go straight to the US from Sharm El-Sheikh, which would have saved us some time, but others wanted to get home at least briefly, or to stay if they were not in the group going to the US. Our early arrival at the airport did us no good. We were left sitting on the tarmac in the plane for many hours, and eventually were literally the last plane to leave. The taoiseach and all the team were fuming and a strong diplomatic complaint was made, but that didn't do us much good. This put all our plans out of kilter, particularly for the taoiseach, who had practically no sleep at all, getting home to Dunboyne from Baldonnel and back after just a few hours for the flight to Washington – a lack of sleep for which he was to pay.

After the long flight we landed in Washington, and had to be raced straight to the hotel where Bruton was scheduled to speak to a packed event for the American Ireland Fund, before the Speaker's lunch and the bowl of shamrock for Clinton. It was a glittering affair, with the great and the good of Irish Americans and key Washington figures in attendance. Bruton was at the top table with First Lady Hillary Clinton, Northern Irish Office junior minister Baroness Denton, John Hume, David Trimble and others. Bruton was thoroughly exhausted, he hadn't been able to sleep on the plane, and should have stuck strictly to reading his script, supplied by the Irish embassy, which I advised him to do. But, as was his habit, he improvised, and it wasn't his finest hour by some distance. I had some explaining to do to journalists and former Congressman Bruce Morrison who wanted to know why the speech was so bad – mainly because he was improvising while suffering from exhaustion and lack of sleep.

14

'GATEWAY' ELECTION AND ALL-PARTY TALKS

The multilateral talks on the Northern election began in Stormont on 4 March 1996. They were jointly chaired by Sir Patrick Mayhew and Tánaiste Dick Spring. It was an inauspicious start; the two main unionist parties decided to boycott the jointly British–Irish chaired sessions. Sinn Féin's leaders turned up, demanding their right to take part in the talks, but they were not allowed to pass a barrier on the roadway. Journalists and camera crews were there in force and there was a continuous clatter of photos by newspaper 'snappers' in the background of the TV news stories, as Gerry Adams denounced this 'undemocratic' treatment. 'We're being denied the right to go in and talk about peace,' he said. This overshadowed the talks with the SDLP, Alliance, and loyalist UDP and PUP. It was a public relations failure not to have anticipated what Sinn Féin would do and to make provisions for it. They could have been let in to talk to officials or some other formula. Leaving them outside with the media was an own goal.

In the middle of this first week in March, the taoiseach's programme manager, Seán Donlon, went north to meet personally with his friend John Hume. He knew Hume well, having worked in Northern Ireland as an emissary from the Department of Foreign Affairs in the early days of the Troubles. Later, as Irish ambassador to the United States, he and

Hume collaborated to steer Irish-American support away from the IRA towards the non-violent constitutional politics of the SDLP and the Irish government. Donlon's mission was to discuss with Hume a formula to restore the ceasefire. It was suggested that, on top of the summit communiqué just announced, with a fixed date for the round-table talks on 10 June, a nationalist 'consensus' agreement was required to restore the ceasefire. The secretary general of the Department of the Taoiseach, Paddy Teahon, felt that a package could be put together, negotiating with Sinn Féin and the SDLP on a joint nationalist position for the talks. Donlon spoke to Hume about this idea, but the SDLP leader appeared to throw cold water on it when he said to Donlon, 'The taoiseach did not appear enthusiastic about this plan for peace.'

Hume wanted the meeting with Donlon to be private, but then he himself told Dick Spring about it at Stormont the next day, where Spring was engaged in the talks with the Northern parties. At first Spring expressed concern about this back channel, but afterwards told the taoiseach that he had 'overreacted'. Later I heard that Sinn Féin's Rita O'Hare expressed her concern about it to Seán Ó hUiginn. According to my note of the exchange, she asked: 'If Seán Donlon is coming back into the loop does that mean something?' I wondered if that question was really about Seán decades before, in very different circumstances, working against the IRA agenda in the US. Paranoia is always lurking in the wings.

The taoiseach himself met with Hume at Greencastle in County Donegal on Sunday 31 March. En route to Dublin, he told me on the phone the meeting was 'good, positive-sounding, but nothing definitive'.

Paddy Teahon, Seán Donlon and I would have been enthusiastic about a 'nationalist consensus' if it was the route back to a ceasefire, but with 'nothing definitive' emerging from the meeting with Hume, that idea appeared dead. Bruton had spoken in his controversial speech to the Meath Association in London the previous November about his responsibility to present Northern nationalist grievances and wishes to the British government under the terms of the 1985 Anglo-Irish Agreement. He repeated this now, saying that he had a responsibility to represent those Irish people who were 'beyond the borders of the Republic'. So I felt Bruton's concern about 'pan-nationalism', declining an impromptu meeting with Hume and Adams at the Dublin Castle Forum was unnecessary, but republicans' reaction to it was over the top. He was troubled by the fact that the moderate Alliance Party leader John Alderdice had just left the Dublin forum saying that the SDLP and Sinn Féin were not taking it seriously, and a meeting with Adams and Hume alone at the forum might further upset Alderdice. I understood his wish not to alienate unionists and others, but that should not foreclose on nationalists of different parties and opinions coming together on the peace process. Addressing fears of unionist majoritarianism after an election, Bruton said the role of the Belfast forum to be set up by the British after the election would be 'insulated' from the all-party talks. The election purpose was to provide delegates for the all-party talks. Bruton declared that there was 'no question of the government I lead conforming to, or acquiescing in, any unionist agenda of domination'. He had worked heroically to get the twin-track policy and the International Body on arms set up, as well as securing British agreement for all-party talks to start after the election, but, with the 'dialogue of the deaf' reigning again, there was no positive reaction by Sinn Féin or the IRA.

The UUP leaders David Trimble and John Taylor came to Dublin on 11 March to talk to the Irish government during the multilateral talks. While the visit was an important symbolic gesture, indicating that the two were interested in a form of co-operation, it did not advance what we already knew of the UUP positions. Bruton challenged them about any strategy to 'logjam' the talks on decommissioning. The exchanges appeared to deliver a gain later that month when Trimble said there would be no 'logjam' if the parties associated with paramilitaries agreed to the Mitchell report. Major and he had promised at the press conference announcing the June date that they would not allow logjamming of the all-party talks, but Bruton continued to hammer away at the subject.

There was no consensus in the multilateral talks on the form of an election, so a week after the deadline for those discussions, as insisted by the Irish side at the February summit, the British government announced that the Forum proportional representation election would be held on 30 May based on 5 seats allocated to each of the 18 Westminster constituencies. The election plan included a novel idea that two extra seats would be given to the ten most successful parties in the election, which ensured that the fringe unionist parties associated with paramilitaries would be represented, as well as the relatively recently formed Northern Ireland Women's Coalition. The SDLP turned down Sinn Féin's proposal of a joint boycott, so when the SDLP decided to contest the election, Sinn Féin decided to run as well. It was clear that, in truth, opposition to an election was more of a Hume–Fianna Fáil bandwagon.

It proved very beneficial for Sinn Féin that the party did take part. As I expected, their vote substantially increased. Sinn Féin closed the gap with the SDLP, reaching their highest ever vote of 15.5 per cent, 17 seats and 116,377 votes, despite the ceasefire having ended. Paul Bew and Gordon Gillespie, in their *Chronology* on the peace process, made this judgement: 'Sinn Féin appeared to be the main winner in the election with its best ever showing.' This result was in an election they had denounced and vilified. If the ceasefire had been maintained or restored, the Sinn Féin vote would have been higher still. I believed the vote was a reward for the long ceasefire, and a push for more. The other votes in the election were: UUP 24.2 per cent, 30 seats; SDLP 21.4 per cent, 21 seats; DUP 18.8 per cent, 24 seats; Alliance Party 6.5 per cent, 7 seats; UK Unionist Party (UKUP) 3.7 per cent, 3 seats. Four other parties, the loyalist PUP and UDP, the Northern Ireland Women's Coalition and Northern Ireland Labour, took part in the election, but did not win any seats, so were allocated two each anyway as part of the top ten.

Sinn Féin was up 5.5 per cent on their 1992 election result of 10 per cent; they were just four seats short of the SDLP, though the latter did not get its due proportional share, taking just 21 seats, while the DUP got 24, with a 2.6 per cent lower share of the vote. The 18 separate constituencies skewed the proportionality of the results. It made the SDLP look weaker than it was at a critical time for the party, which was battling on two fronts: strongly supporting Sinn Féin in the peace process as well as that party's entry into the coming all-party talks; and fighting against them politically in elections. They were ultimately to pay a heavy political price as the divided people of Northern Ireland became more politically polarised, driving up support for the more extreme parties on either side, Sinn Féin and the DUP.

The UUP was still the largest party but it suffered a sharp drop of 10.3 per cent from 1992; they won 30 seats, which meant they would be a key part of any agreed settlement, but this was not considered a good result for them. The DUP was advancing, and the unionists fragmenting, with the UK Unionists, led by MP Robert McCartney, taking three seats with 3.7 per cent of the vote. David Trimble attacked McCartney for an 'ego trip' that undermined unionism in his constituency of Upper Bann, making way for Sinn Féin to win a seat. The centrist party, Alliance, trying to appeal to both communities, came off worst, with 6.5 per cent of the vote and seven seats. All these seat totals included the two extra seats allocated to each of the 'top ten' parties. Four other parties who won no seats were allocated their two each under this system. They were, in order of their share of the poll, the PUP (associated with the UVF), the UDP (associated with the UDA), the Northern Ireland Women's Coalition and a Labour group. This meant in particular that the fringe loyalist parties could take part in the all-party talks.

Over the course of the election campaign, and immediately after the result, there were several detailed phone discussions between Bruton and Major dealing with the chairmanship of the all-party negotiations, particularly the central plenary sessions and the key North–South Strand 2, important for the reassurance of nationalists and republicans that the all-Ireland dimension was included in any settlement. A Council of Ireland was included in the British Government of Ireland Act in 1920 that set up Stormont, but it was never established. The Council included in the Sunningdale Agreement similarly never happened due to the unchallenged loyalist rebellion that caused the collapse of the power-sharing government.

Bruton and Spring were determined to get George Mitchell again as an overarching chairman of the plenary sessions to which the strand negotiations would return. In a call with Bruton on 8 May, Major indicated that he saw a role for Mitchell 'playing a significant part' on the decommissioning issue. A note on the call by Paddy Teahon said: 'As regards the chairs issue in general, the prime minister said he did not believe the two governments could chair at the plenary level.' He mentioned General de Chastelain and two others, 'but not in a definitive way'. On the 20 May phone call, Major had come round to George Mitchell as chair of the plenary, with a decommissioning committee or strand reporting back to it. 'I would very much like Mitchell to chair it, a weighty political figure. I'm not at all keen on George Mitchell doing Strand 2 (North–South) for pragmatic reasons. It would look like the US taking over the whole shouting match, and the unionists would not wear it without grudge and difficulty.' He put forward General de Chastelain as the chair of this strand. Bruton said there was a problem with a 'two-headed' chair operation, 'there has to be a chairman of the chairmen' and this was the role he wanted for Mitchell. Major agreed that all the strands would report back to the chairman of the plenary. Bruton responded, 'George Mitchell as chairman of the plenary and overall external chair, but his deputy would be de Chastelain who chairs Strand 2.' To Bruton's surprise, Major revealed that the British had already approached George Mitchell, but Mitchell had expressed a preference for an approach from the two governments together. This lengthy phone discussion also revealed that Major was insisting on parallel decommissioning taking place, while Bruton argued strongly that the Mitchell Report proposed that the parties 'consider' parallel decommissioning, so that consideration could not be pre-empted. The text reads: 'The parties should consider an approach under which some decommissioning would take place.' Bruton said, 'My big concern is to persuade Sinn Féin they're not being asked to walk into a trap where once they got in, the only thing they'll be hearing about is decommissioning.' Major responded: 'I've got backbenchers writing to me, I've got meetings up to the eyeballs, with people saying "are you about to betray the unionists, sell out the unionists?" and ten thousand other things ... Sinn Féin have been trying to blackmail us with that sort of stuff for the last three years. We all know who sits on the Provisional's army council high command and they'll be sitting in the negotiations wearing Sinn Féin hats.' Parallel decommissioning remained as an issue on the British side, and was endorsed by Tony Blair initially, until it was sidelined in the negotiations and had not occurred when the Belfast Agreement was reached.

After the election, early on 4 June, a team of high-level Irish civil servants, including Paddy Teahon, Seán Ó hUiginn, Secretary General of the Department of Justice Tim Dalton, and David Cooney, head of the Foreign Affairs Unit in Maryfield, Belfast, travelled to London with Dick Spring, accompanied by his adviser Fergus Finlay, a member of the Anglo-Irish Liaison Group, for discussions with Sir Patrick Mayhew and his team to wrap up some key issues about the ground rules for the all-party talks. Spring would go on afterwards to join President Mary Robinson on her official visit to Britain. This was a very significant moment. Nationalist fears centred on the use of a majority vote by unionists to drive the forum and, more importantly, the talks, so the ground rules would have to ensure that this did not happen.

Fergus Finlay in *Snakes and Ladders* explained that the key issue to be resolved was that of 'sufficient consensus' as a procedural rule for issues to be agreed in the talks. Defining what that actually meant was of far-reaching importance because this concept, in the divided communities of Northern Ireland, would also be important in the future underpinning of any agreed form of Northern administration. Any legislative or other proposal would have to have the support of a majority in both communities. The governments' proposals for this rule were in a paper called 'How we Envisage Business Proceeding'. Unanimity would be great, but in reality, 'sufficient consensus' would be needed to keep the show on the road, and to consign unionist majoritarianism to the bin of history. We all had some fears that Major, dependent as he was on the good will of the unionists in the House of Commons, might be inclined to tweak the 'consensus' rule in their favour, or leave the process open in a way that meant unionists could lay down procedures for delivering majority rule. Finlay describes how they expected that the talks over dinner with Sir Patrick and his advisers would last only a couple of hours, but it spun into the early hours of the next day, with the 'overarching' role of Senator George Mitchell in the talks also being hammered out. The team would have to stay overnight and tie up loose ends the next day.

The text on 'sufficient consensus' was this:

> A particular proposition may be deemed to have sufficient consensus where the Chairman is satisfied, having regard to the political parties' voting strengths according to the percentage of the valid poll each received in the Northern Ireland-wide elections on 30 May 1996, that it is supported by parties which, taken together, obtained a clear majority of the valid poll, and which between them represent a clear majority in both the unionist and nationalist communities in Northern Ireland respectively. With the exception of Strand One, both Governments must also endorse the particular proposition for it to be deemed to have achieved sufficient consensus.

But the debate was not over, it would arise in the talks.

The loose ends did not require the ministers, so Dick Spring was free to attend to his duties with President Robinson at Buckingham Palace and elsewhere as she made the first official visit of an Irish President to Britain. But when the team appeared at the Northern Ireland Office to finish the agreement the next day, they were told that the previous night's agreement had been ditched. Major had written his own formula and that was 'a final offer'. Fergus Finlay records in his book that Seán Ó hUiginn took the lead, responding to this démarche by telling the British officials the negotiations were over, and they would report failure to the political leaders. A shocked British official asked him if they were 'refusing to even consider the Prime Minister's proposal'. Ó hUiginn replied with one word: 'Yes.'

Dick Spring stood by his team and the agreement with Mayhew. That same day a late evening phone call was arranged between Bruton and Major. Bruton succeeded in re-establishing final agreement with Major on Senator Mitchell's 'overarching' role, and no change was made to the formula for 'sufficient consensus' in the all-party talks already agreed by Spring and Mayhew. Major relented with only days to go to the launch of the talks. The ground rules for the talks were announced the next day in London, 6 June, by Dick Spring and Sir Patrick Mayhew. President Clinton rang Bruton and Major to congratulate them and once again promised to support the process. But, dampening our expectations, there was no still no reinstatement of the IRA ceasefire, despite continuing official contacts with Sinn Féin. Even if it had come at the last minute on Monday morning, 10 June, the party would have been admitted.

It was a very busy week. The day before we had had to fly to Bonn for a meeting between the taoiseach and German Chancellor Helmut Kohl on EU business, with Ireland taking over the EU presidency on 1 July. The incoming presidency visited all the EU capitals for meetings with the leaders. While Germany was already reunited after the collapse of the Soviet Union and the fall of the Berlin Wall, the new Chancellery in Berlin was still under construction, along with the entire remodelling of the centre of the city. Potsdamer Platz had been left as a wartime bombed-out zone, and the Reichstag a war ruin pocked with rifle and machine gun bullet holes, as well as artillery damage. So the political centre of a united Germany was still the small, charming city of Bonn, notable as the birthplace of Beethoven, the old house where he was born is preserved as a remarkable little museum, while the Chancellery was a dull modern office building. The taoiseach was formally greeted by Kohl, and he reviewed an army squadron of the Chancellery guard. Unlike other premiers of the EU, Kohl wanted the luncheon talks to be attended by himself and the taoiseach, with only a translator and note-takers. So the rest of us were treated to lunch in the Chancellery staff canteen, similar to that of any small company, for which we were supplied with vouchers.

We were accompanied by one of Kohl's friendly officials, who asked us about the Northern Ireland peace process, so we brought him up to date. When I compared this self-service canteen experience with our Government Buildings' red carpet welcome for foreign visitors, top chefs providing an exceptional wining and dining experience, I was bemused, to say the least. Since Germany was the biggest contributor to EU funds, and Ireland then a big net receiver of EU benefits under the Common Agricultural Policy and EU Structural Funds, I joked with my colleagues on the way out, 'We obviously know how to spend their Deutschmarks better than the Germans!'

The taoiseach regularly met Kohl at meetings of the Christian Democrats group in the European Parliament, called the European People's Party, of which Fine Gael was a member. Their prime ministers gathered separately once or twice a year. At one, I recall that Turkey's application to join the EU was discussed and Kohl declared forcefully that it would never happen when he was chancellor and should not happen. He was invited during the Rainbow years to make an official visit to Ireland, but when he came in October 1996, in his address to the Houses of the Oireachtas, he gave great praise to former Fianna Fáil Taoiseach Charlie Haughey, for his efforts in late 1989 and during Ireland's EU presidency in the first half of 1990 to get support for the reunification of Germany. The British and French, Margaret Thatcher and François Mitterrand, were, understandably because of the last war, initially strongly opposed to quick reunification. Kohl said that Ireland's support was 'decisive' in swinging EU endorsement. 'Germany would never forget' the role played by Ireland and Haughey. Kohl did nothing during the visit to help or support his European People's Party colleague. Bruton was displeased.

In the early hours of 7 June a brutal IRA attack took place in the Republic. Detective Garda Jerry McCabe was shot dead by an IRA gang as he and Detective Garda Ben O'Sullivan were escorting an An Post van carrying £80,000 in Adare, County Limerick. O'Sullivan was seriously injured, hit many times, and 53-year-old McCabe died from three of the 15 bullets fired from a Kalashnikov AK47. It was a shocking attack. McCabe left behind a widow, Anne, and their five children. The IRA Army Council quickly denied responsibility in a brief statement: 'None of our volunteers were in any way involved in this morning's incident in Adare. There was absolutely no IRA involvement.' This was a lie. The bloody attack was stunning, just three days before the all-party talks were to start. Instead of a ceasefire, here was a dreadful armed assault on the gardaí, on duty to protect An Post's cash delivery. There was no doubt among the gardaí that it was the work of the Limerick unit of the IRA, despite the IRA denial with the usual code signature of 'P O'Neill'. No one else had access to a Kalashnikov AK47 at the time. The IRA generally did not deny actions by its units, so its swift official misinformation denial, together with reminders by Sinn Féin that the IRA handbook for volunteers specifically ruled out attacks on members of An Garda Síochána, had only one conceivable purpose. This misinformation broadside was aimed at giving protection to Sinn Féin, which intended to use their non-admittance to the talks on Monday 10 June for a huge media stunt, massing their 17 delegates outside the Stormont barriers to protest about their exclusion. They might have been mauled by the media if the IRA had told the truth.

Adams and McGuinness were both able to repeatedly use the IRA denial to deflect media questions. They had another strategy used at the Stormont gate, and elsewhere, about IRA actions, past or present, or about Sinn Féin's response to them: politicians or journalists who posed hard questions would be accused of 'mischief-making' or 'undermining' Sinn Féin's efforts in the peace process, or of being willing to damage the peace process in some way. The strategy was successful at inhibiting probing questions or comments, painting questioners and critics as 'the bad guys'. Adams and McGuinness complained bitterly that their mandate was not being treated 'like the other parties'. The 'other parties' did not support paramilitaries who used political violence, and the loyalist paramilitaries had maintained their ceasefires. The IRA had brought its ceasefire to a bloody end in the London Docklands, and now, by killing a detective garda and seriously wounding another, it was acting against even its own internal rules.

The *Irish Times*' exhaustive and courageous coverage of the vicious IRA attack, the very next day, led with the headline: 'Reputed Head of Munster IRA Arrested over Killing', with the report saying that IRA denial was being rejected by other IRA sources in Belfast and that no 'disciplinary' measures would be taken against those involved. There was an extensive Garda and army hunt under way in the Limerick area after the attack, and five people had been detained. The Munster IRA group were hardened militants. They were believed to be in charge of most of the IRA bunkers of weaponry, and obviously were not concerned about the impact of such a brutal attack on the peace process, or on the Sinn Féin leadership. The *Irish Times* security correspondent, Jim Cusack, also reported that the IRA had continued with many armed robberies after the ceasefire, which was about ceasing 'military' activities.

The next night, 8 June, the Gardaí decided to end the misinformation campaign and rebut anyone intending to constrain them in identifying the perpetrators of the brutal Adare attack. The Garda commissioner, Patrick Culligan, gave a short statement to the media:

> As far as we are concerned, I and members of the Garda Síochána have no doubt whatsoever that it was carried out by members of the IRA. It was an appalling and dastardly crime, sending shock waves throughout the length and breadth of the state.

Journalists asked me to respond. I gave them the agreed statement: 'The Commissioner's word on this must be taken as absolutely authoritative and there can be no doubt that the IRA was involved. This is accepted by the Government.' Journalists caught up with Gerry Adams at a meeting in Dublin to ask him about the commissioner's statement. His response, reported by the *Irish Times*, was again equivocal: he 'believed the IRA statement to the effect that it had not been involved'; and he added that in the past, when it was very unpopular for the IRA to claim responsibility for actions, they did so. Asked if he would condemn the killing of Detective Garda Jerry McCabe, he said it was utterly wrong: 'I repudiate and renounce it.' The choice of the last words was strange, but Adams had admitted it was utterly wrong – that was a condemnation.

Within 24 hours of the Garda Commissioner saying that they had 'absolutely no doubt whatsoever' that the IRA carried out the deadly Adare attack, the IRA issued another statement admitting that its members had carried out the attack, but it was not authorised. This statement was an admission of what was incontrovertible then – that IRA men were involved. Much later, Adams was reported, in the *Sunday Business Post*, to have said that the attack was authorised at a lower level than the IRA Army Council. However, this statement could also have been made to get the killers covered by IRA prisoner release procedures settled in the Belfast Agreement.

The situation caused by the IRA denial, and IRA sources denying the denial, led to a story in the *Sunday Tribune* on 9 June alleging the government had told the Gardaí to 'play down' the IRA involvement, just a day before the Belfast talks were to begin. Bruton rang me at 9.30 that morning about this report. He was 'extremely concerned', I noted. I told him that the Minister for Health, Michael Noonan, from Limerick, was going on RTÉ's *This Week* programme at lunchtime, so I asked him to speak to Noonan. He asked me to speak to him. I was delayed briefly by another call on the same matter from Paddy Teahon, so when I got to Noonan, the taoiseach had already spoken to him. Noonan and I had discussed his interview the previous afternoon and I'd mentioned the 'playing down' rumour to him. Afterwards, he had spoken at length to Tim Dalton at the Department of Justice, and Paddy Teahon, about that issue and others. I felt the government could not be seen as ambivalent. I believed that departmental officers overused traditional civil service caution, insisting on making no quick judgements on the attack. Teahon informed me that he had told Michael Noonan to say 'nothing was ruled in or ruled out on IRA involvement, the most important thing was for the public to assist the gardaí to catch the killers'. Teahon told me the Gardaí were now 'not so sure about the IRA'. I wasn't sure that was the Garda view at all, which was later confirmed by the commissioner. Did this lead to someone telling the Gardaí to 'play down' the IRA involvement?

Knowing civil service caution about prejudicial judgements in the public arena and a desire not to impede a renewed IRA ceasefire, there was, unfortunately, 'something to the story', as Noonan said to me. But I believe it was more about caution, not a deliberate 'playing down' operation. Noonan said on *This Week* that his 'first impression' after hearing about the Kalashnikov AK47s and the 'modus operandi' was that the well-known IRA group in the Limerick area was involved, but, he said, we 'must not speculate'. The Gardaí were now widening the inquiry, he said, but if the IRA was involved, or those associated with the IRA, then there were 'difficulties posed for Sinn Féin'. There was no truth, he said, in the *Sunday Tribune* story about the Gardaí being told by the government to 'play down' the IRA involvement – by that he meant there was no ministerial involvement.

An estimated 50,000 people lined the streets of Limerick for Detective Garda McCabe's funeral. Four IRA men, Pearse McAuley, Kevin Walsh, Jeremiah Sheehy and Michael O'Neill, were eventually convicted of manslaughter by the Special Criminal Court in 1999. Two of the four killers, Pearse McAuley and Kevin Walsh, who would serve more than ten years in jail for the brutal killing of McCabe and the wounding of O'Sullivan, were met by the Kerry Sinn Féin TD Martin Ferris when they were released from the light regime prison of Castlerea on 5 August 2009.

I went with John Bruton to Belfast for the official opening of the first session of the all-party talks at Stormont with John Major. It is important to note that the venue was not the imposing old Northern Stormont parliament building on the top of a hill, often seen on television, but the unattractive nearby office block, Castle Buildings, seat of the Northern Ireland Office. Our mood was sombre and serious. There was no sign of any ceasefire, despite the requirements of Sinn Féin and the IRA being met. We were still struggling in an atmosphere of outrage caused by the IRA killing of Jerry McCabe, while Ben O'Sullivan was still having treatment for his multiple wounds as the summit communiqué was being implemented. President Clinton had called for the ceasefire to be reinstated: 'I call on those who have resorted to violence to heed the voice of the people and cease their campaign of terror,' he had said, also expressing his 'admiration' for Bruton and Major, 'who have shown so much courage and determination in the cause of peace'. He had been joined by Senator Edward Kennedy in calling for a ceasefire 'so that Sinn Féin may participate in these talks', as reported by Seán Cronin in Washington for the *Irish Times*. The day arrived and they were both ignored.

The business of getting the all-party talks going was a serious challenge even without Sinn Féin. We expected unionist attempts to frustrate the instalment of Mitchell as the chairman of the plenary sessions of the talks, to stop or limit the role he was to play. Unionists would likely seek opportunities to skew the ground rules in their favour, as well as using Mitchell's six principles required of all parties to the talks, and the decommissioning issue, for their own ends. A warning of troubled waters over Mitchell's role came when he announced in New York the previous week that he was accepting the role as chairman of the plenary sessions of the talks. Unionists protested loudly in Northern Ireland, and one of Major's backbench MPs, Terry Dicks, threatened to resign the Conservative whip, which would have weakened Major still further. None of this agitation reached the former senator. In his book *Making Peace*, he wrote, 'Nothing was said about any opposition to me. Wrapped in a cocoon of naivety, I flew to Northern Ireland expecting an easy, non-controversial entry into serious negotiations. I could not have been more wrong.' He expected to be home before Christmas. It took 22 months, to Easter 1998, for the talks to conclude.

Bruton's objective was to counter and parry the unionists' efforts so that the talks process was capable of achieving the objectives of an inclusive cross-community settlement dealing with the three strands – North internal, North–South, and London–Dublin – with decommissioning in a fourth strand where it could not be used to block the political negotiations. The blueprint for agreement was already there in the Framework Documents. A business committee, to which disputes could be referred from the plenary sessions, was to be set up quickly. It comprised one representative of each of the parties, representatives of both governments, and General de Chastelain as chairman. He was also to chair the formal Strand 2 North–South negotiations. The former Finnish Prime Minister Harri Holkeri, who had also been a member of the International Body on Decommissioning, would act as an alternate for any of the independent chair roles. Walkouts from any aspect of the negotiations when they got under way were dealt with in the ground rules; if a delegation withdrew either temporarily or permanently from the talks, the chairman was empowered to continue the business with the remaining participants.

Denis Coughlan, political editor of the *Irish Times*, summed up the background to the opening of the talks. He wrote that the circumstances in which negotiations were due to take place were 'less than perfect'. John Major led a 'wounded government' at Westminster, and Ulster unionists were being advised to hold off on serious negotiations until 'after the expected change' in the British government. Gerry Adams had 'threatened to show up at the talks in the absence of an IRA ceasefire. Should republicans persevere in this approach, the two governments will have no option but to go ahead without Sinn Féin. In such circumstances it will be vital that there should be no weakening of the demand for an IRA ceasefire.' The forum to which the parties were elected was intentionally sidelined by the Irish government and the SDLP, to unionist chagrin. The election was just the gateway to the negotiations. The parties had to appoint delegates to the all-party talks and get ready for that challenge.

I think the election results inspired a certain euphoria in Sinn Féin and the IRA, which made key figures think they could ride both horses, war and peace. Michael Ancram, the North's Minister for Political Development, said publicly that even an eleventh-hour IRA ceasefire would secure admission to the talks for Sinn Féin, but to no avail. On the day, the parties started showing up at Stormont throughout the morning. As expected, Gerry Adams turned up with all his elected members of the forum and protested to the world's media that it was anti-democratic and denying their electoral mandate to refuse Sinn Féin entry to the talks. The journalists joked about the 'circus' and the 'pantomime', but it was drama that suited the media, which thrives on conflict. A Sinn Féin delegation led by Martin McGuinness was allowed into Stormont to hear from officials why they had been excluded. Later, a Northern Ireland Office official went to the gateway to read a statement for the assembled media on behalf of the two governments. It reiterated that it had been the consistent position since the February Docklands bombing, included in paragraph 9 of the 'Ground Rules for Substantive All-Party Negotiations' that 'a resumption of ministerial dialogue with Sinn Féin and their participation in negotiations requires the unequivocal restoration of the ceasefire of August 1994'.

Dick Spring had gone to Belfast a day early to join Patrick Mayhew in liaising with the political delegates, and for discussions with George Mitchell about his 'overarching' chairmanship in the talks. We learned that the three main unionist parties – the UUP, DUP and UKUP – had met over the weekend to co-ordinate the strategy of opposition to the Mitchell chairmanship, and what was seen as the two governments dictating the agenda and procedures. Paisley, in particular, struck a hardline note – none of this was 'acceptable'. It was worrying, to say the least. George Mitchell was sanguine about the situation. He had met the unionist party leaders and was now fully aware of the opposition, particularly Paisley's outright rejection, and Bob McCartney's opposition to him being 'imposed' by the governments. In his memoir George Mitchell said the 'more significant' factor for him was David Trimble's silence. 'Trimble could have made it impossible for me to assume the chair by joining them in outright disapproval. But he didn't. He held his fire.' It's a great credit to Mitchell that he took all this on, and persevered.

The intention was that, in the afternoon, Spring and Mayhew would jointly host the introduction to the talks in the main chamber, and addresses to the delegates by Major and Bruton would mark the formal opening of the all-party talks. When it happened, unionists, of course, raised objections to a 'southerner' in this role. Spring courteously left his chair and the chamber to promote some harmony, which was in short supply. Mayhew alone then introduced Major and Bruton to the delegates of the nine political parties assembled there.

Major spoke first, making it clear that the way ahead for the talks was not straightforward, there were bound to be difficulties, but they could be resolved in agreement. Bruton addressed the need to heal divisions and remove the causes of conflict. He twice cited the Framework Documents as the basis for a new accommodation. 'In exercise of our leadership role, the two Governments have described a shared understanding of the parameters of a possible outcome to the negotiations in the document, "A New Framework for Agreement".' Bruton also made an apology to nationalists in the North for the historic southern neglect of them and their rights, and pledged that the talks should achieve equality and parity of esteem for both communities. I believe this was the first such significant apology by any taoiseach:

> To Northern nationalists, I say that we in the South, no less than others, failed in the early decades of the construction of our own State to give adequate practical, as distinct from rhetorical, attention to the protection of your rights, including the expression of your identity. If the future is to be one of peace and of hope, there can be no domination of nationalists by unionists and, equally, none of unionists by nationalists. In our view, there is a need for substantial and significant change, in accordance with the principles set out in that Joint Framework Document agreed with the British government. Northern Ireland can only work successfully if it inspires, for the first time, an equal sense of ownership on the part of unionists and nationalists. There must be parity of esteem and of treatment in all spheres for Northern nationalists and for unionists.

The taoiseach was repeatedly interrupted by unionists calling for points of order, which Mayhew dismissed. The plan was for Mitchell to take the chair after the two leaders formally launched the talks, but the mood indicated that caution was needed because of unionists' vehement hostility to his chairmanship. Instead, there was a short adjournment after Major and Bruton had spoken; then the session continued with Mayhew chairing a session on the role of George Mitchell, outlining the objectives of the governments, while the unionist parties continued their protests. Mitchell, de Chastelain, and Holkeri had to listen to all this on an internal sound link to Mayhew's office, where they were waiting across the hall. 'We stayed there for two days, while my role was being discussed – a strange experience. Both governments were painfully embarrassed, having believed that the opposition could easily be overcome,' wrote Mitchell in *Making Peace*. 'But it was proving to be more difficult and messier than anticipated.'

I had warned Tony Lake in Sharm El-Sheikh, at Clinton's Summit of the Peacemakers, that there would be difficulties at the outset of the talks, which would have to be overcome. I think officials were being as polite and apologetic as they could be, and possibly Mitchell wasn't warned, particularly by the American and Irish sides, because everyone wanted him to be in the chair, so nothing was said that would unsettle him. However, it was no surprise to many of us that these hostile criticisms were being made. Outside the chamber the unionists boasted that they had prevented the governments from imposing a chairman or an agenda. The *Irish Times* reported that Trimble had asserted that the agenda drafted by the governments had been 'binned'. But the unionists badly underestimated the determination of the governments to push through the chairman, the rules and the agenda. This was emphasised strongly by Dick Spring during the evening. He said that the only alternative to Mitchell in the chair, with his overseeing role intact, was for the British and Irish governments to jointly chair the talks – and that would be anathema to the unionists.

In his memoir Mitchell said that Trimble's motives were two-fold. The UUP leader feared that if unionists blocked his chairmanship of the talks, agreed by the two governments, and which had the full support of seven of the ten political parties eligible to take part, the peace process would collapse and unionists would be blamed, 'especially his party'. Trimble wanted to use the controversy about Mitchell's chairmanship to get rid of the 'ground rules' and all the other procedural guidelines and scenarios that the governments had agreed, as well as his 'overarching' powers that the governments had proposed, and start with a blank sheet, with the parties themselves deciding on the rules, agenda and powers of the chair.

In mid-afternoon, the focus shifted, with Major and Bruton giving a joint news conference in Stormont Castle buildings. Both were strongly insistent that Mitchell would remain their chosen candidate to chair the talks. Bruton made a prophetic comment: 'In these all-party talks we have something in place now which has enormous potential for the future of Northern Ireland. It is truly an enormous opportunity.' It was these talks, which Sinn Féin joined the following year, after a renewed ceasefire, that led to the Belfast Agreement. Major said that many people had predicted that the governments would never even get to this stage. Quoting Churchill, Major said: 'In many ways it's the end of the beginning.' In a UK TV interview afterwards Major was also prophetic, saying that the negotiations would be slow, and could outlast his government's term of office.

I found it bizarre that a former Irish Labour Party Minister for Posts and Telegraphs in the Fine Gael–Labour coalition of 1973-7, Dr Conor Cruise O'Brien, was now a delegate for Bob McCartney's tiny unionist party. O'Brien was an intellectual led astray by his brilliance and warped logic, and he got his free seat in Stormont because of the clever government plan – the extra two seats for the top ten parties. Here was the 'Cruiser' telling journalists that his party objected to Mitchell's 'overarching' role. Get rid of this 'supremo' thing, O'Brien said. McCartney, who was the only one in the party to have won a seat in the election, joined with the other unionist leaders demanding a sub-committee to decide the chairmanship and the agenda – a less flexible line than Cruise O'Brien.

The first day of the talks was adjourned at about 6 p.m. and Spring and Mayhew started another round of bilateral talks with the parties. The Cruiser now advised Mitchell to think about dropping the job, while his party leader said Mitchell would be ousted. Paisley denounced the governments' plan for the talks. Hume defended the role of Mitchell and the governments' agenda. Things looked a bit bleak. After taking in the atmosphere and temperature at Stormont, I went to the Portakabin that had been set aside in the grounds for the principals, joining Major and Bruton there. As they settled down to talk, I was taken aback when Major started what turned into a long diatribe about how the other prime ministers and presidents of the European Council had treated Britain over mad cow disease. The British government had gone through the horrors for the past few months since their [Bovine] Spongiform Encephalopathy (BSE) Advisory Committee had finally announced in March the new evidence of a link between BSE and a similar disease, which affected the human brain, Creutzfeldt-Jakob disease. It proved to be a disaster for the beef industry in Britain and a major crisis for the British government. There were extensive cattle herd culls all over the country, and sales of beef and beef products collapsed. There was widespread panic that many people might already have eaten contaminated meat and could potentially face a terrifying brain disease that might take up to ten years to appear. Many people, according to the popular press, were already living on 'borrowed time'. Finding answers to all the questions that were raised was an impossible task since so little was known about the disease.

The UK did take many actions to counter the disease. The widespread use of meat and bonemeal, made from sheep carcasses, as cattle feed had been banned for cattle in 1988, and later bans were introduced on the use of beef brains, spinal cord and intestines for food products. The British took further action, as advised, to require the deboning of meat from older animals and also ban the use of meat and bonemeal as pig and poultry feed. But despite these actions, there was little that could be done about public fear, which was not confined to Britain, but spread across Europe, North Africa and the Middle East. Major admitted that advice was provisional, and kept changing. However, he maintained that the scientific advice was that the risk of transmission of BSE to humans was either non-existent or infinitesimal. John Bruton and I got a demonstration of Major's deep anger about his fellow European leaders. It was all very fresh and recent; we had been at the Turin EU summit with him just a few weeks before, where BSE had been on the agenda, and Major had been pushing the scientific evidence hard.

In late March the EU had imposed what was to be a temporary ban on the export of British beef products to the rest of the world. It was still in force as we listened to Major pour out his feelings. He was furious, denouncing the European Commission and his fellow members of the European Council for pandering to people's 'irrational' fears, rather than acting on the basis of scientific evidence. It was particularly rankling for him that the ban was for the rest of the world, but not for Britain, which he said meant that the 'EU understood that British beef was safe for consumption'. Otherwise it would be banned in Britain.

Major was using the opportunity to express his annoyance about all this to the taoiseach because Ireland was to assume the presidency of the EU in July. He said there had been 'hysteria' in European countries about BSE, which was let run out of control, and the ban now was deeply unfair. He said the other leaders were protecting their own beef industries and farmers at the expense of the British. The ban implied that other countries' beef was safe. The 'beef war', as it became known, was to cost the British government billions of pounds in compensation for the huge culls of animals (to be extended now to older animals), and in lost industries and jobs.

As a believer in the EU, no wonder Major was very angry. Bruton and I listened, more or less in silence and sympathy for his predicament, but the hard reality was that other EU countries, including Ireland, *had* to protect their beef industries in the atmosphere of intense fear. Bruton told Major about Ireland's export difficulties to Egypt and elsewhere because of BSE, and raised questions about his retaliation against the EU, just three weeks before the all-party talks, taking the drastic step of using the veto on every EU measure that required unanimity. This action delighted the Tory Eurosceptics and the popular press; Major was seen as taking the 'beef war' to Europe.

The ban included beef derivatives, gelatine, tallow and semen, important products to Britain. That very day, Major told us, he had succeeded in getting these products removed. He believed his plans to have the entire ban removed had begun to gain traction within the EU as well. So, after using the veto to block 74 decisions, he ceased it in late June, to our relief, before Ireland's presidency. However, the EU export ban on British beef was not finally ended until August 1999. Major had no space in his head left that evening for more on the missing ceasefire and the all-party talks. He knew Patrick Mayhew could well carry that burden.

The next day, when the talks reopened, Mayhew and Spring, who maintained constant links with the party leaders and delegates, proposed on behalf of the two governments that George Mitchell should take the chair and proceed in plenary session, while in parallel a rules and procedures sub-committee could discuss how the process should be conducted. But the UUP, DUP and UKUP objected to this proposal. The UUP counter-proposal was that the sub-committee be established to discuss the powers of the chairman as well as the rules and procedures, and that no chairman be appointed until the sub-committee had finished its work. After some exchanges, the session was adjourned in little more than ten minutes. However, the negotiations between the parties and the two governments' representatives went on all day, with the discussions continuing on the issues of the chairman, his role and the procedures of the talks. The Irish and the British were adamant that Mitchell would take the chair, but tried to improve the possibilities of getting progress on the basis of what a sub-committee might achieve with the UUP, since all three were proposing its establishment.

Nora Owen, Minister for Justice, and Proinsias De Rossa, Minister for Social Welfare, accompanied by foreign affairs Second Secretary Seán Ó hUiginn went to a meeting in a small room with David Trimble, John Taylor, Ken Maginnis and Reg Empey where the unionists made clear their objection to what they saw as dictation by the governments over the talks' chair and plenary agenda; Trimble was waving the agenda in his hand. Dick Spring was delayed, so Owen started the discussion, saying that once the chairman was in place, the agenda would be open to the participating delegates (which included the two government representatives) to change. It was a draft agenda to get the talks going with the chair filled, but obviously the delegates would have a role in what was discussed 'in their own talks'. She felt that this was received well, with a distinctive change in the atmosphere, repeating this several times in response to questions. The Irish group were asked to another broader meeting of the full party delegation and officials later in the day. Nora Owen said there were about 40 people, and the same message was repeated to them. While Taylor was asking for a guarantee, she ignored that, and stressed again that the participants together were the ultimate 'owners' of the agenda, after George Mitchell had taken the chair. She believed it was important for the unionists to feel that they had won a concession. Mitchell then was still in Mayhew's office with his colleagues. He wrote: 'Mayhew and Dick Spring repeatedly apologised to us, saying they would understand if we chose to leave, but that they hoped we would stick it out to the end, although they couldn't be certain of the outcome.' He pointed out that no one was objecting to his colleagues, who were understanding and supportive. Mitchell told Mayhew and Spring that he would stay until the chairmanship was resolved 'one way or the other'. The peace process was more important than his feelings. 'Privately, my two colleagues and I were apprehensive. There seemed to be a reasonable chance that we would have to leave before we got started.' He felt it was 'humiliating' that he might not get the chance to serve and prove that he would be as fair and impartial as he had reassured all the parties in meetings with them. But the three stayed, listening and joking about their plight to keep up their spirits, he revealed in *Making Peace*.

Bruton had to go to Brussels that Tuesday for discussions with Jacques Santer, president of the European Commission, about Ireland's forthcoming presidency of the EU, but first he had to take the morning's questions in the Dáil. He was deeply upset by the performance of Pat Doherty, the vice-president of Sinn Féin, during RTÉ's *Question Time* the previous night. Doherty had refused to condemn the IRA killing of Jerry McCabe and serious wounding of Ben O'Sullivan, hiding behind the 'politics of condemnation' cliché. Public anger at what the IRA had done was palpable. In the Dáil, Bruton said he found it 'appalling' that Pat Doherty was unwilling to condemn the killing of Detective Garda Jerry McCabe. Bruton resisted a Progressive Democrat call to break off even official contact with Sinn Féin, saying that he must maintain some margin of discretion and a flow of information, if it could help achieve a ceasefire. Talking to the media in Brussels, he said that Doherty's attitude 'disgusted' him.

Back at Stormont Castle, the UUP discussions made some more headway after the two governments' paper, 'A Possible Approach to Resolving Procedural Issues', was drawn up and shown to them. The negotiations between the governments and the UUP continued late into the night. The basic solution found was an agreement that George Mitchell would take the chair and open the plenary session. Participants could submit written proposals on the role and powers of the chairman and the plenary agenda. The following week, delegates from each party were to be chosen to form a group to try to agree with Mitchell on his role and powers, and the plenary agenda.

The stage was set for the former majority leader of the US Senate to fulfil the wishes of the Irish and British governments and President Clinton by taking the chair at the all-party talks. Dan Mulhall, who would later become Irish ambassador to the US, was then the senior press officer in the Department of Foreign Affairs; he told me on the phone about the extraordinary midnight drama and stormy scenes before Mitchell was at last installed in the chair. Patrick Mayhew had despaired at one stage, saying in exasperation, 'Send them home!' It wasn't clear who he thought should be banished. The final text, Mulhall told me, was an Irish government document.

Between 11.30 and 11.45 p.m. both the UUP and the SDLP agreed to support the document. Paisley realised that something was happening when he went to Trimble's room to find it occupied by the Irish government delegation. He stormed up the stairs at Stormont Castle Buildings with his delegation, shouting that he was 'not having a republican toady' in the chair; he was 'not going to be treated like this'. Mayhew was already in the main chamber getting things ready for Mitchell, as the chamber filled with delegates. Paisley ran in and started ranting. John Alderdice, the Alliance Party leader, put up his hand to make a tongue-in-cheek point of order: 'Has the meeting started yet?' Just after midnight, Mitchell recounts in *Making Peace*, Mayhew informed him and his colleagues that they were 'going in'. To Mitchell, 'it sounded uncomfortably as though we were embarking on a military invasion of foreign territory. At 12.32 a.m. on Wednesday morning we entered the meeting room. It was a bizarre scene.'

Paisley stood and repeatedly shouted 'No. No. No! You're not welcome here! I won't be attending any meetings chaired by you.' Just before Mitchell arrived in the room there had been a battle over his chair. A hostile delegate made an attempt to take over the chairman's seat, grabbing the chair. There was a shout of 'fucking scum'. British minister Michael Ancram got the chair back, instructing a young official to sit in it to reserve it for the chairman. Mitchell recalled in *Making Peace* that the occupant waited until he was almost on top of him before he got up. 'He quickly explained to me that he had "protected" my seat from

Paisley's and McCartney's people ... as I sat down and listened to that story my unease grew.'

Paisley shouted 'Lundy!' at David Trimble, the worst insult that can be thrown at a unionist. 'You ... remember what happened to Brian Faulkner!' he shouted. This was the UUP leader in the 1970s who signed up to the Sunningdale power-sharing agreement, and lost his leadership of the party because of it. 'This is selling Ulster out! The worst negotiation ever for unionists! You're finished in East Belfast!' – a stronghold for unionists. Paisley then raised strong formal objections to Mitchell taking the chair. In the official transcript of the talks on formal business he is recorded as saying, 'The ultimate say in the appointment of any chairman belonged to the participants.' He asserted that Mitchell was put in 'without any opportunity to voice an opinion'. Paisley then led the DUP in a walkout, followed by Bob McCartney and his group. Mitchell wrote that he was extremely uncomfortable and had a fleeting urge to get up and go home, 'leaving these people to their feud', but his sense of duty and his understanding of the crisis that would envelop the peace process made him stay. He took the chair in a formal plenary session, trying to remain calm after his first exposure to the full brunt of Paisley's loud, intimidating tactics; he wanted to avoid 'betraying his swirling doubts'. Mitchell made some short remarks that were perfectly suited to this purpose and quickly raised the tone and changed the atmosphere:

> On behalf of my colleagues, General de Chastelain and Prime Minister Holkeri, I thank you. We are honoured by the invitation to participate in these historic proceedings. We commend Prime Ministers Major and Bruton, Secretary of State Mayhew and Minister for Foreign Affairs Spring, those of you here today and the many others across Northern Ireland who have contributed to this process.
>
> Our prior participation in this process has brought us into extensive contact with the people of Northern Ireland. We have come to know and admire them. We assure you that we are motivated solely by a desire to be of help to you and to them.

We will meet our responsibilities in a totally fair and impartial manner. We recognise that it is you who must make the decisions on which these proceedings will advance. We will do all we appropriately can to be of assistance. But ultimately agreement in these negotiations is a matter for the participants. That is why the success of these proceedings rests on your shoulders and in your hearts. That is an immense responsibility. It is also a great and noble challenge. I hope that everyone involved can rise to meet that challenge. As we said in the report we submitted to the Governments on January 24th, in words we believe are even more relevant today: 'The risk may seem high but the reward is great: A future of peace, equality and prosperity for all the people of Northern Ireland.'

I have devoted much of my time and effort over the past year and a half to encouraging trade with and investment in Northern Ireland. I have met with many of you, some many times, and many others all across Northern Ireland. That experience has provided me with first-hand knowledge of the importance of peace to economic growth and the creation of jobs. It has also left me with the conviction that there is enormous potential in Northern Ireland for economic growth and broadly-shared prosperity. We have no interest – no interest whatever – other than to help make possible that promising future for Northern Ireland. We pledge our total commitment to that effort.

His words received generous applause from the tired but welcoming delegates, who wanted the talks to proceed, and they had a calming effect. To engage in the all-party talks, the governments required full party pledges to the six principles of non-violence and democratic behaviour identified in Mitchell's report from the International Body on Decommissioning. So, making up the procedure on the spot to at least conduct some business in the first plenary session, Mitchell read out the six principles and asked for commitment from each of the parties present. The pledges were given by all seven parties. It was now Wednesday 12 June, and a new day for the talks was dawning. A critical hurdle had been overcome, and a process begun which was to deliver real peace in 22 months. At the time Mitchell thought the start was not promising, but he wanted to continue quickly so he called a plenary meeting for later that morning.

Outside, Paisley and McCartney were protesting angrily about a 'sell-out' to the waiting media. Trimble represented the agreement as a victory for his UUP; he said he had regained control of the process for the Northern Ireland parties, his main objective, and he called on the other unionist parties to accept UUP leadership on this matter. McCartney condemned the UUP, saying they were gutless, unprincipled and a disgrace. Trimble rejected the accusations and maintained a dignified position trying to calm the Paisley–McCartney abusive rhetoric, which was dividing unionists. Later in the day the attacks continued. As Trimble was finishing a live TV interview at Castle Buildings, William McCrea of the DUP burst in, shouting that Trimble and his party were 'surrendering Ulster and lying to the people. Ulster is not for sale!' It was excruciating to watch it broadcast. Trimble was taking substantial risks to keep the peace process moving forward.

Tánaiste Dick Spring welcomed the agreement, saying it was very important to have Senator Mitchell installed as chairman of the talks. He said that David Trimble had behaved responsibly in the discussions, and he called on the IRA to renew its ceasefire so that Sinn Féin could take part in the talks. Sir Patrick Mayhew said the agreement to put Mitchell in the chair was an extremely important turning point. There was elation among the Irish team after the enthroning of George Mitchell; a hugely significant hurdle had been crossed, and the talks were underway. So the political team, including Dick Spring, Nora Owen and Proinsias De Rossa, returned with all the officials involved to the Irish outpost at Maryfield, where they were staying for security, and a 'wonderful' dinner and fine wines were laid on by the chef at 2 a.m. for these hungry negotiators who rightly celebrated their day's achievement.

In the morning before the plenary session, Mitchell met Paisley and McCartney to try to persuade them to return to the talks, and both agreed. When the plenary began, the DUP and the UKUP were not there, but during the day both Paisley and McCartney, with party delegates, slipped into the conference room in session, at which Mitchell was officially the chairman, and pledged their parties to the six Mitchell Principles. A statement welcoming this new development was issued by the two governments. The two more radical unionist parties attempted to maintain that this was not a recognition of Mitchell as chair and they had their own 'seventh' principle – the old unionist 'majority rule'. Majoritarianism in the talks is what the governments had binned. The two parties also refused at first to call Mitchell 'Mr Chairman', thereby denying his role. Gradually more of them used 'Mr Chairman' and, as time passed, they became more friendly.

Bruton had an intensive confidential discussion with Trimble on the eve of the talks, which I believe helped influence the UUP leader to bravely take on the more extreme unionists and thus assist the establishment of the talks process. Trimble would also be crucial to the achievement of the Belfast Good Friday Agreement. Bruton's engagement with him during the Rainbow government on the need for unionists and nationalists to reach an agreement for peace demonstrated to Trimble, as Bruton said, 'that there was at least one senior figure in Irish politics who understood their case'.

The IRA had more up its sleeve. Just before 9.20 a.m. on 15 June 1996, a beautiful sunny Saturday, the central streets of Manchester were already filling with shoppers and football fans when two men in hooded anoraks and sunglasses left a heavily loaded Ford Cargo van outside Marks & Spencer on the corner of Cannon Street and Corporation Street. It was parked on double yellow lines with its hazard lights flashing. Three minutes later the van was given a ticket by a traffic warden. It contained 1,500 kilos (3,300lb) of home-made explosives, including Semtex, similar in make-up to the London Docklands bomb. The two bombers walked away, ringing an IRA contact in Ireland to let them know the job was done. The pair escaped in a burgundy Ford Granada, later abandoned in Preston.

The events of the day were described in a 2016 article by Jennifer Williams in the *Manchester Evening News*. From 9.40 a.m., Granada, a

Manchester TV station, Sky News, North Manchester General Hospital, a Manchester university, and the Gardaí in Dublin were called by a man with an Irish accent warning that a bomb had been planted in Manchester, giving the location and an IRA code for the Special Branch. The man said the bomb would explode in one hour. Manchester police began an urgent emergency evacuation of an estimated 80,000 people from the centre of the city, complicated because Manchester was hosting a Euro '96 soccer championship game between Russia and Germany the following day. Fans had to be evacuated from their central hotels and sent to lodgings away from danger. Many foreign television crews were in the city for the game.

Shops were closed. Mancunians were used to false alarms, so there was some resistance, but slowly people began to move, a trickle becoming a flood as word spread that the scare was real. Police identified the large white Ford van outside Marks & Spencer and the Arndale Shopping Centre, both of which were evacuated. On their CCTV camera in Bootle Street station, police watched anxiously as footage showed a crowd of people pushing up against the van and sliding along the side of it, badly parked on one of the city's busiest shopping streets. Just after 11 a.m. a British Army bomb disposal squad, which had rushed to Manchester from Liverpool, was preparing to detonate the device from 200 yards away. The officer co-ordinating the police and the army told colleagues by radio that there would be two blasts: a smaller one as the robot blew a hole in the side of the van, followed by the second, which would disable the IRA bomb. At 11.16 a.m. the first small blast went off. At 11.17 a.m. they ran out of time. The bomb exploded, devastating the entire city centre, causing damage for half a mile, well beyond the quarter-mile cordon of the city centre. It left a 15-metre crater in the road and injured 212 people, 16 of them seriously.

The blast created a mushroom cloud 300 metres high and could be heard up to 15 miles away. Glass and masonry were blown high into the sky and rained shards and debris down on people and buildings well beyond the security cordon, causing damage and injury. The powerful blast force travelled laterally and dangerously around the streets.

A pregnant woman was blown 15 feet into the air and was unconscious when the ambulance team reached her. The following day she and her unborn baby were 'doing well'. Another woman had a seven-and-half-hour operation and needed 300 stitches for life-changing wounds to her face and body from shards of glass and wood. One big piece of glass had cut a 'tongue' of skin off her face. A 51-year-old woman evacuee from the city centre had a heart attack after the bomb went off.

The damage was estimated to cost £700m. Nearly twice that was spent over the next few years rebuilding the city centre.

Five days later, the IRA admitted that it was responsible for the bomb and regretted the civilian injuries. Their statement included this:

> The British Government has spent the last 22 months since August '94 trying to force the surrender of IRA weapons and the defeat of the republican struggle. We are still prepared to enhance the democratic peace process. We appreciate the efforts of those who have made a genuine contribution but if there is to be a lasting peace, if the conflict is to be resolved in Britain and Ireland, then the British Government must put the democratic rights of all of the people of Ireland before its own party political self-interest.

Condemnations didn't wait for the IRA admission. John Major called it 'callous and barbaric'. He told the *Lancashire Evening Telegraph* that it was a 'cowardly' act to bomb a shopping centre filled with innocent people and children. It was the 'work of a few fanatics' and caused 'absolute revulsion in Ireland, as it does here'. John Bruton said Sinn Féin were 'struck mute' on the attack in the immediate aftermath, reacting to a fact noted in the *Irish Times* by Geraldine Kennedy when she reported that 'without mentioning the Manchester bomb', Adams said, 'This is a time for everyone committed to the objective of a lasting peace in Ireland to dig deep and apply ourselves with greater determination to restore the peace process.' Bruton said it was 'a slap in the face to people who've been trying, against perhaps their better interests, to give Sinn Féin a chance to show that they could persuade the IRA to reinstate the ceasefire'. The bombing made it harder to get Sinn Féin into the talks, as Bruton said. 'What is needed now is an unconditional and irrevocable ceasefire. There can be no going back this time, no looking back over the shoulder to the option of violence if politics doesn't go their way. This time they must come irrevocably into the political process.'

The day after Geraldine Kennedy's comment and Bruton's 'struck mute' remark, Adams was quoted in the British *Independent* as saying that he was 'shocked and saddened' by the bombing, and his party was still committed to achieving a peace settlement. It would be 'folly' to return to 'isolating republicans'. The two small loyalist parties, the PUP and UDP, called on Dublin to isolate Sinn Féin after the two IRA attacks. David Irvine of PUP said he was disappointed that the Irish government did not sever all contact with the party. On the BBC's *Breakfast News*, Major said that a role in the peace talks was still open to Sinn Féin 'even after Manchester'. But he warned that if Sinn Féin thought the IRA could call a ceasefire and walk into the talks the next day (which was the situation before the bomb), 'that clearly isn't the case. Sinn Féin and the IRA are isolated by their own actions.' In a speech given in Ennis, County Clare, former Taoiseach Albert Reynolds lashed the IRA, denouncing the killing of Detective Garda Jerry McCabe as a cold-blooded murder, and the bombing of Manchester as appalling. Gerry Adams, he said, had a moral responsibility to go to the IRA and get the peace process back in place again; a ceasefire was the only way forward.

In the US a tougher line was noticed by the *Irish Times*'s Joe Carroll and *Newsweek* magazine. President Clinton said he joined Bruton and Major in 'utterly condemning this brutal and cowardly act of terrorism'; he was 'deeply outraged' by the bomb explosion. Senator Edward Kennedy said bluntly: 'The terrorists do not have the support of the friends of Ireland in the United States. Whatever are the goals of the IRA, they are gravely mistaken to believe that they can achieve them by killing police officers and bombing shopping malls.' *Newsweek* suggested that the administration, already impatient about the delay in restoring the ceasefire, might give up on Gerry Adams and Sinn Féin:

'If Adams cannot deliver the IRA, he is of little use to anyone,' the magazine said. Ironically, *Newsweek* had an interview before the bombing with Martin McGuinness, who praised the installation of George Mitchell as chairman of the all-party talks; he would create a 'much more conducive atmosphere for republicans to be associated with in any process he is chairing'. That achievement was of course the result of a lot of hard work and determined pressure by Bruton, Spring and the Rainbow government, not given any credit by McGuinness, and never properly recognised by republicans. I was not alone in wondering if there was something of a split in the republican movement, with the hardliners having the upper hand, leading to the bombings in England and the possibility, after the second IRA statement, of a breakaway group in the Munster/Limerick IRA. I had repeatedly been told by officials that Martin McGuinness was believed to have remained on the Army Council of the IRA, and that lines between Sinn Féin and the IRA were blurred, so there was an issue of trust.

History is littered with republican splits, from the first in Sinn Féin in 1921 over the Anglo-Irish Treaty to the creation of Provisional Sinn Féin and IRA, and they in turn splitting over the decision to end abstentionism from the Dáil. Adams wanted to be trusted, and I felt it was his due after his lengthy talks with John Hume and the first ceasefire, but not everybody trusted Adams and McGuinness since the ceasefire had been broken.

Was Adams capable of putting himself in the shoes of Bruton and Spring? How did republicans think these appalling acts would advance the peace process? Was Adams capable of convincing people that he wasn't riding both horses, war and peace? Tánaiste Dick Spring, on the BBC's *Breakfast with Frost*, spoke of this dilemma:

> The Adare killing was carried out by a breakaway group from the IRA. That leaves us facing a new difficulty. We always felt we were dealing with a leadership, people who were trying to bring the IRA into democratic politics. The situation could be very different, that we don't know who we are dealing with.

The government held a detailed cabinet review of its relationship with Sinn Féin as a result of these two atrocities and posed two questions to the leader of the party. Adams was asked to state publicly if he had gone to the IRA to ask for a reinstatement of the ceasefire. If he had not done so, why not? The second question was to ask Adams to state publicly if his party still supported the IRA's 'armed struggle'. Adams would not respond directly to either question. He claimed that the Department of the Taoiseach knew what he was doing in relation to a ceasefire, but that was just not the case in relation to specific details. In an indirect response to the second question, he repeatedly said that Sinn Féin wanted to end all armed action. The government would also require further official contacts with Sinn Féin to be 'substantive' on a ceasefire or related issues.

In the Dáil on 18 June, the taoiseach repeated the question to Sinn Féin: did the party still support the IRA 'armed struggle'? No question could be simpler or more fundamental. He said Sinn Féin's increased vote in the election was on the basis of a peace strategy – they would not have got that vote if they had indicated to people in Northern Ireland that they supported an IRA armed strategy that included the bombing of Manchester and armed robberies in the Republic. The all-party talks would continue, he said, because they were the best hope for the Irish people. He denounced the IRA as anti-Irish. The leader of Fianna Fáil, Bertie Ahern, said the bomb assault was 'callous' and that all the elected members of the Dáil condemned the unwarranted attack on the entire civilian population of Manchester; this and the killing of Detective Garda Jerry McCabe in Adare had undermined the peace of Ireland. He called for the restoration of the ceasefire as an absolute necessity. The Progressive Democrats' leader, Mary Harney, said it was time to get tough on Sinn Féin, and called repeatedly on Bruton to cut off all official contacts with the party. Labour's Pat Magner called on her to 'stop sniping' at the taoiseach and tánaiste.

Adams said in an *Irish Times* article: 'I am asked if Sinn Féin support the armed struggle of the IRA. I want to see an end to all armed actions. Some members of Sinn Féin, like those in other parties, may have a different view, but Sinn Féin policy on the conflict is contained in our peace strategy.' He did admit for the first time that there 'may be some' in Sinn Féin who were not in favour of the peace strategy. On the question of whether or not he had gone to the IRA asking for a ceasefire, he wrote: 'I have been in regular contact with representatives of the IRA leadership in an effort to restore the peace process,' which was not an answer to the question as posed. Republicans wanted all-party talks, and they were now under way. Adams said in his article that, although he understood the 'difficulties facing the government', he was surprised at how the question was put. 'Perhaps they thought there wasn't enough progress, or in the wake of the killing of Garda McCabe [sic] that they could do no more at that time.'

Certainly, there was sheer dismay in government that the ceasefire was not reinstated to allow Sinn Féin to enter the talks, so there was a distinct lack of trust. My belief is that the IRA's desire to cause political harm to the Rainbow government played a role. It was simply impossible for Sinn Féin to demand to be let in to the talks without a cessation of the IRA campaign. The result of that would have been everyone else walking out, except perhaps the SDLP, and the collapse of the talks. It would be naive of any republican to think otherwise. We all thought that the 17 months of the ceasefire without talks was disgraceful, but Bruton had done everything in his power to get the British to drop the arms precondition and start the talks earlier.

'Up until the tragic killing of Garda McCabe the engagement with the Irish government was particularly constructive,' Adams wrote in the *Irish Times*. 'We were making progress. It was also my view that the government was much more focused recently than at other times, especially in their negotiations with the British, particularly in the run-up to the agreement of 6 June.' (This was the agreement on the ground rules for the talks.) He said that his interaction with IRA representatives showed him that 'they view the British government's stance as the biggest obstacle to any effort to bring about the restoration of the cessation.' In fact, Major had conceded to Irish government pressure in the November and February summits in London, despite extremely difficult conditions; and also in the organisation of the all-party talks now under way, as well as with the appointment of

George Mitchell. Adams, like McGuinness, with his extraordinary falsehood about the Joint Framework Documents, was once again short-selling the achievements of Bruton and the Rainbow government.

The international talks team issued its own statement. Mitchell, de Chastelain and Holkeri said: 'We strongly and unequivocally condemn today's bombing. This reprehensible act comes at a crucial time, just days after the multi-party talks began. We believe that the way to peace is not through violence, but rather through meaningful dialogue.' It was the first of many such appeals they were to make, Mitchell wrote, adding, 'Those opposed to the peace process could not disrupt it through the use or threat of violence.'

Meanwhile, the row about the ground rules and procedures for the talks, as well as the authority of the chairman, rumbled on. The document prepared from all the parties' suggestions on the procedures had led to agreement on many points.

There was clarification and an extension of the requirements for 'sufficient consensus'. It needed the support of parties representing a majority of the total valid poll in the election; a majority of both communities in Northern Ireland as represented in the negotiations; and a majority of the parties involved in the multi-party talks. The smaller loyalist parties were happy with the third step, which meant that they had a greater involvement. The second step now included the phrase 'as represented in the negotiations', taking into account both the absence of Sinn Féin and its inclusion at a later date.

Mitchell conceded in his book *Making Peace* that Trimble's tactics did work: 'The unionists prevented the ground rules and the related documents from being adopted intact, and they kept out of the rules of procedure what they regarded as the most offensive provisions of the ground rules.' However, Mitchell said that during these discussions he felt that 'ultimately my ability to be effective would depend more upon my gaining the participants' trust and confidence than on the formal description of my authority'. In time he certainly gained their trust. The governments' main preoccupation was to ensure that amendments did not substantially curtail the overarching role originally envisaged for

Mitchell in the ground rules published on 6 June, and that the principle of 'sufficient consensus' was preserved as the means of burying unionist majoritarianism. Both objectives were achieved.

Despite these teething issues, the multi-party talks were sustained, and this vital talks process continued, with Mitchell in the chair, until the Belfast Agreement was reached. The key importance of establishing and sustaining this critical pillar of the peace process, despite the difficulties involved, has been widely overlooked, just like the hard-won November 1995 summit leading to the Mitchell Principles, the dropping of Washington 3, and the fundamental importance of the Framework Documents. These three pillars of the peace process on the Rainbow's watch required a huge personal commitment from Bruton and Spring. Ministers Nora Owen, Mervyn Taylor, Hugh Coveney, Proinsias De Rossa and Attorney General Dermot Gleeson spent many days at Stormont. There was also great dedication and tenacity shown by key officials, combined with the extraordinary patience, tolerance and intelligence of George Mitchell, who dealt with what he called the 'twin demons of violence and intransigence', facing personal threats, the ongoing IRA campaign, and radical political negativity, particularly from the Paisley and McCartney unionists, to keep the talks going. The talks were strongly supported by the two governments and the participants, until Tony Blair and his New Labour Party won the British general election in May 1997. Thus this hard-fought round-table talks train was ready and waiting for Blair and Sinn Féin to get on board.

As Mitchell astutely noted, the June 1997 election in the Republic, called by the Rainbow government, 'backfired', so Bertie Ahern was able to join Blair on that train. Mitchell wrote tellingly in *Making Peace* that Blair and Ahern 'now had the opportunity to enter the history books as the men who brought peace to Northern Ireland. In both cases, they owed that opportunity to their predecessors who had begun the peace process and kept it going.' That was certainly the truth.

15

VERONICA GUERIN'S MURDER

THE TAOISEACH SPOKE TO JOHN Major on the phone about the killing of Jerry McCabe and the Manchester bomb. They both strongly agreed that the talks must proceed, and that an unambiguous ceasefire was what was required from the IRA. They also discussed the forthcoming Irish presidency of the EU and the BSE issue. Major looked favourably on EU Commissioner Jacques Santer's plan for the ending of the ban on the export of British beef and he indicated that the British would end their veto on important EU decisions before Ireland took over the presidency on 1 July 1996. The veto was finally dropped on 21 June at the Italians' final presidency summit in Florence, which Bruton and Spring attended. It had been a decade since I visited Florence, and I was glad to be able to take some time over lunch each day to look around this beautiful city again, one of the wonders of the world. We were relieved that Major had ended his 'mad cow' veto on important EU decisions, so it wouldn't blight our presidency. The BSE agreement at Florence included IR£160m extra compensation for EU farmers, and Ireland expected to get about 10 per cent of that sum.

The British did not win any friends by doing a heavy media briefing in Florence, claiming that the framework for ending the British beef export ban would not be a 'climbdown' by the other member states, when it was nothing of the sort anyway, proved by the fact that the ban would not be ended for another three years. The briefing was really meant for British home consumption – the hostile popular press needed to be fed propaganda on who had won the 'beef war'. Other leaders openly criticised the British to the media, dismissing these claims. The agenda for the Irish presidency was growing so much that at Florence it was decided that there would be a second special EU Irish summit in October as well as a December summit. The taoiseach briefed the Irish and other media about the agenda, which included preparing a new EU treaty for consideration at the Intergovernmental Conference (IGC); preparations for an economic stability pact after the launch of the euro to underpin the single currency; adjustments to the pre-euro exchange rate mechanism; and, on top of all that, substantial reports on employment and illegal drugs.

The preparations for the launch of the Irish presidency with Jacques Santer at the new Meeting House Square in Temple Bar were well advanced. The summer evening show would be a glittering programme of Irish performing artists. Singer Virginia Kerr would begin with a performance of Seán Ó Riada's 'Mná na hÉireann'; then there was The Band, a melding of some of the finest Irish musicians, including Steve Cooney, Máire Breatnach and Máirtín O'Connor with composer Shaun Davey and others; Anúna, The Corrs, and the National Symphony Orchestra's brass and percussion sections. The three entrances to the square could be managed with a flow of people in and out and around the edge of the plaza, and seating was provided for the invited guests in the central area.

While we were in Florence, we got news of a marching season confrontation in Belfast, a harbinger of more trouble on that front during the summer, which would intensify into a sharp clash between the Irish and British governments. There were many deliberate provocations of Catholic neighbourhoods by the Protestant Orange Order insisting on marches commemorating 'victories' in the seventeenth century over the Catholic King James II by William of Orange, who had been installed as the British king by the Protestant Parliament. William, ironically, was married to James II's daughter. On 21 June in Belfast, a huge force of RUC men had sealed off an area around a Catholic neighbourhood while hundreds of nationalist protesters sat or lay on the Cliftonville Road to prevent a march. RUC men in riot gear cleared the road by dragging people off it. This was followed by petrol bomb attacks and stone-throwing, with at least one vehicle set on fire. An elected Sinn Féin representative, Gerry Kelly, who tried to gain access to the area as a public representative, was among those held by the RUC. He succeeded in escaping. There was widespread sympathy in the Republic for Northern Catholic nationalists exposed to triumphalist intimidation.

On the same day, in the early hours, while we were at the summit in Florence, armed gardaí made a raid on a farm near Clonaslee in the Slieve Bloom area of County Laois, after receiving a tip-off during the ongoing search for the killers of Detective Garda Jerry McCabe. They found a substantial bomb-making factory for the IRA. The *Irish Times* reported that a number of arrests were made, with two known IRA figures involved, one connected with the shipment of weapons from Libya on board the vessel *Eksund*, seized at sea, the other suspected of being a long-time bomb-maker. Gardaí found mortar bomb components, including timers, Semtex, home-made explosives, electrical parts and batteries. Two weeks later there was an IRA mortar attack on a British base at Osnabrück in Germany. No one was injured but property was damaged.

Bruton held a bilateral meeting with Major at the Florence summit, joined for part of the time by Dick Spring, at which they discussed support for the continuing multi-party talks and complimented the Garda success in discovering the IRA bomb factory. The Gardaí were getting substantial intelligence from their widespread investigation of the brutal killing of Jerry McCabe. They had arrested more than twenty people. The Semtex haul was large, with 16 finished mortars. Gardaí thought this bomb factory was the main facility for the IRA and finding it dealt a severe blow to its operations. Semtex had been used in the Docklands and Manchester bombings, together with easily acquired home-made fertiliser explosives. Semtex had also been planted under Hammersmith Bridge in April 1996, but the bomb had not gone off. RUC Chief Constable Hugh Annesley had warned of possible loyalist paramilitary retaliation, particularly if Northern Ireland was targeted. Spring, speaking to the media, praised the 'stoic' and responsible behaviour of the parties representing the loyalists in the multi-party talks and he hoped that their ceasefires would hold. The taoiseach said the manufacture of mortars was inconsistent with Sinn Féin's acceptance of the six Mitchell Principles. If the party was committed to peace, why were these bombs being made?

But there was an alternate world. Republicans held the annual Wolfe Tone Bodenstown commemoration that solstice weekend of June 1996. Talking to journalists, Martin McGuinness did not think the bomb factory discovery would make it more difficult for the governments to talk to Sinn Féin since they were sitting in Stormont with loyalist party delegates who had been arrested on arms charges. He ignored the critical difference – the loyalist paramilitaries were still on ceasefire.

On 26 June, back from Florence, I heard a news flash on RTÉ radio reporting that the investigative journalist Veronica Guerin, who wrote extensively in the *Sunday Independent* on the drug barons and their criminal gangs, had been killed. She was shot dead at point-blank range by one of two men on a motorbike who pulled up beside her car, stopped at the Boot Road traffic lights on the Naas dual carriageway. I was shocked beyond description. I didn't know Veronica personally, but I was very familiar with the extraordinarily courageous work that she had been doing for the newspaper. She had a string of exclusives on the raw underbelly of criminal Ireland, which was crying out for a much more intense policing intervention. Now she had lost her life for exposing this dark underworld. All this crowded into my mind as I hastened to the taoiseach's office. He was in shock, having already heard what had happened.

Bruton's office was establishing contacts for Veronica's husband and family so he could express his sympathy. I suggested he should make a phone call to the editor of her newspaper. We got through to the *Sunday Independent* news editor, Willie Kealy, at 3 p.m. The taoiseach told him he wanted to express 'profound sympathy to you and all journalists at the *Sunday Independent*. People in Leinster House were shocked speechless at what has happened. There's a pall of gloom and grief. I've never seen such an atmosphere.' He said that he would visit the paper's offices later to talk to the editorial staff in person, which he and I did, speaking to the deputy editor, Anne Harris, and her colleagues – the editor was in London. All were still in shock. Something had to be done; a line had been crossed and there had to be severe consequences.

In the Dáil that evening Bruton attacked the savage murder as 'sinister in the extreme'; 'that a journalist should be callously murdered in the line of duty is an attack on democracy, because it is an attack on one of the pillars of our democracy.' He promised that the government would bring forward measures to combat powerful and wealthy criminals. On 29 June the taoiseach and I attended Veronica's funeral. Minister for Justice Nora Owen, who knew Veronica Guerin very well, was in New York to speak at a session of the UN about drug crime when she heard the news of Veronica's murder. She was upset and shaken by the news. The murder became part of the discussion at the UN meeting, with a strong reaction by delegates. Veronica Guerin had been threatened before, and in a gun attack on her home she was wounded in the leg, and Nora Owen had visited her in Beaumont Hospital. Veronica was truly fearless. She had an armed garda escort for a while, but the arrangement had ended. A huge Garda investigation was launched, which continued for a number of years, and the government anxiously sought ways to increase vigilance on criminals, improve the conviction rate, and tackle the wealth of crime bosses and their gangs. These criminals delighted in flaunting their wealth, showing off to the youth of deprived areas as a means of recruiting new gang members.

The day after the funeral, I delivered some papers to the taoiseach's country home at Dunboyne. He and Finola asked me to stay for lunch, so we could continue talking about the issues. Over a fine bacon and cabbage Sunday lunch, Bruton told me that he had received a suggestion from an adviser that the powers of the Special Criminal Court should be strengthened to deal with the criminal gangs. I had been thinking along the same lines. For some years, members of the IRA could be imprisoned on the sworn testimony of a garda superintendent that the person was a member of the organisation. Volunteers would never renounce the IRA, so the law was successful, until the IRA changed its rules and allowed its members to deny membership in court.

The entire country was appalled at Veronica Guerin's murder, and there was outrage too at the way the criminal gangs publicly displayed their wealth, driving BMWs and Mercedes, buying houses, mansions and farms, and in one case a large country house with horse stables and a jumps circuit. It seemed to ordinary people that these criminals now felt so safe that they could get away even with murder. The gang lords, and their rank-and-file thugs, had the upper hand because the laws of evidence made it hard for the Gardaí to put them behind bars. The mood of the people, I believed, would welcome strong emergency action against these criminals.

I suggested to Bruton that it would need a garda superintendent or other senior officer giving evidence of his belief that an accused was a member of a criminal conspiracy – on top of whatever other evidence could be produced. That belief would be treated as incontrovertible proof before the Special Criminal Court, where judgments were made by three judges, not a jury. It would be extremely controversial. Bruton was concerned about the suspension of civil rights involved, and clearly was unwilling to go that far. He also cited the fact that emergency legislation, when enacted, can survive for many years after the emergency has passed. It could also undermine Garda willpower to put in the almost superhuman effort necessary to gather evidence that would stand up in court.

In Dunboyne, our discussion turned to the other proposals to deal with crime gangs, which had been mooted for some time. Among these was the seizure of criminal assets and the creation of a special unit of the Garda Síochána to carry this out. Bruton had spoken to Ruairí Quinn, the Minister for Finance, the day after the murder of Veronica Guerin about the need for government action. Quinn told Bruton that two Labour TDs, Joe Costello and Róisín Shortall, had proposed a system to confiscate criminal illegal wealth and channel the money back into disadvantaged communities. In the previous year the Rainbow government had sought an improvement in Garda action on the criminal gangs and their wealth. Though Garda Commissioner Pat Byrne was keen to improve his force's performance, it was patently clear that new laws and a new agency were needed. Nora Owen was determined to rapidly bring forward the Proceeds of Crime Act, and the Department of Finance would sponsor the Criminal Assets Bureau Act. Together these Acts would provide for the investigation and seizure of criminal wealth. In his memoir, Quinn wrote that the word 'agency' was not used because of Garda sensitivities about the word 'agents'.

Barry Galvin, the state solicitor for Cork, had already made a public impression in the media as a man who wanted to take on the drug barons – he had spoken on the topic on RTÉ's *Late Late Show*. Quinn contacted him to see if he might take on the job of heading up the Bureau, which would involve members of An Garda Síochána, the Revenue Commissioners, Customs and Excise, and officials from the Department of Social Welfare. However, Garda sensibilities about taking instructions from a civilian led to 'a compromise whereby Detective Chief Superintendent Fachtna Murphy was the chief executive officer and Barry Galvin the chief legal officer', a dynamic that was outlined by Ruairí Quinn in his 2005 book. Both Acts went through the Dáil in record time. By October CAB was already operational, with its new powers. Now, instead of a conviction being required before assets could be seized, which had been the law until then, CAB just had to prove, on the balance of probabilities, that the assets were the proceeds of crime. CAB has done sterling work for the state ever since it was set up.

The state's first witness protection programme was also established. This has had mixed results over time. It was used to cater for those turning state's evidence during the Veronica Guerin murder trials. The use of the Special Criminal Court for criminal gangs was put on a secure footing. The government agreed to a Fianna Fáil amendment allowing the freezing of drug barons' assets on the word of a Garda superintendent. As Nora Owen rightly observed, the anger of the Irish people over Veronica Guerin's brutal murder acted as a catalyst for the passage of badly needed tough measures, which she delivered in record time. A special midsummer sitting of the Dáil was scheduled for 25 July to legislate for the main elements of the anti-crime legislation.

The three party leaders – the taoiseach, the tánaiste, and Proinsias De Rossa – met with Owen a number of times about the anti-crime issues. Bail was a thorny problem because a number of crimes had been committed by accused persons out on bail. The party leaders agreed that a referendum would be held later in the year to provide for the refusal of bail if there was a danger of other crimes being committed. The government would also legislate to require bail to be lodged either in cash or its equivalent; the bail provider must guarantee the good behaviour of the accused on bail; and the bail money could be confiscated if the accused committed another offence while on bail. The Criminal Justice Act of 1984 would be amended to provide for consecutive sentences to be served if additional offences were committed on bail.

Another controversial issue was the right to silence. The three leaders agreed with Owen to amend the law to allow inferences to be drawn by the court in drugs cases where accused persons did not divulge to the investigating gardaí alibis or other evidence that they later relied upon in their defence in court, but that could have been given to officers during questioning.

As the Gardaí continued to investigate Veronica Guerin's murder, the focus was on a drugs gang led by John Gilligan, who had left the country just before the attack. After the murder, members of Gilligan's gang were arrested, and one, Charles Bowden, turned state's witness. He gave evidence against four other gang members, including Gilligan himself, at their trials in the Special Criminal Court. None of these cases was ultimately successful on foot of Bowden's evidence, but in 1999 Brian Meehan was convicted of murdering Veronica Guerin when the court accepted evidence given by another gang member, Russell Warren. Meehan was sentenced to life imprisonment. Gilligan was tried and acquitted of the murder but was later convicted of importing 20 tonnes of cannabis, and was sentenced to 28 years in prison, reduced to 20 years on appeal. CAB seized his assets, including a farm and stables, despite Gilligan's legal bid from jail to stop it from happening.

During this time, I had dinner with a Sinn Féin acquaintance. He told me that the ceasefire was always a limited affair, but the IRA did not want to return to the full war. Sinn Féin and the IRA knew that a united Ireland would not be possible in their lifetime. 'The IRA attracts people who are psychopathic killers,' he told me. At an IRA inquiry into a punishment shooting that this man attended, where the victim allegedly was shot accidentally as he attempted to run away, the victim had his jacket with him with obvious 'gunshot blast burns' in the material, which he threw onto the table. 'Is that the jacket of a person shot accidentally, running away?' demanded the victim.

It was the IRA quartermaster who was against the ceasefire, my dining companion told me, empowered by the decommissioning issue, and refusing to give up weapons. Come the election, Sinn Féin could, with the right candidates, win Dáil seats in Sligo–Leitrim, Cavan–Monaghan and Louth, he said. Fine Gael's problem was poor candidates. My Sinn Féin contact said that Fianna Fáil could be deeply divided over the election agreement with the Progressive Democrats, a split that did not materialise. He wasn't a fan of the Fianna Fáil front bench. The Labour Party, he predicted, was in trouble. I agreed with that, and all the polls showed it. He said that there *must* be a ceasefire again before the general election the following year. There would have been if the Rainbow government had not made the tragic mistake of holding an early general election.

16

BRITISH DEBACLE AT DRUMCREE

As we have seen, a major point of conflict between the two communities in the North was the Orange Order parades. Unionists and loyalists delighted in marching provocatively behind pipe bands through Catholic nationalist areas and streets, banging Lambeg drums, and sporting their sashes, flags and banners. They'd commemorate King William III's victory over King James II at the Boyne in 1690, the breaking of the siege of Derry or local Protestant heroes and their exploits. Catholics felt these events were a warning to the 'Fenians' that Protestants were in charge in Northern Ireland and Catholics and nationalists should 'know their place'. This was 'a Protestant state for a Protestant people'. On the other hand, the unionists and loyalists maintained that they had a right to march anywhere in Northern Ireland.

One of the most contentious of these flashpoints was the annual Orange parade through the nationalist Catholic Garvaghy Road after a service at the Drumcree parish church in Portadown, Co. Armagh. In the summer of 1995, the Upper Bann MP David Trimble was seeking the leadership of the UUP. Controversially, he joined the Rev. Ian Paisley in leading the disputed parade down the Garvaghy Road, to the anger of the residents. It came as a shock to me and others in the Department of the Taoiseach that Trimble would brazenly lead this triumphalist, intimidatory parade. But it was the MacNaughton rule at work – that unionist would-be leaders must bend to the wishes of the Orange masses. Trimble succeeded Molyneaux as leader of the UUP in September of that year, and his action on the Garvaghy Road was almost certainly a significant boost to his leadership victory over John Taylor.

The British State Papers for 1996 show that the Orange Drumcree parade was the subject of a meeting on 17 May between Sir John Wheeler, the security minister at the Northern Ireland Office, and the then RUC deputy chief constable, Ronnie Flanagan, just before the all-party talks began. Flanagan warned that there was increasing unionist resentment at marches being banned. RUC intelligence indicated that a ban on the Orange Order parade down the Garvaghy Road could result in a large number of Orangemen laying siege to Portadown and creating serious public order difficulties.

It appears that the RUC was softening up the Northern Ireland Office on the issue of a ban, which the Garvaghy Road residents were demanding after the affront visited on them the previous year. Wheeler noted that Trimble's action 'had to be seen in the context of his leadership bid' and it was hoped he could be more statesmanlike this time. However, Flanagan indicated that the MacNaughton rule still applied, saying there were rumblings within the Orange Order that Trimble was 'going soft by going down to Dublin', a reference to his recent visit to the taoiseach in Dublin to discuss the all-party talks. Wheeler met Trimble later that same day and the UUP leader expressed concerns about large-scale disorder, predictably blaming Sinn Féin for raising tension when there would be none if the parade's intimidation and bullying was stopped. However, he did favour a dialogue.

In fact, the RUC chief Hugh Annesley did ban the Orange parade planned for Sunday 7 July on the Garvaghy Road. Preparations were made to close the road into Garvaghy, with concrete barricades at Drumcree church and a strong defence by a substantial number of RUC officers armed with rubber bullet guns and other weapons. David Trimble raised the temperature by accusing Annesley of making a 'grossly irresponsible' decision. Orange leaders made appeals for members to come to

Drumcree to join 'the siege', recalling the 1689 siege of Derry. A huge crowd, estimated at 10,000, assembled before the RUC and the barricades, with reports of many thousands more coming to join the demonstration. A serious confrontation seemed unavoidable. There had already been loyalist disturbances all over the six counties, with riots, vehicles burned, roads blocked and Catholic families fleeing their homes in north Belfast.

Over the years, British forces, police and army, clearly discriminated against nationalist demonstrations and gave in to unionist/loyalist demonstrations. I've already mentioned the 1968 violent RUC attacks on peaceful nationalist civil rights marchers in Derry and the 14 innocent people killed in 1972 by British Army paratroopers on Bloody Sunday in Derry. The previous year, the same British regiment had killed 11 innocent civilians in Ballymurphy, Belfast. Then there had been the British Labour government's disastrous capitulation to the Ulster Workers' Council, in effect loyalist road blocks, barricades, and the shutting down of electricity supplies destroying the Sunningdale Agreement's five-month-old power-sharing Northern Ireland Executive in 1974 led by Unionist leader Brian Faulkner, SDLP leader Gerry Fitt and Alliance Party leader Oliver Napier. It was the first of its kind, not repeated for 25 years.

Garret FitzGerald, who was Minister of Foreign Affairs at the time, described the dynamic in his 1991 autobiography, writing that the Irish government 'regarded it as breathtaking, the abdication of responsibility for law and order in Northern Ireland by the British government in favour of an illegal body'. Nationalists, North and South, he said, 'believed at the time that had the British Army been willing to take prompt action against road blocks, barricades and overt intimidation when these features first made their appearance, the strike could have been broken'. The North's state electricity company staff were largely Protestant, discriminating against Catholics, and complied with the UWC diktat. Disgracefully, BBC Northern Ireland became 'dominated by the views of those challenging the British government's authority,' said Dr FitzGerald, who feared the 'emergence there of a fascist-type political entity run by extremist unionist politicians and loyalist paramilitaries'. The morale of the Executive, 'both unionist and nationalist members, was shattered by what they saw as their betrayal by a British government that seemed to them – and to us – to be fearful of its own army, the unwillingness of which to act was made plain by leaks to the press from their headquarters in Lisburn'. Now, at Drumcree, there was about to be another cave-in to unionists and loyalists threatening violence. It outraged the nationalist community, North and South.

I was in Paris with the taoiseach at a meeting with French President Jacques Chirac at the Élysée Palace on 11 July in a splendid, gilded room with enormous windows overlooking the city and a huge baroque eighteenth-century tapestry, when the RUC reversal was about to happen at Drumcree. The meeting was about the Irish presidency of the EU, which had just begun, and the taoiseach and Chirac were discussing the issues to be resolved.

At Drumcree church the situation was getting ugly. It had been a four-day stand-off between the RUC, the British Army, and thousands of angry unionists and loyalists, with exchanges of fire between the RUC and the mob, the RUC firing rubber bullets at shouting and screaming Orangemen, who were throwing bottles and stones at them. The line seemed to be holding before the Chirac meeting, though many thousands more Orangemen were expected to join the protesters. When the meeting with Chirac finished, Paddy Teahon told us that the British had U-turned and allowed thousands of unionist and loyalist demonstrators, not just the Orange marchers, down the Garvaghy Road, to an outburst of anger from the upset residents who had felt assured that the ban would hold.

We heard that about two hundred residents had sat down on the road and a number had been hit with batons as the RUC cleared the way. Trimble and Paisley were there but did not lead the marchers; however, they had clapped them as they strode down the road. Teahon rang John Holmes in Downing Street to protest, saying we were 'very concerned' and wanted to know why the decision about the ban had been reversed. Holmes said, 'It was in the interest of saving lives.' This volte-face turned the unrest in loyalist areas of Northern Ireland to angry scenes and confrontations with the RUC in nationalist areas across the North.

When we emerged from the Élysée Palace, RTÉ's Brussels correspondent, Tommie Gorman, was waiting with a film crew. Tommie wanted the taoiseach's reaction to Garvaghy on top of his interview about the Chirac meeting before Bruton spoke to other journalists.

I had scribbled down a few notes as the story unfolded. The key point was 'British/RUC given in to threat of violence – signal to paramilitaries = Brits only give in to force', but I didn't get to speak to Bruton before the interview began. I was unhappy with some of his comments in the interview; I didn't feel they were strong enough. He said that the British should have allowed dialogue to take place; the decision allowing the march through was 'precipitate and mistaken; we have been in direct contact with the prime minister's office', and he would be speaking to him. He did not 'believe the right decisions were taken'. Talking to Patrick Smyth of the *Irish Times* and other journalists, Bruton said similar things, but when he was asked if the RUC, fearing the increasing numbers of protesters, could have changed the situation, he replied: 'No. As leader of the Irish government my view is the state can never yield to force or the threat of force, a cardinal principle in my view, of democratic governments.' Much stronger, but, for this subject, television would have made a greater impact.

Back in Dublin later that evening, I was pleased to get a call from Leo Enright, a former colleague in RTÉ, now working as Ireland correspondent for the BBC. He asked for an interview with the taoiseach for the BBC's *Nine O'Clock News*. I said I would do what I could to get it and made for the taoiseach's office. Bruton said he had already done an interview for RTÉ – wouldn't it be too much to do another? I told him the interview with Tommie Gorman was too soft. This was an important issue, not just in Northern Ireland but for the whole country. People were very angry over the British capitulation to the threat of violence from the Orangemen. The security forces always confronted nationalists and had in the past killed peaceful demonstrators and innocent civilians. This was submission to a violent unionist mob. The interview was an opportunity to get his TV reaction right. He agreed. I phoned Leo to tell him the taoiseach would be strong. He would get a good interview.

A short time later Leo called me back and said the presenter of the *Nine O'Clock News*, Peter Sissons, was going to do the interview, which would lead the bulletin. They would do it from the Dáil television studio, which was in a government building on Kildare Street opposite Leinster House. I went back to Bruton, and he read out the points he was going to make: a sovereign government caved in to people using violence and threatening more; a democratic state can never yield to force or the threat of force; it could not be inconsistent or partial in the way it applied the law; people looked to the police and the government to be impartial, not to be willing to yield to pressure, and to uphold the law; these were principles of democracy and had all been breached in the Garvaghy Road events; the forces of law and order and government in Northern Ireland had failed. He asked me what I thought. I felt it perfectly met the needs of the day, but I was afraid to be too outspoken in case the taoiseach pulled back, so I just said, 'Hmmm, okay, it's fine.' Then I told Bruton about the presenter doing the interview and he agreed to that. During the interview I could see Peter Sissons's reactions – he knew they had a big story, thanks to Leo. In the course of the broadcast, the taoiseach added that there was evidence of a lack of impartiality in the way some residents had been treated when they were removed from Garvaghy Road.

> The peace process depends on politicians who support democracy all of the time, not on an à la carte basis, and take their courage in their hands to make agreements. The British government's authority has been seriously damaged by concessions made to the Orange Order in this matter ... it would be foolish to pretend that very serious damage has not been done.

When we got back to Government Buildings Bruton said he'd talk to Major on the phone. Later, after the broadcast, all hell broke loose on the British side, with angry media interviews broadcast on the BBC and other TV channels; Mayhew was everywhere condemning Bruton for his 'most extraordinary outburst' and claiming that the chief constable had reversed the ban decision and let the march down Garvaghy Road to save lives. Bruton rang me the next morning, angrily saying I had got him into a terrible conflict. I argued that as taoiseach he had no choice – he had to strongly condemn the British volte-face. I told him to wait until he saw the reaction in Ireland.

He rang me again just before lunch to say that he had received calls from cabinet ministers around the country saying that the local reaction to his interview was great. I spoke to Dermot Gleeson, who confirmed that view, and said it was exactly what the situation required. He also spoke to the taoiseach. In the US, former Congressman Bruce Morrison, who was a member of Friends of Ireland, spoke to an Irish diplomat, who wrote: 'He expressed considerable praise for the strong stand which the taoiseach had taken in response to Drumcree, and believed that this had helped to stabilise the response on the nationalist side.' The taoiseach's aide-de-camp, Captain Maurice McQuillan, rang me to express his relief – he had been worried after the Paris interview. It was a national issue; public opinion in the Republic was outraged about Garvaghy Road. Bruton had worked so hard at avoiding nationalist sentiment within himself, believing it had led to so much bloodshed, that he was cautious in reaction to events lest he stir angry nationalism in others.

Some fifty police officers and ninety loyalist demonstrators were injured in the stand-off after the church service. There were injuries in both communities as a result of the riots and violence, but it was a Catholic taxi driver in Lurgan, 31-year-old Michael McGoldrick, who paid the full sectarian price for Drumcree. He was murdered by loyalist hitmen on 8 July, shot in the back of the head. 'Just three days earlier,' a deeply upset George Mitchell wrote, 'McGoldrick had graduated from Queen's University with a degree in English and high hopes. He and his wife had a seven-year-old daughter, and his wife was expecting their second child.'

Years later Pat Farrell, general secretary of Fianna Fáil at the time of the 1997 election, told me they were concerned that the party would lose votes to Bruton over his Garvaghy Road stand and on the other occasions when Bruton appeared to be taking a firm nationalist position. A strong nationalist stand was a vote-getter in the Republic. Charles Haughey, after an interview I did with him in his northside mansion in the late 1970s, chatted amiably about this subject. His charming side was on display after a testy row over the interview, during which he disappeared from the dining room, decorated with paintings and a bust of himself, leaving me on my own at the table. He returned ten minutes later when I was packing up to leave. Haughey's tactic was to throw interviewers off balance. He was very dismissive of the 'low intellectual capacities' of the western world leadership at the time, which included US President Jimmy Carter and British Prime Minister Jim Callaghan. Just before I left, the conversation touched on patriotism and nationalism, and he said the latter 'was without a doubt the greatest political motivating force of public opinion. There are times when you cannot ignore it, and your public will require it of you.' However, this strong motivating effect is also used by those who want to exploit it for meaner reasons, personal gain, power or self-interest. Samuel Johnson coined a cutting phrase for those types: 'Patriotism is the last refuge of a scoundrel.'

Meanwhile, Bruton did not get to talk to Major until 10 p.m. on 11 July, waiting in his office after the BBC interview. He was fuming when Major came on the line, citing the old chestnut of a series of meetings, pleading he was not aware of the arrangement, and he was 'not least dealing with the problems of Northern Ireland and what's now happening in various parts of Northern Ireland all evening'. Testily, Bruton responded:

> Yes, yes, I have been sitting here watching the television and watching the results of the decision that was taken by the Chief Constable this morning, which is very, very serious I have to tell you. I think it is showing force winning the day ... and I have spent my time working with you to demonstrate that there was another way forward apart from force. Here we have force '... on the part of the mass gathering of Orangemen forcing the Chief Constable to change his position on a matter that he had decided earlier in the week ...' The negotiations that were continuing through the churchmen were still continuing and still offered some prospect of success, but they were just swept aside by reversing the ban.

Major insisted that things were more complex than that and cited the Garvaghy Road residents' spokesman, Breandán Mac Cionnaith, who had been convicted and jailed for six years for taking part in an IRA bombing in Portadown. 'One of the problems for much of the last two days is that the churchmen and others have been trying to get the Garvaghy road residents to put up someone to negotiate other than a convicted terrorist convict.'

Bruton interjected, 'He served his sentence.'

'Nobody is going to talk to him,' Major replied.

'Sure David Ervine was a terrorist too,' said Bruton. (Ervine served time in jail for a UVF linked offence and was at the multi-party talks representing the PUP which had links with the UVF. The loyalist cease-fire still held.)

Major continued, 'The trouble here is on both sides. I am not defending the Orange Lodge, God help me I'm not, but it isn't all one-sided on this occasion.'

'I don't think that it is reasonable to use the excuse that this man was convicted,' Bruton responded. 'If he was convicted, he served his sentence and he has been released. A number of people in politics in this country on both sides of the border and on both sides of the political divide were in jail at some time or other. I'm in government with a man ... the Minister for Social Welfare was interned for a lengthy period.' (Proinsias De Rossa was interned without trial or conviction. He is a strong opponent of the use of violence.)

'We have been trying to get agreement, John ... the decision taken by the chief constable was his and his alone ... He did it to avoid the loss of life. Tomorrow there would have been lives lost.' According to Major, the few thousand Orangemen there would have increased to 50,000, 'to take part in the marches'. He did not take part in 'operational decisions' but he could see why the chief constable 'did what he did. Fifty thousand people would have overwhelmed the RUC, overwhelmed the army.' Many of the Catholics of Garvaghy would be at risk, he said.

'Well this brings back the same type of argument that was used to capitulate to the Ulster Workers strike in 1974,' Bruton replied. (The

British Labour government allowed loyalists to block the streets of Belfast and shut down power stations, causing the collapse of the Sunningdale Agreement first power-sharing government in the North.)

'I don't want to get into a squabble with you,' Major continued. 'I have had the last two or three days trying to deal with this in the most discreet way possible. What would you have done? Would you have overruled the RUC and then face the risk tomorrow that there would have been 50,000 people in a mass loss of life?'

'Who made the decision then to block the road in the first place?' Bruton asked. 'What happened here is that the appearance has been created that the RUC started off to block this march but when the numbers on the other side – in other words when the force on the other side – got too large, they decided to back off. I mean this is not something that happened for the first time. We had a previous experience of this issue last year, so we had twelve months to plan for it. Why start off on a route of saying that you are going not to let the march down the road and then, entirely predictable events developed as they did, why did the RUC back off today?'

Major disagreed, 'No it wasn't entirely predictable ... for this reason. Last year, there was a stand-off and then there was a negotiation, and a small number of marches went through. This year Hugh Annesley saw what was happening, wanted to stop it and hoped there would be a negotiated settlement.' Major said he understood that for two days the marchers were prepared to go through in small numbers, but the residents weren't prepared to agree to that, and with the 12 July the next day the RUC's view was it could be 50,000 present; an "unprecedented situation" and if they broke through and a lot of people, including Catholics, were killed, I wonder what would have been said then?'

Bruton remained resolved: 'I don't believe that the British Army is unable, and the British forces are unable to protect people to that degree. It seems to me that starting off on the course of saying that you are going to block the road and then, when the numbers get too large, backing off, does not convey a sense of resolution or a sense that your government is in charge.'

'I resent that, John,' Major responded angrily, 'and if you want to continue the conversation in that fashion you can continue it alone, because I am not going to.'

'No!' exclaimed Bruton.

Major interjected, 'Operational decisions are for the police ... the British government does not interfere with operational decisions either by the General Officer commanding the army, or by the police in terms of street control. It is our habit to take the advice of those people ... unless there is a very strong reason to override it and, in this judgement, I have got no experience of control of that area; neither has Paddy Mayhew. He was absolutely right to take the advice of the chief constable.'

Bruton countered, 'You claim that the RUC were in a very difficult position. To allow them to be the ones that are taking decisions of this nature, I mean these are quite essentially political decisions, they are about order in society and who makes the rules and who ensures that the rules are kept. They are the essence of politics in my view, and to place the RUC in the position that it alone is taking such decisions makes it very difficult for the RUC to win the acceptability that they need to win from the entire community—'

'John,' Major interrupted, 'would you have instructed the Gardaí what to do?'

'Yes, if necessary. Yes, not in terms of individual prosecutions or that sort of thing—'

'No, no,' interrupted Major; 'in terms of control of a street problem.'

'Yes,' Bruton answered. 'I would accept responsibility that at the end of the day the first responsibility of government is to maintain order and if you—'

'That is not what I asked. What I asked was whether you would actually instruct the Gardaí when they are actively in control of a street problem as to what to do and instruct them to act against their professional advice and against the advice of the army.'

'This was not a decision that was taken in a split second,' said Bruton. 'This was a decision that was predictable over several days.'

Major interrupted: 'I'm sorry John, you see, I do not agree with that. The circumstances were changing during the period. The negotiations were going on during the period—'

'They weren't finished when the decisions were taken.'

'They did nothing but negotiate for the last few days.'

'The negotiations hadn't concluded,' Bruton explained. 'The churchmen were actually just leaving the building when they were told that the decision had been taken to allow the march through. The actual negotiations were still on. This decision was taken almost in a way that actually undervalues the future use of church people as mediators because they were stepped aside.'

'John, I don't yet know how the decision was taken, so I'm assuming you don't quite yet know how the decision was taken.'

'Well I know that the timing is such that the churchmen were still in the building having meetings or concluding a meeting when this decision came through.'

'Without success.'

'Without success, yes, but I mean that sort of decision isn't taken in a split second, so plainly that decision had been reached some hours previously. But they were allowed to continue on.'

Major disagreed. 'I don't believe that is the case. I don't yet because I haven't cross-examined the chief constable about his decision, and I wasn't aware we were going to have this sort of conversation about an operational decision by the chief constable.'

'Well I can tell you this,' Bruton returned. 'This has done untold damage to the feelings of the nationalist community in Northern Ireland, and I have to say of the people in this state. People here are appalled at this, and I really want you to understand how strong the feelings are here. You know my record in matters of this nature. I would not speak in a way as to magnify feelings if they were not as they are. The feelings here are very, very strong about this decision and I believe that—'

'The feelings are that strong in the North as well, John, and our job is to try and damp down those feelings, not puff them up.'

'Indeed.'

'And that is what I shall try and do.'

Bruton pressed his point that the RUC making this decision in a conflict between two communities made it hard for them to be accepted in both and it was 'likely to put back relations between the RUC and the nationalist community by up to five years'.

Major continued: 'It is the intransigence of both sides which ensures that there couldn't be normal street policing.' He claimed that people 'had started to have' faith in the RUC, and questioned how Sinn Féin would have responded if they had been put under 'direct political control of ministers' over the last few years.

Bruton said people would have more confidence in ministers who were 'ultimately accountable for making political decisions ... this is a political decision in its effect and nature. It also has a security dimension, but by any standard is a political decision to allow that march through that area where it causes such political offence, and the consequences of it are most certainly political.'

'And the consequences of not letting it through would have been a lot of dead people very probably.'

'Well I find that very, very hard to believe,' Bruton said.

Major returned to the threat of 50,000 joining the marchers. Bruton questioned their getting through, the security forces would have stopped them. Major claimed they'd have come across the fields, not the high street saying, 'Oh gosh there's a soldier, I'll go back.' And he added that the RUC for a very long time had been under attack from a large part of the nationalist community. Being under the control of ministers would not have helped.

'I think that the effect of this decision is political in a major way,' Bruton said. 'However, we can't undo it now that it's taken ... we have just got to try and learn what we can from it.' He said that a commission should be set up immediately to deal with these sort of decisions with a wider consequence and a wider remit than the chief constable. Bruton pressed the commission idea urgently. 'The people of Garvaghy Road feel extremely exposed. The fact that force seems to have won the day on the part of the loyalists in this case makes many Catholics feel extremely insecure in their homes in Northern Ireland at the present time.'

'Well, enough of them are feeling so insecure, they seem to be causing trouble elsewhere.'

'Well some of them are being put out of their homes we know in north Belfast today,' Bruton rejoined. 'And we have a loyalist killing [the Catholic taxi driver]. Perhaps not authorised, I don't know. But there is a deep sense of insecurity amongst the Catholic community now in Northern Ireland and this is a political issue in a strong [way and] is not a matter for the chief constable alone to cope with.'

After rehearsing his 'street control' argument, Major said, 'I do want to find a way to cope with the sensitivities of both communities ... and I hope to say something in a few days. But I need to find out exactly what happened, how it happened, when it happened, and what would have happened if alternative mechanisms had been in force ... though I regret that it is so, marching seems to be something deep in the temperament and we have had over 300 marches this year. This one has caused trouble, the other 299 haven't.'

'I know you can understand that this will be seen as a victory for Dr Paisley and David Trimble – a victory over the nationalist community.'

'I don't think that they see it that way from all I hear ... and I certainly neither expect nor hope for any form of triumphalism from anyone ... I can't control perceptions, but I think those perceptions would be wrong. I think everybody should be shaken by what has happened over the last few days. It makes one realise how fragile everything is ... we have learned to speak fairly frankly to one another and I freely concede that some of the people have behaved appallingly on the Protestant side and I have made that very clear publicly and privately over the last few days ... but I have to say it isn't entirely one-sided ... some of the normal residents of the Garvaghy Road moved away [and] some pretty hardline people took their place. They weren't remotely interested in reaching any accommodation. It was extremely convenient to some people to have this conflict built up and I have no doubt that Sinn Féin and the IRA are rubbing their hands with glee at the outcome ... and I very much suspect that they were involved.'

Bruton pounced. 'Absolutely. That's right. That's why I am beside myself ... and that's precisely why I am so deeply troubled by all this, because it is a victory in practice for the IRA. It is a victory for all the things that you and I have stood against.'

This confrontation with the British continued the next day when my opposite number in 10 Downing Street, John Haslam, rang me at home to say that Major and Mayhew considered the taoiseach's remarks on the BBC 'hugely over the top'. Downing Street thought that in the phone call between the two leaders the taoiseach had been 'very strong – they had accepted that'. But his remarks on the BBC had 'caused quite a stir'. I told Haslam that the phone call was *hours after* the BBC interview – the taoiseach had to spell out the depth of feeling in this country and his clear view that the situation had been mishandled. The points he made were true – and a bad situation has been made worse.' It is not accepted in Ireland that the British government could not have prevented the massing of Orangemen if there was a will to do so,' I told Haslam.

This British debacle led to the acceptance of Bruton's proposal, after an independent review of parades and marches by Dr Peter North, vice-chancellor of Oxford University, agreed on a commission in January 1997. The Northern Ireland Parades Commission, a quasi-judicial body responsible for placing restrictions on parades it deems contentious or offensive, was established by April 1998. The seven-member body can re-route parades to avoid certain areas and ban participants on the basis of previous breaches of its rules. It tries to work through local dialogue, and while progress has been made over the years, parades are still viewed as highly sensitive, and the commission has been criticised by the Orange Order.

Talking to David Dimbleby on BBC *Panorama* on 15 July 1996, Major stuck to his line that Drumcree–Garvaghy Road was an operational matter for the RUC. But Dimbleby was having none of it, putting it to him that it was 'a matter for the government when you have that degree of conflict in the UK over something that has been banned by law'. He cited Bruton saying it was a serious mistake breaching the three canons of democracy, and the Catholic Cardinal Cathal Daly saying he felt betrayed by the British government. Major repeated the RUC operational mantra: he wanted to look to the future and these critical comments were 'behind us now'.

Dimbleby responded, 'It is not exactly behind you, is it? ... The consequence of it is that the unionists are seeing, and indeed claim, once again, to have had a victory in Northern Ireland.' Major dismissed this notion, but Dimbleby said, according to Annesley, that the Orangemen were prepared to bring out 'between 60, 70, even perhaps 100,000, people and they won the day by sheer force'.

Bruton's two widely publicised clashes with Major over the British handling of the peace process – his London speech in November 1995 and his BBC interview about Garvaghy Road in July 1996 – were the two strongest public statements of constitutional nationalist/republican views to a British prime minister by any taoiseach since de Valera's reply to Churchill after the Second World War.

Meanwhile, at the Stormont multi-party talks, in the interim between the start of the ban and its reversal, the DUP and the UKUP blamed the British and Irish governments for the stand-off and walked out until the situation was resolved. Mitchell wrote in *Making Peace*: 'We had been in talks for less than a month, and these two parties were walking out for the second time. An intense discussion followed. But all of the remaining parties wanted the process to continue; they feared that if there were a lengthy adjournment the talks might never resume.' Mitchell came up with a good plan to continue the process with bilateral/trilateral meetings, two or three parties meeting together or with the chairman, but there would be no meeting in plenary session or in a large informal discussion until he felt it would be productive.

When the violence broke out at Drumcree, Mitchell's wife, Heather, left Northern Ireland on the advice of the security services. Mitchell joined her some days later. When the plenary session had been suspended for nearly two weeks, the streets had calmed down, and Mitchell called all the parties to a meeting on Monday 22 July.

> The meeting was long and very contentious. The DUP and UKUP returned along with all of the seven other parties. The delegates hurled insults and invective at each other. I had learned a valuable lesson about the fragility of the process and the sensitivity

of the participants to external violence. The memory of this day was with me nearly two years later when, fearful of the effects of a new surge of violence, I decided to propose a final, rigid deadline for the talks.

Mitchell was concerned near the end of July, having not even agreed the rules of procedure after two months, that the talks would never get anywhere if it recessed for the month of August with nothing achieved. So he, his two colleagues and the key party leaders privately reduced their differences to four rule provisions. The trio decided on these and prepared a rules document circulated to all parties for the plenary meeting on Wednesday 24 July. It was leaked immediately, but despite that they had two effective days to enact the rules, if agreed fully, and set an agenda for the remainder of the opening plenary. Mitchell then faced a number of tough challenges. The first was over the method of voting for the rules – one-by-one or as a package using 'sufficient consensus' as the determinant. It could make or break them. As luck would have it, Paisley's DUP was still in the process, and the party asked for a meeting led by the deputy leader, Peter Robinson. They wanted to take the one-by-one route, starting with 'sufficient consensus'. Then they could vote on the rules they wanted, and then against the whole package. They wanted the rules vote taken at the following plenary, on Monday 30 July.

After discussion with his colleagues, Mitchell decided that Robinson's date was the best chance of getting agreement, so he announced it at the end of the informal debate on Thursday 26 July. The SDLP members were upset by the decision and a group went to confront Mitchell at his office. They had wanted the vote that very evening or before the end of the week. They feared that Paisley would use the delay to attack the deal and that Trimble would back out. The former Senator describes in *Making Peace* how he began to worry about his judgement, and this intensified when he discovered that the staff of all three chairmen opposed the decision, feeling that the trio had 'caved in to those who opposed us and abandoned those who supported us'. He respected the staff, and his worry intensified so much that he couldn't sleep thinking about it, replaying his meeting with the DUP and pondering if he'd got it right, or if it was a betrayal.

Then he took a long-distance phone call from his brother Robbie's wife, Janet, in the US, telling him that Robbie, who had been diagnosed with bone marrow cancer some years before, was in a very bad condition. Mitchell spoke briefly to his brother on the phone, but he wanted to be by his side. He was faced with a terrible conflict. He could leave straight away and see his brother for the last time, but if there was a hitch in the rules being approved, it might mean the end of the peace process. What was the right thing to do? He couldn't save his brother's life, but the success of the talks could save others' lives. It was a poignant dilemma. Mitchell spoke to his brother's doctor, who did not think the end would come at the weekend, so he decided to stay and leave immediately after the vote on the Monday. But he was still haunted by doubts. His brother died on the Saturday morning.

Mitchell recounted what happened in *Making Peace* on the Monday morning:

> ... in less than an hour with brief, unemotional discussion, seventeen votes were held. The rules of procedure were adopted without a hitch. When Sinn Féin entered the talks in September 1998, Paisley led his party out for good, vowing to wreck them from the outside, which did not succeed. But they had just now helped to keep the peace talks on the rails. Unfortunately, the parties were unable to agree on an agenda for the remainder of the opening plenary session. But the peace process was still alive.

17

BRUTON ADDRESSES THE US CONGRESS

John Bruton is never going to have a day like it again – no matter how long he is Taoiseach. He got three prolonged standing ovations when he addressed a joint session of the Senate and House of Representatives on Capitol Hill ... he was interrupted by applause more often than if he was at a Fine Gael Ard Fheis. Then the great, the powerful and the good honoured him by turning up for a dinner hosted by Ambassador Dermot Gallagher and his wife Maeve at the redbrick Irish Embassy Residence.

WHEN JOHN BRUTON ADDRESSED THE US Congress on 11 September 1996 it was indeed a historic day for the Irish in Washington, celebrated in this *Irish Independent* opinion piece by Chris Glennon, the paper's political correspondent. Bruton was only the fifth Irish leader to be given this honour; the previous two had been Fine Gael taoisigh – Liam Cosgrave in 1976 and Dr Garret FitzGerald in 1984. Two presidents of Ireland, Seán T. O'Kelly and Éamon de Valera, completed the quintet.

Considerable protocols are involved in the ceremony surrounding an address to Congress. When Bruton arrived at the Capitol he was met by the two sergeants at arms of the House and the Senate, and escorted to the Speaker's Ceremonial Office, where he met Speaker Newt Gingrich, the first Republican to hold the job since 1955 – the Democrats had controlled the House for the next forty years. After President Clinton's poor performance during his first two years in office, the Democrats suffered a heavy defeat in the 1994 congressional elections, losing control of both House and Senate. However, Clinton had now recovered and had a 20-point lead over the Republican Presidential candidate, Senator Bob Dole, winning a second term in the coming election in November 1996. At the Capitol, Senator Dole gave the taoiseach a plaque with a Republican pledge to support the Irish peace process.

After the speaker left to take his chair on the chamber podium, the sergeants at arms escorted Bruton to the podium to make his address. His work on the speech paid off. He had written it himself over a number of weeks, reading widely on US history, its revolutionary times and its constitution. He charted the Irish lineage of a number of presidents, starting with the man who succeeded George Washington, John Adams. Three lesser-known presidents, Andrew Jackson, Chester Arthur and James Buchanan, he said, 'were sons of Ulster emigrants'. And, he added, 'The present distinguished President also, of course, follows in this line.'

He said Ireland was inspired by America. Irish people had found refuge there from both famine and want. Irish Americans had contributed much to America, in business, education, literature, law and politics. 'These successes have given all Irish Americans more confidence than ever now to proclaim their Irish heritage, and more interest than ever in Ireland itself. They have been especially helpful to us in the search for a solution to the problem in Northern Ireland.' It was a skilfully crafted speech that struck all the notes that would resonate with his audience, but there were political messages for home as well. Bruton said that Ireland had followed the American economic model – 'a free market subject to rules, combined with a democracy based on the rule of law' – and that provided the world with the best method of meeting 'the population, environmental and the resource challenges of the twenty-first century'. If anything, these great issues have become more extreme in the three decades since this speech. The global warming crisis is already acute, the world's population is out of control, chiefly in the poorest, most underdeveloped regions, and the scramble for resources like rare earth metals, lithium and others needed to combat global warming is intense. There were six billion people on earth in 1996, when Bruton spoke; now there are eight billion, with UN experts expecting that world population will peak at 10.4 billion in the mid-2080s. Hope springs eternal.

In his research, John Bruton discovered that on the day he spoke to Congress, 210 years before, almost to the hour, delegates of revolutionary America met at Annapolis near Washington to set in motion the convention in Philadelphia that gave Americans the Constitution of the United States of America, making it the 'pioneer of that most powerful of all political ideas – democracy under the rule of law'. He spoke as president of the European Council, which 'is seeking in its Inter-Governmental Conference to do for the fifteen members of the European Union what the men who met at Annapolis and Philadelphia did so long ago, for the thirteen former colonies of America' – that is, to write a new constitution for Europe 'to add new member states to its east, just as your constitution of 1789 allowed this American Union to add so many new states to its west'. There was a thunderous standing ovation in the packed chamber.

Americans, he said, came together because of necessity, not inspired by theorists such as Montesquieu or Locke to build the perfect state, 'but to solve practical problems about shipping on the Potomac, how to pay for the revolutionary army, who was going to pay taxes and who would collect them, how they could get goods to market, and how their frontiers would be protected'. They knew that to do all this, they would have to make political reforms in a constitutional conference. They came together as people who were loyal first to their states, but they knew that loyalty and allegiance could find their best expression as part of a wider American continental identity and loyalty.

Bruton compared the American experience with that of Europe, which also came together out of necessity – the necessity of reconstruction in the wake of the Second World War, the need to resolve national conflicts that had led to three wars in the previous eighty years, and the necessity of resisting communism. Rather than politics and politicians serving the needs of commerce, the emerging union did the opposite and 'made commerce the servant of a great political objective'. (Later, the EU had to drop the use of the word 'constitution' when referendums in May and June 2005 on the proposed constitution of the European Union were defeated by 55 per cent of voters in France and 61 per cent in the Netherlands. Referendums in Spain and Luxembourg supported the constitution and it was ratified by 16 of the then 25 member states of the EU, with two more near ratification, but the European Council decided on a pause for reflection, and essentially the same text was signed by all members of the Union as the Treaty of Lisbon, becoming law on 1 December 2009.)

Bruton signalled awareness of the risks and dangers involved for European constitution-building. While 'national chauvinism' was overcome by the EU bringing together wartime enemies, he said, the 'psychological base of national chauvinism remains a threat'. The problem of 'bringing existing members closer together, while also expanding membership – is one that is familiar to anyone who has studied the history of the United States'. Europe's task of constitution-building, Bruton said, was particularly difficult. 'Europeans were on different sides in past wars, whereas the American founding fathers, whatever their differences, had all been on the same side. But we are determined to make the EU work – to make it work for peace, to make the European Union a firm friend and partner for this great American Union.'

'This Union – the United States – has worked because it is based on freedom', Bruton said, quoting the third president, Thomas Jefferson, who declared, 'error of opinion may be tolerated, where reason is left free to combat it'. The taoiseach continued:

> Conformism of thinking, political correctness if you will, is the great enemy of democratic discourse. We must not be afraid to disagree. We must not dismiss other people's opinions just because they have chosen the wrong words to express them. Equally we must accept that some people's views are so profoundly different from ours on some things that they will never, ever, agree with us.

The arrival of social media over the following twenty years has made these problems far more complex. Reason, the facts and the truth are much more difficult to defend and promote in the 'post-truth society'. An outrageous lie is embraced and believed by a great section of the world's population much more quickly and deeply than the mundane truth.

> Living with difference. That's the challenge for the United States today. It's the challenge for Europe. And it is also the challenge for Ireland as a whole, and for Northern Ireland in particular – living with difference. Two communities, each feeling itself to be a minority – a minority that has been oppressed, or a minority that fears it may be oppressed in the future, the fears of each mirror those of the other ... each tradition must be willing to sit down for long enough, and to listen for long enough, to the views, worries and concerns of the other tradition – to uncover the common ground.

Bruton then thanked the efforts of President Clinton, Vice-President Gore, Speaker Gingrich, other leaders of both Houses of Congress, and many people in the US, for their contribution to the establishment in June of the multi-party talks in Belfast, where most of the parties had been sitting down together 'under the able chairmanship of former Senator George Mitchell, whose skill and commitment I salute today'. More sustained applause from the members of Congress.

The multi-party talks, due to resume in a few days in Belfast, had achieved a breakthrough on some procedures before a summer adjournment. Bruton told Congress that full agreement would take time, and would come in stages, but he emphasised that the Irish government strongly believed that the talks had to move past procedure to substantive matters.

> Almost as much as the Irish themselves, Americans welcomed the political efforts that gave us a ceasefire of 17 months. But now they want the IRA to stop for good. True negotiations can only take place in an atmosphere of genuine peace. The all-party

talks, for which we have worked so hard, have been delivered; we must have everyone there at those talks. That means a cessation of violence that will hold in all circumstances. I know I have the full support of the United States Congress for that vital objective. We are asking nationalists and unionists to agree a political framework which will allow them, together, to take on responsibility for solving the day-to-day problems that affect the lives of the million and a half people who live in Northern Ireland, and to do so in harmony and co-operation with the people of Britain and with the rest of Ireland. Such an agreement is within reach. The Irish and British governments were able to agree last year on a detailed model or Framework of a possible agreement ... agreed institutions for Northern Ireland must be ones that enforce fairness and check the arbitrary excesses of whoever happens to be in the majority in any area at any given time.

Bruton quoted the second US President John Adams's remarks, which could have been said about the fifty years of total control by unionists dominating Northern Ireland, ignored by the British parliament and government: 'The people, when unchecked, have been as unjust, tyrannical, brutal, barbarous and cruel as any king or senate possessed of uncontrollable power. The majority has eternally, and without exception, usurped over the rights of the minority.' Bruton said that that was why the enforcement of fairness through law had been one of the keystones of the American Constitution, and 'that is why we need rules, and a balanced system of institutions, in Northern Ireland. Rules that require people to share power ... rules which recognise that people are different from one another, and that people's allegiances are many and varied.'

His words were met by more applause then, but how times have changed in the US. Today, the enforcement of fairness through law that has been a keystone of the American Constitution, is itself under grave threat from the wholesale politicisation of the Supreme Court, lies about the 2020 presidential election, and a coup attempt made on Congress itself. A society that created the richest and most powerful country in the world is in danger of destroying itself by its acute, seemingly unbridgeable divisiveness. In the US, strong beliefs about subjects like religion, ideology, politics and philosophy could be freely debated, moderated by arguments based on facts and intelligent reasoning. Those who believed in an afterlife and a god could discuss their convictions with atheists and agnostics without descending into fury and insult. Now belief has drilled deeper into a dark hardcore where a lie becomes the truth, and the facts are lies.

The EU, Bruton said, reflected the concept of multi-allegiances, giving the example of a person who can at the same time owe allegiance to Flanders, to Belgium and to Europe and can work and live with someone who had a different set of allegiances. 'If such a model can work for Europe, it can work for Northern Ireland. And if we can get that right, we will be setting a model for similarly divided communities across the world, just as men of Irish descent set a model for the world, two hundred and ten years ago, when they helped draw up the constitution of this great state.' With those words, Bruton ended his address, to a prolonged standing ovation. His speech had been delivered perfectly and was received with much more warmth and enthusiasm, and with greater impact, than that of Garret FitzGerald a decade before. Let us hope that the concept of a peaceful acceptance of multiple allegiances in a divided community can survive.

The Irish ambassador's dinner that evening was a splendid occasion. Just a few of the names give a flavour: Senator Ted Kennedy and his wife, Victoria (he was very complimentary about Bruton's address); and two senior members of the US cabinet, Secretary of Commerce Mickey Kantor and Secretary of Education Richard Riley. From the administration, National Security Advisor Tony Lake, Jack Quinn, Counsel to the President, and Nancy Soderberg, deputy assistant to the president (she and I sat together talking of international affairs, her specialism – she had played a role in President Clinton's engagement with Sinn Féin and the IRA in the run-up to the 1994 ceasefire); Republican Senators John McCain and Mitch McConnell. From the House, Richard Neal (Democrat) and Peter King (Republican), co-chairs of the Ad Hoc

Committee on Irish Affairs. From the business world, Bill Flynn, chairman of Mutual of America and winner of the Irish American of 1995 award, and Don Keough, the first person of a Catholic background to become chairman of Coca-Cola, based in Atlanta, Georgia.

Before the dinner, the taoiseach met a group in the Capitol hosted by Ben Gilman, the chairman of the House Committee on International Relations, including members of Friends of Ireland and the Ad Hoc Committee on Irish Affairs, of which Gilman was also a co-chairman. He was a Republican Congressman for the Rockland County area of New York, which had a strong Irish-American community. In his opening remarks he complimented Bruton on an 'excellent speech' which got a 'great reception'. He also criticised the British government for 'giving in to mob rule' at Drumcree. He asked Bruton about the prospects for a ceasefire, and Bruton replied, 'I have no reason, beyond hope, for achieving a ceasefire. There's no solid piece of paper – but the logic of the position is pushing in that direction.' Gilman then asked, 'If the IRA declare a ceasefire tomorrow, are there any conditions for Sinn Féin getting in the talks?' Bruton replied: 'No condition – they go straight in. It will cause problems for others in the talks, but the ground rules are there.'

Peter King from New York had for years maintained a close relationship with Sinn Féin and Gerry Adams and was very well-informed on the issues. He had criticised the cancellation of direct ministerial talks with Sinn Féin after the London Docklands bomb, but privately had pressed Sinn Féin for a restoration of the ceasefire. He complimented the 'brilliance' of Bruton's address. 'You feel you must reassure unionists and loyalists', he added, 'but others don't show an outreach to nationalists. John Major would not say anything critical of the marches. Republicans feel they're walking down a dark alley.' Bruton said that Major was a 'good friend', and it was on the record that the British government had stated that it had no selfish or strategic interest in Northern Ireland – if people want to leave it was okay. Furthermore, 'the British government had agreed in the Framework Documents that there should be and must be a North–South arrangement in a settlement – the British government policy as well as the Irish government policy is in the Framework

Documents.' On Drumcree, Bruton said the British intention was that the Orange march shouldn't have happened – the problem was that 'they didn't hold to it'. The underlying evidence was that the British government 'do want to move in the right direction', the intentions are 'not unambiguously in the wrong direction'. King interjected, 'Adams is trying to get a ceasefire, but the republican movement is not getting reassurances.'

> Bruton: On a day-to-day basis you could probably demonstrate that is true, but what I've stated is about long-term policy – we must keep bringing them back to the principles. Sinn Féin have a better chance of change in the talks, not with bombs in Manchester.
>
> King: The British ambassador met with us and he said the handling of Drumcree was a disaster. In the House of Commons John Major ridiculed John Hume. Hume said he was discouraged by the talks. Drumcree moved people away from moderate positions. Banbridge people who were moderates told me that it proved why the IRA didn't hand in guns. There's very little that republicans could bring back to their constituents after two years. And there's still a unionist veto on the ground.
>
> Bruton: The first thing is politicians make mistakes from time to time. We've got to go back to the fundamentals of their policy. If you can hold them to it, it will make them even-handed. There's a problem with the RUC: it's 90 per cent Protestant, because of the violence. In 1919 the old RIC was mainly Catholic in Stormont. A British officer said the only way the Drumcree marchers could be stopped was to shoot them. I think he should have stopped them; it was fundamental to civil organisation. If ten Orangemen were shot, we don't know what would have happened. The British retreated – history will tell us if they retreated to regroup or make a change in policy. They crumpled under pressure. That was wrong, but it happened.
>
> You met John Hume two to three weeks ago. I met him last week, and movement is possible. Let's wait and see. Yes, nearly

two years of a ceasefire and nothing happened. That's wrong, but it's not altogether wrong. The British, Irish and the US governments met them, and we achieved round-table talks. We're dealing with a problem that is four centuries old. These people don't like one another, they don't intermingle very much. To some extent the delay *has* caused problems, the British government handling is not perfect, but don't give them any reason to back off the principles. The veto – there's a focus on that word. Both sides have a veto, the word is used far too easily – it's about consent. Gerry Adams says remove the unionist veto. It's asking us to force them to accept something they won't accept. We won't send our forces North, we don't have the force needed, we'd need ten times the British forces. Lastly, I think that David Trimble's behaviour at Drumcree was unacceptable.

This visit to the United States for Bruton's address to Congress had begun three days earlier with a White House meeting with President Clinton to discuss the peace process and the multi-party talks, coinciding with former Senator George Mitchell's return to Belfast for the reopening of the talks on 9 September. Bruton thanked the president for Mitchell's continuing patient chairmanship and sought a renewal of support and commitment for the Belfast talks, the peace process, and any agreement that would be reached in the talks. All were readily given at the meeting. The president repeated his support for the efforts of the two governments and said it was a 'must' that the IRA reinstate the ceasefire. The taoiseach said he cautiously hoped that would happen and it would be permanent and lasting, not tactical.

They discussed the heightened sectarian animosity in the North during the marching season in the wake of Drumcree. The taoiseach hoped that would dissipate with the resumption of the Belfast talks. The president asked about the attempts to exclude the two loyalist parties from the talks, and the taoiseach assured him that this was partly a political ploy by Paisley's DUP that would not succeed as long as the loyalist ceasefires continued. Paisley had made a complaint about the presence of the two small loyalist parties because of a death threat against two loyalist paramilitary members by the CLMC, and the talks had to be adjourned while that was investigated. Bruton emphasised the important role David Trimble could play in an agreement, and he told Clinton he believed the US administration should encourage him, perhaps by inviting him to visit the US. Bruton had met the SDLP at Government Buildings before setting out for the US and he was encouraged that the UUP and the SDLP were meeting in advance of the reopening of the multi-party talks that might identify subjects for 'compromise and agreement'. It was a change from June, when relations between the two parties had not been that good.

Clinton and Bruton spoke to the media directly afterwards. Clinton was questioned about the prospects for the talks against the background of sectarian clashes and violence of the summer. He said:

> I can see circumstances under which we can make some real progress there, if we got one or two good breaks – so we are going to keep working on it ... I just believe that we are still on the right side of history and I can also see the development of events in a way which would make it possible for us to make some real progress, but you know they are just beginning. I have a lot of confidence in Senator Mitchell and his team there, but mostly I believe that the people in Northern Ireland want peace.

The headlines next day told the story. 'Progress possible in the North talks, says Clinton' (*Irish Times*); 'Clinton in push to salvage the peace' (*Irish Independent*); 'End the stalling, demands Clinton' (*Cork Examiner*). Clinton's 'good breaks' included a restored ceasefire, but neither the IRA nor John Major would make the necessary steps.

At the same time, the UUP were also having bilaterals with both the British and the Irish governments at the talks. The Irish delegation was led by Hugh Coveney. The taoiseach got a report about these Belfast discussions on 9 September. The UUP was clearly preparing for the entry of Sinn Féin to the multi-party talks. Reg Empey said that if Sinn Féin came into a sub-committee on arms it would never reach a conclusion; 'They would obstruct the work.' The UUP wanted to deal with the issue as quickly as they could and have it out of the way. The UUP would be 'at risk' if the negotiations entered the three strands without the decommissioning legislation in place. Empey said, 'to put it in cold political language', they did not want to be in the three-strand negotiations when Sinn Féin entered the talks, and then Sinn Féin said they would never agree to decommissioning. He said the UUP and the SDLP had a common basic problem – 'neither believed the other's stated position' – and the UUP was trying to address this, or it would be impossible to make progress. The UUP were assured that Irish legislaton on a legal basis for decommissioning was well advanced. There was some good news from Belfast. Reports that Mitchell would be leaving the talks because of their slow progress were dismissed by the man himself.

The day after the Congress speech was a welcome day of rest. The taoiseach, Finola and delegation were invited to visit the nearby historic town of Williamsburg, the pre-revolutionary centre of British power, which had been restored with great care. Then we visited the nearby site of Jamestown, the initial British settlement, where we saw the excavation of the remains of a seventeenth-century teenage sailor and heard about the early contact between the settlers and the Native Americans. Finally, we hurried to the fine restored colonial-era city of Charleston. The city and its many wooden buildings had been destroyed by a hurricane some decades before. After a packed day, it was back to Williamsburg for a gala dinner in honour of Bruton, and the next morning we left from Williamsburg airport for Casement aerodrome at Baldonnel.

18

EU PRESIDENCY SEALS EURO DEAL

I RECRUITED TWO OFFICIALS FROM within the civil service to collect presidency press material from all Departments for a regular media newsletter on the presidency's work, and I appointed the former Fine Gael press officer, Peter White, who had become a high-profile media consultant, to edit the newsletter for the six-month term from July to December 1996. I also arranged an initial press briefing at Government Buildings, hosted by the taoiseach over a lunch in the elegant Italian Room and attended by invited journalists from the then 15 countries of the Union, and EU correspondents based in Brussels. The purpose was to outline the Irish agenda for the presidency. The lunch went well; then the journalists converged on Bruton for an off-the-record session. The key question sceptical journalists posed to him was whether or not the common currency could ever actually happen, given the economic divergence of member states. This debate had gone on for many years, the single currency had its champions and sceptics. But the path was already well mapped, and it had a name – the euro. Bruton told them it would happen, 'largely on time because it is a political project for the European Union, not based solely on economics'. He said it was an important bonding project as the European Union grew, and it would contribute to a shared fiscal discipline.

The core 11 countries that adopted the euro from the start were Germany, France, Italy, Spain, the Netherlands, Belgium, Austria, Finland, Ireland, Portugal and Luxembourg. They would set a standard for other members to follow. Britain and Denmark opted out, though Denmark strictly pegged its krone to the euro. Bruton's prediction was correct; the final agreement on the introduction of the euro, at first electronically, came on 1 January 1999. Greece joined a year later, and the notes and coins became legal tender, replacing national currencies, in 2002. No one could foresee that Greece would falsify its financial accounts to become a core country, which backfired on the country when the great financial crash came in 2008.

The rotating presidency was a unique way of sharing the importance of EU summitry at that time, with each country providing a venue or venues for these grand city occasions, with ministerial councils, such as finance, agriculture and health, held at venues around the country. There was 'glory' then attaching to the achievements of each presidency in relation to the significance of the measures agreed, as well as the treatment of delegates, ministers, officials and journalists with hospitality, facilities and gifts. The European Community grew from nine states in 1973, when Britain and Ireland joined, to 28 states after the collapse of the Soviet Union and communist Yugoslavia. Those enormous geopolitical changes freed eastern European and Balkan states to join the renamed European Union. It became more practical after enlargement to centralise the summits in Brussels, though the presidency still rotates around the now 27 states (after Brexit). During our presidency the number of states had already grown to fifteen, with three more states, Austria, Finland and Sweden, becoming full members in 1995.

For me the job of press secretary for the presidency meant that I had to host European and international correspondents for briefings on the agenda items, and, in general, other journalists assigned to cover various aspects of European business. I held a succession of events after the first 'political euro' briefing in Dublin. Boris Johnson, then working for the *Daily Telegraph*, turned up as a sceptical interlocutor at one of these events in Dublin Castle. I set up a committee of departmental press officers and relevant officials to plan for the summits, most particularly for the second Dublin summit in December 1996, where we were expecting up to two thousand journalists – a daunting task, and I would have to give a number of press conferences for them. An additional burden and opportunity were presented to me before our presidency began. I was approached by a BBC2 producer seeking to make a 'fly on the wall' documentary about the EU presidency while Ireland was in possession. When I discussed this initially with the taoiseach, he was reluctant, feeling it would be very intrusive and could be inhibiting; it would require a lot of access to previously confidential meetings and discussions. However, after some gentle persuasion, he eventually came round, with the proviso that the BBC crew would have to obey tight instructions on access and leave if there was a confidential matter to be discussed. It was a broadcasting success.

The biggest issue for Ireland was going to be advancing the single currency, which had been named the euro at the Madrid Summit in late 1995. The finance minister, Ruairí Quinn, chaired the Economic and Financial Affairs Council (ECOFIN), the EU's council of finance ministers, so he would play an important role in delivering an agreement on the strict financial rules on debt and borrowing that would govern the eurozone states. Bruton put it in simple terms: 'This was to enable us to launch the euro on a solid basis, providing that no member state could borrow and spend euro in a way that would devalue the coins in everyone else's pockets.' The agreement was called the Stability Pact.

Quinn, Bruton and Spring were at the European Council meeting in Madrid that formally adopted the euro as the name of the new common currency. The embattled British prime minister, John Major, fought a rearguard action to reject the name, arguing that it would upset British sensitivities and be seen as overtly political. According to Quinn, the German chancellor, Helmut Kohl, responded briskly and dismissively: 'John, this project is political. The single currency is the necessary bridge to a united Europe, and we all have to cross it. It will be called the euro!' I was with Bruton in Madrid when I learned about Major's failed attempt to block the 'euro' name. I hadn't been a fan of the name beforehand, but since I was very much in favour of the European Union, the argument was impressive and made the 'euro' more appealing to me.

Germany had the strongest currency in Europe, the Deutschmark. This was supported by a traditionally disciplined people and government, with good labour relations and little industrial strife. Selling the euro as a replacement for the German Deutschmark was not going to be easy. Helmut Kohl agreed to the euro project with Jacques Chirac in part to win French support for German unity after the fall of the Berlin Wall. France aspired to lead Europe but was not as fiscally or politically disciplined as Germany, so the franc was weaker, and France frequently undermined itself (which it has even up to the present day) by at times appearing ungovernable. Italy, the fourth largest economy in Europe, suffered from political instability, with frequent changes of government, and over-borrowing.

Britain, always something of an outsider, struggled through the 1970s with terrible industrial strife. The trade unions were very powerful. I worked for both the *Newcastle Evening Chronicle* and BBC North-East in Britain during the 'three-day week' in 1973, when big industries were forced to partially shut down by Conservative Prime Minister Ted Heath because the miners were on strike and coal-fired power stations were disabled. Heath called an early election in 1974 demanding to know 'Who governs Britain?' and lost. I had returned to Ireland in time to do an RTÉ TV *7 Days* programme about what the miners wanted. In one of the great Welsh valleys I interviewed a miners' leader beside a strike-closed pit. He told me that they should have a wage 'equivalent to that of brain surgeons'. In fact, what happened was that many of the coal pits were permanently closed in the coming years. Labour returned to government from 1974 to 1979, but the excessive abuse of power by the unions saw the streets of London piled high with rubbish in strikes during the 'Winter of Discontent', which brought Margaret Thatcher to power. She then broke the power of the unions and put the Labour Party out of government for 17 years.

Ironically, the British upheaval gave an impetus to economic and monetary union in Europe. The subject had been on the European agenda since the 1960s, but the focus had been on various schemes to limit member states' exchange rate volatility, bizarrely called 'the snake in the tunnel'. Britain's Home Secretary, Roy Jenkins, angry at excessive far-left and trade union power within his party, resigned in 1976 after coming third in a ballot for both the party leadership and the prime minister's job. Harold Wilson had resigned early, and Jim Callaghan became prime minister. Jenkins became president of the European Commission, and in 1977 he gave an important speech in Venice which injected new life into the idea of economic and monetary union in Europe. I went to Brussels in mid-December 1977 to interview Jenkins on the subject for RTÉ's *This Week* programme. I unfortunately let slip that the interview would be broadcast in early 1978, at which Jenkins said imperiously, 'I'm not going to be canned for that long' and started rising from his chair. Thankfully I was able to talk him out of it. He told me that an economic and monetary union was an imperative for the then European Community (EC) to unlock the full potential of the common market. Jenkins' initiative was followed by the creation of the European Monetary System put forward by the French president, Valéry Giscard d'Estaing, and Helmut Schmidt, the German chancellor, in 1978 with a new and lasting exchange rate mechanism (ERM) in the following year.

The former French finance minister, Jacques Delors, became President of the Commission in 1985 and brought a fresh authority and dynamism to the role. He wanted the EC to be a powerhouse for economic development in member states, using its ability to spread wealth through its programmes. Ireland was a big beneficiary, receiving more than IR£6 billion from the European Structural Funds. The Delors Report on economic and monetary union proposed three stages for achieving this goal. The first stage started in July 1990 with the abolition of exchange controls, thereby enabling free capital movement in core countries. The Maastricht Treaty in December 1991 agreed on the common currency as a formal objective of what was to become the European Union and set the 'convergence criteria' for member states on public finances, interest rates, inflation and exchange rate stability. The UK and Denmark negotiated opt-outs from the common currency.

Britain became a serious victim of the exchange rate discipline on 'Black Wednesday' in 1992, when the pound sterling had to crash out of the ERM. That cost the country billions – money spent trying to bolster sterling in the market. Famously, financier George Soros bet billions of pounds that the UK could not keep sterling above the floor, and he won. It was a huge international embarrassment for Britain, and a shock to right-wing Tory Eurosceptics. The Maastricht Treaty, which came into force on 1 November 1993, also included political elements of a union, citizenship and moves towards common foreign and internal policies.

The second stage began on 1 January 1994 with the establishment of the European Monetary Institute in Frankfurt, the forerunner of the European Central Bank. National central banks had to be made independent of government, and the institute had the task of improving monetary co-operation between member states. By 1996 the way was being prepared for the third and final stage, which would be the launch of the euro digitally in 1999, locking the currencies into the ERM, and finally launching euro notes and coins in 2002. It was a historic journey for the euro, which has defied its many critics and doom-mongers, surviving an existential crisis during and after the great financial crash in 2008.

A lot of the technical work on co-ordinating the currencies, and the fiscal requirements of member states, was carried out by an advisory monetary committee of expert officials, but the key political and monetary decisions were dealt with at ministerial level in ECOFIN. In late September 1996, during Ireland's presidency, the monetary committee reported to the ministers. Enough progress was made on the Stability Pact governing member states' debt in the eurozone for it be completed at the second Dublin summit. There was media speculation at home and abroad about the countries capable of meeting the pact's financial restraints between national debt and a country's annual economic output (gross domestic product, GDP) to sustain a new currency related to the Deutschmark. There was some doubt that Ireland would be able to make it. Ruairí Quinn, in his memoir, describes how during an ECOFIN debate about establishing a group of eurozone currency ministers within the

EU, there was some opposition to this 'club within a club'. Quinn had his doubts too. The German finance minister Theo Waigel, sitting beside him, asked in a whisper what he was worried about since Ireland was going to be in the founding group of countries. This was a great reassurance to Quinn and the secretary of the Department of Finance that the success of the Irish economy was being recognised abroad.

The first Dublin EU summit was held on 5 October 1996 and its focus was mainly on the IGC of EU member states, which was the method of agreeing changes to EU treaties, which have to be formally ratified by national parliaments, and which in some cases, including Ireland, are the subject of national referendums. There is always a time-lag between the formal agreement of changes at an EU summit, and the full ratification of a new EU treaty, as there was with Maastricht. In Dublin Castle, the leaders arrived one by one with their teams in limousines to the Upper Yard before St Patrick's Hall. I got a mild shock when a Mercedes bus with only one passenger drove up to deliver Helmut Kohl to the castle. As he struggled to get off the bus, like a giant with bowed head negotiating the bus steps, I realised what an enormous man he was. He was assisted off the bus by the waiting attendants, then threw back his head and marched into the castle.

Bruton told the European Council that ECOFIN was now confident of finalising the Stability Pact for the December Dublin summit, and he gave reassurances that a draft treaty for the IGC would be presented for agreement by June 1997, so that enlargement of the union to the east could take place. During the session he pressed his fellow leaders for progress on measures to deal with criminal drug gangs. The murder of Veronica Guerin had intensified his wish to see EU action against such gangs, and other members of the council were supportive. At the meeting, Kohl dismissed media speculation that the German appetite for EU reform had cooled. Bruton promised to bring forward a treaty chapter on employment, despite British opposition, and the way was cleared for further majority voting. Chirac, who had been reluctant, agreed to a number of extra matters, including immigrants, asylum and visas, for majority vote. The German foreign minister, Klaus Kinkel, said the national veto on the development of EU foreign and security policy had to go, and an EU foreign policy unit with a secretary general was required. Speaking to the media, John Major had a long list of items the UK would oppose – practically the full agenda. Major knew he had to keep his Eurosceptic 'bastards' on side. At the council Major got involved in a row with the president of the European Parliament, Klaus Hänsch, who said that Britain was not committed to Europe. Major said this was offensive – the British were good Europeans. To Major's chagrin, Hänsch advised the other 14 EU member states to go ahead with necessary reforms if Britain was obstructive.

Ireland's superb ambassador in London, Ted Barrington, wrote a confidential message about Major's precarious position:

> The political strains on this Government are enormous. In the Commons the Prime Minister has a majority of only one. He is expected to lose that majority in the by-election of 12 December in a safe Labour seat. Within the [Tory] Party the Prime Minister faces an undeclared contest for the leadership ... already the Prime Minister's enemies are marshalling their forces and are prepared to use any issue to embarrass and harass their leader. Their two most convenient issues are Europe and Northern Ireland – issues that stir deep emotions and evoke deep resonances in the Party.

Hostility to the EU, he noted, largely coincided with those most sceptical about Major's policy on Northern Ireland. Michael Portillo was one of two ministerial EU sceptics who did *not* use the North 'as a battleground within the party'.

Just two days after that first EU summit, on 7 October 1996, the IRA made its first major attack in Northern Ireland since the ceasefire in 1994, with an extraordinary double bombing of the Lisburn headquarters of the British Army in Northern Ireland. Two IRA men succeeded in getting into the Thiepval Barracks – named after the memorial in France to the 72,337 British soldiers, many from Ireland, who died in the Battle of the Somme – using forged passes based on an identity card of a former British soldier. They drove two 800-pound (360kg) car bombs into the barracks. One exploded near an administrative building, injuring many, and the second shortly afterwards, destroying the military medical centre, catching some victims of the first blast as well as medical staff. There were 31 injured, and a British soldier, Warrant Officer James Bradwell, died four days later of multiple wounds, the first British soldier to be killed in Northern Ireland since the 1994 ceasefire. The IRA admitted responsibility the next day. Gerry Adams said, 'There has been a protracted political vacuum here. If we don't fill that vacuum with real talks then it will be filled with the sort of serious incidents we saw yesterday.'

Bruton denounced the attack in the Dáil as a 'cynical betrayal of the peace process' by the IRA. They had 'completed a terrible triangle' of bombing, from the London Docklands to Manchester and Detective Garda Jerry McCabe's killing in Adare, and now Lisburn. John Major wrote to the taoiseach on 11 October commending his Dáil statement: 'You said exactly what needed to be said in the aftermath of the cynical and despicable bomb attack in Lisburn … Sinn Féin have excluded themselves from the talks and will have a hard task now to convince anyone that a new ceasefire is credible.' It certainly didn't help the efforts that were going on at the time to make progress out of the political 'vacuum'. John Hume had been working on a document with Gerry Adams about what was needed to achieve a restored ceasefire and the admission of Sinn Féin to the ongoing multilateral talks at Stormont chaired by Mitchell. The document was given to the British by Sinn Féin on 10 October and a key question posed was the period of 'quarantine' after a ceasefire before Sinn Féin could enter the talks on a fixed date.

Bruton was convinced by officials' reports on Adams's views, and those of John Hume, that there were grounds for the ceasefire to be restored if Sinn Féin could be admitted to the talks swiftly after a restored ceasefire. In a lengthy phone call with Major on 26 October, the first of several, Bruton tried to get Major to drop the British proposal of a three-month probation for Sinn Féin after a ceasefire. He explained Seamus Mallon's fear that a three-month waiting period would be disastrous for the SDLP in the coming British election: 'Sinn Féin would, in those circumstances, have enormous sympathy among all nationalists in Northern Ireland in the run-up to the election, whenever it will take place. Nothing would suit Sinn Féin better than to be in the sin-bin during that period.'

Major was interested, but maintained that his intelligence services said, 'There is a lot of evidence that the IRA are ready to place more bombs.' Bruton argued that the Adams peace process group had been in a 'more confident mode' within the republican movement since the previous August and this led him to believe that Adams had 'the capacity to deliver'. Major replied: 'I'm disinclined to believe anything from them, a timeframe is really not a new hurdle.' Bruton let his frustration at Major's unrelenting attitude show: 'But really, what more would you know in three months? These people have been engaged in a campaign of violence for 25 years. If they want to, they can turn it off for the three months and then resume preparatory action.' Major replied: 'What will be said, and believed in the House of Commons, if we let Sinn Féin in without such a test period, is that every time Sinn Féin get irritable, they let off a few bombs and that the government then rush to accommodate them.'

Bruton tried again to get Major to consider a fixed date to get Sinn Féin into the peace talks with an hour-long phone call on 6 November. 'We are coming close to decision points in regard to the discussions that have been going on through John Hume with Sinn Féin and the possibility, I think the likelihood in fact, of an IRA ceasefire,' he told Major. 'My understanding is that the package ... that has been put forward with our support, is one that will involve Sinn Féin entering the talks just to accept the Mitchell Principles initially.' This would be followed by a period to 'verify' that the commitment to Mitchell's six democratic principles 'was real and not cosmetic'. This democratic pledge by Sinn Féin would be made possible by the declaration of an IRA ceasefire which 'would be much stronger than anything we have seen before,' Bruton said, with the leadership saying 'they can't foresee any circumstances in which the conflict would be resumed'. Bruton told him: 'I think it is very important that we take this opportunity now.' Major parried, saying that they had 'moved away' from the explicit three-month probation period in their response to the Hume–Adams initiative over Irish concerns, but the 'immediate entry of Sinn Féin into the talks would not be seen as credible and would not run at all here'. Unionists would not be there to talk to them. While Major was willing to discuss the issues, his baseline was summed up on the phone when he said: 'In terms of the way people are feeling over here, I have no difficulty whatever in standing pat because nobody believes a word Sinn Féin/IRA say.' During the lengthy calls, Major wanted Sinn Féin and IRA language about 'permanence' in a ceasefire declaration, 'positive words' on Mitchell's suggestion of parallel decommissioning of arms during the peace talks together with some acceptance of consent for constitutional change. The words in an IRA statement would be important. Major maintained they needed to see evidence of this in advance for him to convince his cabinet and the Commons. Bruton wanted a believable 'unequivocal ceasefire', and that nothing was done 'inconsistent with this ceasefire or the Mitchell principles'. Then Sinn Féin should be admitted to the talks 'at the earliest moment' provided for in the ground rules for all-party talks and the February 1996 summit communiqué. Major said the IRA bombs had changed the situation. Bruton pushed intensely for a fixed entry date, setting out a plan to Major in a letter on 28 November – Sinn Féin, after a ceasefire, to briefly enter the talks process just to sign up to the Mitchell Principles, then the Stormont talks would adjourn over December through the holidays and all of January, with Sinn Féin to fully join the resumed all-party talks on 30 January 1997, after a ceasefire 'proving' period of two months. But there was a sharp rift between them: an entrenched Major would not agree. That rift remained after a London summit on 9 December 1996. Major told the media afterwards that he was now 'blue in the face' saying that he would not agree a talks entry date for Sinn Féin after a ceasefire, reiterating a public British statement at the end of November replying to the Hume–Adams initiative. Bruton was deeply disappointed. As this record shows, he was also 'blue in the face' pushing Major to stop stonewalling. It proved to be the end of serious ceasefire negotiations with Major after he passed up this real opportunity.

In the next Bruton phone call with Major on 31 January 1997 they discussed the implementation of the North Report into marches and parades commissioned after the Drumcree debacle, and the taoiseach raised the 25th anniversary of Bloody Sunday that month, informing Major about fresh evidence on Channel 4 TV, ignored and rejected by Lord Widgery in 1972 showing the culpability of British Army paratroopers. Bruton told the Dáil he wanted a 'comprehensive and unequivocal British statement that the victims were totally innocent'. Major told Bruton that he had 'an open mind' on any significant new evidence. The taoiseach said officials would compile a report on new developments and the outcome given to the British.

Back to the EU summit. Ruairí Quinn had scheduled another meeting of ECOFIN for 12 December, the day before the EU summit started, to see if the Stability Pact could finally be agreed: there was a stand-off between the Germans and the French over key elements. Predictably, the issue was the Germans insisting that the euro had to have strict financial safeguards, while the French wanted more flexibility. The haggling convinced Quinn that it would have to go to the European Council meeting the next morning. In his memoir, he revealed that he had another distraction at the meeting, which made him very angry: 'I was being gazumped and bushwhacked right at the time of the critical discussions which were going on at ECOFIN.' He had been informed by Dick Spring that he and the taoiseach had agreed the national pay deal. Quinn and his officials had wanted to stretch the negotiations into the new year; he was looking for public sector productivity and economies to ensure that budgetary discipline was maintained and Ireland continued to meet the criteria for joining the euro. It was an odd clash. Spring and Bruton were preparing for the politics of a coming electoral year. The next morning Quinn said he had an 'intense, awful row' on the phone with Spring. Later he joined Bruton and Spring at the European Council while I was there with the camera crews, taking a little longer with the BBC documentary team before ushering them out.

Bruton as president then opened the session, which heard a report from ECOFIN the previous night, so the Council would have to sign off on the Stability Pact. The taoiseach recalled:

> Early in the day it became clear that we were heading for a deadlock in a dispute over the pact that pitted Helmut Kohl of Germany against Jacques Chirac of France. Helmut Kohl wanted the penalties imposed on those who exceeded borrowing limits to be automatic. Jacques Chirac wanted escape clauses, political flexibility and an emphasis on employment. The deadlock was so complete that, after an hour or so, I had to adjourn the meeting to allow private discussions between the protagonists, so the French and Germans went off into a huddle accompanied by the multilingual prime minister and finance minister of Luxembourg, Jean-Claude Juncker.

Quinn said that Bruton asked him if the finance ministers could have one last go at a solution and he had acted on that, so the discussions were carried out in a room found for Quinn by the ever-helpful David Byers, manager of Dublin Castle.

Bruton described how it ended:

> After much animated discussion, the trio, Juncker, Chirac and Kohl, returned to the table with the makings of a deal. Countries which were in recession, defined as an annual fall in gross domestic product (GDP) of 0.75 per cent, would be exempted from the penalties for excessive deficits, and the word 'growth' would be added to the title of the pact. This deal was accepted by all.

Thus the Stability and Growth Pact was formally agreed by the Irish presidency and was hailed in the media, nationally and internationally, as a great success for Ireland. A strong foundation for the euro was in place. The exemption from the penalties won by the French was a considerable loosening of the draft rule that required a recession fall of 1.5–2 per cent in GDP to escape punishment for breaking the budget deficit rule limited to 3 per cent of GDP.

My notes at the time said that it was an attempt to soften a 'rigid automatic definition' of a recession to make a case, and Jean-Claude Juncker was 'pivotal' in achieving agreement between Chirac and Kohl.

He was a fluent French and German speaker with financial experience. 'Of all the prime ministers, he was the only one who knew in minute detail the technicalities involved,' said Quinn in his memoir. The Irish draft reform of the Union Treaties for the Inter-Governmental Council was also seen as another substantial success. It included the Union as an area of freedom, security and justice; citizens' rights and benefits; the need for a common foreign and security policy and structure; the EU's institutions and voting methods for an enlarged European Council; and the still controversial veto. Another significant success was the advances made during the presidency, pushed hard by the taoiseach, to increase EU states' co-operation against organised crime, drug gangs, trafficking in persons, mainly women, and the sexual exploitation of children. The European Council wanted Europol, the new European police body, to have 'operative powers' to work in conjunction with national authorities on these issues 'of serious concern to citizens in all member states'.

The *Irish Times* European correspondent Patrick Smyth hailed three major summit achievements on the road to European integration: clearing the road to the euro; the draft reform of the Union treaties; and 'in turning the painfully cumbersome EU system of co-operation in justice and home affairs into a functioning arm of the Union'. It was Bruton and the Rainbow who succeeded in getting the full approval of the EU for Ireland's 12.5 per cent business tax rate, unique in the EU, and a critical foundation of Ireland's huge success in attracting foreign investment, particularly from US companies. Bruton's standing with the EU, not least in the presidency, clinched that key tax policy, and he had negotiated it in a 'bipartisan' way with his two left-wing coalition partners, as he told RTÉ's *The Week in Politics*.

We gave the summit's departing journalists a side of Irish smoked salmon and a bottle of whiskey each. That went down well.

19

THE HEPATITIS C DISASTER

ON 21 FEBRUARY 1994 THE Blood Transfusion Service Board (BTSB) announced that women who had received a blood product called anti-D between 1970 and 1994 should have blood tests for hepatitis C. It was the start of an unfolding nightmare for more than 1,600 women, and for one in particular, Brigid McCole, from County Donegal, a mother of six daughters and six sons, who would become a pivotal victim of this medical disaster, and the nemesis of the state in its reaction to the scandal. The then Fianna Fáil–Labour government's reaction was both appallingly slow and incomplete. The BTSB report presented to the Department of Health contained evidence that some women who might have received anti-D as far back as 1977 were now testing positive for hepatitis C. There was also primary evidence from a London laboratory that plasma taken from an Irish donor in 1977 was linked to cases of hepatitis C.

Apart from the screening of women given anti-D over that period, Minister for Health Brendan Howlin established a three-person expert group the following month to investigate what had happened in the BTSB. The group reported ten months later, in January 1995. His Rainbow successor, Michael Noonan, was forced by public outrage at the scandal, which resulted in the death of Brigid McCole, to establish a legal tribunal of inquiry in October 1996. The tribunal reported in half the time, just five months. It was a big error not to have established a tribunal of inquiry immediately after the BTSB report to the Department of Health in February 1994. It was also a shame that the government then did not immediately establish a sympathetic response policy, demonstrating some understanding of the serious illness that hepatitis C can cause, and caring for women who had been infected by contaminated blood products from a state body. Since the previous Fianna Fáil-led government had set up the expert group, which did uncover many of the facts, Noonan had resisted their belated political calls in opposition for a tribunal. He cited the costs of the Beef Tribunal into the meat industry, and its lack of clarity.

Michael Noonan, as the Rainbow government's Minister for Health, depending heavily on legal advice, adopted a legalistic approach to this highly emotional situation. That stoked anger and bitterness, not just among the more than 1,000 people shown to be affected out of 60,000 given blood tests, but in the public generally. Noonan had established a compensation tribunal based on the 1986 scheme of compensation for personal injuries suffered in the Stardust night club fire disaster of 1981. This did not prove to be the good immediate solution he wanted, though it was eventually used by a majority of the victims. Mrs McCole, who was seriously ill, wanted to expose all the facts of how she and many other women were contaminated with this disease by blood products from an important state body, so she chose to go to the courts to discover the truth.

The minister said, both in the Dáil and outside it, that his legal advice was that the responsible party was not the state but the BTSB itself. However, Mrs McCole's lawyers were having none of that, and sued the BTSB, the Department of Health, the National Drugs Advisory Board, Ireland and the attorney general. Noonan wanted the infected women to go to his compensation tribunal, so Positive Action, the group formed by the affected women to represent the victims, was told by the chief state solicitor's office that if they didn't go there, they would face 'uncertainties, delays, stresses, confrontation and costs'. That legalistic statement, misinterpreted as a threat, poured acid on the wounds and fed cynical attacks on the minister from Fianna Fáil, now in opposition, but carrying shared responsibility for the minimalist approach for most of

1994. In addition, the state mistakenly opposed Mrs McCole, taking her case under a pseudonym to protect her identity. Haemophiliacs taking cases against the state for contamination with HIV due to blood transfusions a few years earlier had been allowed to remain anonymous.

The BTSB lodged a sum of £175,000 with the court in May 1996, and admitted liability to Mrs McCole in September, offering this sum as a settlement. However, the BTSB's legal advice was to defend an action pressing for aggravated damages and Mrs McCole was warned that if her case failed, she would be liable for the entire costs. That was projected by Fianna Fáil and the media as a threatening legal device aimed at forcing a settlement, but it is a legal fixture in cases where there is a compensation offer. Mrs McCole's condition worsened rapidly and she died on 2 October, just days before the trial was to start. In the hours before her death, she felt she had to accept the settlement of £175,000 from the BTSB.

The hepatitis C scandal was a tragedy that haunted Michael Noonan at every turn and seriously damaged his political reputation at the time as a 'safe pair of hands'. Fourteen days after Mrs McCole's death, Noonan was in the Dáil speaking in a debate about the BTSB affair, and he asked if Mrs McCole's solicitors would not have 'served their client better if they had advised her to go to the compensation tribunal early this year'. This led to a protest walkout by Positive Action members, the group representing the victims, who were listening in the public gallery. I was alerted by Brian Dowling from the 'pol corrs' rooms when I rang to say the briefing would be late, because I was at a meeting about the December EU summit. I flicked on the RTÉ *Six One News*, which confirmed the story, and then went straight to the taoiseach and told him that Noonan would have to apologise in the Dáil. Bruton agreed, ringing the chief whip, Jim Higgins, to come quickly. Seán Donlon, Attorney General Dermot Gleeson and Jim Higgins gathered in my office and we drafted an apology, which Higgins brought to Noonan:

> In my remarks earlier this afternoon I made a reference to the late Mrs McCole's legal proceedings which I now realise has caused understandable offence to her family, to other victims and to

those in the associated organisation. I would like to avail of this opportunity to apologise unreservedly for the offence caused. It was unintended. I certainly did not mean to question in any way the right of Mrs McCole and her legal team to take the course of action which they did. This is a great personal tragedy for the family of Mrs McCole and I apologise again for any hurt which I may have caused.

It was an embarrassing moment in the Dáil. Mrs McCole was only 54 when she died. She had been ill for almost a decade, and she had 'gone through hell' in the latter stages, her daughter Bríd later told the tribunal. I called the taoiseach in his car – he was on the way to see the President, holding the phone up to the Dáil proceedings so he could hear the apology. After the debate Noonan, Gleeson, Mary Kenny, an assistant to the minister, and Richard Green, his adviser, gathered in my office. Gleeson was worried about the lawyers, because the minister's original statement was also an insult to them. Michael Noonan wanted to issue another statement. We drafted one, but I was unhappy with issuing a second formal statement. Noonan had to go to a vote in the Dáil, and when he returned, he was buoyed up by personal comments made around Leinster House about his apology. The Labour Minister for Education, Niamh Bhreathnach, 'had heard his speech and didn't see anything wrong with it', my note says. The second statement idea was dropped.

Noonan was committed to an interview on Vincent Browne's late-night RTÉ radio programme later that evening, which I said would give him an opportunity to extend the apology to the lawyers involved, but Noonan was adamant: there would be no further apologies. Later the taoiseach rang me at home, and first agreed that there should be no further formal statement. Later still, Bruton rang me again. Dick Spring had called him after a dinner with former Attorney General John Rogers, who was counsel for Mrs McCole. Spring said Michael Noonan had made 'a complete mess of hepatitis C and he'd have to watch his back the next day'. The taoiseach wondered if the lawyers issue had prompted the call. I told him I would ring Noonan at the RTÉ studio, where he was going through a tough interview with Vincent Browne, and tell him to include the lawyers in his apology live on the programme. I got the minister on the phone during a commercial break in the programme and Noonan's extension of the apology to the lawyers fitted in perfectly.

Just before all this, Michael had invited me for a drink at his club on St Stephen's Green. We had an interesting talk about politics in general and more specifically about the government. He told me that in politics 'it's a business of good day, bad day'. This was certainly a bad day. But it was far from the end of his story. Noonan went on to become a Fine Gael leader during the first decade of the new millennium, unsuccessfully, with a Fianna Fáil-led government insulated in office by the roaring Celtic Tiger, then from 2011 to 2016 a much-praised Minister for Finance in Enda Kenny's Fine Gael–Labour government, which had to sort out Ireland's financial disaster inherited from the Fianna Fáil–Progressive Democrats–Green governments. All the banks had been bankrupted by their insane international borrowing to fuel an equally mad property bubble which predictably burst. Fianna Fáil was exposed and crushingly ejected from office by the people in 2011. The financial crash had revealed appalling economic mismanagement during the housing 'bubble' years. Noonan ended his political career on a 'good day' for him.

The human cost of the BTSB's incompetence and negligence, revealed in the report of Mr Justice Thomas Finlay's tribunal, was immense and the financial cost to the state enormous. Within seven years, Noonan's compensation tribunal had already made over 1,500 awards to individuals and paid out €300 million. The largest award was reported to be over €3 million, and hundreds of victims were appealing tribunal awards to the High Court, where awards could be many times greater. One out-of-court settlement of a case was reported in April 2002 to be in excess of €2 million. These cases show the disgraceful meanness of the BTSB offer of about €210,000 to Brigid McCole, and the insensitivity of the warning about aggravated damages. Politics is 'red in tooth and claw', and that was seen in political charges made during the hepatitis C scandal. Having made political capital out of this scandal in opposition, accusing the government of directing an insensitive, aggressive 'jackboot' policy on the legal approach to Mrs McCole's case, Fianna Fáil, back in power at the end of June 1997, launched an inquiry by an independent counsel into the records of the Rainbow government's handling of the case. However, the balanced report of that counsel to the new Fianna Fáil Minister for Health, Brian Cowen, in August 1997 said there was no evidence of such a government policy. What happened was the ordinary working of the adversarial system of justice, which is also 'red in tooth and claw'.

A Fine Gael statement, obviously written by a legal expert, cautioned that 'political value judgements should not be used to influence the conduct of court cases, it was a highly questionable principle for any minister to adopt. It would have far-reaching implications in other cases.' On foot of the counsel report, Cowen announced a review of the other cases being taken to the High Court and said he was authorising state legal teams to begin settlement negotiations. The objective was that nobody would be required to prove negligence to get compensation. But, as Health Correspondent Alison O'Connor reported in the *Irish Times*, the legal advice remained that the state should not admit liability.

> The minister was less than clear on what any new option would mean for women who are talking court action in pursuit of aggravated damages. There were echoes of legal fudging in his explanation and a reluctance, not unlike his predecessor, to say anything that might open the floodgates to further claims for aggravated damages.

The political cynicism was exposed, and Brian Cowen was hoist with his own petard.

20

LOWRY'S FALL AND HAUGHEY'S MONEY

THE REVENGE OF THE 'COSY CARTELS'. That was how some wits described a report on 29 November 1996 in the *Irish Independent* that Dunnes Stores Group had paid more than £200,000, approved by Ben Dunne, for a substantial renovation of the Tipperary home of Michael Lowry, the Minister for TEC. It had happened some years before he became a minister. We have already met the 'cosy cartels'; that was how the minister described bands of businessmen who, he had alleged the previous year, were able to hoover up state contracts. If there were any political or other motivations in the leaking of details of the payment, within days it was having unintended consequences. Mr Justice Brian McCracken, who presided over the Tribunal of Inquiry (Dunnes Payments) established on 7 February 1997 by the Rainbow government, described what happened next in his remarkable report: 'Within days, further articles appeared in the media, possibly as a result of a leaking, that referred to payments of over £1 million allegedly made by the late Mr Ben Dunne to a retired politician. There was speculation that the politician might have been Mr Charles Haughey.'

Mr Justice McCracken's report, for all its carefully written language, was an astonishing read, telling the story of how his tribunal heard Haughey's naked denial of the allegation. But the former Fianna Fáil taoiseach was caught out in his lies. He was forced to write a grovelling apology not only to Justice McCracken and the tribunal, but also to his legal team, whom he had misled in relation to his multiple payments from Ben Dunne, totalling £1.3 million while he was taoiseach. He had to thank the lawyers for agreeing to see out the tribunal with him.

I rely heavily on the report of the McCracken Tribunal of Inquiry in telling this story. It was the shortest ever productive tribunal in Ireland, taking just over six months to reveal the scandal of Haughey's money from Ben Dunne and lay bare Lowry's 'under the counter' rewards for working with Dunne.

The information about payments to Lowry and Haughey were put in writing in a number of documents because of a disagreement within the board of Dunnes Holding Company about some of the policy decisions and trading methods of Ben Dunne, the chief executive and a major family shareholder through the family trust. These differences in the Dunne family grew wider and deeper when his personal problems were publicly exposed during the early 1990s. In February 1992, he was charged by police in Florida after they discovered cocaine in his hotel room. Dunne was on a golfing holiday and, after a game, back in his hotel room at the Hyatt Regency Hotel, he rang an escort agency for some company. He had over 30 grams of cocaine with him, and when his escort arrived, they started taking it together. Dunne had a severe panic attack and started shouting, so the woman fled the room. She warned hotel security that the occupant of the room was behaving in a strange way and yelling. The security guards went to check and found Ben Dunne roaring at the top of his voice. The police were called and found the cocaine in the room. Dunne was charged with both possession and trafficking cocaine because of the large amount in his possession.

This escapade attracted an enormous amount of publicity in the Irish media, but Dunne was well advised by his lawyer, Noel Smyth, that on his return to Ireland he should do a series of media interviews confessing to the whole story and apologising for the distress and hurt he had caused his family. Thus, he won some sympathy for his human failings and for his regrets about the pain he had inflicted on those close to him, rather than being gleeful about a rich man in trouble. Noel Smyth had gone to

Florida to do plea-bargaining for Dunne, and had succeeded in getting the serious trafficking charge dropped. Then Dunne faced a well-reported trial, which might have meant time behind bars, but he was ordered to spend only a month in a rehabilitation clinic in England. The tribunal report says, 'After this, the personal and policy differences on the board became aggravated and in February 1993 Mr Ben Dunne was removed as Chairman of Dunnes Holding Company, and in July, he was removed as an executive director of the company.'

Ben Dunne then issued two sets of legal proceedings, one as an 'oppressed shareholder', and the other against the Dunnes Settlement Trust, according to the tribunal report, 'claiming certain reliefs against them, and in effect alleging the trust was a sham. The object of these proceedings would appear to have been to force the other members of the family to acquire his interest in Dunnes Holding Company for as high a price as possible.' Documents were drawn up by both sides for the legal actions. Ben Dunne's assertion that he had made payments to Charles Haughey of over £1 million, while he was taoiseach, between 1988 and 1991 was in correspondence of the legally termed 'Particulars' of his claim against the Dunnes Trust, delivered to the family solicitors as part of the litigation process by his lawyer, Noel Smyth. Payments to Lowry and others were detailed in a report drawn up by the accountancy company Price Waterhouse for Dunnes Stores Group, and hence for the other members of the family. Dunne was threatening to use the Haughey payments as a means of undermining and discrediting the family trust, telling a member of the trust that he would say that the payments were to influence Haughey to change the trust law to the advantage of the Dunnes trust. He later disavowed this claim: it was a 'stupid' allegation, which he made 'under ferocious pressure to try and get what I felt was mine'. The subsequent Moriarty Tribunal found that there was evidence that Dunne got a benefit from Haughey who organised a meeting for him with a senior Revenue Commissioner.

The family row was intense. Both actions were listed for hearing on 16 November 1994, but negotiations took place and a settlement reached, so neither the contents of the Price Waterhouse report nor the Smyth correspondence was made public. Then the leak about Lowry's house burst the dam and led dramatically to the exposure of Haughey's method of financing his extraordinarily expensive lifestyle, which had puzzled journalists and the public for a generation. After the McCracken report, Haughey was called before the new Moriarty Tribunal, which was held over many years. The whole unseemly, shocking but fascinating story was further dragged out of him and others, all because of Michael Lowry's house extension. Lowry was under investigation for his extension and its related payments (which were exposed in the McCracken Tribunal) and over the deeply disputed award of the second mobile phone network licence to Denis O'Brien, supervised by the Department of TEC, of which Lowry was minister.

I was with Bruton preparing for an event he had to attend at a Dublin hotel the morning the Lowry extension story broke. I was convinced, before we learned any more, that this would be curtains for the minister. Bruton had already spoken to Lowry on the phone, who said it was about matters before he became a minister and asked for time to look into it. In the car on the way to the event, I warned Bruton that the media would be gathered at the event, and he should be brief, factual and not speculate. I was worried that his regard for Lowry's loyalty during the attempted heave against him would subconsciously bring a defensive note to what he would say. At the group doorstep he said:

> I'm very confident that when the details are presented everyone will be satisfied. The issues go back a number of years, and he resigned his directorship of his company. I spoke to him. He said he needed time to talk to his financial advisers. I think he's entitled to the time to look into the matter, to say whatever he needs to say from his personal point of view.

On the way back to Government Buildings we briefly discussed the timescale for a full explanation – at the very most it should be 48 hours. I was convinced from the start that there had to be a tax issue involved in this house extension payment. We were both back in the office the next day, on a Saturday, preparing for developments. Lowry, knowing that the clock was running down, told Bruton on the phone that he was going to resign. The taoiseach alerted me that Lowry was resigning and would issue a statement, and that he himself would make a statement on the resignation.

While putting out the taoiseach's statement by fax, I was surprised when Lowry turned up at Government Buildings in the November gloomy darkness looking for a meeting with the taoiseach, surrounded by the doorstep media bristling with cameras and microphones. I went to the taoiseach's office and advised him that he should not meet with Lowry because the media were there in force. My view was that this would only damage him. Lowry wanted further identification with Bruton, who had a deserved reputation for honesty and playing a straight bat. Bruton's loyalty to the man who had stood by him at a difficult time won out. He wanted to do something. I proposed a photo call in the Sycamore Room. I would bring in the media and Lowry, and then the taoiseach would make a very brief appearance, but say nothing and answer no questions – it was just a photo opportunity. That was my serious mistake. When the cameras were filming and flashing, Lowry said, 'My best friend, my best friend for ever.' Bruton was snared. The clip was repeated many times during the continuing fallout from the extension story.

Lowry's resignation statement claimed that there had been no impropriety on his part in respect of any payments made for work carried out on his house; it was not possible to fulfil his departmental obligations and at the same time deal with 'sustained attack' from certain quarters; he did not want to embroil Dunnes Stores in 'what is in reality a political issue'; and he had a responsibility to protect Streamline Enterprises (his company, which installed refrigeration units for Dunnes Stores, and was set up and paid for by Dunnes). I wondered how he expected TDs and the public to swallow that. He said he did not want to prolong the distress to which his family and friends had been subjected. In truth, he resigned because he knew he would have to be fired if the matter was not fully resolved quickly. Accepting Lowry's resignation in a statement, Bruton acknowledged that he had to deal with the public disclosures of matters connected with his business career before he became a member of the government. He said Lowry had been a loyal personal friend and good colleague, as well as a hard-working minister. He hoped space would be given to him and his family, and that Lowry's natural good humour and strength under pressure would help them through this difficult time. Later, Bruton called former Fine Gael leader Alan Dukes and offered the vacancy at TEC, which Dukes was happy to accept. The rift over the heave against Bruton was finally closed. Asked by the *Irish Times* about their rivalry, Dukes replied 'What rivalry?'

Three weeks later in the Dáil, Lowry made a 25-minute personal statement in which he confessed that at the time of his appointment as a minister, his statement to the taoiseach that his tax affairs were in order and up to date was not true:

> I made a declaration to the Taoiseach to the effect that I had availed of the tax amnesty and that, in so far as I was aware, all my tax affairs were up to date and paid. I now accept that some of my tax obligations are still outstanding. I apologise to the Taoiseach, the House and the public for failing in that regard.

Dealing with the extension to his house, he claimed that there was a dual payment scheme for his work in Dunnes: to his company, and to him directly. 'As I was personally owed a considerable but undetermined sum of money, Mr Ben Dunne proposed that Dunnes Stores would undertake renovation of the house. Dunnes Stores appointed the architect. Dunnes Stores appointed the contractor.' It may seem incredible, Lowry said, but the total value of the work had yet to be determined to his satisfaction. 'As recently as yesterday afternoon, Dunnes Stores, through their solicitors, stated that payments to their contractor, Faxhill Homes Limited, in respect of alterations to my house amounted to an extraordinary £395,000. I totally reject this figure.' He maintained, 'It was not a loan, it was not a gift, it was not a handout, it was income.' He claimed it was not a tax evasion scheme designed by him.

Mr Justice McCracken concluded that there was 'no doubt' that Dunnes had paid £395,107 for the work that was carried out, and continued: 'In the books of Dunnes Stores Group the payments for the work on Mr Michael Lowry's house were treated as having been payments for work done for Dunnes Stores at the Ilac Centre in Dublin.' This was queried by the chief accountant of Dunnes, Michael Irwin, because if the payments were for Streamline Enterprises and/or Michael Lowry for work done by them, it would have been tax-deductible by Dunnes Stores, 'but Mr Ben Dunne insisted that this was the procedure which ought to be followed'. McCracken observed in his report:

> It is also significant that the method of payment used ensured that there was no record of these payments being made for the benefit of Mr Michael Lowry, and this seems to have been the clear intention of Mr Ben Dunne when he insisted that the payments be made in this way.

Lowry claimed in the Dáil that the first time he learned of the 'offsetting internally in Dunnes of the payments for the house extension to the Ilac Centre' was from the media reports of 29 November. He continued to insist that the value of his work for Dunnes had 'yet to be determined', while the new regime at the company told him that no money was due to him personally, and payments mentioned by Lowry were 'irregular'. In his Dáil statement Lowry made the following remarks, which the tribunal later found astonishing.

> I did not make any secret of the fact that Dunnes Stores paid me for professional services by way of assistance towards my house. If someone were trying to hide income, would he or she not be more likely to put it in an offshore account? The last thing such a person would do would be to spend it on a very obvious structure of bricks and mortar for all the world to see.

Mr Justice McCracken responded:

> In the light of the fact that Mr Michael Lowry had had two offshore accounts in his own name, one in the Bank of Ireland in the Isle of Man, and the other in an Allied Irish Banks subsidiary

in Jersey, and had held money in an Isle of Man account in the name of Badgeworth Limited, this part of his statement must be viewed with some astonishment.

The tribunal, Mr Justice McCracken said, was 'entitled to take into account his apparent lack of candour' in assessing the motives behind the financial arrangements Lowry had with Dunnes Stores, and with Ben Dunne in particular.

In his conclusions Mr Justice McCracken drew attention to many payments over the years from Dunnes and Ben Dunne to Lowry or Streamline, including some for bonuses to Streamline Enterprises staff, and some payments for the company which Lowry cashed, or lodged to accounts in his own name. McCracken found that bonuses were paid to staff members. But he also dealt with sums amounting to £155,000 that Ben Dunne paid to Lowry between October 1990 and May 1992 as personal bonuses. 'Two of these payments were made into bank accounts in the Isle of Man, one in the name of Michael Lowry, and the other in the name of Badgeworth Limited,' which was a company that had been set up on Dunne's instructions for Lowry's benefit. The accounts were opened and the monies paid in this way, McCracken wrote, 'with the intention of enabling Mr Michael Lowry to have money in an offshore account, contrary to the exchange control legislation then in being, and to assist him in evading tax'.

Lowry, McCracken concluded, also had an account in his own name and the names of his three children in the Jersey subsidiary of AIB, 'into which one of the cheques in an amount of £34,100 sterling paid to Streamline Enterprises in respect of work done in England was paid'. This account, McCracken said, did not have the assistance of, or was even known by, Ben Dunne, 'and again was an attempt by Mr Michael Lowry to evade the payment of tax'. The whole system by which Lowry would be paid substantial sums on a personal basis, and have a large sum of money spent on his house 'were designed to, and did, assist him in evading tax' was the conclusion of the tribunal, and it was 'also satisfied that Mr Ben Dunne knowingly assisted Mr Michael Lowry in evading tax'. When this was put to Ben Dunne at a tribunal hearing, he said: 'Mr Lowry is old enough and mature enough to be able to take care of his own tax problems, and I wouldn't have been involved in anything like that.' This response was described in the tribunal report as 'a completely naive and unacceptable explanation'. It was preceded, McCracken wrote, by Dunne's acknowledgement that 'people got small Christmas bonuses under the counter. The Tribunal is satisfied that these were very large bonuses, but still were being paid, in effect, under the counter.' The McCracken Tribunal went on to dismiss an argument that the large savings Dunnes made with Streamline Enterprises could in any way justify the Lowry payments, which it called 'clandestine'. It said this was an 'extraordinary' relationship, allowing Dunnes to have 'virtually complete control over the business of Streamline Enterprises', and allowing payments to be made to Lowry in 'a completely unorthodox fashion which facilitated tax evasion. Putting it at its mildest, it was an unhealthy business relationship, leaving aside the political implications altogether … the potential consequences of it are extremely disturbing.' McCracken cited three consequences.

First, by evading tax in this way, Lowry made himself vulnerable to all kinds of pressure from Dunnes Stores, had they chosen to apply these pressures. The threat to disclose payments and the offshore accounts could have been used by Dunnes Stores to obtain favours, as indeed could a threat to cut off this source of income to Michael Lowry.

Second, should the existence of these accounts become known to a third party, apart from Dunnes Stores, political or financial favours could have been sought in return for silence. The disclosure of these matters had a catastrophic effect on Lowry's personal and political life. 'The threat of disclosure would have been a powerful weapon in the hands of any third party', leaving Lowry 'open to blackmail of various kinds'.

Third, and perhaps the most damaging aspect of this relationship:

> There could be a public perception that a person in the position of a government minister and member of Cabinet was able to ignore, and indeed cynically evade, both the taxation and

exchange control laws of the State with impunity ... and it is an appalling situation that a government minister and Chairman of a Parliamentary Party can be seen to have been consistently benefiting from the black economy from shortly after he was first elected to Dáil Éireann. If such a person can behave in this way, without serious sanctions being imposed, it becomes very difficult to condemn others who similarly flout the law.

The findings of the McCracken Tribunal about former Fianna Fáil Taoiseach Charles Haughey, reported on 25 August 1997, were dramatic. In a few short sentences of introduction to the story of Haughey's money from Ben Dunne, a big lie was demolished:

> Mr Charles Haughey has now admitted that he received five payments from Mr Ben Dunne amounting in all to £1.3 million. However, when asked at the early stages of the Tribunal of Inquiry whether he had received the benefit of any of these monies, Mr Charles Haughey denied any knowledge of them and denied having obtained any benefit from them.

As a result of these denials the tribunal undertook extensive investigations to trace the monies Ben Dunne had paid, and the sources of Haughey's income. The devastating revelations came in sober tribunal language:

> The result of these investigations was that the tribunal became satisfied beyond all reasonable doubt that all of the monies paid by Mr Ben Dunne were received by or on behalf of Mr Charles Haughey for his benefit, or in one case, for the benefit of a member of his family.

Colm Keena, an investigative journalist with the *Irish Times*, wrote an extraordinary book, *Haughey's Millions: Charlie's Money Trail*, which is a masterpiece in charting how Haughey managed to live the lifestyle of a wealthy man in a large mansion in north County Dublin with extensive grounds, on the income of a government minister at first, a backbench TD for a number of years, and latterly as leader of Fianna Fáil and taoiseach, having come from a modest background with no inherited wealth.

I was at Haughey's first press conference as taoiseach in Leinster House in December 1979 after he won the vote of the parliamentary party ahead of George Colley, the candidate backed by Jack Lynch, who had resigned early. I was waiting at the door of the conference room in Leinster House to see Haughey coming, which he did with a noisy band of his cheering supporters triumphantly striding towards the room down the long hallway. A door opened from a room on the left side of the hall and out of it came Jack Lynch, who obviously wanted, however painful it might have been, to congratulate his successor, whom he had fired from his job as Minister for Finance during the Arms Crisis nine years earlier. Haughey did not miss a step. Turning a look of contempt at Lynch, nodding faintly with a grimace, he strode forward. A mortified Jack Lynch was literally pinned to the wall as the mob following Charlie pushed roughly past him. I ducked back into the room, shocked at this naked display of the transfer of power. During the press conference, Vincent Browne bluntly asked Haughey where his money had come from. Quick as a flash, Haughey retorted that the question presumed he was rich, which might not be the case: 'Ask my bank manager!' This brought laughter from some among the assembled journalists, and Haughey got away with it. In fact, at that time, his AIB bank manager was struggling to pin him down to repay debts of many hundreds of thousands of pounds. A huge sum was written off later because AIB considered Haughey a 'key influencer'.

Colm Keena revealed in his book that Haughey was deeply concerned about the leak to the *Irish Independent* in November 1996 about Ben Dunne's payment for Lowry's extension, afraid that he too would feature in the Price Waterhouse report, so he contacted the solicitor Noel Smyth. Haughey was well practised at using Smyth for information about the Dunnes affair, because in early 1994, when it appeared that the Dunnes' bitter family dispute was going to feature in court, Smyth suggested to Ben Dunne that Haughey should be informed of what was being alleged about him – the £1 million plus given to him by Dunne. 'This development was to become a central element in the later destruction of Haughey's reputation, in which Smyth was to play a leading role,' wrote Keena. Smyth called Haughey in 1994 and a meeting was arranged at his mansion. In the early 1970s Haughey had bought Abbeville, a large eighteenth-century house redesigned by James Gandon from an earlier building on the site, with 250 acres of grounds. The purchase greatly accelerated rumours and mystery about where Haughey was getting his money. 'It would appear that he enjoyed a lavish lifestyle, although he denied this in evidence, and there is no doubt that the upkeep of Abbeville must have required considerable funds,' McCracken wrote in his report.

Smyth told Haughey at Abbeville that 'he was satisfied the research he'd carried out while preparing for Ben Dunne's case would support' the £1 million plus allegations. Haughey's response was that he had never received the money. Despite all that was involved, Smyth wasn't alarmed by this reaction – 'He didn't believe him,' wrote Keena. Later, Haughey rang Smyth and said that he wanted to talk to him 'as a matter of urgency'. When they met, Haughey, having considered the matter, thought this was an attempt to destroy him. Smyth said it was nothing of the sort, nothing personal; they were 'stuck in a situation whereby these events had occurred'. Haughey feared that if the allegations became public, it would be 'devastating' for him, after his long career in public life. Anxiously, Haughey also unsuccessfully tried to get Ben Dunne's sister, Margaret Heffernan, to settle the legal actions, and urged Ben Dunne to drop his case against the Dunnes Trust. Relief came when the Dunnes' cases were settled on 19 November 1994. But it did not last, because the Dunnes' solicitor wrote to Haughey several times demanding the return of the money that had been 'improperly diverted' to him. Haughey called Smyth repeatedly, because he was stumped about what to do. Smyth advised him to get a solicitor, but Haughey did not respond.

Two years later, in November 1996, while Lowry was still reeling from his exposure, Haughey was worried again that he would be next. It was clear that the circle of those who knew about the payments had grown, and the

Price Waterhouse report was being seen as the source of the information. Haughey started calling Smyth again. All his calls to Smyth's office were systematically logged and later this would prove to be important evidence that Haughey was lying about his contacts with Smyth. Haughey wanted to meet. Smyth, as Ben Dunne's solicitor, suggested a neutral venue in a friend's house near Haughey's mansion. Haughey took some comfort from the fact that the payments to him did not appear in the Price Waterhouse report, though there were small payments to his wife, son and brother as well as a payment of £85,000 to the Fine Gael party as a political donation. The Price Waterhouse report was being examined by Judge Buchanan for the Dáil Committee on Procedure and Privileges. The government had to wait until Buchanan reported before setting up the McCracken Tribunal of Inquiry. Buchanan had no tribunal powers to compel witnesses and access documents to discover the full facts. The media hunt was now on for evidence that the £1 million plus was given to Haughey. The details of the allegation by Ben Dunne in the 'Particulars' of his case against the family Trust were sent by Noel Smyth to the family solicitors on 4 November 1994, ramping up pressure about the looming court hearing on 16 November.

Ben Dunne, facing a witness examination before the McCracken Tribunal in 1997, recalled a significant event when he *personally* gave money to Haughey, having said three years before that the money was given to siblings. In November 1991 Dunne had asked his solicitor, Noel Smyth, to get 'three bank drafts for him of £70,000 sterling each from Tutbury Limited in the Isle of Man', a company he had set up to hold Dunnes cash. The drafts were made payable to fictitious names. Dunne's tribunal evidence was 'that some days later' after he got the drafts from Smyth, he was playing golf at Baltray, County Louth and had the three bank drafts in his pocket. When the game was over he rang Haughey and arranged to go to Abbeville on his way home. There he felt that Haughey 'was not himself but looked down and depressed'. As he was leaving, the tall, large-framed man took the three bank drafts from his pocket and famously handed them to Haughey saying, 'Look, that is something for yourself.' Haughey responded, 'Thank you, big fellow.' These three drafts, totalling £210,000 sterling, were to prove fatal for Haughey's reputation.

Mrs Margaret Heffernan gave evidence to the tribunal that she had made attempts to find out if her brother had given money to Haughey, but when she asked Ben about it, he denied having done so. Later she went to Abbeville and asked for the return of the money, and Haughey said he was surprised at the request, and he couldn't be responsible for what her brother said, raising questions about the mental stability of Ben Dunne. Heffernan told the tribunal that Haughey had diverted the conversation, and did not answer her question. She also went to Des Traynor, who had actually negotiated the £1 million plus with Ben Dunne, but her evidence was that Traynor told her that he knew nothing about it. Traynor, who had become Haughey's bagman, died aged sixty-two years in May 1994, leaving a huge gap in Haughey's fundraising. His death also left Haughey without a master at devising money trails that kept special clients' money secret from the prying eyes of Revenue inspectors but still accessible to Haughey.

Traynor was a chartered accountant who started his career in Haughey Boland, the accountancy company founded by Haughey, with Harry Boland, after his qualification in the late 1940s. Haughey also qualified as a barrister-at-law. Traynor was the company's first clerk 'articled' to Haughey in 1951, becoming a partner in 1961. Haughey started his political career in 1957 when he was first elected to the Dáil, continuing to win a seat until his retirement in June 1992. The bond between Des Traynor and Haughey, both northside Dubliners educated by the Christian Brothers, was established in these formative years. Traynor went on to establish a career as a businessman and banker, and in December 1969 was appointed a director of Guinness Mahon Ltd, a licensed bank. It was established in Ireland in 1836 but moved its headquarters to London, and the Irish bank became a subsidiary. One of Traynor's earliest jobs at the bank was to establish a small investment subsidiary in the Cayman Islands, the Guinness Mahon Cayman Trust Ltd. The Caribbean islands would over the years develop a reputation as a tax haven and destination for hot money. In 1976 Traynor became de facto chief executive of the Irish bank as deputy chairman and he retained that position for the next ten years, according to the McCracken report. After resigning from the job, he became chairman of Cement

Roadstone Holdings (CRH), which was to become a very successful international Irish construction materials enterprise.

As both their careers flourished – Haughey had become a Fianna Fáil government minister in the 1960s – they remained close and Traynor was in a position to advise Haughey on his financial affairs. In the 1980s the Cayman operation was sold by the Irish bank first to its parent in London, then to a consortium led by Traynor, which in turn sold a large share of the Cayman operation to a London bank, Henry Ansbacher. So the name of the bank changed several times, ending up as Ansbacher Cayman Ltd, fully owned by the London bank. McCracken discovered that huge sums of money Traynor gathered for Haughey were stashed in an account in the Cayman Islands, but the money could be accessed in Ireland through a scheme Traynor ran whereby customers could make withdrawals and take out loans in Ireland, backed by the offshore accounts. To fund that, Ansbacher Cayman deposited money from Irish clients in its own name at Guinness Mahon. In 1989 there was £38 million in this Ansbacher account. McCracken wrote:

> This was a very ingenious scheme whereby Irish depositors could have their money offshore, with no record of their deposits in Ireland, and yet obtain an interest rate which was only one eighth of one per cent less than they would have obtained had they deposited it themselves in an Irish bank.

It was Traynor who operated this 'ingenious' system. Traynor and a couple of close associates were the only people who knew the clients' names, identified by codes and various forms of accounts. While some monies shifted location after Traynor's death to Hamilton Ross, the Poinciana Fund and Irish Intercontinental Bank, McCracken was able to match two code names to Haughey. S8 was a sterling account and S9 a Deutschmarks account, 'out of which payments were made for his benefit'. The latter appeared to have been used 'exclusively' for Haughey. In 2002, a report identified 200 holders of Ansbacher accounts, including Haughey and eight members of the board of CRH. Revenue investigations into the accounts had yielded over €112 million in unpaid taxes and penalties, according to the *Irish Times*. When the tribunal began hearing evidence about the alleged Dunne payments in April 1997, a lot of the Ansbacher money in Dublin departed.

When Haughey became taoiseach again in 1987, he was once more in a position to fundraise. Traynor rang Noel Fox, an accountant and partner in the firm of Oliver Freaney, auditors in some companies of the Dunnes Stores Group. Fox knew Traynor slightly. Traynor told him he was dealing with a 'significant problem, a business problem' concerning Haughey, and he was seeking about 'half a dozen people to contribute £150,000 each towards settling his problem'. He asked Fox, 'a financial adviser to Dunnes Stores and in particular a trusted adviser and close personal friend of Ben Dunne', to approach him to see if he would become part of the bailout consortium for Haughey. Fox attended a Dunnes management meeting every morning at eight, so at the next day's meeting he spoke to Ben Dunne about Traynor's approach to him. Ben Dunne's recollection was that he took a few days to consider the matter, and then spoke to Fox about it after another morning meeting. Fox had pressed the need for confidentiality and, on hearing this, Dunne said: 'I think Haughey is making a huge mistake trying to get six or seven people together … Christ picked twelve apostles and one of them crucified him.' Dunne 'then agreed to pay the entire amount, which he recollects as £700,000, while Noel Fox recollects it as being about £900,000,' according to the McCracken report.

A short time later, Traynor again contacted Fox to say that Haughey 'urgently required the sterling equivalent of £205,000, and asked that it be provided by way of a cheque made out to Mr John Furze, whom he said was the banker looking after the transaction.' Furze was one of Traynor's associates in Cayman. Fox had never heard of him, 'nor did he know what bank he was connected with'. McCracken reported that Fox was contacted 'on three further occasions by Mr Desmond Traynor seeking money on behalf of Mr Charles Haughey':

> In July 1988 he asked for £471,000 sterling, in April or May 1989 he asked for £150,000 sterling and in February 1990 he asked for

a further £200,000 sterling. In each case Mr Desmond Traynor specified the manner in which the payments were to be made, the name of the payee and the account into which they were to be paid.

Fox passed on each of the requests to Ben Dunne, along with the details Traynor had given him. In each case Dunne 'provided the necessary payments'. McCracken went on to deal with each of the payments in fine detail, where the money came from and how it had entered Traynor's magical international money roundabout, which made it secretly available in Ireland for Haughey's benefit; for example, paying for his general day-to-day expenses, all the while carried out by Haughey Boland accountants; paying off a £105,000 due loan from a state bank, the Agricultural Credit Corporation, which could have deeply embarrassed a taoiseach if he had failed to pay it; and even more funds were withdrawn in cash.

McCracken's tribunal team 'made extensive enquiries throughout the public service as to any possible instances in which Mr Charles Haughey might have used his influence for the benefit of either Ben Dunne personally, the Dunne family, or the Dunnes Stores Group. The only request for special favours which the tribunal has been able to uncover was a request by Mr Ben Dunne for a personal meeting with the chairman of the Revenue Commissioners. The Tribunal has heard evidence of this meeting, at which nothing specific was requested by Mr Ben Dunne.' The tribunal therefore concluded that Haughey had carried out no 'wrongful use of his position' in this regard.

However, in 2006 the Moriarty Tribunal, which followed the McCracken Tribunal, took a different view after digging out more details and context. Colm Keena reported in the *Irish Times* that Moriarty had found that Haughey's intervention with the Revenue had led to an offer to cut Dunnes Stores' potential tax bill by millions. This 'real and tangible benefit for Mr Dunne' was 'directly consequent on Mr Haughey's actions', the Moriarty Tribunal found. However, Dunnes took the tax issue to the Appeal Commissioners and won, so the tax question did not arise. The

Moriarty Tribunal also revealed additional Dunne payments to Haughey in early 1987, solicited by Traynor, coinciding with fears amid the Dunnes Trust and family that the enormous growth of the business could lead to a huge tax bill for the Trust, threatening the Dunnes Group itself.

In late April 1997, just three weeks before the general election was called, sensational headlines were splashed across the front pages about the tribunal hearings. 'Dunne Business Associate Confirms Haughey got £1.3m'; 'Dunnes Tribunal To Reveal New Facts Regards Payments'. The *Irish Times* reported that Fianna Fáil leader Bertie Ahern wanted the election delayed until after the tribunal ended. The party's ard fheis was taking place and members were in fear and turmoil about the electoral danger to them from the revelations about their famous boss. Ahern was deeply concerned, claiming that the tribunal could be 'manipulated', getting 'Ben Dunne in, and Charlie Haughey in and a few other Fianna Fáil people' and an election then called. It was a strange statement. The tribunal was doing its job in calling both Dunne and Haughey to give evidence, and it was wrong to suggest this could be pre-election manipulation.

I was more interested in Ahern's demand that the election be delayed until the tribunal was over. I agreed wholeheartedly and hoped that government members would see the substantial advantage in letting the tribunal finish its work. But no, the tribunal was to deliver its hammer blow to Haughey a matter of weeks after the Rainbow left office. I had been with Bruton when he appeared before McCracken to answer questions about Ben Dunne's £180,000 ordinary political donations to the Fine Gael party, first through Alan Dukes when he was the party leader, and then via Bruton after Lowry set up a meeting between him and Ben Dunne. Bruton had to explain why he had told the Beef Tribunal that party leaders rarely know anything about fundraising, but he had met with Dunne because the party was in dire financial straits. The tribunal found no impropriety in these donations.

A dramatic development started on 25 April. Noel Smyth, Ben Dunne's solicitor, raised a legal question about the admissibility of evidence he could give to the tribunal. This evidence was the record of his conversations with Haughey during five meetings since the '£1 million plus' speculation started in 1996 after Lowry's exposure. On the advice of his barrister, he had written a statement about these meetings and posted it to himself; the envelope was still unopened. Smyth considered that this evidence might be 'inadmissible due to the confidential nature of the conversations'. This was a bombshell, but Mr Justice McCracken handled it brilliantly and with great care. He decided that 'natural justice' required that Haughey see this record, and make what arguments he wished on its admissibility as evidence. So the document was delivered to Haughey unopened and he was invited to be represented or appear personally in three days. On 28 April, counsel for Haughey finally appeared, just to deal with the admissibility of Smyth's statement. He requested an adjournment to prepare and consider the legal position. The tribunal had evidence to analyse from its investigations, and had to hold hearings in London and the Cayman Islands, so McCracken decided the tribunal would resume its sittings on 30 June. The government did not perceive any electoral advantage in waiting for its own tribunal to report on these stunning revelations, so the election bandwagon rolled on.

Haughey sought and was granted full representation on 30 June, four days after the Rainbow left office. His counsel said it was Haughey's intention to give documents to the tribunal on 4 July dealing with all matters before the tribunal and these would acknowledge the evidence that, 'as a matter of probability', £1.3 million was paid into accounts managed by Traynor on behalf of Haughey, but without his knowledge. His counsel said the documents would 'clarify that it is not the case' that Haughey personally received three bank drafts 'made payable to fictitious persons' from Ben Dunne. The Haughey statement did not arrive until minutes before the tribunal sitting on 7 July. Counsel for Haughey indicated that he was not going to challenge Smyth's statement about his conversations with Haughey, so Smyth's statement was given to the tribunal.

At the start of the investigations, Haughey had denied receiving any monies from Ben Dunne. Now, he admitted he got the benefit of the money, but claimed he had no knowledge of it. But he also claimed that Dunne's story of the three bank drafts was untrue. In his statement,

Haughey said: 'I say no such meeting ever took place.' In relation to Smyth's statement about their conversations on these matters, he disputed everything that Smyth had recorded in his sealed envelope and claimed that Smyth had made each phone call requesting that they meet. It was his word against Smyth's – he thought. This proved to be a fatal error. The following day Noel Smyth pulled the pin on the grenade, effectively telling the tribunal he could prove that Haughey was lying. Every phone call Haughey made to him had been duly registered in his office in an official log with details and dates. There was some consternation among Haughey's legal team about this new information and his counsel requested an adjournment for 24 hours to consider the position while the tribunal, by consent, sought and received Smyth's records.

When the tribunal sat the next day, 9 July, Haughey's counsel said he wanted to read a statement from his client. In the statement, Haughey finally accepted the truth – he had received the £1.3 million from Ben Dunne and he had known all along from 1993 that Dunne was the donor. In another stunning reversal, he now accepted that the meeting with Ben Dunne at Abbeville, which he had said 'never took place', did in fact take place. He accepted that Ben Dunne gave him the three cheques for £210,000 sterling at his home in November 1991. It was an extraordinary climbdown, but that wasn't all. Haughey had to make a humiliating admission: 'I wish to make it clear that until yesterday I had mistakenly instructed my legal team. They have however agreed to continue acting for me for the duration of the Tribunal.' He also apologised to the tribunal for his obstruction.

It was the end for Haughey. The next day in person he gave a humiliating statement of apology and confession. In his report McCracken had to devote four and a half pages of commentary on Haughey's evidence, because he said 'regrettably, in relation to many of these matters, the tribunal considers Mr Charles Haughey's evidence to be unacceptable and untrue'. All this was in the Rainbow's tribunal report just weeks after the government left office.

McCracken cited the law about obstruction of the tribunal. He sent the relevant papers to the Director of Public Prosecutions, who duly charged Haughey with obstruction. The former taoiseach had lied repeatedly, and had tried to block, confuse and confound McCracken's investigation. The evidence of obstruction was damning; it should have been an open and shut case – necessary for Ireland's democracy. But what actually happened was dumbfounding. After a number of hearings by Judge Kevin Haugh, preparing for a trial during 1999/2000, the judge rejected Haughey's attempts to stop it by claiming that a fair trial could not be held while there was adverse publicity about him arising then from the Moriarty Tribunal. However, finally Judge Haugh did impose an indefinite stay on the case and it never resumed, after the Progressive Democrat Tánaiste, Mary Harney, called for Haughey to be put in jail. Harney clarified that she was not speaking about the obstruction trial; she was referring to new information then emerging from the Moriarty Tribunal that Haughey had received some £8 million from business persons in Ireland, worth the equivalent of €65 million at the time. It was a heavy irony since Ms Harney's party, the Progressive Democrats, arose out of opposition to Haughey's leadership within Fianna Fáil and was founded by senior figures who had either been ejected from or had left the party.

Bruton, Spring and De Rossa, now in opposition, in July 1997 pushed Bertie Ahern hard for another tribunal to be established after McCracken reported, to follow the leads his tribunal had uncovered about Haughey's finances that needed further investigation. The three party leaders could still have been in government celebrating the success of McCracken's exposures, politically benefiting from the Fianna Fáil scandal and embarrassment, and setting up the new tribunal. On top of that, a new IRA ceasefire was on the way. Still taoiseach until nearly the end of June, Bruton and the newly elected British prime minister, Tony Blair, had already agreed the terms for Sinn Féin to enter the Northern Ireland all-party talks. Finally, Ruairí Quinn could have been preparing his second budget for a general election in the autumn. Even if the autumn election had been lost, these would all be significant achievements, but I believed the Rainbow would have won.

I was already in Turkey trying to forget, to get away from all that had been unnecessarily lost, looking for ancient ruins and delighting in the wonderful Turkish Mediterranean coast.

21

A PEACE DEAL WITH TONY BLAIR

AFTER THE CHRISTMAS AND NEW Year holidays of December 1996–January 1997, I talked to colleagues in the Department of the Taoiseach about a date for the general election. The previous government had been formed in mid-December 1992, so the election had to be called by the same date in 1997. The longest possible campaign from then would have meant an election in the second half of January 1998. It was possible but not necessary since late October or November was possible and preferable. I made my view clear to my colleagues in the Department, that autumn would be best after a *second* election budget, because we were adopting the European system of autumn budgets, with two budgets in 1997. It was a unique opportunity. Ruairí Quinn delivered a well-received budget in January, which was considered *the* election budget. We could surprise the electorate with a *second* popular budget. I had a conversation in mid-January with a senior Labour official, who had spoken of 'nineteen weeks to victory', which would put the election in June. Both the Labour Party and Democratic Left had organised April annual party conferences, which appeared to be springboards for an election soon afterwards. Labour hoped for a 'reset' with the Irish people after rejecting collaboration with Albert Reynolds in the 1992 election campaign and then joining him in government. Polling showed that the electorate was waiting to punish them. I learned much later that Ruairí Quinn was in favour of a June election for fear of demands from special interests and Labour backbenchers later in the year. I was very disappointed that he wasn't a cheerleader for autumn.

I had lunch with Senator Pat Magner, a senior and well-respected Labour figure, to suggest that Dick Spring should make a serious speech apologising to the Irish people for a breach of faith in 1992, in advance of the coming general election, putting the apology in the context of the policies that Labour had succeeded in implementing. Spring could say he had allowed his interest in delivering those policies to dominate, and he had learned a good lesson the hard way. He should ask for forgiveness and understanding. It was worth doing – the Irish people are forgiving. I don't know if Pat, whom I admired, ever put the proposition to Spring, but he did say 'Dick might not do it,' and it never happened.

Early in the new year, I spoke in the Dáil bar to Renagh Holohan, who wrote the Quidnunc column for the *Irish Times*. She asked me about the election date. I told her I didn't know, but I made the case strongly for the Rainbow election to be called after a second good budget in the autumn. She wrote about it, but her other informants had convinced her it would be June. She said that an autumn date after the second budget was considered a spin to confuse the opposition. At a reception around the same time in the Department of the Taoiseach, attended by a number of Fine Gael ministers, Hugh Coveney said he was in favour of a November election, but I was the only one to agree with him. Coveney asked his comrades, 'Do you not want at least to be ministers for another six months?' He got only subdued mutters, but Coveney was right. During Bruton's lengthy autumn 1996 phone talks with the British PM, Major asked about the date of the general election in Ireland and Bruton replied: 'We are working on October next year.' Realising the cat was out of the bag on his view, he qualified his statement, saying 'it could possibly be earlier' and later scribbled changes covering every option on a transcript, early and late. The final transcript dropped all reference to the election.

I went to the taoiseach early in the new year to push for holding the election in the autumn, after a second 'popular' budget, which the booming economy could afford, and a cast-iron certainty that Tony Blair's New Labour would win the British election in May, greatly improving prospects for the peace process and a restored ceasefire. I was expecting to have a significant discussion but as soon as I had said all this, Bruton told me abruptly that a senior Fine Gael minister had told him a snap election should be held in April, and then quickly moved on to other matters. I was dismayed, but I still canvassed anyone who would listen and was shocked at negative or non-committal responses. Much later I learned that a close adviser and confidant of Bruton favoured a June election, and unfortunately he carried great weight with the taoiseach. Ruairí Quinn wanted June, and Agriculture Minister Ivan Yates also wanted June, claiming farmers would be up in arms by autumn.

On 14 May, the day before the election was called, the *Irish Independent* printed its editorial across the top of its front page beneath the masthead. 'It was to become the most infamous editorial in the history of Irish newspapers,' was the judgement of Matt Cooper, broadcaster and journalist, in his book *Who Really Runs Ireland?* It was jaw-dropping partisan propaganda which had no place in any newspaper, let alone on the front page. The Independent News and Media was controlled by businessman and former rugby star Tony O'Reilly. It advocated ditching the Rainbow coalition of Fine Gael, Labour and Democratic Left in favour of the Fianna Fáil–Progressive Democrat opposition, saying it was 'Payback Time' and approving the last two parties' tax rate cuts that would favour those with bigger salaries. Spring called it 'disgraceful and despicable, a new low in Irish journalism', and Bruton said it was a perverse political opinion, 'urging people not to vote for a government which had succeeded in recording a nine per cent annual growth rate during its term of office'. Since the *Irish Independent* was the biggest-selling Irish daily newspaper, there is little doubt that the editorial damaged the government.

Cooper's book traces the business background as the potential 'motive' for this ugly and biased political attack, which 'included a contentious and highly significant personal meeting between Bruton and O'Reilly'. The key item at that testy meeting in O'Reilly's holiday home in Glandore, west Cork, in July 1996, was a business wrangle over illegal

TV deflector masts in the country, which were able to supply British TV channels to households with TV aerials, free or at a very low cost. The later disgraced Fianna Fáil minister Ray Burke had given out 29 Multichannel Multipoint Distribution Service (MMDS) licences, a costly technology whereby foreign TV channels could be distributed around the country. Seven went directly to the Independent group and eleven more to companies in which the group had stakes. Burke gave assurances via 'a letter of comfort' to a senior executive of the Independent group promising a vigorous clamp-down on illegal services, but the letter contained 'a coding rarely used by civil servants to indicate that the content came from the minister and not from the department', wrote Cooper. O'Reilly had made clear in his chairman's letter in the Independent group annual report his upset with the Rainbow government that the continuing deflector services were costing a subsidiary company millions. There was a national campaign then under way by deflector users against being forced to use a more expensive service. Why were the deflectors not tolerated or licensed in some form by the Fianna Fáil administration at the time, instead of trying to impose the expensive MMDS system? Cooper's independent and fascinating account of this whole affair includes an 'intriguing' political payment, the second mobile phone licence, and Irish oil exploration and mining. It is an extraordinary look behind the scenes of politics, power and money then in Ireland. While I was keenly aware of the MMDS versus deflectors issue and its potential impact on the election, it was being handled by a colleague of mine at the time, and it was never raised by the political correspondents.

The taoiseach called the general election on 15 May for 6 June 1997, agreed with the coalition partners. An opinion poll in the *Irish Independent* that day gave the Fianna Fáil–Progressive Democrats alliance a nine-point lead over the Rainbow coalition parties. This confirmed the findings of a poll published in the *Irish Times* two weeks earlier, when the election decision could have been revisited. It gave a ten-point lead to Fianna Fáil and the Progressive Democrat parties over the combined parties of the Rainbow. At the same time the British Labour Party won a landslide victory over Major's Conservatives with a gigantic 179-seat majority, sweeping Tony Blair into 10 Downing Street on 2 May. The *Irish Times* poll and Blair's election made no impact on the juggernaut of the June election. It left me despondent. All my experience of elections told me that this early call was incomprehensible. There had been an expectation by some that the two groupings would be more or less equal, or the Rainbow just slightly behind, neither of which I believed, because of the Labour Party's troubles. Apart from the second budget and Tony Blair replacing Major, a third reason for delaying the election until the autumn was the growing problems for the former Fianna Fáil leader and taoiseach Charles Haughey at the McCracken Tribunal. From the smoking gun created by the leak targeted at Lowry six months before, Haughey was now sensationally walking the plank at the tribunal. Ben Dunne gave his evidence on 22 April 1997 that he'd paid the £1.3 million to Haughey – all the required bailout funds, citing the betrayal of Jesus by Judas out of the 12 Apostles. He decided 'for confidentiality purposes to do it *myself* for Mr Haughey'. The colourful story was laden with irony. The Dunne family dispute led to Ben Dunne *personally* exposing Haughey.

I spoke again to my predecessor, Peter Prendergast, about the role of a press secretary during an election. It was a party-political event, and the taoiseach's party had its own press office. Peter told me that the Fine Gael press office would be the main office for the campaign, and would deal with all related matters. I should confine my role to ongoing government business. He suggested that's the way the party officers would want it, and I could step back and let them at it, but be available for media advice if it was sought. I had already done two hour-long preparatory interviews with the taoiseach, throwing tough questions at him across a range of issues including hepatitis C, Lowry, the breakdown of the IRA ceasefire, and governing behind a 'plate of glass'. Eoghan Harris was brought on board to prepare Bruton for the RTÉ television debate with Bertie Ahern.

Before calling the election, Bruton had an election think-in at his house in Dunboyne, which he asked me to attend. It was there I learned, to my surprise, that he was going to have a special campaign train to travel around the country. The question came up about who was going to be with him to handle the media. I said I'd be happy for the party press office to take on the role. But Finola spoke up at the meeting, saying that the taoiseach wanted me to go, because he was used to me being with him and dealing with the media, so I said I'd be happy to go. But when the campaign was about halfway through, the party secretariat thought there were too many men about the taoiseach, particularly for TV shots of the campaign, and a young female press officer, Majella Fitzpatrick, joined us. I was very happy to stand back, and Majella became a vivacious and lively performer at Bruton's side. Finola had spoken at the Dunboyne meeting about the last election in 1992, when Bruton was under too much pressure trying to whip up enthusiasm for the Fine Gael campaign. She said the train would be a calming campaign experience. However, it proved too slow and limiting in terms of covering the country. Bruton got a great reception everywhere he went – this time he was taoiseach, not a recently chosen leader trying to make an impact. The polls consistently showed a high level of public approval for the government, about 57 per cent, and Bruton's personal ratings were comparatively high. The problem with the train was that he didn't get to visit enough locations and meet and greet the people, which would have created more of a campaign atmosphere. Bertie Ahern was travelling by bus and was able to do just that.

Another disadvantage in the campaign was the presentation to the electorate of what was being offered by the three parties that were seeking the return of the Rainbow government. The parties had agreed a 21-point masterplan of the shared principles and pledges for a new government, launched by the three party leaders in the Shelbourne Hotel on the day the election was called. It sank like a stone, because it lacked the specifics that the electorate and the media wanted to hear. The points were general: a tax system targeted to help people on middle and lower incomes; a radical reduction in long-term unemployment; greening everything the government would do; a safe and secure society, and so on. Each party in the Rainbow government launched its own campaign over the next few days, to promote what they had achieved for their constituencies in the Rainbow. Common to all parties was the commitment to widen tax bands, at a cost of about £1.5 billion, a progressive way of delivering more gains to low and middle-income earners than making simple tax rate cuts, which bring most gains for those on higher incomes. Both Fianna Fáil and the Progressive Democrats were promising about the same amount of money by slashing tax rates. Of course the headline figures for tax cuts were easy for the electorate to understand. Widening the tax bands was fairer but needed a pre-emptive debate for months beforehand to explain the rationale.

In the last week of the campaign, my colleagues John Foley and Tony Heffernan and myself on Bruton's train became the intermediaries for the rather anxious party leaders to agree a one per cent tax cut to the rates, as an extra offer to the electorate, when the polls were still showing the Rainbow would lose. I was dismayed watching RTÉ TV to see how poor the Fine Gael political broadcasts were; there was little mention of the party's best asset, John Bruton himself, who was polling higher than the party. So, in my only intervention in this space, I rang Peter White and got him to make a film about Bruton, as president of the EU Council, with Bill Clinton in Dublin, with Major and other world leaders and so on. Peter did a good job and I believe the film had a strong impact in the limited time that was left. Bruton tried unsuccessfully to inveigle Ahern into a second TV debate in Cork, and Dick Spring agreed to a TV debate with Mary Harney. The main TV debate just a few days before the election was given as a win for Bruton across the media, and could have helped Fine Gael in the closing stages.

In the 28th Dáil, both Fianna Fáil and Fine Gael increased their number of seats on their 1992 numbers by nine each, to 77 and 54 respectively. However, the Labour Party suffered severely, losing all the gains of the Spring tide in 1992, losing 16 seats and sharply dropping their numbers from 33 to 17. Democratic Left held its numbers to the four seats it had won in 1992, but lost its by-election gains of an additional two seats. The Progressive Democrats saw a collapse of more than half, from ten to just four. So the two blocs were Fianna Fáil–Progressive Democrats with 81 seats; and the Rainbow with 75. There were 166 seats in the Dáil. The Greens had two seats, Socialists one, Sinn Féin one, and there were six Independents, mainly with a Fianna Fáil DNA. Bruton did meet with the Independents, but it was a stillborn overture. The new Dáil opted for a Fianna Fáil-led minority government, with Bertie Ahern winning the vote for taoiseach by 85 votes to 78.

But before and after all that, Bruton's government continued during the critical months of May and up to 26 June 1997. Our system is different from the UK, where the transfer of power and office was made immediately after the election on 1 May; the Irish system takes some weeks. Most important, there was swift and significant engagement with the new British prime minister, Tony Blair, about the peace process. His brilliant campaign and youthful charm conquered all, and his landslide victory gave his party a historic majority. Speaking to journalists in the wake of the British election, the taoiseach called it 'stunning'. 'The fact that we now in Britain have a government with a strong majority will be very good from an Irish point of view. It will enable it to tackle Northern Ireland issues with resolution.' The two leaders used their time together very effectively. Sinn Féin had won two Westminster seats for Gerry Adams and Martin McGuinness, so Bruton said they should take that as a political mandate to move ahead with the peace process. He believed that the new British government would inject more energy and purpose into the talks process, and, to achieve that, 'we stand ready to work with them on an agreed basis'. He had last met Blair in Dublin during the December EU summit; he would be more favourable and practical for Ireland on EU issues as well as the North. Bruton paid tribute to former prime minister John Major for his 'immense' contribution to the search for a peaceful settlement in the North, while Spring said Major's efforts 'deserved a better outcome than they received'. The multi-party talks had continued from the autumn of 1996 until March 1997, making some progress on decommissioning, as we've seen, and technical issues. Major's unwillingness to agree a date for Sinn Féin to join the talks after a ceasefire had stalled the Hume–Adams initiative which led to Sinn Féin's document of 10 October 1996, but it was to be dramatically revived by Tony Blair and approved by Bruton.

February 1997 had seen something of a media campaign by Hume and Adams to keep the process alive, an article on a ceasefire in the Belfast *Irish News* by Hume, followed by Adams in the *Irish Times* setting out Sinn Féin's position on a political settlement after a ceasefire. It came ten days after the shooting dead of British soldier Stephen Restorick, the last soldier to be killed before the peace settlement. Major's private secretary John Holmes wrote a private memo, which can be found in the CAIN Archive at Ulster University, describing the Adams article as a PR effort to 'throw the ball back into our court'. It was 'a big story in Dublin'. He went on to say that Adams appeared to be putting 'greater emphasis on the need for, and possibility of, a new ceasefire than in recent months'. Major handwrote a comment on the memo 'Clever little devil, isn't he? But is it genuine?'

Bruton upset uninformed officials on both sides of the Irish Sea by 'bouncing' ideas on the phone with John Major to inject some life into the peace process. One was a very good idea, later adopted by both Tony Blair and George Mitchell, that a deadline should be set for the all-party talks. Major, no doubt in a skittish mood during an election campaign that he was bound to lose in six weeks' time, was proving hard to get on the phone before Bruton went to see Clinton in Washington for the St Patrick's Day celebrations. It was a ridiculous affair, but kept officials occupied, lunching and writing memos for a week or so, before the two talked for 25 minutes on 13 March. At about the same time, former Taoiseach Albert Reynolds wrote to Major, pleading with him to name a date for a ceasefire and for Sinn Féin to join the peace talks. Major rebuffed the request, in a response that can also be found in the CAIN Archive, making the point to Reynolds that first 'the IRA must call an unequivocal ceasefire'. The Irish government position had been to stand by the February 1996 communiqué: that a restored ceasefire would lead directly to the admission of Sinn Féin to the negotiations. But the Docklands bomb, followed by the Manchester bomb just days after the opening of the all-party talks, had hardened Major. If the IRA thought the bombs would soften him up, they were badly mistaken. Some republicans and others foolishly believed that the Docklands bomb moved the governments to launch the talks, but that was spurious. Sinn Féin had their chance at the opening of the talks to enter with a ceasefire, but the IRA spurned the offer. Republicans worried afterwards that a new ceasefire without clarity on their swift admittance to the talks could split the Republican movement. Major would have to fix a date for their admittance, but he wanted republicans to move first with a ceasefire.

I had lunch with a diplomat from the British embassy. He strongly agreed with the outgoing chief constable of the RUC, Hugh Annesley, who predicted that another IRA ceasefire was 'still possible within a year', a timing that looked beyond the British election. Annesley was retiring, he said, and 'wanted to be able to say that his analysis of the situation was right', which it was. The British official told me they were getting signals through 'indirect' contacts that the ceasefire would be restored. The British believed that 'Adams and McGuinness still want to go the peace road'. He claimed 'IRA morale was on the floor' and *that* was spurring violent acts.

Prime Minister Tony Blair took over Downing Street on 2 May 1997. Six days later, Bruton and Spring went to London for a meeting with Blair and Mo Mowlam, the new secretary of state for Northern Ireland. I met my new opposite number, Alistair Campbell, for the first time and we chatted while the leaders talked. Bruton was the first foreign leader to meet the new British prime minister. Blair made it clear that he was anxious to move the peace process forward, sweeping the board clear of any blockages. He was very glad and complimentary that the multi-party talks process, started the previous year, had been kept alive by the continued efforts of the Rainbow government and the passive willingness of the outgoing British administration. Bruton stressed the importance of former US Senator George Mitchell still holding the chair. Mo Mowlam had wasted no time: she had already been out and about on the streets of Belfast meeting and greeting people, and she had issued a statement that had messages for both republicans and unionists. A 'new settlement' would reiterate that there would be no constitutional change without the consent of a majority; arrangements for a new government would need cross-community support; policing would be reformed; there would be equality in employment; and she wanted to see Sinn Féin in the negotiations with a restored ceasefire.

After the hour-long meeting, Bruton was positively glowing with the media about the vigour and determination of Blair's approach to

Northern Ireland. He was sure that there would be a major change and improvement in Anglo-Irish relations. He said Blair understood there was an 'urgent' need to deal with the issues in the way of a restored ceasefire, and that developments would quickly be forthcoming. Blair had the freedom of a commanding majority and a determination to solve the outstanding issues. Officials were put to work on a practical scheme to get a renewed ceasefire so that Sinn Féin could enter the talks. Blair saw the chance to get that 'hand of history' on his shoulder. Blair and Bruton got on well together; in his autobiography Blair said Bruton was a 'great guy'. But Bruton did not win the election, so Blair had years to develop a strong personal and political relationship with Ahern as taoiseach, which was essential for maintaining the Belfast Agreement, and for the peace process – which did not end on Good Friday 1998. According to Alistair Campbell's *The Irish Diaries*, Blair had doubts about Ahern after his first meeting with him as taoiseach a week after he took office: 'BA was a nice enough bloke, and very affable, but TB felt he was basically putting the Sinn Féin line most of the time, Bruton basically was hostile. TB said after they went [Ahern and officials] he was worried the peace process had taken a setback.' Bruton's attitude was much more nuanced than 'hostile'; he supported republicans who fully supported the peace process. Mo Mowlam, speaking to journalists, was anxious to dispel worries about violence at the Orange Order Drumcree march in mid-July. She said the government would uphold the law. In fact, the RUC forced the march down Garvaghy Road, illustrating the difficulties involved.

Blair then surprised the Northern Ireland parties by turning up in Belfast on 16 May to make a significant speech of reassurance to unionists. He said he was committed to Northern Ireland and the principle of consent, which he was to repeat during the speech, and went on to spell out a message that took republicans aback: 'My agenda is not a united Ireland and I wonder just how many see it as a realistic possibility in the foreseeable future.' He placed Northern Ireland along with England, Scotland and Wales as a part of the United Kingdom and declared, 'I believe in the United Kingdom. I value the Union.' He couldn't see that changing: 'None of us in this hall today, even the youngest, is likely to see Northern Ireland as anything but a part of the United Kingdom.' But he leavened the message for republicans by saying that if they won a majority without coercion, that would be respected, and he revealed that he was allowing his officials to meet Sinn Féin.

Blair arranged two important meetings of his senior officials with Sinn Féin, starting five days later, with a follow-up on 28 May so that he could carefully analyse the situation to make sure there would be no misunderstandings on the part of the government or Sinn Féin. Blair, Bruton and Spring had another meeting on the margins of the pre-summit European Council gathering in The Hague on 23 May to review progress. Things were moving very fast. Blair briefed them privately on the British meeting with Sinn Féin two days before. It was part of his strategy, he said, to move quickly, trying to get a new ceasefire and Sinn Féin into the talks. Bruton told him that confidence-building was important. Decommissioning would be back on the all-party talks agenda using the Mitchell report, but, he said, it could not be allowed to stop progress in the talks on substantive issues. Blair indicated that a timeframe for the talks to end would impose some discipline; he thought May 1998 in legislation could suffice. 'How long a wait must there be after a ceasefire before Sinn Féin get into the talks?' he asked rhetorically. 'They are thinking four weeks or less, but they must fulfil conditions; it's subject to them meeting the ground rules,' i.e. agreeing the six Mitchell Principles, with no breaches on the ground. Bruton told Blair, 'We don't know how genuine this is. The last time people at the top engaged, they hadn't brought the movement with them.'

Blair said he 'was sorry if this initiative took him slightly by surprise, but as it happened, it turned out okay'. There was no need for any apology; Bruton and Spring were delighted with his energetic approach, Bruton was just cautioning about trust. Blair took the point. 'Genuine? I don't know, we'll put them to the test. It's better to get them into peace talks, and put the onus on them to keep the ceasefire. My strategy is, don't leave Sinn Féin with any vestige of excuse. I want, if I can, to get them into the talks then crack on with the process.' He wanted an agreement on all three strands and he repeated one of his messages from his Belfast speech:

'I don't believe that anyone believes that a United Ireland is coming out of this.' Bruton said, 'It would be much harder to deal with if Sinn Féin is a major party.' He was referring to their success in the Westminster election; Adams had held his Belfast seat, which he had taken from the SDLP; and Martin McGuinness had ousted the DUP's William McCrea in mid-Ulster. With their vote growing, Sinn Féin was threatening the SDLP. Blair said, 'I felt I had to act quickly because of the views of what is happening on the ground. If people feel Sinn Féin has a grievance, then they'll vote for them – but if they're [the IRA] faced with hard choices …?' Spring asked about the role of David Trimble. Blair said, 'he's interested in the notion of himself and John Hume being two engines' of agreement.

The meeting had to break there to get back to the European Council. It was so dramatic and dynamic compared to what we had to deal with over two years with John Major. Afterwards, talking to journalists, Bruton complimented Blair's 'tremendous' determination to give republicans an opportunity to embrace peace and join negotiations on a settlement. Nothing else was said publicly at the time. While the Irish election was in full flood, Bruton and Blair stayed in touch on the phone about developments and the British second meeting with Sinn Féin. Blair wrote a 'confidential and personal' letter to the taoiseach on 11 June.

> Dear John,
>
> It was good to talk to you on the phone earlier this week, and to share our concerns about renewed IRA violence. The attack on the army patrol yesterday, and today's killing of a Loyalist terrorist, only increase my fears, although the responsibility for the latest incident is not yet clear.
>
> As you know, I want to get Sinn Féin into the talks if I can. We have had two meetings with them at official level to clarify our position on various issues of concern to them, and to set out our own. I now want officials to send them a short piece of paper by the end of this week, so that they can be in no doubt of where we stand. I attach a copy of what we propose to send. I would be grateful if you could treat this in strict confidence for the

moment. We may want to arrange a further meeting of officials with Sinn Féin early next week, but that is seriously threatened by continuing IRA violence.

In any case I plan to make a statement about our position, probably next week. This would explain again our position on confidence-building, decommissioning, and the time-frame for negotiations. It would also set out that we have in mind a period of some 6 weeks to assess a ceasefire. In other words a ceasefire in mid-June would lead, if it were satisfactory in word and deed, to Sinn Féin's formal entry into the talks by the end of July.

I should add that I propose to ensure that the substantive political talks get under way in September, whether Sinn Féin are in the talks or not. I am not prepared to allow further delay. So Sinn Féin need to make up their minds whether they want to be part of the political process or not.

I hope you will be ready to support fully this approach and that we can also reach agreement rapidly on decommissioning, to enable the talks to move forward. I am prepared to make a reasonable offer to Sinn Féin, despite the risks this entails. I hope they will not misunderstand the position or my determination. I will not tolerate an approach from them which claims to be political but remains underpinned by violence or the threat of it. Their current twin-track strategy leaves me genuinely alarmed about their sincerity.

I want to make rapid progress this summer and will do everything I can to achieve this. I know I can count on your influence to help me to do so. If the two governments are together, we are best placed to move others.

Yours ever,

Tony

AIDE-MEMOIRE
MEETINGS WITH SINN FÉIN

The purpose of the meetings on 21 and 28 May was to ensure there was no misunderstanding of the Government's position or of Sinn Féin's. This note sets out the Government's position, in particular on the points raised by Sinn Féin.

First, Sinn Féin's participation in talks. The entry of Sinn Féin into the talks requires an unequivocal restoration of the IRA ceasefire. Negotiating while violence continues, or under the threat of violence, is unacceptable.

The British Government wants to see the talks proceed on an inclusive basis, and move on to the substantive political issues as soon as possible, and in any case by September. It wants to see Sinn Féin participating in these talks. Sinn Féin's entry is governed by the legal requirements set out in paragraphs 8 and 9 of the 'Ground Rules for the All-Party Negotiations'. The Secretary of State is legally obliged to issue an invitation to Sinn Féin when she considers those requirements are met, having made a political judgement of all the circumstances in the round.

Some time will be needed to assess a ceasefire to see that words and deeds are matching before such a judgement can be made. We understand that an open-ended time period gives rise to accusations of bad faith. We are prepared therefore to remove any misunderstanding by saying the period of time for such a judgement is some 6 weeks. If an unequivocal ceasefire is in place by mid-June, and is satisfactory in word and deed, Sinn Féin would be invited to a plenary session of the negotiations by the end of July. That would be the occasion for Sinn Féin to make clear its commitment to the Mitchell 6 principles.

In the period immediately following a ceasefire, we expect participants might wish to consider adjourning the talks. As was said by the previous Government and this Government, Ministerial meetings with Sinn Féin would be possible, as well as bilateral and other meetings in Castle Buildings, including the Independent Chairmen and Sinn Féin. Sinn Féin would also have access to an office in Castle Buildings.

Second, timeframe. Because of its concern to get this process going, the Government believes the talks should not continue beyond May 1998, the date envisaged by current legislation, and that a settlement should be achieved by then. There will be regular reviews of progress.

Third, decommissioning. The talks participants are currently addressing the issue of decommissioning. The Government has always made it clear that it supports parallel decommissioning as recommended by Mitchell, and that it wants to resolve this rapidly to the satisfaction of the participants so that it does not block the start of substantive political negotiations in September. It is working with the Irish Government to do so. This can only be on the basis of implementing all aspects of the Mitchell report. As mutual progress is made on political issues and decommissioning, this can create growing mutual trust and confidence on all sides.

Any agreement on decommissioning seems likely to include a commitment by each participant to work constructively and in good faith to implement all aspects of the Mitchell report; an independent commission, to be established in parallel with the launch of substantive negotiations; a dedicated committee of the plenary to advance all aspects of the Mitchell report; and a review mechanism for progress across the spectrum of the negotiations.

Fourth, confidence-building. The Government wants to build confidence on all sides of the community, based on principles of equality of opportunity, equity of treatment and parity of esteem. Measures already announced include incorporation of the ECHR [European Court of Human Rights] into domestic law, a review of training opportunities for young people; a commitment to equality of opportunity in the labour market; a commitment to legislate this year on the North report; and a commitment to implement proposals to develop a policing service capable of securing the support of the whole community, including a more independent complaints system.

Confidence-building is of course a two way street. A genuine and lasting abandonment of violence would do more to rebuild confidence across the community than any other step. Other paramilitary activity such as intimidation through so-called punishment attacks should also stop, on all sides. This would help the Government to respond imaginatively in areas such as security force deployments.

Sinn Féin's concerns were set out in its paper of 10 October. This note answers those concerns fully. An immediate and unequivocal IRA ceasefire is now needed to enable Sinn Féin to enter the talks as set out above. If Sinn Féin do not enter the talks, the substantive negotiations will be taken forward in September in any event.

This substantial programme for peace, which Bruton shared with Ahern, was given to Sinn Féin two days later on 13 June, answering all the party's questions in the document of 10 October 1996. A new renewed ceasefire would be 'proved' over just six weeks.

Three days after the aide-memoire was given to Sinn Féin, the IRA shot two young RUC policemen in the back of the head while they were on a midday foot patrol in a small lane called Church Walk in Lurgan, County Armagh. This brutal double murder was carried out by two IRA men wearing wigs and windcheaters who ran up behind the officers and shot them at point-blank range. They escaped in a car which was found later burned out in a Catholic estate nearby. It was a shocking attack: the two young men were community policemen with young families. Constable Roland John Graham was married with three daughters aged ten, seven and two; Reserve Constable David Andrew Johnston was married with two sons aged seven and three. As community policemen, they were regularly seen on foot patrol.

Both Tony Blair and John Bruton were attending the Amsterdam Summit of the European Union when we got the news about these dreadful murders. Everyone in our delegation room at the summit centre was dumbfounded, speechless. Contacts were immediately made with the British delegation. We went first to their delegation room, where the British team were also in shock, but we were told that Blair was on the third floor, so we went down to his room. Tony Blair was horrified at what the IRA had done, visibly distraught and angry. He and Bruton talked together briefly and agreed to go together to give their reactions to the media already assembled outside. As we went to take the lift, Blair turned to me, the closest person to him, and said emotionally, 'It's a personal affront when I've been doing all I can to bring them into the talks. I might not be able to bring them in after this.' Numbly, I said, 'It's appalling, unbelievable.'

Bruton said, 'They're trying to intimidate you,' to which Blair responded, 'They've picked the wrong person.' Bruton said 'I know that. I've always doubted Sinn Féin/IRA sincerity,' and Blair said, '*Everything* was being done.' Seán Ó hUiginn added: 'They have been told this was the best package on offer, they have a response on all that they asked. It could be a group wanting to upset the apple cart.' Bruton commented, 'But the leadership is the same – and they can't deliver.' Blair replied, 'And if they can't deliver a ceasefire, what's the use in talking to them? I can deal with the [Labour Party] hard left, but these people are gangsters.' In the room before we started down to the lobby, Blair had told us, 'I expected to be savaged by unionists over what I have offered to Sinn Féin.' In the lobby, Alistair Campbell and I were emphatic that the two leaders should make their statements and then answer just a couple of questions. There were many requests for TV interviews to be done. The two leaders then strode out together to face the cameras, and denounced the senseless, brutal murders.

A furious taoiseach, with Blair at his side, had this to say:

> I condemn in the most stringent terms possible the murders of John Graham and David Johnston, a politically motivated crime, and a setback to the peace negotiations in the most deliberate way possible. The British prime minister was reaching out to the republican movement to restore the ceasefire and join the talks process, and these efforts are thrown back in his face. There are five children today who have no father anymore, three girls and two boys, and all this has been done in the name of so-called politics, to achieve a political objective. These things don't happen by accident. It's a thoroughly organised movement with a political wing and a military wing – they operate to the same agenda. They work hand in

glove; to believe in anything else is to believe in a myth. I'm aware of the extent of Mr Blair's efforts to bring the republican movement into the peace process. I'm appalled by this calculated act. Sinn Féin should cut all links with the IRA, and say they disavow the activities of the IRA and any linguistic insults to the intelligence of decent people. The republican movement is adept at avoiding responsibility, they are experts in the use of the language of evasion.

I welcome the fact that the new British government is attempting to inject new momentum into the peace process in meetings with Sinn Féin, and the IRA send in the assassins, a calculated act of intimidation. If there are divisions within the republican movement, it's time for those who want a peace deal to remove themselves from any connection with those carrying out these actions. Gerry Adams, quoting the poet John Donne, said this event 'diminishes' us all. These two men were diminished for ever. They have ransacked the dictionary to find new words in order to avoid condemning this brutal murder. For him to say that this diminishes us all is the height of hypocrisy. I reject his use of these weasel words to evade his responsibility.

Blair said:

> This was absolutely an appalling act of brutality, a totally callous murder, and it is all the more appalling because we were working hard to build momentum back into the peace process to find a lasting settlement for people in Northern Ireland. It is difficult to interpret this latest attack as anything other than a deliberate attempt to frustrate that process working, a signal that Sinn Féin and the IRA are not interested in peace and democracy and prefer violence. I would like to see Mr Adams face up to the responsibility of condemning it, condemning it outright, no hesitation, no weasel words, but condemning it as any decent human being would do. There is obviously no question of a further meeting with Sinn Féin in these circumstances.

Blair also called on Sinn Féin to end all connection with the IRA. From Washington, President Clinton delivered a harsh attack on the IRA: 'I condemn this brutal act of terrorism in the strongest possible terms. There is nothing patriotic or heroic about these cowardly killings.' Campbell quotes Bill Clinton as saying later that what Adams said was 'stupid'.

When they had finished their statements and interviews for RTÉ, BBC and Channel 4, we went back to the lobby where Tony Blair complimented and thanked Bruton, saying his words were very strong and would have a powerful effect. They, like all of us, were still in shock. The two leaders had to return to important EU summit business shortly afterwards, which in a way was a diversion from the gloom and horror provoked by the murders. Before the news conference, I met John Holmes, Blair's principal private secretary. He asked me if we would agree with their suspension of meetings with Sinn Féin. I said we would, divining the taoiseach's mind.

Just two weeks earlier Holmes had been involved in a statement on the Great Famine that became controversial decades later. The 150th anniversary of the Famine was being commemorated from 1995 to 1997, one of the worst years of the Famine being 1847, though it continued to the end of that decade. A junior minister, Avril Doyle, was given responsibility for co-ordinating events to remember this dreadful Irish holocaust. The commemorations provoked unworthy and frankly disgraceful reactions in Downing Street. The Anglican rector of Liverpool, Canon Nicholas Frayling, was planning 'a service of contrition' in Liverpool's Anglican Cathedral at which 'Britain can express its deep regret for its treatment of Irish citizens 150 years ago'. Members of the British government and the royal family were expected to attend and the Irish President Mary Robinson would also be present. However, John Major vetoed any official British participation in this proposed ecumenical service. Major believed that the service in Liverpool 'would look like an apology for the Famine' and would offend unionist sensitivities in Northern Ireland.

Senior British officials had considered Avril Doyle's decision to go ahead with a concert by the Liverpool Philharmonic Orchestra in 1996 as 'very awkward'. The British ambassador to Ireland, Veronica Sutherland, was allowed to attend this concert as a low-key British involvement. She had attended several Famine events in Ireland, including an ecumenical service in Tuam, County Galway, where Archbishop Lord Robin Eames, the Protestant Primate of All Ireland, had given the address. At a dinner hosted by the ambassador, Avril Doyle had suggested a similar event at Liverpool Cathedral. Sutherland in turn had recommended the idea, and it was endorsed by Sir Patrick Mayhew, who said it 'might do a lot of good' – all these events are noted in the CAIN Archive, Ulster University's superb collection of source material on the Troubles. Mayhew was right, but the cancellation by Major demonstrated that even the most decent of Britons can be insensitive about serious wrongs committed under British rule in Ireland.

Organisers of a major televised Cork Famine commemorative event scheduled for early June 1997, backed by Avril Doyle, pushed the British government hard to make a formal statement to be included, and Holmes, the oracle of Downing Street, was the man who wrote the 'Blair' statement on the Famine, read at the event by actor Gabriel Byrne. It was based on a draft by others, and reported in both Ireland and Britain as an 'apology' for the Famine. Pressed by the deadline, Holmes tried to reach Blair for approval, but did not succeed. He got Alistair Campbell and others to read the text before sending this out in Blair's name:

> The Famine was a defining event in the history of Ireland and Britain. It has left deep scars. That one million people should have died in what was then part of the richest and most powerful nation in the world is something that still causes pain as we reflect on it today. Those who governed in London at the time failed their people through standing by while a crop failure turned into a massive human tragedy.

Bruton complimented Blair for the 'thought and care' of the statement. In UK government papers released in 2021, and discussed in *The Guardian* in July of that year, there was a Holmes note to Blair explaining that he had approved the wording off his 'own bat' and that 'the key sentence in your message is the acknowledgement that the British government at the time could have done more to prevent the tragedy. This is no more than a statement of fact, and falls well short of an apology.' It was well short of what was needed, to be sure, but after a century and a half of British government silence on their culpability, it was a start. The full resources of the 'richest and most powerful nation in the world' were needed but deliberately not used, leaving a million dead and millions more emigrating in desperation. It should be admitted that there were racist views of the Irish peasantry at play; and there was a crude, inhumane attitude towards 'surplus Irish people' standing in the way of a more efficient use of the land – a 'clearance' that would allow more productive use, a deadly view disgracefully expressed by the senior British official in charge of Irish Famine relief, Charles Trevelyan. The former chief prosecutor of the International Criminal Court, Luis Moreno Ocampo, stated in August 2023 that 'starvation is the invisible genocide weapon'. More open-minded and critical historical research is needed, not to stir emotions, but to arrive at the truth. I was not involved in the Famine commemoration plans and did not agree with the subdued government approach.

At the EU summit, the Germans were happy that the Stability Pact for the euro agreed at Dublin was endorsed without change. The Commission chief, Jacques Santer, declared that the message from Amsterdam was that the EU was well on the road to monetary union. Ireland opted out of the Schengen passport-free travel area for 13 states of the 15. We could not join because the UK was not going in, fearing mass immigration. Ireland wanted to maintain the historic Common Travel Area with Britain, recognised by the EU, and did not want to provide a 'back door' into the UK. There was a confirmation of the Declaration on Employment, with new powers for the EU, already substantially prepared in Dublin, and agreement on a relationship between the EU Council of Finance Ministers and the new European Central Bank to ensure that the bank understood the political need for growth and jobs.

As further reactions to the murders of John Graham and David Johnston came in, Adams admitted his shock at the killings, according to RTÉ News, adding, 'they should be a spur to those involved in the peace process.' The North Armagh brigade of the IRA admitted responsibility for the murder of the two policemen the day after the attack. The wave of disgust and condemnation did help propel the IRA to establish a renewed ceasefire and that did ultimately lead to a split in the republican movement that Adams had sought to avoid. One group was the 'Real IRA', whose claim to shame was the appalling brutality of the Omagh car bombing in August 1998, four months after the Belfast Agreement. It killed 29 people and injured 220 others, making it the deadliest single atrocity of the Troubles.

The year 1997 was also the 25th anniversary of another ghastly British event – Bloody Sunday. This anniversary also caused consternation in Downing Street. Released British government files show that an angry Sir Patrick Mayhew phoned the prime minister's office in February 1997 to express his distress about Major's 'unwillingness' to sign a letter to John Hume 'regretting Bloody Sunday'. Secretary of State Mayhew wanted Major to express his 'profound regret' for what happened in the Bogside on 30 January 1972, saying that this was different from an apology, 'which would effectively accept responsibility and open the door to calls for prosecutions'. He considered it important, and he was upset that his carefully considered advice was rejected. Mayhew believed an expression of regret would lower tensions around the anniversary. John Hume was looking for a meeting with the prime minister, accompanied by the families of victims. John Holmes wrote to Major saying that the killing of 14 people by British Army paratroopers was an 'inglorious episode which we genuinely can regret. But the politics of saying so are not straightforward.' He warned that the distinction between an expression of regret and an apology 'may not be entirely apparent to the great British press'. There could be headlines about apologies, sops to nationalists and U-turns. He also said there was the 'probability' of more evidence about the killings soon from the families and the Irish government, and 'if we are going to edge in their direction' it would be better to do it then. His advice was that Mayhew meet the families 'in sympathetic listening mode'.

Major's reaction was a handwritten note on the memo. 'I am not at all attracted to this. It's got big downsides and small upsides.' Shortly afterwards Downing Street wrote to Mayhew agreeing that *he* meet with Hume and the families, but the prime minister was not in favour of being drawn down the road towards 'apologising for Bloody Sunday'. Major 'would certainly not wish the government make a formal expression of regret'. However, Holmes thought it would 'not be easy' to stop Mayhew using the word 'regret' in talking to John Hume. But Holmes thought it would be 'liveable' if it was in the context of regretting all deaths – and if Mayhew did not make it public afterwards. Major agreed with that approach. But that approach just caused further anger and disappointment among the relatives of the dead after the Mayhew meeting went ahead on 14 February 1997; Mayhew expressed his regret, but the following day he said there would be no official apology or new inquiry.

In the last week of the Rainbow government, Bruton sent a file on Bloody Sunday to Blair that drew attention to new evidence which had emerged on the UK's *Channel 4 News* in four key programmes broadcast between January and May 1997. The credibility of the Widgery Tribunal, which found no fault in the British military killings, was shredded in these broadcasts, so much so that Bruton told Blair in an accompanying letter that the dreadful injustice to the innocent victims of Bloody Sunday was multiplied by the second injustice of Lord Widgery's 1972 report. The Irish government had made a deep analysis of the multiple failings of Widgery, revealed in the new evidence, and that analysis was sent with Bruton's letter. This was reported by Geraldine Kennedy in the *Irish Times* on 25 June 1997, quoting Bruton's call for all who had been affected by past acts of violence to have a means of achieving peace and justice. Bruton wrote:

> I believe that establishing the truth about what happened on Bloody Sunday will represent a major step in this direction; will make an important contribution to the cause of peace and reconciliation; and will offer hope to all those who grieve as a result of the violence of the past three decades ... there is now

an opportunity to lay to rest this most troubling and disturbing episode of the terrible history of the past 27 years.

The Channel 4 investigation was extraordinary and, once again, devastating about the British system of justice in Irish cases. Eyewitness evidence that there was shooting from the old city walls above the marchers, rejected by Widgery, was backed up by ballistics evidence that the shots could not have come from paratroopers at ground level. Intercepted radio recordings of the British Army, rejected by Widgery as illegal, confirmed that the British Army fired from the Derry walls. A soldier of the Royal Anglian Regiment told *Channel 4 News* that he was in a 14-man patrol on the walls and described how a sniper from the Anglians opened fire, claiming he'd seen a man with a gun – he recalled the sniper saying, 'Bloody hell, I've got two with three shots.' A paratrooper told *Channel 4 News*, 'Command and control was absent, noticeably absent for a period of perhaps fifteen minutes during which the bulk of the injuries occurred,' and that during that period 'decisions were made by individuals on the ground which led to some shameful and disgraceful acts being perpetrated.' He said his statement for Widgery was altered before he signed it. A marksman with the 22nd Light Air Defence Regiment, operating alongside the Parachute Regiment, said he was not aware they were being fired on and no rounds were fired at him; 'If there'd have been incoming fire, I'd have heard it.' He said paratroopers fired from the hip into a crowd of people, in contrast to the official account that said all shots were aimed at threatening targets. This superb Channel 4 TV investigation was by Lena Ferguson and Alex Thomson.

The damning evidence from the four key *Channel 4 News* investigation reports was analysed in the Irish government's file. In his covering letter, Bruton welcomed indications from Blair's new government that it would look again at Bloody Sunday. Bruton said this approach would assist the removal of profound distress, not alone for relatives but for all the nationalist community. On *Channel 4 News* in January 1998, Tony Blair formally announced a new inquiry into Bloody Sunday to be carried out by Lord Saville of Newdigate. In June 2010, Prime Minister

David Cameron eventually apologised on behalf of the British government for Bloody Sunday, following the publication of the Saville report into the killings. Campbell revealed in *The Irish Diaries* that Blair was 'always reluctant to hold the inquiry' and only when it concluded and David Cameron apologised 'were sceptics like TB finally persuaded of the merits'.

Just three days before Bruton left office, he and Blair met in New York at a special assembly of the United Nations on the Earth Summit. They completed their work on the decommissioning issue, agreeing a 12-page document that would be sent to the parties in the Stormont talks the next day. It was based on work developed by the two governments from the autumn of the previous year. This was the last piece of the jigsaw to achieve a new IRA ceasefire that could lead to Sinn Féin's admission to the all-party talks now in September, when they recommenced after the August break. It proposed that paramilitary weapons be decommissioned during political talks, as recommended by the Mitchell report, dropping the demand for prior decommissioning. Blair wanted it to be kept under wraps (he was to speak on it in parliament), but that was too much to ask of a man who had only days left in office. Bruton briefed journalists in New York, and then he spoke by phone to the *Irish Times*. Bruton expressed confidence in a renewed ceasefire: 'We have provided every possible conceivable clarification for the republican movement. They can put forward no remaining reason for continuing the IRA campaign. It allows for decommissioning to be dealt with seriously without blocking the talks.'

Blair told the House of Commons: 'The report foresaw mutual progress on decommissioning and substantive political issues leading to a progressive pattern of mounting trust and confidence. That is what the two governments want to see.' Most important, this issue would not be permitted to stand in the way of substantial negotiations. He said an independent commission would be appointed by the two governments to oversee and validate weapons put beyond use. It would be independent of both governments. There would be a committee of the plenary talks and a sub-committee to deal with the weapons issue, and there would be a sub-committee on confidence-building measures. In the wake of the Lurgan atrocity, a determined Blair also repeated his statement that the 'settlement train' was leaving, with or without Sinn Féin and the IRA.

This was the moment of decision for republicans. Blair had effectively given the IRA an ultimatum with a deadline just weeks away in mid-July to restore its ceasefire, in order to meet the six weeks required to prove it, so that Mo Mowlam, secretary of state for Northern Ireland, would, under law, invite Sinn Féin to pledge their adoption of the six Mitchell Principles and then join the multi-party talks in September. The IRA declared a renewed ceasefire on 19 July. They knew, from Blair's mid-May speech, the 'partitionist' nature of any settlement, with unity requiring full consent North and South. Mo Mowlam repeatedly stressed that a settlement would be based on the Downing Street Declaration and the Framework Documents, as indeed the Good Friday Agreement was; and it came about after Tony Blair took personal charge of the Easter week negotiations. Bruton's outreach to unionists played a subtle role, I believe, in the outcome, and my focus is on that in this account.

Blair went to Belfast for just one day on Tuesday 7 April 1998 to endorse an expected settlement, making the famous 'hand of history on his shoulder' remark. But he was shaken to find the talks in a doldrum. The Alliance Party leader, John Alderdice, told him that 'the thing was a non-starter for David Trimble'. Then he met the talks chairman, George Mitchell, who 'unnerved' him, saying 'the deal was undoable', wrote Blair in his autobiography. 'I took the decision then and there to take complete charge of the negotiation.' He stayed working in the dreary Castle Buildings for four days, 'engaging intimately in the detail of one of the most extraordinary peace negotiations ever undertaken'. John Holmes wrote a report by letter to Blair on what happened, day by day, over this historic week. Blair met Trimble at Hillsborough to hear his problems. The Irish side had injudiciously put on the table *all* the extensive texts about North–South bodies that Bruton and Major had agreed in 1995 about what might be achieved through continuous co-operation; that and decommissioning were the key issues, but others were 'not insuperable', wrote Holmes. Blair decided that 'radical change' was necessary.

George Mitchell agreed, and he was to phone Ahern early on Wednesday morning to alert him. Blair also told Trimble that morning, before his breakfast with Ahern, that he would be 'pressing him for radical change'. Ahern, who was returning to Dublin afterwards for his mother Julia's funeral, made clear that he and his team would have a 'crack' at amendments, 'in particular the North–South parts'. But Ahern expressed fears that the UUP would pocket any gains and raise other issues. After a good tripartite meeting between the two governments and the UUP, with Ahern indicating a willingness to compromise, the UUP and the Irish agreed a joint meeting later. Holmes says that relations broke down completely between the Fianna Fáil delegation and the Ulster Unionists at that meeting on Wednesday evening. He wrote, 'Bertie Ahern commented that it had finished just in time, before blows were exchanged.'

On Thursday morning Blair rang Trimble to tell him that a deal on the North–South text was possible, and he should 'engage quickly' with the SDLP on the internal Northern Ireland government issue. The British had expected the UUP and the Irish delegation to have worked all night on the texts, but it had not happened. 'It gradually became clear that the two were not capable of solving their problems bilaterally – the mutual distrust and hostility was too great. From now until virtually the end of the talks, we negotiated with them both by proxy, and kept them apart,' wrote Holmes. They carried out this shuttle diplomacy on the North/South Ministerial Council, with implementation bodies reduced to a 'minimum' of six, with a longer list of potential bodies. (Two examples of these North–South bodies are Tourism Ireland and Waterways Ireland.) The council and bodies were critical to the Irish side, who wanted them covered by Westminster legislation, because unionists had not delivered on the agreed Irish dimension in 1921 and 1973. The Irish government was going to replace articles in the constitution laying claim to the North, with unity only by consent, and there had to be something substantial in return. Once the North–South Council and implementation bodies were agreed, in just a few hours the SDLP and UUP agreed on a ministerial cabinet-style government for Northern Ireland, rather than the UUP's wish for Assembly committees to run every department.

Holmes noted that Ahern 'spent hours with Adams trying to persuade him that the deal was worth accepting', and listening to his demands, among which was that all prisoners had to be 'out in a year'. Later Ahern and Blair together faced down this Sinn Féin demand – it would be two years. Meanwhile, according to Holmes, Trimble had told Blair that 'decommissioning would be a showstopper unless we got right the link between this and Sinn Féin's ability to sit in the new Northern Ireland government.' The late Seamus Mallon describes the countdown in the talks in his memoir *A Shared Home Place* using the content of Holmes's letter – saying it was in 'serious doubt' whether an agreement would be reached right up to the last minute, late in the afternoon of Good Friday, 10 April 1998. Holmes describes the final impasse: 'It quickly became clear that Trimble's troops were in general revolt, particularly his young staffers, but also major figures like [Jeffrey] Donaldson.' (Donaldson later became leader of the other major unionist group, the DUP, to which he had defected. He has now, many years later, stepped down while historic sexual charges are investigated.) Holmes wrote:

> Faced with the prospect of selling to their community a deal involving Sinn Féin at the Assembly Government table with no guarantee of decommissioning; with all prisoners out in two years, at least severe doubts about the future of the RUC, a new relationship with Dublin [the North/South Ministerial Council and bodies], and a nationalist hold on major Assembly decisions, they were losing their nerve … it began to look hopeless and despair took hold.

According to Mallon, decommissioning was the chief issue that emerged from a meeting of Blair with all the UUP heavyweights: Trimble, John Taylor, Reg Empey, Ken Maginnis and Jeffrey Donaldson. They said the deal was 'unacceptable and unsaleable'; they could not sit at a cabinet table with Sinn Féin when there had been no decommissioning. Holmes described the moment:

> The prime minister let his despair show but said he was ready to help if he could, but not by reopening the text itself. When they

had left, we concocted a letter to Trimble making it clear that, if after six months of the new Assembly, the present rules to promote non-violent methods had proved ineffective, we would support changing the rules to give them teeth.

This was sent to Trimble 'without much hope', said Holmes. But Trimble, who wanted a solution, managed to carry the day with a majority of his party's team that afternoon, and the Belfast Agreement was a done deal – but Jeffrey Donaldson walked out. It would eventually cost Trimble his leadership of the UUP and his party's loss of unionist leadership, about which Mallon was scathing, as we saw earlier, blaming the governments' subsequent mishandling of the decommissioning issue. Holmes wrote that, as they left for London, the British delegation was 'scarcely able to believe what had happened'.

Deaglán de Bréadún, who covered the all-party negotiations right to the end, concluded in his book *The Far Side of Revenge*, 'Without David Trimble there might well have been no possibility of agreement.' Bruton's relationships with Trimble and other unionists, I believe, helped influence him towards striking a deal with nationalists, which Bruton constantly advised. The grounds for success were also improved by the hard road Bruton travelled on the peace process, an integral part of the full story. It would not have happened without the key building blocks that had been put in place.

Gerry Adams and Martin McGuinness now faced their 'Michael Collins' moment, supporting an agreement that could potentially, in time, be a stepping stone to a united Ireland. It was a silent acknowledgement that the IRA's 25-year violent campaign to force a British withdrawal from Northern Ireland had failed, and in reality had made the agony of the North more difficult to end. In an *Irish Times* interview in December 2023 by Mark Hennessy, Ireland and Britain editor, former Tánaiste Dick Spring had this to say to Sinn Féin/IRA: 'Certainly I would like to see Sinn Féin expressing some empathy about the problems they've caused through the campaign of violence ... if they admitted at some stage, you know, that the campaign should never have happened.' Freya McClements,

Northern editor of the *Irish Times*, interviewed senior IRA man Frankie Quinn on the August 2019 anniversary of the first 17-month ceasefire. He gave a forthright analysis of why they adopted the peace process:

> We were saying the armed struggle's failed, it can't win, the jails are filling up, people are dying left, right and centre and the British are getting the better hand on us. Obviously we knew in our hearts that we were deeply, deeply infiltrated at a very high level. The armed struggle had to stop. We'd dump weapons, call the ceasefire, and then go into talks.

I've outlined the facts about the substantial work done on the peace process by Bruton, Spring and the Rainbow government. The political missteps were minor in comparison and understandable. Bruton's critics, for the most part, were either seriously misjudging him and his actions on the peace process, or playing up partisan politics, indulging in propaganda, and attacking him because of his detestation of the IRA, and his outreach to unionists. There was a lot of that in republican media in the context of the general election. Bruton did not ever let that stop him from working hard on the peace process. On 26 June 1997 the Rainbow government handed this fully completed work to the incoming Fianna Fáil–Progressive Democrat administration. There was nothing of significance to be done on the peace process – all the elements were in place for a ceasefire; it was time to keep pressing and encouraging Sinn Féin and the IRA to do the right thing. Blair had made it clear that he had put forward a finished package, a ceasefire was required very shortly, and the IRA complied on 19 July 1997. Six weeks later in early September, Sinn Féin joined the talks.

The new government's first real challenge was to deal with the deeply embarrassing exposure of former Fianna Fáil Taoiseach Charles Haughey as a continual liar. Almost daily, as they took up office, he was being forced by dramatic evidence at the McCracken Tribunal to admit that he *had* been given £1.3 million by Ben Dunne and he had lied to both the tribunal and his own lawyers. Haughey was facing serious charges of obstruction. It was incumbent on the new government to see that justice was done, but as we've seen, it later failed on that score. There was now a need for another tribunal to further investigate Haughey's sources of wealth, following the revelations of McCracken. There was heavy pressure from the opposition on Fianna Fáil, and from their own coalition partners, who had suffered under Haughey's rule in the party, the key figures either being expelled or leaving to form the Progressive Democrats. Ahern appointed Mr Justice Michael Moriarty to preside over a tribunal, which was to last for 14 years, on Haughey's wealth as well as more investigations of Michael Lowry and the award of the second mobile licence. It would have been much more expeditious in my view to separate the two – McCracken, or another with his team to continue on Haughey, having unearthed the truth about Dunne's payments, and Moriarty to deal with the mobile licence and Lowry. In the meantime, Blair and Ahern had seized the opportunity created by their predecessors, as George Mitchell said, and got on board the 'settlement train'.

AFTERWORD

BEN DUNNE, WHO FEATURES HEAVILY in this work with his highly 'irregular' financial arrangements with both Michael Lowry and Charles Haughey, died in November 2023. His death was the subject of an informed and insightful analytical article by Fionnán Sheahan, the Ireland editor of the *Irish Independent* on 20 November of that year entitled 'From Rainbow to Ruin: How Ben Dunne shaped the definitive election of our times'. It *was* a critically important election for the future of the Republic. Ben Dunne's murky financial largesse with Haughey and Lowry did harm to the two civil war parties, and Fine Gael lost the moral high ground with Lowry, as Sheahan says.

But at least he was gone quickly. The Haughey revelations were more spectacular because he had been taoiseach for years. The Rainbow's mistake was to cut across its own tribunal, leaving its full extraordinary exposure of Haughey until after the election. Dunne's personal funding of Haughey, and the exposure of the Ansbacher affair where money for Haughey was channelled in a corrupt, complicated Cayman Island offshore banking tax evasion scheme was damning, set up by his business colleague and 'bagman'. The scheme was used by, as Sheahan wrote, 'a golden circle in the highest ranks of politics, society and business who operated under different rules from "the little people"'. It would have been a different election if it had taken place after the McCracken report.

The Republic's economy achieved an unprecedented growth rate of 9 per cent a year during the Rainbow's tenure, not to be equalled in the 'boom' years that followed, creating 1,000 new jobs every week. I believed the Rainbow would win in autumn 1997, which as we saw, Bruton first favoured. People were more convinced that times were lastingly good with each day that passed, and the economic forecasts were all very positive. Sheahan's judgement: 'The Rainbow coalition of Fine Gael, the Labour Party and Democratic Left was only in office for two and a half years, yet was a progressive, balanced and purposeful alignment, despite bringing together the polar opposites on the political spectrum.' He concluded: 'The significance of this election was encapsulated by the optimistic outlook the new government inherited, which yielded staggering dividends in peace and economic terms within a year. But the shape of that government also ensured a greater focus of economic over social affairs, with reliance on property taxes and lack of robust regulation sowing the seeds of the collapse just over a decade later. It's a great "what if" to wonder if events would have played out differently had the Rainbow returned.'

I have no doubt that the growing wealth of Ireland would have been shared in a fairer way, mending serious social problems with the input of two left-wing parties, also encouraging enterprise and ensuring high-quality regulation. Bruton's warm intellectual relationship with Proinsias de Rossa convinced him of the imperative of social inclusion. Pat Rabbitte, the former super-junior minister, spoke of the 'rancher' from Meath engaging deeply with the 'inner city radical', saying: 'By the time he [Bruton] finished in that government he was quite a convinced social democrat.'

While I did not feel any great angst about the fall of the Rainbow in the summer of 1997, I became very disillusioned when I saw what I considered to be serious mismanagement of the economy over the following decade. Within a relatively short time under Bertie Ahern's government, the inflation rate was driven up from the stable 1.5 per cent of the Rainbow to over 6 per cent. In 2010 the *Wall Street Journal* reported that between 1998 and the crash in 2008 Irish government spending increased by 138 per cent against economic growth of 78 per cent, an annual average of 13.8 per cent, more than double the average annual increases of the Rainbow. Meanwhile, government allowed the banking sector during that decade to recklessly borrow billions to invest in property, a good deal of it jerry-built, without responding to the admittedly muffled warnings of the Central Bank about the property bubble as early as 2002. I recall being frustrated at a Central Bank briefing, pressing a senior official in an RTÉ interview afterwards to put their warnings in plain English, but the obfuscation continued. The Bank was frightened of upsetting the government. I was not shocked when it ended with an enormous property crash, something that I, and others, had been predicting for years. It was extraordinary that a talented government, in slightly differing makeups over that decade, could not see this coming and make contingency plans for a crash, as well as taking action to avoid it.

What I did not see was that the government would make the ordinary taxpayers of the country pay for the collapse, borrowing billions to rescue the banks and also insulating thousands of reckless borrowers and lenders from what would have been their fate otherwise, causing widespread alienation, which is not entirely resolved yet, even though the economy has recovered. The three-party government of Fine Gael, Fianna Fáil and the Greens had no choice but to pay billions for the many seriously defective 'celtic tiger' buildings. A continuation of the Rainbow's prudent economic and financial approach would not have allowed the excesses that contributed to the crash, and responsibility would have been reinforced in banks, businesses and borrowers. There would still have been a boom, as there was between 1994 and 1997, but without excess and so disastrous a crash, I believe.

I am not alone in this view. The political editor of the *Irish Times*, Stephen Collins, wrote during the crash that the 'prudence' of the Rainbow could have handled the economy better. Ireland took a turn for the worse, leading to a decade of excess and a disastrous crash leading to loss of economic sovereignty through submitting to IMF and ECB financial control. From 2011, a new Fine Gael–Labour government had little choice but to take the painful path of mending the broken economy – and paid a severe electoral price for that heavy task in 2016. Fine Gael recovered somewhat, but Labour support remains splintered to this day. Citizens, apart from the various policies and promises of change or largesse, should always consider the 'what if' factor. It never goes away.

ACKNOWLEDGEMENTS

My thanks to John Bruton, Roy Dooney, Seán Donlon, Jonathan Williams, Conor O'Clery, Michael Heney, Dermot Gleeson, Nora Owen, Ivan Doherty and Deaglán de Bréadún; the CAIN Archive at Ulster University for its superb documentation of the Troubles in Northern Ireland, particularly British state papers; the National Archive of Ireland and its ever-helpful staff for Irish state papers; and the *Irish Times* Archive, for its important role as the paper of record, the first draft of history.

Finally, I would like to thank Patrick O'Donoghue, Margaret Farrelly, Iollann Ó Murchú, Charlie Lawlor and the entire team at Gill who have been so marvellous and helpful throughout this process.

SELECT BIBLIOGRAPHY

Adams, Gerry, *Free Ireland: Towards a Lasting Peace*. Kerry: Brandon, 1995.

Bew, Paul and Gillespie, Gordon, *The Northern Ireland Peace Process 1993–1996: A Chronology*. London: Serif, 1996.

Blair, Tony, *A Journey*. Random House, 2010.

Bowyer Bell, J., *The Secret Army: History of the IRA 1916–1979*. Poolbeg Press Ltd., 1989.

CAIN Archive (online) *Conflict Archive on the Internet*. Ulster University.

Campbell, Alistair, *The Irish Diaries: 1994–2003*. Dublin: Lilliput Press, 2013.

Channel 4 News, 'Bloody Sunday inquiry rules in favour of ITN', 12 February 2004.

Collins, Stephen and Meehan, Ciara, *Fine Gael: From Collins to Varadkar*. Dublin: Gill Books, 2020.

Coogan, Tim Pat, *The Famine Plot*. Palgrave Macmillan, 2013.

Cooper, Matt, *How Ireland Really Went Bust*. Dublin: Penguin Ireland, 2011.

Cooper, Matt, *Who Really Runs Ireland?* Dublin: Penguin Ireland, 2009.

de Bréadún, Deaglán, *The Far Side of Revenge: Making Peace in Northern Ireland*. Cork: Collins Press, 2008.

English, Richard, *Armed Struggle: The History of the IRA*. Oxford University Press, 2004.

Ferriter, Diarmaid, *The Border: The Legacy of a Century of Anglo-Irish Politics*. Profile Books, 2019.

Finlay, Fergus, *Snakes and Ladders*. Dublin: New Island, 1998.

FitzGerald, Garret, *All in a Life: An Autobiography*. Dublin: Gill & Macmillan, 1991.

Garvin, Tom, *1922: The Birth of Irish Democracy*. Dublin: Gill Books, 2005.

Heney, Michael, *The Arms Crisis of 1970: The Plot That Never Was*. London: Head of Zeus, 2020.

Holmes, John, *Letter on Easter Week negotiations*. Made available by Eamonn Mallie.

Irish Times, 'British move on terms for SF talks welcomed', 28 February 1995.

Keena, Colm, *Haughey's Millions: Charlie's Money Trail*. Dublin: Gill & Macmillan, 2001.

Kehoe, Emmanuel, 'The turbulent ghost of Jerry McCabe', *Sunday Business Post*, 11 June 2006.

Kennedy, Geraldine, 'Bruton must learn from past errors to become a custodian of the peace process', *Irish Times*, 17 February 1996.

Key, Robert, *The Green Flag: A History of Irish Nationalism*. Penguin, 2000.

Major, John, *John Major: The Autobiography*. London: HarperCollins, 2000.

Mallie, Eamonn and McKittrick, David, *The Fight for Peace: The Inside Story of the Irish Peace Process*. Heinemann, 1997.

Mallon, Seamus and Pollak, Andy, *A Shared Home Place*. Dublin: Lilliput Press, 2019.

Mitchell, George J., *Making Peace*. New York: Alfred A. Knopf, 1999.

Mitchell, George J., *The Negotiator*. Simon & Schuster, 2016.

Murphy, David and Devlin, Martina, *Banksters*. Hachette Books Ireland, 2009.

Ocampo, Luis Moreno, 'Expert Opinion: Genocide against Armenians in 2023', https://luismorenoocampo.com/wp-content/uploads/2023/08/Armenia-Report-Expert-Opinion.pdf, 2023.

O'Clery, Conor, 'Christopher calls for NI disarmament to begin', *Irish Times*, 28 February 1995.

O'Toole, Fintan, 'Burke family values are reflected in Irish Constitution', *Irish Times*, 18 March 2023.

Quinn, Ruairí, *Straight Left: A Journey in Politics*. London: Hodder and Stoughton, 2005.

Rafter, Kevin, *Fine Gail: Party at the Crossroads*. Dublin: New Island, 2009.

Rafter, Kevin, *Martin Mansergh: A Biography*. Dublin: New Island, 2002.

US National Archives transcript release to the William J. Clinton Presidential Library in Arkansas, and *Irish Times*, 6 September 2019.

Williams, Jennifer, 'Manchester bomb: June 15, 1996. A day that changed our city forever', *Manchester Evening News*, 15 June 2016.

INDEX

A

abortion information 67, 86
Adams, Gerry
    arms decommissioning 11, 52, 64–5, 97, 164
    attacks Bruton's stance 193
    constitutional politics 25
    cordite whiff, 66
    deflects questions on IRA actions 232
    dialogue with John Hume 1
    Docklands bombing 178–9
    Garda McCabe murder 233
    reaction to Framework 45–6, 51
    relationship with Mansergh 19
    shocked by Manchester bombing 253
    weasel words accusations 357
Adams, John 287, 291
Adare 231
Ahern, Bertie
    abortion information 67
    Coveney controversy 85
    fears about Haughey revelations 335
    inflation rise 372
    meets Blair in Belfast 366
    peace role overstated 1, 258
    prisoner release 367
    questions Bruton 160–1
    supports business news service 93
Alderdice, John 124–5, 224
Aldergrove 36
American-Ireland Fund 221
Ancram, Michael 36, 77, 97, 125, 164–5, 237
Anderson Management 117–8
Anglo-Irish Agreement 26, 31, 33, 163–4
Anglo-Irish Liaison Group 127
Anglo-Irish Summit 1996, 196–8, 202–6
Anglo-Irish Treaty 41
Annapolis 288
Annesley, RUC Chief Constable Hugh 164, 261, 269, 348
Arafat, Yasser 211
arms decommissioning
    international commission 103, 105, 109–10
    long delayed 129, 156
    Mayhew's stance 28
    Nordic involvement, 52, 105
    single item agenda 10–11
    six principles 44
arms sales to Iraq 197, 205
Armstrong, John 23

INDEX

Arthur, Chester 287
Articles 2 and 3
   removal 21, 28, 46, 366
   unionist attitude 30

B

Balcombe St siege 209
Baldonnel aerodrome 36, 50, 139
Ballybunion 151
Ballymurphy atrocity 131, 270
Balmoral Centre 39
bank rescue, cost of 373
Barrett, Seán 17, 85
Barrington, Ted 305
Barry, Gerald 134
Bashir, Inam Ul-Haq 175, 176, 181
Beef Tribunal report 4, 83, 313
Berezag, Gemma 177
Berezag, Zaoui 175, 176–7
Berlin Wall 230
Bew, Paul 28, 127, 148, 167, 198, 225
Bhreathnach, Niamh 315
Bhreatnach, Lucilita 110, 153–4
Bird, Charlie 56
Black Wednesday 303
Blair, Tony
   backs Union 349–51
   brings Sinn Féin into talks 194, 349
   confidential letter to Bruton 351–5
   Famine statement 359
   Northern Ireland approach 348–9
   restores ceasefire 2
   role overstated 1, 258
   supports all-party talks 258
   takes charge of negotiations 365
   visits Bruton 112
   wins 1997 election 342–3
Blood Transfusion Service Board 312, 313–4, 316
Bloody Sunday 129, 131, 270, 361–4
Bodenstown Wolfe Tone commemoration 262
Bogside Inn, Derry 124
Boothroyd, Betty 20
Bord Gáis contract 80–3
Bowden, Charles 266
Bowman, John 136
Bradwell, Warrant Officer James 306
Brando, Marlon 59
Brennan, Martin 118
Brexit 33
British beef, EU ban 242–3, 259–60
British Telecom 119
Brooke, Peter 1, 26
Browne, Noël 41
Browne, Vincent
   doubts about coalition 7
   interviews Noonan on hepatitis C 315–6
   questions Haughey about his wealth 328;
Bruton, Finola 36, 65, 150, 344
Bruton, John
   abortion information 67–8
   ad libs in White House 64
   addresses Congress 286–92
   apology to nationalists 239
   attitudes to media 12–3
   Billy Fox murder 65, 122
   Canada visit 116–7
   cancels Chequers summit 112–4

commitment to peace process 72–3
condemns Garvaghy Road cave-in 273
condemns Lurgan RUC murders 355–7
Coveney crisis 80–3
decommissioning issues, 55–9, 64–5
defends Lowry 321, 322–3
Derry visit 121–4
detests IRA 55, 122
divorce campaign 134–5
excessive concern for unionists 107
foundations for peace 1
Garvaghy Road 275–81
general election train 343–4
Hillsborough summit 36–40
leadership heave, 66
Lee Clegg case 100–3
marks end of WWII 74
meetings with Jim Molyneaux 30–1, 99
meetings with John Major, 9–10, 35, 95–9, 101
meets Mo Mowlam 11
meets Tony Blair 11
Moscow visit, 95–6
1916 'a mistake' 122
pane of glass government 8–9, 12
press assessments 78
press secretary offer 8
Prince Charles visit 88
prisoner releases 56, 100, 102
refuses to meet Trimble 157–8
relationship with Clintons 65
restores ceasefire 2
social inclusion 372
Speaker's Lunch, 63

testy meeting with Tony O'Reilly 341–2
visits Terenure synagogue 74–5
warns Sinn Féin on need to end violence 114–5
White House 1995 visit 55
Bruton, Richard 69, 82, 83
BSE/mad cow disease 241–3, 259
Buchanan, James 287
Building Blocks' 126, 204–5
Burke, Liam 72
Burke, Ray 342
Burntollet Bridge 131
Butler, Sir Robin 114, 138
Byers, David 310
Byrne, Gabriel 359
Byrne, Garda Commissioner Pat 264

C

CAIN Archive 347
Callaghan, Jim 275, 302
Calleary, Dara 16
Cameron, David 131, 364
Campbell, Alistair 112, 348–9, 364
Campbell, Gregory 124
Cannes EU Summit 104, 186
Carey, Donal 6
Carey, Governor Hugh 62
Carter, Jimmy 62–3, 275
Cassidy family 152
Cassidy's pub, Camden St 153
Castle Buildings, Belfast 235
Castlerea prison 235
Catholic Church 41, 67, 134
Cayman Islands 331
Cement Roadstone Holdings 331–2
Central Bank of Ireland

INDEX

muffled warnings 373
property crash 373
timidity 373
Chamber of Commerce, Derry 124
Charles, Prince 88
Charleston 297
Chequers 54, 110
Chilcot, Sir John 54, 192
children's shoes tax 8
Chirac, Jacques 100, 216, 271, 301, 304, 310
Chrétien, Jean 116–7
Christopher, Warren 51–2, 210, 212–13
CIÉ
   appointments 69
   chairman's New York visit 71, 109
   controversial property deals 109
civil rights movement 123, 131
Civil War 41
Clegg, Paratrooper Lee 100, 101–3
Cleverly, James 177
Clinton, Bill
   addresses Dáil 149
   backs Mitchell 149–50
   College Green event 150–2
   condemns Lurgan RUC murders 357
   decommissioning 63–4
   Docklands bombing 178
   freedom of Dublin 152
   invites Adams to White House 55
   IRA ceasefire 184
   Irish-American economic conference 77
   ongoing commitment to peace 217–21, 295–6
   outraged by Manchester bombing 253
   prioritises Northern Ireland 52
   Sinn Féin fundraising 55
   visits the Republic 1995 2, 122, 139, 142, 148–53
   visits Northern Ireland 146, 148
Clonaselee bomb making site 261
Clongowes Wood College 85
Cluskey, Peter 173–4
Colley, George 328
Collins, Michael 88
Collins, Stephen 78, 373
Combined Loyalist Military Command 189, 215, 296
Common Agricultural Policy 231
Common Travel Area 360
Communicorp 118
Confederation of British Industry 75
Conlon, Michael 80, 82, 87
Connell, Archbishop Desmond 67
Cooney, John, 92–3
Cooper, Matt 341–2
Cosgrave, Liam 13, 42, 286
Costello, Joe 264
Coughlan, Denis 78, 148, 199, 237
Coulter, Phil 65
Council of Ireland 22
Coveney, Hugh
   Bord Gáis controversy 80–6
   demotion 84–6
   inexperience 66
   meets UUP 296
   untimely death 86
Cowen, Brian 317
Craig, William 34
Cran, James 173
Cranbourne, Viscount 22

Crawford, Robert 146
Creggan 124
Criminal Assets Bureau 265
Cronin, Seán 235
Cruise O'Brien, Conor 241
Culligan, Garda Commissioner Patrick 178, 233
Culloden Hotel 75
Cusack, Jim 233

D

d'Estaing, Valéry Giscard 302
Dalton-Chilcot Group 54, 105, 113
Dalton, Tim 23, 54, 105
Daly, Cardinal Cathal 282
de Bréadún, Deaglán 192, 193–4, 200–1, 368
de Chastelain, General John 139, 140, 147, 191, 227
De Rossa, Proinsias
    Coveney controversy 81, 85
    interned 276
    Minister for Social Welfare 6
    prisoner releases 11
de Valera, Eamon 41, 283, 286
Delors, Jacques 302
Democratic Left, Soviet Union funds 6–7
Denton, Baroness 221
Derrylin 6
Desmond, Dermot 118
Dicks, Terry 236
Dimbleby, David 282–3
direct rule 40
divorce referendum
    carried 135–6
    Church opposition 134
    No campaign 134
    preparation 133
    significance 136

Docklands IRA bombing
    advance planning 145–6
    IRA warning 173–4
    Sinn Féin talks exclusion 237–8
    victims 175–7
Docklands Victims Association 176
Docklands, London 111
Doherty, Ivan 5–6
Doherty, Pat 77, 132, 245
Dole, Bob 287
Donaldson, Jeffrey 157, 367, 368
Donlon, Seán
    ambassador to US 62, 222–3
    hepatitis C scandal 314
    Hillsborough meeting 37–8
    Northern adviser 36
    peace setbacks 24
    programme manager 17, 222
Donoghue, David 137–8
Dooney, Roy 17, 116, 157
Dowling, Brian 89, 90, 91, 94, 314
Downing St Declaration
    drafts 20
    peace pillar 1, 26
    Sinn Féin refuse to endorse 25, 27
    unionist exclusion 22
Doyle, Avril 358, 359
Doyle, Roddy 152
Drapier 147
Drugs Advisory Board 69
Drumcree march, Portadown 268, 269, 271–3, 294, 349
Dublin and Monaghan bombings 42
Dublin Castle 26, 107
Duignan, Seán 9, 14, 92
Dukes, Alan 66, 323

INDEX

Dunbar, Liam 68
Dunboyne 80, 106, 263–4
Dunlop, Frank 86
Dunne, Ben 121
   cocaine possession 319–20
   death 371
   donations to Fine Gael 335
   family disagreements 319–20
   funds Lowry home renovations 318, 320
   Lowry tax issues 326
   payments to Haughey 318–20, 327–31, 333–4

E

Eames, Archbishop Robin 58, 359
Earth Summit 364
Edward VII, King 96
Empey, Lord Reg 177, 297
Enniskillen bombing 3–4
Enright, Leo 272
Ervine, David 276
Esat Digifone 117–20
Esat Telecom 119
EU Constitution 289, 291, 292
EU expansion 299
EU Presidency 298–305
EU single currency 298–304, 309, 310
EU: Russian fears of expansion 100
   single market 34
Europa Hotel 148
European Central Bank 303, 373
Europol 311
exchange rate mechanism 302, 303

F

Farrell, Brian 93
Farrell, Pat 274

Faulkner, Brian 34, 247, 270
Faxhill Homes Ltd 323
Feeley, Frank 152
Feeney, Brian 106
Feeney, Peter 92
Ferguson, Lena 363
Ferris, Martin 235
Finlay, Fergus
   Chequers meeting 54
   decommissioning 54–5
   downplays inter-government row 113
   Hillsborough summit 38
   on John Foley 10
   Spring adviser 5
   summit cancelled 111
Finlay, Judge Thomas 316
Finner Camp 7
Fitt, Gerry 270
FitzGerald, Garret
   addresses Congress 61, 286
   Anglo-Irish Agreement 27
   briefing procedure 158
   children's shoes tax, 8
   first coalition collapse 8
   Sunningdale 42
   UWC strike 270
Fitzpatrick, Majella 344
Flanagan, Deputy Chief Constable Ronnie 137–8, 269
Florence EU Summit 259
Flynn, Bill 59, 293
Foley, John 10, 14, 70
Foley, Tom 63, 84
Forum for Peace and Reconciliation 125, 158
Foster, Arlene 34
Fountain Estate, Derry 124
Four Horsemen 61–2

Fox, Billy 65, 122
Fox, Noel 333
Framework Documents 50, 58, 98, 206–7
Frayling, Canon Nicholas 358
Free Derry Corner 124
Friends of Ireland 274, 293

G

Gaddafi, Muammar 175, 177
Gahan, Francis 59
Gallagher, Ambassador Dermot 60, 64, 286
Galvin, Barry 265–6
Ganesh, Jonathan 176–7
Garvaghy Road Orange march 193, 268
Garvin, Tom 34, 49
Gateway elections 224–8
Gaza 211
Gillespie, Gordon 127, 148, 225
Gilligan, John 266
Gilman, Ben 293
Gingrich, Newt 59, 63, 286–7
Glandore 341
Gleeson, Dermot
    acts for Larry Goodman 90
    advises author on legal action 93
    Brendan Smyth controversy 89–90
    Bruton Q&A sessions 79
    Coveney controversy 81–2
    Docklands bombing 180
    hepatitis C scandal 314–5
Glenn, George 124
Glennon, Chris 91
Golfgate 16
Good Friday (Belfast) Agreement
    foundations 1–2, 25
    34
    self-determination 43, 46, 156
    Trimble's role 250, 368
Goodman, Larry 90
Gore, Al 125, 210
Gorman, Tommie 271–2
government leaks
    budget 14–15
    junior ministers 13
    Molyneaux meeting 31–3
Graham, Constable Roland 355
Great Famine 358–60
Greece financial crash 299
Green, Richard 315
Greencastle, Co. Donegal 223
Guerin, Veronica
    crime reporting 262
    drug barons' target 262
    drug gangs 304
    funeral 263
    murder 262
Guildford Four 209

H

Halappanavar, Savita 41
Hammersmith Bridge bomb 261
Hanora's Cottage 72
Hänsch, Klaus 305
Harding, Ted 82
Harney, Mary 255, 338
Harris, Anne 262
Harris, Eoghan 147–8, 343
Harris, Simon 7
Harte, Paddy 68
Hartley, Tom 75
Haslam, Jonathan 212–3, 281–2
Haugh, Judge Kevin 338
Haughey Boland Accountants 331
Haughey, Charles

INDEX

Abbeville 329
ACC loan 334
AIB loans written off 328
Ansbacher offshore account 332, 371
arms crisis 328
biography 94
denies knowing of Ben Dunne payments 336–7
early career 331
Garvaghy Road 274
implements Bruton's budget 8
intervenes with Revenue re Dunnes Stores tax liability 334–5
Kohl's gratitude 231
lavish lifestyle 327–9
lies to and obstructs McCracken 337–8, 369–70
opinion of Carter and Callaghan 275
payments from Ben Dunne 318–9, 327–31, 333–4
Smyth logs all phone calls 337
Heaney, Seamus 153
Heath, Ted 42, 301
Heffernan, Margaret 329, 331
Heffernan, Tony 13, 84, 135
Hendron, Joe 174
Heney, Michael 123
Hennessy, Mark 368
hepatitis C scandal
  Brigid McCole court case 313–4
  Judge Finlay report 316
  Noonan apology 314–5
  origins, 68–9, 312
  Positive Action 313, 314
  tribunal of inquiry delay 312–3
  victims' compensation 316
Higgins, Jim 18, 85, 314

Hillsborough summit 35–40
Hogan, Phil
  budget confidentiality 15–8
  EU Trade Commissioner 16
  resignations 16, 18–9
Holkeri, Harri 105, 147, 236
Holland, Mary 170–1, 192, 194
Holmes, John 271, 347, 358, 359, 361, 367–8
Holohan, Renagh 340
Howlin, Brendan 67, 71, 312
Hume, John
  decommissioning 122
  dialogue with Adams 1
  1916 'a mistake' 123
  Nobel Peace Prize 40
  peace process role 1
Hunter, Andrew 172–3
Hurd, Douglas 104, 142

I

IMF control 373
Independent Commission on Policing 49
International Body on Decommissioning
  British doubts 143–5
  Canada's involvement 117
  creation 44, 132, 139, 143, 147
  issues report 162–4, 217
  members 147
  Sinn Féin submission 153–5
IRA
  arms decommissioning 10
  attracts 'psychopathic killers' 266–7
  Billy Fox murder 65
  bomb Manchester 250–4
  bomb Thiepval barracks, Lisburn 305–6

ceasefire prospects 1, 2, 9, 26, 53, 107–8
denies then admits Garda McCabe murder 231–4
Docklands bombing 173–82
end ceasefire 111, 173–4
Hume–Adams meetings 207–8
infiltration 369
litter bin bombs 215
Munster militants 233
murder RUC men in Lurgan 355–7, 360
post-ceasefire robberies 232
prisoner releases 12, 102
punishment attacks 146
quartermaster opposes ceasefire 267
renew ceasefire 365
return to war 142, 145
secret British contacts, 74
seeks to damage Rainbow government 256
Irish College of General Practitioners 86
Irish Congress of Trade Unions 104
Irwin, Michael 324
Iveagh House 35

J

Jackson, Andrew 287
James II, King 267
Jamestown 297
Jefferson, Thomas 289
Jeffries, John 175, 176, 181
Jenkins, Roy 302
Johnson, Boris 74, 299
Johnson, Samuel 275
Johnston, Reserve Constable David 355
Joint Framework Documents 20, 21, 23, 24

consent essential 29
delayed 34–5
key elements 43–5
Jordan, Neil 152
Juncker, Jean-Claude 310–1

K

Kantor, Mickey 292
Kealy, Willie 262
Keane, Conor 104
Keane, Fergal, 8
Keena, Colm 327, 328
Kelly, Donal, 64
Kelly, Gerry, 77
Kelly, Paddy, IRA man 201, 212, 218
Kennedy, Edward 62, 292
Kennedy, Geraldine
   Bruton ad libs 64
   Bruton's failings 185–7, 189–91, 208
   government 'secretive' 105–6
   Northern elected body 169
   praises Bruton 147
   Widgery failings 361
Kennedy, Hugh 34
Kennedy, John F. 152
Kenny, Mary 315
Kenny, Pat 152
Kenny, Ronan, 68–9
Keough, Don 59–60, 293
King, Congressman Peter 63, 292, 293–4
Kinkel, Klaus 304–5
Kohl, Helmut
   Bonn Summit 230
   physique 211, 304
   single currency issues 300–1, 310
   Turkey's EU application 231

INDEX

L

Lake, Anthony 125, 202, 210, 213, 214–6, 292
Lawlor, Éamonn 104
Lennon, Joe 15
Lisbon, Treaty of 289
Little Island 82
Little, Joe 56
Liverpool Anglican Cathedral Famine service 358
Loftus, Lord Mayor Seán 150
Lowry, Michael
    assists Denis O'Brien on phone licence 120
    bizarre meeting with author, 70–1
    business cartels, 71
    CIÉ problems, 69, 71, 109
    cosey cartels accusation 117
    Coveney controversy, 82, 83
    Hogan controversy 17
    home renovations paid by Dunnes 318, 320, 323–4
    inexperience, 66
    McCracken Tribunal 318, 323–5
    ministerial demise, 69
    offshore accounts 324–5
    on Albert Reynolds, 70
    on Labour politicians, 71
    on Phil Hogan, 70
    payments from Denis O'Brien 120
    potential leader, 69
    reliance on PR, 70–1
    resignation 322–3
    role forming coalition, 69
    Streamline Enterprises 322
    surveillance claims 108–9
    tax evasion 323–7
Lynch, Jack 328
Lynch, Kathleen 81
Lyne, Rod 24, 103

M

Maastricht Treaty 20, 302, 303
Mac Cionnaith, Breandán 275–6
MacNaughton, Captain E.L. 34
Maginnis, Ken 30, 51
Magner, Pat 9, 255, 340
Maitland, Olga 173
Major, John
    BBC broadcast 24–5
    decommissioning 20, 96–8, 130
    Docklands bombing 183
    elections before all-party talks 166–7
    meets Bruton 9–10, 35, 96–9, 101
    National Concert Hall ovation 157
    panders to Eurosceptics 305
    prisoner releases 100
    reliance on UUP 20
    Tory opponents 103, 142
    triple lock 50
    vetoes Famine commemoration in Liverpool 358–9
    visits Northern Ireland and the Republic 155–6
Mallie, Eamonn 33, 145, 184
Mallon, Seamus 43, 156, 367
Manchester IRA bombing 250–4, 257
Mansergh, Martin
    adviser to Ahern 150
    briefs Bruton on the North 20, 58–9
    elections in North 160, 162
    marching season confrontations 260–1
    relationship with Adams 19;

Martin, Micheál 7
Maryfield Anglo-Irish Secretariat 31, 130, 137, 164, 192
Mayhew, Sir Patrick
   attends War Memorial Gardens 75
   Bloody Sunday 361–2
   disarmament, 52
   Hillsborough summit 38
   meets Adams, 77–8
   North–South bodies 35
   restricts Sinn Féin/IRA talks 52–3, 75–6
   Sinn Féin/IRA talks invite 28, 52
   united Ireland 23
McAuley, Pearse 235
McCabe, Detective Garda Jerry 231–5, 245, 255–6, 261
McCain, John 292
McCann, Prof. Seán 68–9
McCartney, Robert 226, 238
McClements, Freya 368–9
McCole, Brigid 312–6
McConnell, Mitch 292
McCracken, Justice Brian 318
McCracken Tribunal 318, 323–7, 329, 330–4, 337
McCrea, William 249, 351
McElhatton, Shane, 87
McGoldrick, Michael 274
McGuinness, Martin
   Army Council member 254
   character 47
   decommissioning issues 125
   deflects questions on IRA actions 232
   Deputy First Minister 47, 121
   IRA ceasefire 28–9, 55, 110
   opens talks with British 77
   takes mid-Ulster seat 351

McKenna, Justice 133
McKittrick, David 33, 145, 184
McLaughlin, Mitchel 97–8, 159, 196
McMichael, Gary 126
McQuillan, Captain Maurice 274
McSharry, Ray, 8
Meánscoil Feirste 11
Meath Association, London 128–9
Meehan, Brian 266
Meehan, Paula 152
Meyer, Christopher 10, 35, 37, 114, 165–6, 168–9
Millar, Frank 46, 130, 148
Mitchell Principles 57, 307–8
Mitchell, George
   accepts talks chair 246–9
   all-party talks 2, 191
   arms question 127
   chairs decommissioning body 139, 140, 147
   Clinton's special advisor 144
   gains unionist trust 257
   multi-party talks 283–5
   praise from Bruton in Congress 290
   unionist opposition to roles 144, 237–40
Mitchell, Heather 283
Mitchell, Jim 5
Mitchell, Robbie 284–5
Mitterand, François 231
Molloy, Philip 92
Molyneaux, Jim
   Anglo-Irish Agreement 33
   attitude to Framework 24, 51
   meetings with Bruton 99
   North–South bodies 30–1
Moriarty Tribunal 118, 120–1, 320–1, 334–5, 370

Morrison, Bruce 59, 221, 274
Mowlam, Mo 11, 159, 348–9
Moynihan, Daniel Patrick 62
Mubarak, Hosni 210, 211, 212
Mulhall, Dan 246
Murphy, Detective Chief Superintendent, Fachtna 265
Murray, Frank 158

N

Napier, Oliver 270
National Drugs Advisory Board 313
NATO 100
Neal, Richard 292
Nelson, Brian 154
Nicholas II, Tsar 96
Noonan, Michael
    abortion information, 67–9
    abortion 'price list', 86–7
    apologises to McCole family 314–5
    Coveney controversy 83
    delays hepatitis C inquiry 312–3
    Fine Gael leader 316
    Garda McCabe murder 234–5
North Report 309
North-South bodies 29–31, 35, 44–5, 366
North-South Ministerial Council 366
North, Dr Peter 282
Northern Ireland Assembly 51, 156, 160–2
Northern Ireland Parades Commission 282
Northern Ireland Protocol 34
Northern Ireland Women's Coalition 225, 226

O

Ó hUiginn, Seán 20, 179, 180
O'Brien, Denis
    donations to Fine Gael 120
    mobile phone licence 117–9
    payments to Michael Lowry 120
O'Callaghan, Owen 109
O'Clery, Conor 51–2
O'Connell, Joe 209
O'Connor, Alison 317
O'Donovan, Declan 192
O'Dowd, Niall 59–60
O'Gorman, Hugh 7
O'Hare, Rita
    concerns about Donlon 223
    Docklands bombing 179
    IRA ceasefire ends 174
    Mitchell report 158–9
O'Kelly, Seán T. 286
O'Malley, Desmond 4
O'Neill, Michael 235
O'Neill, Representative John 61
O'Neill, Tip
    opposes IRA violence 61–2
    St Patrick's Day lunch 60
    united Ireland 62
O'Reilly, Emily 70, 72
O'Reilly, Tony 341
O'Sullivan, Detective Garda Ben 231
Oakden, Edward 146
Ocampo, Luis Moreno 360
Oireachtas Golf Society 16
Omagh car bombing 361
Orange Order
    concessions 273
    Garvaghy Road trouble 268–9, 271, 275–81
    parades 268

power 34
Orr, Rev. Cecil 124
Osei, Barbara 175, 176
Owen, Nora 81, 82, 180, 244
    criminal assets 264
    Guerin murder 263, 265
    right to silence 266

P

Paisley, Ian
    attacks Mitchel 246–7
    attacks Trimble 247
    DUP expulsion 47–8
    First Minister 47
    greets Major in Ballymena 155
    opposes Anglo–Irish Agreement 39–40
    opposes Framework 46, 51
    US visit 125
Patten, Chris 49
Peres, Shimon 211
Pheonix, Dr Éamon 187
Portillo, Michael 305
Prendergast, Peter 32, 158, 343
PSNI
    establishment 49

Q

Quinn McDonnell Pattison 133
Quinn, Frankie 369
Quinn, Jack 292
Quinn, Ruairí
    accepts coalition 71
    Council of EU Finance Ministers 300, 303–4
    Guerin murder 264
    Hogan's budget leak 16–7
    national pay deal 309
    presents budget 14
    Prince Charles visit 88

R

Rabbitte, Pat
    Coveney controversy 85
    Docklands bombing 174
    super junior minister 6
Rabin, Yitzhak 129
RAF Northolt 9–10, 140
Rafter, Kevin 19, 58
Ráth Mór 124
Reagan, Ronald 60–1
Real IRA 361
Redmond, John 122
Reid, Fr Alec 110–1, 160
Reilly, Karen 100, 102
republican splits 254, 361
Restorick, Stephen 347
Reynolds, Albert
    Brendan Smyth extradition 17
    export guarantees 4
    meets Major at Chequers 54
    peace process role 1
    historic compromise government 4
    slams IRA 253
Riley, Richard 292
Robinson, Mary 136, 149, 228, 229
Robinson, Peter 46, 127, 125
Rogers, John 315
Rosney, Bride 136
Ross, William 46
rotating taoiseach 7
RUC
    armed gendarmerie 49
    B Specials 47, 49–50, 131
    reforms 48–9
    replaced 49
    sectarian nature 49
Russell, Matt 89

INDEX

S

Sam Maguire trophy 151
Santer, Jacques 245, 259, 260, 360
Saville Inquiry 363
Schmidt, Helmut 302
Sharm El-Sheikh 209–10
Shatter, Alan 66
Shaw, George 36, 37, 82, 116
Sheahan, Fionnán 371–2
Sheehy, Jeremiah 235
Shortall, Róisín 264
Sinn Féin
    access to governments 29
    approach to media 13
    deny IRA murder of Garda McCabe 232
    do not accept Downing St declaration 25, 27, 160
    threat to SDLP 351
    US fundraising 52
Sissons, Peter 272–3
Smith, Jean Kennedy 59, 60, 152
Smyth, Fr Brendan 4, 5, 17, 83, 89–90
Smyth, Noel 319–20, 328–30, 335–6
Smyth, Patrick 272, 311
Smyth, Sam 87, 92
Soderberg, Nancy 292
Soros, George 303
Speaker's St Patrick's Day Lunch 60–1
Special Criminal Court 235, 263, 264, 266
Spring, Dick
    accompanies Prince Charles 88
    backs Bruton as taoiseach 71
    Coveney demotion, 81
    decommissioning proposal 105
    foundations for peace 1
    Hillsborough summit 38–40
    meets Jim Molyneaux 30–1
    welcomes Mitchell report 166
    unionist perceptions 38–9
St Brendan's College, Killarney 105
St Columb's Cathedral, Derry 124
Stardust fire 69, 313
Structural Funds 231
Summit of the Peacemakers 210–16
Sunningdale Agreement
    Council of Ireland 226
    damages Faulkner 34
    destruction 270
    excludes unionist coercion 27
    hostility 22
    IRA opposition 42
Sutherland, Veronica 358–9

T

Tavern on the Green, New York 59–60
Taylor, John 162, 170–1, 269
Taylor, Mervyn 133
Teahon, Paddy 23, 36, 38, 82, 91, 104
Telecom Éireann 119, 121
Telenor 118
Terenure synagogue 74–5
Thatcher, Margaret 26–7, 33, 231, 301
Thomas, Quentin 187
Thomson, Alex 363
Top 100 Awards 59–60
Traynor, Des 331–2
Trimble, David
    attacked by unionists 247–9
    Garvaghy Road march 268–9
    Good Friday Agreement 250
    loses UUP leadership 34, 368
    new Assembly 106

Nobel Peace Prize 40–1
    seeks meeting with Bruton 157–8
    supports Mitchell 238, 240
    tells loyalists to disarm 126
Tubridy, Ryan 94
Turkey, EU application 231

U

U2 152
Ukraine invasion 100
Ulster Folk Museum 77
Ulster Workers' Council 22, 41, 270, 276
US Constitution 288
US Supreme Court 291

V

Vanguard movement 34
Varadkar, Leo, 7

W

Waigel, Theo 304
Wall, Mary and Seamus 72
Walsh, Kevin 235
War Memorial Park, Islandbridge 74, 76
Ware, John 102–3
Warren Buffett group 114
Warren, Russell 266
Washington, George 287
West Bank 211
Wheeler, Sir John 269
Wheeler, Sir Roger 138
Whelehan, Harry 4
White, Peter 298, 345
Widgery Report 309, 361
William J. Clinton Presidential Library 179
William, King 267
Williams, Jennifer 250–1

Williamsburg 297
Wilshire, David 213
Wilson, Gordon 3–4
Wilson, Harold 42, 302
Wilson, Marie 3–4
Wilson, Peter 3, 4, 5
witness protection programme 265
Women's National Council 150

X

X case 67

Y

Yates, Ivan 4, 83
Yeltsin, Boris 95, 96

Z

Zaoui, Farid 176
Zhukov, Marshal Georgy 96